WOMEN, POVERTY, EQUALITY

The stark reality is that throughout the world, women disproportionately live in poverty. This indicates that gender can both cause and perpetuate poverty, but this is a complex and cross-cutting relationship. The full enjoyment of human rights is routinely denied to women who live in poverty. How can human rights respond and alleviate gender-based poverty? This monograph closely examines the potential of equality and non-discrimination at international law to redress gender-based poverty. It offers a sophisticated assessment of how the international human rights treaties, specifically the Convention on the Elimination of Discrimination Against Women (CEDAW), which contains no obligations on poverty, can be interpreted and used to address gender-based poverty. An interpretation of CEDAW that incorporates the harms of gender-based poverty can spark a global dialogue. The book makes an important contribution to that dialogue, arguing that the CEDAW should serve as an authoritative international standard setting exercise that can activate international accountability mechanisms and inform the domestic interpretation of human rights.

Women, Poverty, Equality

The Role of CEDAW

Meghan Campbell

·HART·
PUBLISHING
OXFORD AND PORTLAND, OREGON
2018

Hart Publishing
An imprint of Bloomsbury Publishing Plc

Hart Publishing Ltd
Kemp House
Chawley Park
Cumnor Hill
Oxford OX2 9PH
UK

Bloomsbury Publishing Plc
50 Bedford Square
London
WC1B 3DP
UK

www.hartpub.co.uk
www.bloomsbury.com

Published in North America (US and Canada) by
Hart Publishing
c/o International Specialized Book Services
920 NE 58th Avenue, Suite 300
Portland, OR 97213-3786
USA

www.isbs.com

HART PUBLISHING, the Hart/Stag logo, BLOOMSBURY and the
Diana logo are trademarks of Bloomsbury Publishing Plc

First published 2018

© Meghan Campbell 2018

British Library Cataloguing-in-Publication Data
A catalogue record for this book is available from the British Library.

ISBN: HB: 978-1-50990-974-2
       ePDF: 978-1-50990-977-3
       ePub: 978-1-50990-972-8

Library of Congress Cataloging-in-Publication Data

Names: Campbell, Meghan, 1985- author.

Title: Women, poverty, equality : the role of CEDAW / Meghan Campbell.

Description: Oxford [UK] ; Portland, Oregon : Hart Publishing, 2018. | Includes bibliographical
references and index.

Identifiers: LCCN 2017048795 (print) | LCCN 2017049126 (ebook) | ISBN 9781509909728 (Epub) |
ISBN 9781509909742 (hardcover : alk. paper)

Subjects: LCSH: United Nations. Committee on the Elimination of Discrimination Against
Women. | Convention on the Elimination of All Forms of Discrimination against Women
(1979 December 18) | Women (International law) | Women's rights. | Sex discrimination against
women—Law and legislation. | Equality before the law. | Poverty—International cooperation.

Classification: LCC K3243.A41979 (ebook) | LCC K3243.A41979 C36 2018 (print) |
DDC 342.08/78—dc23

LC record available at https://lccn.loc.gov/2017048795

Typeset by Compuscript Ltd, Shannon

To find out more about our authors and books visit www.hartpublishing.co.uk. Here you will find extracts,
author information, details of forthcoming events and the option to sign up for our newsletters.

Acknowledgements

I am profoundly thankful to Sandra Fredman for her guidance throughout this project. She has had unwavering patience in helping me form and shape my ideas. Her perceptive questions and steadfast support have been invaluable. I am eternally grateful for all the kindness, challenging questions and laughter over the years.

I have had the privilege of participating in Sandra Fredman's weekly research group. I am sincerely indebted to the time, energy and helpful guidance of: Shreya Atrey, Jason Brickhill, Max Harris, Barbara Havelková, Laura Hilly, Miles Jackson, Galina Kostadinova, Jaakko Kuosmanen, Karl Laird, Fiona de Londras, Tom Lowenthal, Richard Martin, Chris McConnachie, Yishai Mishor, Victoria Miyandazi, Ndjodi Ndeunyema, Justice Dhaya Pillay, Nomfundo Ramalekana, Anup Surendranath and Helen Taylor. These friends and colleagues with infinite patience have read numerous drafts of this project. They have given me companionship, enthusiastic support, encouragement and insightful suggestions. Words cannot express my appreciation to them.

Thank-you to Nazila Ghanea-Hancock, Denise Réaume, Cathryn Costello, Catherine Redgwell and Frances Raday who at the earlier stages provided helpful guidance.

My heartfelt thanks to my parents Gerry and Lori Campbell and my sister Amy Campbell. At an early age they introduced me to social justice and are always challenging me to think critically on gender and poverty. Even from a distance they have given me infallible love and support.

Thank-you to Geoffrey Swenson, Francesca Ward, Jonathan Neve and Alice Neve who have made me laugh throughout this project and have offered many words of kindness.

Chantal Boutin and Silvia Pittner have offered unflinching and loving support before, during and undoubtedly after this book. Words are inadequate to capture my appreciation for all these two have done for me. So I offer my sincere and simple thanks.

Contents

Part I

1

Mapping the Problem

POVERTY IS AN obstacle to human flourishing. The UN Office of the High Commissioner for Human Rights (OHCHR) explains that the 'defining feature of a poor person is that she has very restricted opportunities to pursue her well-being'.[1] Throughout the world, women disproportionately live in poverty.[2] The evidence, thus, suggests that being a woman both causes and contributes to poverty. Women's role in reproduction; their almost sole responsibility for care-giving; women's limited access to sexual and reproductive health services, educational opportunities, property and forms of credit; deeply entrenched sociocultural attitudes, prejudices and stereotypes on the role and value of girls and women; the segregation of women into low-paid and precarious work; and the exclusion of women from public life create a unique experience for women in poverty that is different from that of men who live in poverty. To put it plainly, poverty, like violence, is a gendered phenomenon.

It is crucial, then, that a spotlight be shone on the gender-based aspects of poverty. On the positive side, there is increasing attention being paid towards women's poverty: from the high-profile Poverty is Sexist campaign[3] to the Sustainable Development Goal's global political commitment both to achieve gender equality and end extreme poverty.[4] These initiatives, however, approach gender-based poverty as charity or development. A human rights lens offers a new and exciting perspective on gender-based poverty. Women in poverty are denied their human rights on a tragically routine basis. The UN Special Rapporteur on extreme poverty and human rights argues that: '[P]overty is an urgent human rights concern ... it [is] characterized by multiple reinforcing violations of civil, political, economic, social and cultural rights.'[5] For women who live in poverty, these human rights violations are almost invariably

---

[1] Office of the High Commission for Human Rights (OHCHR), 'Human Rights and Poverty Reduction: A Conceptual Framework' (2004) HR/PUB/04/1 [15].

[2] UN Special Rapporteur on extreme poverty and human rights, 'Final Draft of the Guiding Principles on extreme Poverty and Human Rights' (2012) A/HRC/21/39 [23].

[3] 'Poverty Is Sexist', www.one.org/us/take-action/poverty-is-sexist/.

[4] 'Sustainable Development Goals: 17 Goals to Transform our World', www.un.org/sustainabledevelopment/sustainable-development-goals/.

[5] ibid [3].

linked to patriarchal gender norms.[6] Recognizing that the interaction between poverty and gender results in severe human rights violations, the question becomes: can human rights be a tool to redress gender-based poverty? The promise of human rights is tantalising. Unlike charity campaigns, economic policies or development programmes, human rights set normative standards and place duties on the duty-bearer to respect, protect and fulfil these standards towards the rights-holder.[7] Conceptualising women's poverty as an issue of human rights means women living in poverty are not passive recipients of largesse or aid but are empowered rights-holders who can draw on human rights standards to hold the duty-bearer accountable.[8] It has been argued that a human rights approach to gender-based poverty provides 'a framework for the long-term eradication of ... poverty'.[9]

There is a plethora of human rights forums in which to begin to develop the relationship between gender, poverty and human rights. At first glance, focusing on a specific domestic human rights instrument would be the most compelling starting point because of the direct impact it could have on domestic laws, policies and programmes on gender-based poverty. While incorporating gender-based poverty into domestic instruments is crucial, it is of equal importance to understand how the UN human rights framework can meaningfully engage and address gender-based poverty. Initial steps have already been taken to unpack the relationship between gender, poverty and human rights. Prominent actors in the UN human rights system, specifically UN Special Rapporteurs, have been vocal advocates for using human rights to ameliorate gender-based poverty.[10] To move forward it is crucial to situate gender, poverty and human rights in binding international *legal* commitments. Focusing on international human rights law is attractive. The UN international human rights treaties have near global ratification. Understanding that there is a legal human rights obligation to address gender-based poverty can spark a global dialogue, serve as a legal, political and cultural focal point for discussions on gender-based poverty, and give domestic legislators, policy-makers and judges a toolkit to ensure that women in poverty are able to enjoy their human rights.[11]

---

[6] World Bank, 'Voice and Agency: Empowering Women and Girls for Shared Prosperity' (2014) https://openknowledge.worldbank.org/handle/10986/19036 and World Bank, 'The World Development Report: Gender Equality and Development' (2012) https://openknowledge.worldbank.org/handle/10986/4391.

[7] OHCHR, Who Will Be Accountable: Human Rights and the Post-2015 Development Agenda' (2014) HR/PUB/13/1 ix.

[8] UN Special Rapporteur on extreme poverty and human rights, 'Guiding Principles' (n 2) [45].

[9] ibid [6].

[10] UN Special Rapporteur on extreme poverty and human rights, 'Guiding Principles' (n 2); OHCHR, 'Poverty Reduction' (n 1).

[11] M Nussbaum, 'Women's Progress and Women's Human Rights' (2016) 38(3) *Human Rights Quarterly* 589; S E Merry, *Human Rights and Gender Violence: Translating International Law into Local Justice* (University of Chicago Press, 2006) 16.

Adopting a human rights-based approach to gender-based poverty raises a new host of challenges. There are nine core UN human rights treaties, but none of them explicitly create obligations on gender-based poverty or even on poverty. Traditionally, poverty has been addressed through socioeconomic rights: rights to food, health, shelter and an adequate standard of living.[12] There is a case to be made for examining how the socioeconomic rights in the International Covenant on Economic, Social and Cultural Rights (ICESCR) can be used to tackle gender-based poverty.[13] The protection of socioeconomic rights in ICESCR, 'impl[ies] a commitment to social integration, solidarity and equality and include[s] tackling the issue of income distribution ... [which] ... are indispensable for an individual's dignity'.[14] Notwithstanding this promise, the role of gender in creating and perpetuating women's poverty points towards an overlooked human rights treaty. The Convention on the Elimination of All Forms of Discrimination Against Women (CEDAW) is the pre-eminent legal instrument on women's human rights.[15] It has been described as a 'landmark treaty in the struggle for women's rights'.[16] CEDAW is the only international human rights instrument exclusively focused on women. The treaty is unique in that it investigates from an asymmetrical standpoint how gender discrimination and inequality negatively impact women's human rights and proposes tailored obligations to remedy the gendered aspects of human rights violations. The strong commitment to eliminate discrimination against women and achieve gender equality in CEDAW offers a new and sophisticated way of using human rights to redress gender-based poverty that specifically captures the gender dimensions.

Despite a strong commitment to women's rights, there is a gap in CEDAW. There is no specific obligation in CEDAW on gender-based poverty. There is only a passing reference to women's poverty in the preamble, but there is no substantive provision on gender-based poverty in the treaty. Even though CEDAW is silent on the matter, it remains the ideal human rights treaty to address gender-based poverty. As mentioned, CEDAW has a nuanced understanding on the role of gender in human rights.[17] The wide scope of the treaty is another factor pulling in favour of using CEDAW to combat

---

[12] UN Special Rapporteur on extreme poverty and human rights, 'Socio-economic Rights and Poverty' (2016) A/HRC/32/31.

[13] International Covenant on Economic, Social and Cultural Rights (adopted 16 December 1966, entered into force 3 January 1976) 999 UNTS 3.

[14] JK Mapulanga-Hulston, 'Examining the Justiciability of Economic, Social and Cultural Rights' (2002) 6(4) *International Journal of Human Rights* 29, 34.

[15] Convention on the Elimination of All Forms of Discrimination Against Women (adopted 18 December 1979, entered into force 3 September 1981) 1249 UNTS 3.

[16] C Chinkin and M Freeman, 'Introduction' in M Freeman, C Chinkin and B Rudolf (eds), *CEDAW: A Commentary* (Oxford University Press, 2013) 2.

[17] Art 5(a) CEDAW.

gender-based poverty. Women in poverty experience a reinforcing web of human rights violations, including violations of their civil and political rights.[18] Due to the gender pay gap, women in poverty are often unable to afford information communication technology, thereby severely limiting their ability to participate in the latest political movements and be competitive in the labour market. In this example, gender-based poverty underpins women's lack of participation in public life (civil and political rights) and low position in the labour market (socioeconomic rights). Unlike ICESCR, CEDAW protects both civil and political, and economic and social rights. States are required to eliminate discrimination against women in *all* fields of life, public and private, civil and political, social, economic and cultural, so that women can enjoy their human rights.[19] Bringing gender-based poverty into CEDAW gives us a comprehensive tool. It requires the state to redress how gender-based poverty acts as an obstacle to women's civil, political, social, economic and cultural rights.

The gender-based poverty gap in CEDAW brings into focus our central inquiry. Given the absence of any specific obligation, can CEDAW be amended or interpreted to bring gender-based poverty within the auspices of the treaty? After canvassing and dismissing the possibility of amending CEDAW or drafting an optional protocol, an evolutionary interpretation of CEDAW that incorporates gender-based poverty is proposed in Part I. There are several potential interpretative routes to incorporating gender-based poverty into the treaty. An interpretation of equality and non-discrimination in CEDAW, two norms that permeate all of the treaty, offers the most persuasive and comprehensive basis to ensure a rich understanding of how gender-based poverty limits women's human rights. Unlike other possible interpretations of CEDAW, conceptualising gender-based poverty as an issue of equality and non-discrimination captures and emphasises the entrenched gendered nature of women's poverty. Moreover, this proposed interpretation unlocks the full potential of CEDAW. Given that a majority of the substantive provisions in CEDAW are based on equality and non-discrimination, an interpretation of CEDAW that connects gender, poverty, equality and non-discrimination ensures that all of the substantive obligations in CEDAW are understood in light of the experiences of gender-based poverty.

One of the strongest arguments in favour of using human rights to address gender-based poverty is that at the heart of human rights is accountability. States are accountable for their laws, policies and programmes that create, maintain and exacerbate gender-based poverty. Thus, it is not enough to provide a rigorous interpretation of CEDAW that incorporates the harms of gender-based poverty. It is crucial to investigate how the proposed

---

[18] UN Special Rapporteur on extreme poverty and human rights, 'Guiding Principles' (n 2) [3].
[19] Arts 1 and 3 CEDAW.

interpretation can be successfully integrated into the treaty's accountability mechanisms. Part II examines the current approach of the Committee, the body of twenty-three independent experts that monitors state implementation of CEDAW, to gender-based poverty. To more fully integrate gender-based poverty into CEDAW, I propose a General Recommendation on women and poverty. A General Recommendation is an authoritative statement from the Committee that provides a legal justification for this new interpretation; gives examples of best practice; and guides domestic laws, policies and programmes. A General Recommendation on women and poverty would be a pioneering evolution in international human rights law. It would be the first Recommendation or Comment by any of the UN treaty bodies that focuses on gender-based poverty and even more broadly, poverty. The General Recommendation on women and poverty proposed in Chapter 8 would place the Committee in a firm position to make from a human rights perspective both persuasive and authoritative recommendations to a majority of the world's states on gender-based poverty.

The purpose of this first chapter is to map the relationship between gender and poverty, to analyse the gaps in international human rights law and outline the proposed evolutionary interpretation of CEDAW. This chapter proceeds in the following manner: although there is a clear understanding that women are disproportionately poor, there is no established definition for gender-based poverty. To tap into the potential of the international human rights framework to address gender-based poverty it is vital both to investigate and define this phenomenon. Section I, relying on women's experiences and theories of social justice, defines gender-based poverty as the redistribution wrongs of not having access to economic resources coupled with the recognition and participation harms that exclude and devalue women and restrict their agency. Section II makes the case for using human rights to redress gender-based poverty. Specifically, it argues that gender-based poverty is a serious obstacle to women's human rights. The obligations and commitments in human rights instruments need to respond to the unique rights violations inherent in gender-based poverty. As of yet there has been no explicit and concerted effort to understand how the UN treaties can address gender-based poverty. Section III explains the gap in CEDAW: that there is no comprehensive obligation requiring states to ameliorate gender-based poverty. This gap is deeply problematic given that gender-based poverty is a serious impediment to women's human rights. Section IV explores in greater detail why CEDAW is the ideal treaty to situate a human rights approach to gender-based poverty. Section V justifies why an interpretation of CEDAW via equality and non-discrimination is the best option to bring gender-based poverty into the CEDAW framework and then maps how the proposed interpretation could be incorporated into the treaty's accountability mechanisms.

I. DEFINING GENDER-BASED POVERTY

Gender-based poverty is complex and very few attempts have been made to capture this phenomenon in a definition. The starting point, then, is to examine definitions of poverty and assess how these can be modified to incorporate the role of gender. Defining poverty has proven challenging for law-makers and policy-makers alike. New and reconceptualised definitions of poverty are moving away from equating poverty exclusively to material deprivation. A broader understanding of poverty incorporates the experiences of poverty and captures the lack of autonomy and power inherent in poverty. Incorporating the experience of poverty is an important shift and ensures that poverty alleviation programmes, laws and policies meaningfully address the complexity of poverty. Not as much attention has been paid to how the causes of poverty influence the conceptualisation of poverty. The root causes of poverty are difficult to articulate with any accuracy. However, it is evident that there is a strong relationship between gender and poverty. A few empirical examples illuminate this connection. In most European countries, women over 65 years old are at 'a higher risk of poverty than men'.[20] In the developing world, approximately one in three married women have 'no control over household spending on major purchases, and about one in ten married women is not consulted on how their own cash earnings are spent'.[21] It is inescapable that gender discrimination and inequality are influential in perpetuating women's poverty. The new definitions of poverty have not explicitly reflected this relationship and there is no established definition of gender-based poverty. To fully grasp how CEDAW can redress the gender-based aspects of poverty, it is crucial to understand the scope of the problem. After canvassing the new conceptions of poverty, examining the de facto experiences of women in poverty and the capabilities theory of Sen and Nussbaum, the recognition and redistribution paradigm as developed by Fraser, and finally the theory of justice developed by Young, a definition of gender-based poverty is proposed.

A. A New Conception of Poverty

Historically, poverty has been 'defined as insufficient income to buy a minimum basket of goods and services'.[22] This definition of poverty focuses on the number of people unable to access economic resources and reveals the dire state of the global population. The UN estimates that one in five people

---

[20] UN Department of Economic and Social Affairs, 'The Worlds Women 2015: Trends and Statistics' (2015) ST/ESA/STAT/SER.K/20 181.

[21] ibid 179.

[22] CESCR, 'Substantive Issues Arising in the Implementation of ICESCR: Poverty and ICESCR' (2001) E/C.12/2001/10 [7].

in the developing world live on less than $1.25 US a day.[23] Reducing poverty to economic want, however, is a limited understanding and does not capture the reality of living in poverty. Poverty has multiple, interlocking and reinforcing dimensions. People who live in poverty repeatedly report that it is more than material disadvantage. Poverty also encompasses powerlessness, exhaustion, exclusion, rejection, isolation, loneliness, insecurity, vulnerability, invisibility, worry, fear, anger, low self-confidence, frustration, stigma, humiliation and shame.[24] People in poverty are trapped in a web of powerlessness and voicelessness.[25]

Organisations around the world, such as the UN Development Programme (UNDP) and the Oxford Poverty & Human Development Initiative,[26] are responding to the empirical evidence and reforming the definition of poverty to reflect the experiences of the people who live in poverty. Our central aim is to investigate how CEDAW can be used to address gender-based poverty. Therefore, while recognising that a variety of individuals and organisations are grappling with how best to define poverty, we only examine how actors within the UN system, where CEDAW is based, are redefining poverty. There is wide agreement that poverty needs to be redefined, but there is no consensus on a broader concept of poverty.[27] Prominent actors in the UN, namely the Office of the High Commissioner of Human Rights (OHCHR) and the Committee on Economic and Social Cultural Rights (CESCR), the treaty body that monitors state implementation of ICESCR and the UNDP Human Development Index,[28] have drawn on the capabilities theory pioneered by Sen and Nussbaum to define poverty. This approach focuses on 'human capabilities and on the choices or freedoms of poor people'.[29] Significantly, consideration of capabilities moves the discussion beyond an exclusive focus on economic want. The aim of this approach is to make the individual a dignified being that can shape her life.[30] As Nussbaum explains, it does not ask: 'How much in the way of resources is Vasanti able to command?' Instead it asks: 'What is Vasanti actually able to do and be?'[31]

---

[23] *The Millennium Development Report: 2014*, 8–9, www.un.org/millenniumgoals/2014%20MDG%20report/MDG%202014%20English%20web.pdf.

[24] D Narayan et al, *Voices of the Poor: Crying out for Change* (Oxford University Press and World Bank, 2000) 31.

[25] ibid 265.

[26] Oxford Poverty & Human Development Initiative, 'Our Purpose', www.ophi.org.uk/.

[27] UNIFEM, 'Progress of the World's Women 2005: Women, Work and Poverty', 15, www.unifem.org/attachments/products/PoWW2005_eng.pdf.

[28] OHCHR, 'Poverty Reduction' (n 1); S Klasen and D Schuler, 'Reforming the Gender Related Development Index and Gender Empowerment Measure: Implementing Some Specific Proposals' (2011) 17(1) *Feminist Economics* 1; S Alkrine, 'The Missing Dimensions of Poverty Data: An Introduction' (OPHI Working Paper Series 00, 2007); OPHI, www.ophi.org.uk/.

[29] UNIFEM, Progress of the World's Women 2005 (n 27) 15.

[30] ibid 72.

[31] One of the women Martha Nussbaum uses in *Women and Human Development: The Capabilities Approach* (Cambridge University Press, 2000).

To be able to create a meaningful life it is necessary for each person to achieve a certain level of capabilities. Nussbaum's list of capabilities required for humanity is comprehensive: life; bodily integrity; sense, imagination and thought; emotions; practical reason; affiliation; other species; play; being able to participate in effective political choices; and being able to hold property.[32] Although there is no provision for economic resources, Nussbaum acknowledges that these capabilities will require a 'greater material equality than exists in most societies, since we are unlikely to get all citizens above a minimum threshold of capability for truly human functioning without some redistributive policy'.[33]

The capabilities approach is being used to reconceptualise poverty within the UN system. The UNDP has used capabilities theory to devise the Human Development Index, where poverty is measured on life expectancy at birth, years of education and gross national income per capita.[34] CESCR also adopts a multidimensional definition of poverty grounded in capabilities theory. It explains that poverty is 'as a human condition characterized by sustained or chronic deprivation of resources, capabilities, choices, security and power necessary for the enjoyment of an adequate standard of living and other civil, cultural, economic, political and social rights'.[35] The OHCHR stresses that poverty is the failure to achieve a basic level of capabilities.[36] It further holds that poverty is 'the absence or inadequate realization of certain basic freedoms, such as the freedoms to avoid hunger, disease, illiteracy and so on'.[37] In all of these new definitions of poverty there is still a role for material disadvantage but it is more nuanced than purely economic definitions of poverty.[38]

B. Recognising and Defining Gender-Based Poverty

A multidimensional definition of poverty is essential to accurately capture what it means to live in poverty. It is only a first step. To truly address gender-based poverty, it is necessary to tailor responses that correspond to the underlying reasons why women in poverty experience human rights violations. The European Court of Human Rights made a similar observation in respect to understanding the racial overtones of violence against minorities:

> Treating racially-induced violence and brutality on an equal footing with cases that have no racist overtones would be turning a blind eye to the specific nature

---

[32] ibid 79–80. Sen chooses not to define a set list of capabilities arguing instead that this should be left to the reasoning of the community; see A Sen, 'Human Rights and Capabilities' (2005) 6(2) *Journal of Human Development* 151–66.
[33] ibid 86.
[34] UNDP, 'Human Development Index', http://hdr.undp.org/en/statistics/hdi/.
[35] CESCR, 'Poverty and ICESCR' (n 22) [8].
[36] OHCHR, 'Poverty Reduction' (n 1) 7.
[37] ibid 17.
[38] ibid 10.

of acts that are particularly destructive of fundamental rights. Failure to make a distinction in the way situations that are essentially different are handled may constitute unjustified treatment irreconcilable with [the non-discrimination provision] in the European Convention on Human Rights.[39]

To meaningfully address poverty it is essential to capture the experience of poverty *and* trace its causes. Poverty is complicated and there are many interlocking factors that explain it. Moreover, the causes and explanations of poverty can reflect political ideologies and be deeply value-laden. Again, the legal literature on poverty within the UN framework is examined as it is most relevant to understanding the relationship between gender-based poverty, human rights and CEDAW. Natural disasters, conflict and post-conflict situations, climate change, endemics, large-scale tax evasions, corruption, global governance structures all cause and contribute to poverty. Gender power relations are also a significant cause of women's poverty. The UN Special Rapporteur on extreme poverty and human rights forcefully holds that '*discrimination and exclusion are among the major causes and consequences of poverty ... persons living in poverty often experience disadvantage and discrimination*' based on their identity status, such as gender.[40] At the same time, it is important to acknowledge that there may be situations where women experience poverty that is not connected to their gender—for example, an epidemic or natural disaster. However, the response to these experiences and situations would have to be carefully analysed to ensure that remedial measures are not based on prejudicial and stereotypical gender norms that create or exacerbate gender-based poverty.[41] While recognising the importance of appreciating all the factors that have a role in poverty, the focus here is on one contributing factor to poverty: gender discrimination and inequality.[42]

Nussbaum's capabilities theory is grounded in women's experience and specifically developed from a gender perspective, but the multidimensional definitions of poverty derived from the capabilities approach have so far been framed in gender-neutral terms. This is problematic as the evidence indicates a close relationship between gender and poverty.[43] Examining both the experience of women who live in poverty and the gender-based causes of poverty, it is possible to arrive at an accurate definition of gender-based poverty.

While the capabilities approach offers important insights, it is important to identify the role of gender in denying capabilities and perpetuating poverty.

---

[39] *Ciorcan v Romania*, [2015] ECHR 84 (European Court of Human Rights).
[40] UN Special Rapporteur on extreme poverty and human rights, 'Guiding Priniciple' (n 2) [8].
[41] The Committee, 'General Recommendation No 18: on Women and AIDS' (1990) CEDAW/C/GC/18.
[42] OHCHR, 'Poverty Reduction' (n 1) 8.
[43] See for example, UN Women, 'Progress of the World's Women 2015–2016: Transforming Economies, Realising Rights', http://progress.unwomen.org/en/2015/.

Burrows writes that for 'most women, what it is to be human is to work long hours in agriculture or the home, to receive little or no remuneration and to be faced with political and legal processes which ignore their contribution to society and accord no recognition of their particular needs'.[44] These factors to varying degrees apply to men in poverty, but they operate differently for women because the reasons for their poverty are different. The gender division of labour in both the formal and informal labour market; the lack of legal regulation of the informal labour market, the concentration of women in low-paying and often precarious jobs, the low valuation of work traditionally assigned to women, unequal pay for work of equal value, gender power imbalances in the home, the disproportionate amount of unpaid care work women perform, and the limited access women have to education, bank loans, sexual and reproductive health services and land all combine to create a unique experience for poor women.[45] It is sociocultural norms on the role and value of women that underpin women's exclusion from public discourse, marginalise their voice within the household and limit their ability to access economic resources. Again sociocultural gender norms dictate that women perform a disproportionate amount of unpaid care work. This means women have fewer opportunities for education and skills-training and so are less likely to be economically independent.[46] In startling numbers women do not have control over resources.[47] If a woman does try to assert her property rights, she may be perceived as egotistical and selfish by the community.[48] Often the lack of control over land or other property is dictated by the law. Family, property and inheritance law are constructed to ensure women do not have control over resources.[49] Marriage, divorce or widowhood can detrimentally effect a woman's financial situation.[50] In both the developed and developing world, women bear a 'greater cost than men upon the breakdown of the family and may be left destitute upon widowhood'.[51] Due to sociocultural norms and power imbalances in the household, women may receive less than men even though there are sufficient

---

[44] N Burrows, 'International Law and Human Rights: The Case of Women's Rights' in T Campbell et al (eds), *Human Rights: From Rhetoric to Reality* (Basil Blackwell, 1986) 82.

[45] G Brodsky and S Day, 'Beyond the Social and Economic Rights Debate: Substantive Equality Speaks to Poverty' (2002) 14 *Canadian Journal of Women and the Law* 184; C Sweetman, *Gender, Development and Poverty* (Oxfam, 2002).

[46] The World Bank, 'World Development Report: Gender, Equality and Development' (n 6) 82.

[47] ibid 80–1.

[48] I Ikdahl, 'Property and Security: Articulating Women's Right to their Homes' in A Hellum and HS Aasen (eds), *Women's Human Rights: CEDAW in International, Regional and National Law* (Cambridge University Press, 2013) 270.

[49] World Bank, 'Voice and Agency' (n 6) ch 5 'Control over Land and Housing'.

[50] World Bank, 'World Development Report: Gender, Equality and Development' (n 6) ch 4 'Promoting Women's Agency'.

[51] The Committee, 'General Recommendation No 29: on Economic Consequences of Marriage, Family Relations and their Dissolution' (2013) CEDAW/C/GC/29 [4].

resources to meet a minimum basic needs standard.[52] Nussbaum illustrates this point by examining the daily life of Jayamma, a woman who lives in southern India. Jayamma 'takes sugar in her tea, for example, while she allows her husband and her children to take the more expensive milk'.[53] Calculating that the home has access to resources cannot account for the fact that Jayamma does not have milk in her tea. Women like Jayamma are often powerless 'to determine the way in which livelihoods are made and money is spent'.[54] Measurements of poverty are often based on household units and rarely pierce the veil and acknowledge the unequal distribution of resources between men and women in the home.[55] The Committee has also recently observed that 'women often do not equally enjoy their family's economic wealth and gains'.[56] As a further example, women and girls may undergo harmful cultural practices which limit their ability to complete their education and fully participate in the community.[57]

Thus, poverty for women is not merely insufficient income but is also characterised by exclusion from social life, political marginalisation, bodily and psychological insecurity, stigma, fatigue and voicelessness.[58] This is consistent with the gender-neutral definition of multidimensional poverty canvassed above. It is imperative to appreciate that the economic disadvantage, compromised autonomy, exclusion and participation harms women in poverty experience are often rooted in gender and gender relations. It is the unique interaction between gender and an inadequate command over economic resources that result in women being denied their capabilities and living in poverty. It is important to conceptualise gender-based poverty as distinct from poverty because for many women the reason they live in poverty is routinely underpinned by patriarchal power relationships between men and women. Fraser's redistribution and recognition paradigm is helpful here in developing a definition of gender-based poverty.[59] Redistribution harms are 'rooted in the economic structure of society' and involve the economic deprivation of the individual.[60] Recognition harms, on the other hand, manifest in cultural domination, non-recognition and disrespect and the remedy lies in 're-evaluating disrespected identities [and] positively valorising

---

[52] S Chant, 'Re-thinking the "Feminization of Poverty" in relation to Aggregate Gender Indices' (2007) 7(2) *Journal of Human Development* 201.

[53] Nussbaum (n 31) 57.

[54] Sweetman (n 45) 4.

[55] UN Department of Economic and Social Affairs (n 20) 180.

[56] 'General Recommendation No 29: on Economic Consequences' (n 51) [1].

[57] The Committee and The Committee on the Convention on the Rights of the Child, 'General Recommendation No 31: On Harmful Practices' (2014) CEDAW/C/GC/31 [14], [56], [61].

[58] Sweetman (n 45).

[59] N Fraser and A Honneth, *Redistribution or Recognition: A Political–Philosophical Exchange* (Verso, 2003).

[60] ibid 13.

cultural diversity'.[61] Fraser argues that: '[T]wo dimensionally subordinated groups suffer both mal-distribution and misrecognition in forms where neither of these injustices is an indirect effect of the other, but where both are primary.'[62] She uses gender as the classic example of a two-dimensional subordinate group. A good example of the synergy between these two different types of harm is the struggle for equal pay for work of equal value. Fredman observes that 'the value system on which pay is based is deeply gendered, reflected in the inferior recognition afforded to women's work in the labour market' which results in lower pay.[63] At the same time, lower pay contributes to the low status of work done by women. Fraser's insights clarify that the definition of gender-based poverty needs to accurately capture the synergistic relationship between economic deprivation and gender norms.

There is one further element that needs to be included in the definition of gender-based poverty so that it accurately reflects the cause and experience of women who live in poverty. Fraser and Young's theory of justice places a primary role on participation. This in turn highlights the harm of exclusion. Fraser's theory places the parity of participation at its normative core. She argues that 'the distribution of material resources must be such as to ensure participant's independence and voice'.[64] Similarly, Young places central importance on participation in decision-making processes.[65] Both Fraser and Young argue that to remedy the redistribution and recognition harms of gender, decision-making processes must be more inclusive and emphasise the importance of participation. It is important to conceptualise participation as including a voice in both public and private decision-making processes because, as the Committee, notes: '[W]omen in both developing and developed countries generally share the experience of being worse off economically than men in family relationships.'[66] This is reflected in the example of Jayamma who does not have access to household resources. Equal participation in the home is vital for women who live in poverty. Participation must also recognise that women do not necessarily speak with the same voice but can have different and even competing voices.

Drawing all these insights together, gender-based poverty is defined as the redistribution wrongs of not having access to economic resources coupled with the recognition and participation harms that devalue women and exclude them from public and private life. It is the combination both of material disadvantage and gendered sociocultural norms that routinely limit the ability of women in poverty to create a meaningful life.

---

[61] ibid.
[62] ibid 19.
[63] S Fredman, 'Redistribution and Recognition: Reconciling Inequalities' (2007) 23 *South African Journal on Human Rights* 214, 219.
[64] Fraser and Honneth (n 59) 36.
[65] I Young, *Justice and the Politics of Difference* (Princeton University Press, 1990) 36.
[66] 'General Recommendation No 29: on Economic Consequences' (n 51) [5].

Before proceeding to assess how the international human rights framework grapples with gender-based poverty, it is important to clarify two issues. The first issue is of terminology. At times there is a distinction drawn between extreme poverty and poverty. Extreme poverty is marked by a prolonged and vicious degree of powerlessness, stigmatisation, exclusion and material deprivation.[67] While poverty has the same features it is generally understood not to engage the same level of severity. The distinction may have some legal significance. Arguably circumstances of extreme poverty could violate rights not engaged by poverty, such as the right to life or the right not to be subjected to cruel, inhumane or degrading treatment. As is explained in detail below, the text of CEDAW does not distinguish between extreme poverty and poverty. Nor are there provisions in CEDAW on inhumane treatment or life. This means the question of which rights apply only in cases of extreme gender-based poverty does not arise in the context of CEDAW. CEDAW is designed to apply to all women regardless of their geographical, cultural, religious, social or economic context.[68] Therefore, for our purposes no distinction is drawn between gender-based poverty and extreme gender-based poverty. It is interesting to note that although the mandate of the Special Rapporteur is extreme poverty and human rights, she emphasises that the guiding principles on extreme poverty 'should not be interpreted as indicating that specific obligations or recommendations may not also apply to persons living in poverty generally'.[69] There is a further important reason gender-based poverty as a whole must be dealt with under an international human rights framework. Extreme gender-based poverty tends to focus on conditions in the developing world.[70] Focusing only on extreme gender-based poverty has the potential to obscure gender-based poverty in the developed world, yet women in both the developed and developing world suffer from gender-based poverty. For these reasons no distinction is drawn between these two conceptions of gender-based poverty. The definition of gender-based poverty, while including cases of extreme gender-based poverty, is broader to include gender-based poverty that is not marked by a degree of severity.

Second, the experience and causes of poverty are intricate and crosscutting. Similarly, gender-based poverty cannot be attributed to one single actor. For women, both private and public actors within the state can create and perpetuate gender-based poverty. There is increasing recognition that actors external to the state can also play a meaningful role in perpetuating

---

[67] UN Special Rapporteur on extreme poverty and human rights, 'Guiding Principles' (n 2) [4].
[68] The Committee, 'General Recommendation No 25: on Temporary Special Measures' (2004) CEDAW/C/GC/25 [14].
[69] UN Special Rapporteur on extreme poverty and human rights, 'Guiding Principles' (n 2) fn 1.
[70] The World Bank, 'Poverty: Data', http://data.worldbank.org/topic/poverty. There is no data on poverty from Western Europe, North America, Australia or New Zealand.

and ameliorating gender-based poverty. The UN Working Group on Discrimination Against Women in Law and Practice observes that:

> [The] mobility of corporations and free trade agreement have resulted in the amassing of political power vis-as-vis host States... the move of production by transnational corporations to export processing zones, the reliance on home and sweatshop sectors, and land dispossession by extractives industries are a locus for corporate abuse and violation of human rights, and most of the victims are women.[71]

Salomon also notes that one of the consequence of the growth of international organisations, such as the World Bank and the International Monetary Fund, 'is that governments have increasingly less control in determining their economic and social policies within their own territories, particularly developing countries'.[72] UN Women argues that international macroeconomic policies 'do not adequately consider the importance of unpaid care and domestic work... they have also artificially constrained the resources available to governments to finance policies and programmes for gender equality'.[73] The international human rights regime was developed within a statist framework; only states are bound by human rights obligations and the treaty bodies only have authority to monitor the actions of state parties. There is increasing attention to how non-state actors such as transnational corporations and international financial institutions can be held accountable for human rights violations and how states can work together to tackle global problems, such as gender-based poverty.[74] It is outside our scope to extensively assess how external state actors can be held accountable. In Chapter 4 there are tentative proposals to developing an obligation to cooperate and accountability mechanisms for non-state actors drawing on the state's obligation in CEDAW to eliminate discrimination against women without delay (Article 2).

II. GENDER-BASED POVERTY AS AN OBSTACLE TO HUMAN RIGHTS

Poverty has long been perceived as a private moral failing and an issue of charity. Poverty alleviation programmes have been based on political

---

[71] Working Group on Discrimination Against Women in Law and Practice, 'Discrimination against Women in Economic and Social Life, with a Focus on Economic Crisis' (2014) A/C/26/39 [69].

[72] M Salomon, *Global Responsibilty for Human Rights: World Poverty and the Development of International Law* (Oxford University Press, 2007) 45–6; UN Special Rapporteur on extreme poverty and human rights, 'The World Bank and Human Rights' (2015) A/70/274.

[73] UN Women, 'Progress of the World's Women 2015–2016' (n 43) ch 4 'Macroeconomic Policies and Gender Equality'.

[74] OHCHR, 'Report of the United Nations High Commissioner for Human Rights on the Responsibilities of Transnational Corporations and Related Business Enterprises with Regard to Human Rights' (2005) E/CN4/2005/91.

commitments, acts of generosity or development programmes, all of which can be withdrawn and subject to change. The UN human rights actors understand poverty differently. The OHCHR holds that poverty is legally relevant when it is causally connected to the denial of human rights.[75] The Human Rights Committee (HRC), which monitors the implementation of the International Covenant of Civil and Political Rights,[76] and CESCR both routinely conceptualise poverty as an obstacle to human rights and a cause of human rights violations. This is explored in greater detail in Chapter 3 when canvassing strategies for constructing a persuasive interpretation of CEDAW. The UN Special Rapporteur on extreme poverty and human rights also refers to poverty as an obstacle to human rights.[77] She notes that poverty is both a cause and consequence of human rights violations.[78] Conceptualising poverty as an impediment to human rights avoids determining if there is a right to be free from poverty.[79] The focus is on how poverty negatively impacts the enjoyment of established human rights. The analysis here adopts this conceptualisation—poverty and gender-based poverty as an obstacle to human rights—and does not investigate if there is right to be free from poverty or gender-based poverty. It focuses on how gender-based poverty interacts and undermines the established legal commitments in CEDAW.

It is helpful to start first by examining how the UN approaches the link between human rights and poverty and then assess the impact of gender. Both the OHCHR and UN Special Rapporteur on extreme poverty and human rights explain that all rights are at stake when understanding and remedying poverty. The Special Rapporteur clarifies that poverty is 'characterised by multiple reinforcing violations of civil, political, economic, social and cultural rights'.[80] People in poverty 'are confronted by the most severe obstacles to accessing their rights and entitlements. Consequently, they experience many interrelated and mutually reinforcing deprivations that prevent them from realising their rights and perpetuate their poverty.'[81] An example helps illustrate this point. If children are undernourished because their family cannot afford food, they are more likely to perform poorly in school.[82] Often due to negative stereotypes and stigmatisation, deprived neighbourhoods are not as well serviced and poor children have to 'travel a

---

[75] OHCHR, 'Poverty Reduction' (n 1) 10.

[76] International Covenant of Civil and Political Rights (adopted 16 December 1966, entered into force 23 March 1976) 991 UNTS 171.

[77] See UN Special Rapporteur on extreme poverty and human rights, 'Draft Guiding Principles on Extreme Poverty and Human Rights' (2010) A/HRC/15/41 [34].

[78] UN Special Rapporteur on extreme poverty and human rights, 'Guiding Principles' (n 2) [3].

[79] T Pogge (ed), *Freedom from Poverty as a Human Right: Who Owes What to the Very Poor* (Oxford University Press, 2008).

[80] UN Special Rapporteur on extreme poverty and human rights, 'Guiding Principles' (n 2) [3].

[81] ibid [4].

[82] UN Special Rapporteur on extreme poverty and human rights, 'Draft Guiding Principles' (n 77) [24].

long way to access public services such as health care, education and sanitation facilities'.[83] People in poverty lack the voice, agency and power to engage the political process to advocate for food subsidies, new schools or high-quality public services.[84] Without being able to access education, these children then find it difficult to gain decent employment and become trapped in exploitative work.[85] This is just one example of many of the interlocking human rights violation that occurs for people in poverty.

The OHCHR holds that ensuring the enjoyment of *all* human rights is necessary to address poverty effectively.[86] They explain that while poverty might be defined by the lack of traditional socioeconomic rights, 'an effective anti-poverty strategy will certainly have to address a much wider range of human rights. This is because human rights can be relevant to poverty in multiple ways.'[87] They identify three: constitutive, instrumental and constraint-based relevance.[88] Constitutive relevance is when inadequate resources result in a denial of the right—for example, inadequate food undermines the right to food. To explain instrumental relevance, the OHCHR draws on Sen's work on famines. Sen's analysis demonstrates that famines never occur when there is 'a reasonable degree of civil-political freedom'.[89] Civil and political rights give the individual voice and allow them to hold the state accountable. Individuals can then demand that the state take all appropriate measures to fully implement socioeconomic rights. The realisation of socioeconomic rights, such as the right to food, ultimately prevents famines. All human rights have the ability to 'promote the cause of poverty reduction'.[90] In relation to constraint-based relevance, human rights can 'have a bearing on the nature and content of poverty reduction strategies by ruling out certain types of actions as impermissible'.[91] A poverty reduction strategy might include population control measures, but 'it would not be permissible to adopt draconian measures such as forced sterilization that violate people's personal integrity and privacy'.[92] The OHCHR insights are returned to when interpreting the text of CEDAW in Chapter 4.

Although there is no explicit definition of gender-based poverty within the UN framework, there is a keen awareness that, for women in poverty, it is the interaction of limited access to economic resources, gender norms and participation harm that creates significant impediments to the realisation

---

[83] ibid [26].
[84] OHCHR, 'Poverty Reduction' (n 1) 13–14.
[85] UN Special Rapporteur on extreme poverty and human rights, 'Draft Guiding Principles' (n 77) [24].
[86] OHCHR, 'Poverty Reduction' (n 1) 11.
[87] ibid.
[88] ibid.
[89] ibid; A Sen, *Development as Freedom* (Oxford University Press, 1999) 188.
[90] OHCHR, 'Poverty Reduction' (n 1) 11.
[91] ibid 12.
[92] ibid 12.

of their human rights. The UN Special Rapporteur on extreme poverty and human rights succinctly observes: '[G]ender inequality causes and perpetuates poverty.'[93] Women 'are disproportionately represented among the poor *owing* to the multifaceted and cumulative forms of discrimination that they endure'.[94] The UN Special Rapporteur on the right to food notes that women face discrimination not only in the law but also in the result of 'social norms or customs, linked to certain stereotypes about gender roles; unequal access to productive resources such as land and to economic opportunities, such as decent wage employment; unequal bargaining positions within the household; gendered division of labour within households'.[95] The UN Working Group on Discrimination Against Women also observes that: '[D]iscriminatory legislation, often through application of personal law systems, continues to create an almost impassable barrier to women's equal economic and social opportunity.'[96] Gender discrimination plays a pivotal role in condemning women to lives of poverty. It is the synergistic relationship between discrimination, gender inequality and poverty that creates serious obstacles to the full enjoyment of women's human rights, such as the right to food, education, employment and land.

III. THE GAP IN THE INTERNATIONAL HUMAN RIGHTS FRAMEWORK

It is imperative to explicitly articulate the unique multidimensional harms of gender-based poverty and to recognise that gender-based poverty is a significant obstacle to women's human rights. As explained above, various UN Special Rapporteurs are beginning to recognise the close relationship between gender, poverty and human rights. The next step is to situate the relationship between gender, poverty and human rights in states' binding international *legal* commitments. None of the nine UN human rights treaties contain provisions on gender-based poverty. How can international human rights treaties best respond to this newly recognised threat to human rights? As of yet, there has been no direct, explicit or sustained assessment on how the UN treaties can address gender-based poverty. Socioeconomic rights are perceived as the strongest tool to tackle poverty.[97] Seemingly the first choice, then, for situating gender-based poverty in the international human rights treaties would be ICESCR, which protects key socioeconomic rights.

---

[93] UN Special Rapporteur on extreme poverty and human rights, 'Draft Guiding Principles' (n 77) [45].

[94] UN Special Rapporteur on extreme poverty and human rights, 'Guiding Principles' (n 2) [23].

[95] UN Special Rapporteur on the right to food, 'Women's Rights and the Right to Food' (2013) A/HRC/22/50 [2].

[96] Working Group (n 71) [14].

[97] D Whelan and J Donnelly, 'The West, Economic and Social Rights and the Global Human Rights Regime: Setting the Record Straight' (2007) 29 *Human Rights Quarterly* 908, 930–31.

This option is not without difficulties as the struggle for the recognition, monitoring and enforcement of socioeconomic rights is well documented.[98] The role of gender in perpetuating women's poverty points towards using new legal tools for addressing gender-based poverty. Perhaps gender-based poverty is best tackled through the equality and discrimination framework in CEDAW?

As mentioned above, CEDAW is designed to eliminate all forms of discrimination and achieve gender equality so that women can enjoy their human rights. It explicitly guarantees women's equality in political life (Article 7), nationality (Article 9), education (Article 10), employment (Article 11), health (Article 12), economic and social life (Article 13) and family life (Article 16). It ensures women's equality before the law (Article 15) and there are special provisions for rural women (Article 14). The aims of CEDAW— eliminating discrimination and achieving gender equality—seem to promise that it is the ideal treaty body to begin to develop states' legal obligations to address gender-based poverty. However, there are some notable omissions from CEDAW. There are no provisions in CEDAW addressing gender-based poverty or gender-based violence. General Recommendation No 19 on violence against women rectified this omission and gender-based violence is firmly interpreted into the definition of discrimination against in women under Article 1 of CEDAW.[99] There is currently no similar established understanding of how gender-based poverty is incorporated into CEDAW.

Initially this concern might appear moot as CEDAW does seem to have provisions to address gender-based poverty, but on closer inspection these fall short. There is one reference to poverty in the preamble to the treaty, namely 'a concern that women in poverty have the least access to food, health, education and employment opportunities'. This concern does not directly translate into any substantive provision. This is not to dismiss the importance of the reference to gender-based poverty in the preamble; it is an important interpretative aid and drawn upon when interpreting the text in Chapter 4.[100] The most promising provision to address gender-based poverty is Article 14 on equality for rural women. Article 14(2)(c) holds that states shall 'ensure... the right: to benefit directly from social security programmes' Article 14(2)(h) creates a right to 'enjoy adequate living conditions, particular in relation to housing, sanitation, electricity and water supply, transport and communications'. However, the chapeau of Article 14 makes it explicit that these rights are only granted to rural women, for the obligation holds that states 'shall take all appropriate measures to eliminate

---

[98] S Fredman and M Campbell (eds), *Social and Economic Rights and Constitutional Law* (Edward Elgar, 2016).
[99] (1992) CEDAW/C/GC/19.
[100] C Chinkin and B Rudolf, 'Preamble' in M Freeman, C Chinkin and B Rudolf (eds), *CEDAW: A Commentary* (Oxford University Press, 2013).

discrimination against *women in rural areas*'.[101] There are no obligations for states to ensure an adequate standard of living or social assistance to urban women. As poverty is not confined to rural areas, using Article 14 to address gender-based poverty is a limited approach. The reasons for confining key socioeconomic rights to rural women are explored in detail in Chapter 2. A similar problem arises under Article 11 on equality in employment. Article 11 guarantees women the right to social security and paid leave.[102] Problematically, these provisions are conditional on some form of employment relationship. Another potential provision is Article 13, which requires the state to ensure equality in economic and social life. CEDAW elaborates that this means equality in family benefits, access to financial credit and participation in the community. While there has been some academic commentary on the potential of this provision to be interpreted to address gender-based poverty, it remains an underdeveloped right.[103] Moreover, Articles 11, 13 and 14 of CEDAW read in isolation do not address the interactions between civil and political rights and gender sociocultural norms that, as explained above, are crucial to understanding and ameliorating gender-based poverty. Thus, while CEDAW with its commitment to addressing gender norms, eliminating discrimination and achieving women's equality still holds significant promise to meaningfully address gender-based poverty, it is necessary to carefully consider how despite no explicit provision on gender-based poverty this promise can be realised.

IV. THE PROMISE OF CEDAW IN ADDRESSING GENDER-BASED POVERTY

The gap in CEDAW might suggest that it cannot address gender-based poverty and it would be more straightforward to approach gender-based poverty through the socioeconomic rights guaranteed in ICESCR. Examining and comparing the content and structure of both ICESCR and CEDAW reveals that there is still significant potential for CEDAW to ameliorate gender-based poverty.

CESCR observes that the rights in ICESCR 'lie at the heart of the Covenant [and] have a direct and immediate bearing upon the eradication of poverty'.[104] ICESCR guarantees rights to gainful employment, fair wages and equal remuneration for work of equal value; social security; maternity benefits; an adequate standard of living; and a continuous improvement in living conditions, health and education.[105] All of these are crucial elements in

---

[101] Emphasis added.
[102] Art 11(1)(e) CEDAW.
[103] B Rudolf, 'Article 13' in M Freeman, C Chinkin and B Rudolf (eds), *CEDAW: A Commentary* (Oxford University Press, 2012).
[104] CESCR, 'Poverty and ICESCR' (n 22) [5].
[105] Arts 6–13 ICESCR.

remedying gender-based poverty. Although the rights are, for the most part, framed in gender-neutral terms, under Article 3 of ICESCR states are required to ensure 'the equal right of men and women to the enjoyment of all' rights in ICESCR. Article 3 'should be read in conjunction with each specific rights guaranteed under' ICESCR. This means, for example, although Article 11 of ICESCR holds 'everyone has a right to an adequate standard of living for himself and his family', CESCR has clarified that this should be interpreted from a gender perspective. The right to an adequate standard of living, as CESCR explains, requires the state to recognise women as the heads of households, to ensure women have the right to own economic resources and control over food production, and to address gender-based social norms that dictate women eat less nutritious foods.[106] This is a nuanced approach as it addresses both the redistribution and recognition wrongs of gender-based poverty. However, there has been criticism that CESCR has not been consistently or comprehensively integrating a gender perspective into its interpretation of ICESCR.[107] The full potential of ICESCR to remedy the harms of gender-based poverty is just beginning to be uncovered.

Turning to CEDAW, it is readily apparent that it is the ideal treaty to initially situate gender-based poverty in binding international legal commitments. The failure of the mainstream international human rights system to take women's human rights seriously prompted the UN to draft a treaty that exclusively focuses on the rights of women.[108] CEDAW has positioned itself as the definitive treaty for addressing women's human rights. It is a sophisticated instrument because in one document it protects civil, political and socioeconomic rights.[109] CEDAW has a very strong mandate to address the interaction between gender social norms and women's human rights. Article 5 of CEDAW explicitly calls on states to remedy negative sociocultural stereotypes and prejudices that disadvantage women. Since gender-based poverty is deeply rooted in gender social norms, CEDAW is in a strong position to uncover the gender-based aspects of women's poverty. The Committee is a strong advocate for empowering women in all aspects of public and private life. It analyses the situation of women in prisons;

---

[106] CESCR, 'General Comment No 16: The Equal Right of Men and Women to the Enjoyment of Economic, Social and Cultural Rights' (2005) E/C.12/2005/4 [28].

[107] H Charlesworth, 'Not Waving but Drowning: Gender Mainstreaming and Human Rights in the United Nations' (2005) 18 *Harvard Human Rights* 1; D Otto, 'Gender Comment: Why Does the UN Committee on Economic, Social and Cultural Rights Need a General Comment on Women' (2002) 14 *Canadian Journal of Women and the Law* 1; S Fredman, 'Engendering Socio-economic Rights' in A Hellum and HS Aasen (eds). *Women's Human Rights: CEDAW in International Regional and National Law* (Cambridge University Press, 2013) 232.

[108] Division for the Advancement of Women, 'Short History of CEDAW Convention', www.un.org/womenwatch/daw/cedaw/history.htm.

[109] HB Schopp-Schilling, 'The Nature and Scope of the Convention' in HB Schopp-Schilling and C Flinterman (eds), *The Circle of Empowerment: Twenty-Five Years of the Committee on the Elimination of Discrimination Against Women* (Feminist Press, 2007) 25.

the exploitation of women in the media; the gendered effects of austerity measures; abortion laws; sex education and bullying; the gender pay gap and affordable childcare; the necessity of temporary special measures to increase the participation of women in legislative bodies, the judiciary and private companies; the economic effects of divorce; the structure of social benefits; and the situation of vulnerable women.[110] CEDAW's attention to a variety of women's issues and its ability to address gendered sociocultural norms makes it the ideal treaty to incorporate the interlocking and complex nature of gender-based poverty.

The strengths of CEDAW become even more apparent in contrasting the structure of the obligations in CEDAW and ICESCR. Under Article 2(1) of ICESCR, states are obligated 'to take steps... to the maximum of [their] available resources, with a view to achieving progressively the full realisation of the rights' in ICESCR. Alston and Quinn explain that there is an immediate obligation to take steps that aim at achieving the full realisation of economic, social and cultural rights and that the 'progressive realisation' obligation and 'maximum available resources' depend on the state's level of economic development.[111] ICESCR is focused on both immediate steps and the progressive development of resources to realise socioeconomic rights. There is a further immediate obligation in ICESCR. Article 3 guarantees equality between men and women in economic, social and cultural rights. CESCR explains that this is 'a mandatory and immediate obligation of [the] State',[112] but it does not explain how this immediate commitment to gender equality interacts with the progressive realisation standard. Reading these two provisions together suggests that all immediate steps taken to progressively realise rights need to further equality between men and women. State measures to realise socioeconomic rights under ICESCR cannot disproportionately favour men. CEDAW, on the other hand, is premised on eliminating discrimination and achieving gender equality. The Committee notes this means that the obligations in CEDAW are to be immediately realised.[113] Using the obligations in CEDAW to alleviate gender-based poverty places the state obligation on a different standard. The UN Working Group on Discrimination Against Women explains that the commitment to gender equality 'concerns the division of existing resources, not the development of resources, and therefore the principle of progressive realisation does not apply'.[114] CEDAW requires the state: (i) to *immediately*

---

[110] The Committee, 'Seventh Concluding Observations: UK' (2013) CEDAW/C/GBR/CO/7.

[111] P Alston and G Quinn, 'The Nature and Scope of the State Parties' Obligation under ICESCR' (1987) 9 *Human Rights Quarterly* 156.

[112] CESCR, 'General Comment No 16: The Equal Rights of Men and Women' (n 106) [16].

[113] The Committee, 'General Recommendation No 28: on the Core Obligations' (2010) CEDAW/C/GC/28 [15].

[114] Working Group (n 71) [8].

assess the de jure and de facto situation of women; and (ii) to *immediately* take concrete steps to formulate and implement a policy that 'is targeted as clearly as possible towards' achieving substantive equality.[115] The state is not setting a timetable for when to progressively realise gender equality, but instead 'the emphasis is on movement forward ... to build on [appropriate] measures continuously in the light of their effectiveness and new or emerging issues, in order to achieve the treaty's goals'.[116] If gender-based poverty can be brought into the CEDAW framework, there is an immediate obligation to remedy the discriminatory and unequal laws, policies and programmes that create and contribute to gender-based poverty. This is an important difference and further justifies examining how CEDAW can immediately incorporate gender-based poverty. The challenge of an immediate obligation to achieve gender equality in relation to gender-based poverty is further explored in Chapter 4.

Initially situating gender-based poverty in CEDAW is not to be taken as marginalising the role of ICESCR in remedying gender-based poverty. A rich understanding of gender-based poverty can and should be incorporated into ICESCR and the other human rights treaties and instruments. Van Leeuwen observes that the UN has a two-pronged complementary approach to women's human rights through the 'principles of non-discrimination and equality in [the] *mainstream* human rights treaties and through these principles in [the] *women-specific* human rights treaties'.[117] A rigorous approach to gender-based poverty situated in the women-specific treaties can feed into the other human rights treaties. There is a strong precedent for this positive relationship. The Committee was one of the first voices connecting violence against women to patriarchy. This understanding has feed into and picked up by CESCR, which now adopts a comprehensive rights-based approach to gender-based violence.[118]

V. MAPPING THE SOLUTION: AN EVOLUTIONARY INTERPRETATION OF CEDAW

CEDAW, with its comprehensive focus on all women's issues—civil, political, socioeconomic and cultural—and its proven track record of being a strong advocate for women's human rights is the model choice, notwithstanding its lack of specific substantive obligations on gender-based poverty. The gender-based poverty gap in CEDAW remains a significant problem.

---

[115] 'General Recommendation No 28' (n 113) [24].
[116] ibid 24.
[117] F Van Leeuwen, 'Women's Rights Are Human Rights!': The Practice of the United Nations Human Rights Committee and the Committee on Economic, Social and Cultural Rights' in A Hellum and HS Aasen (eds), *Women's Human Rights: CEDAW in International Regional and National Law* (Cambridge University Press, 2013) 246. Emphasis in the original.
[118] ibid.

There are several possible solutions to remedy this gap. The first is an amendment to CEDAW or an optional protocol that creates a new obligation on states to combat gender-based poverty, and the second is an interpretation of the existing provisions in CEDAW to incorporate gender-based poverty into the treaty. The latter, specifically an evolutionary interpretation of equality and non-discrimination in CEDAW that incorporates gender-based poverty into the treaty, offers the most coherent and comprehensive approach to using CEDAW and the international human rights framework to address gender-based poverty. This section briefly canvasses the two identified solutions, the methodology that will be used and sets-up the questions that will be investigated in the remaining chapters.

In domestic law when a gap has been identified the natural response is to amend the legislation. Due to the nature of international law, amendments are not straightforward. International law is a horizontal and voluntary system of law. The Committee cannot unilaterally amend the treaty. It is states that must draft an amendment or optional protocol. This would be a very protracted process that would require considerable political commitment. Drafting international treaties takes a significant amount of time and when drafted a threshold number of states have to ratify the treaty for it to have any legal effect. It took almost 14 years to draft CEDAW.[119] The drafting of the Optional Protocol to ICESCR began in 1990. It was adopted by the UN General Assembly in 2008, and only came into force in 2013. The total time for adding a functional Optional Protocol to ICESCR was 23 years.[120] Given the critical need of women in poverty, waiting for an amendment is unacceptable. Preferring an interpretation of CEDAW should not be taken as a wholesale rejection of amending CEDAW, drafting of an Optional Protocol to CEDAW or even a specific UN convention on poverty. These are all important endeavours. Due to the length of time it would take to achieve them, it is crucial to understand how CEDAW can currently respond to gender-based poverty. The interpretative route is not without its own set of challenges. It raises issues of authority and legitimacy. In a horizontal system of law who has the authority to interpret and develop CEDAW? This issue is thoroughly canvassed in Chapters 3 and 4 and here it is only necessary to flag the interpretative role of the Committee.

The more compelling option to address the gap in CEDAW is an interpretation that incorporates gender-based poverty into the treaty. This interpretation can then be used by the Committee as a basis for recommendations on gender-based poverty in the treaty's accountability mechanisms: the General Recommendations, Concluding Observations, Individual Communications and Inquiry Procedure. An interpretation

---

[119] Division for the Advancement of Women (n 108).
[120] 'UN Treaty Database, http://treaties.un.org/Pages/ViewDetails.aspx?src=TREATY& mtdsg_no=IV-3-a&chapter=4&lang=en.

that includes gender-based poverty would not suffer the delays of an amendment.[121] This is not the first time the Committee would be addressing gaps in CEDAW through an evolutionary interpretation of the text. Gender-based violence was not included in CEDAW, but the Committee has persuasively interpreted it into the treaty and states have accepted this interpretation.[122] This proposed solution to the gender-based poverty gap in CEDAW raises many questions. Are there specific terms, phrases or words that can be interpreted to incorporate the harms of gender-based poverty into CEDAW? Is it best to situate gender-based poverty in one specific right in CEDAW or is a comprehensive interpretation which engages the entirety of CEDAW preferable? What impact would such an interpretation have on the nature of the state's obligations and the work of the Committee? It is argued that an evolutionary interpretation of equality and non-discrimination in CEDAW, two norms that infuse all of CEDAW, can be interpreted so as to persuasively and comprehensively incorporate the role of gender-based poverty in obstructing women's human rights. This is a comprehensive interpretation that engages all of the obligations in CEDAW as the majority of the state's obligations are based on equality and non-discrimination.

The next chapter examines the drafting history and seeks to understand why gender-based poverty was not included in CEDAW. Chapter 2 investigates the state's reasoning process in relation to gender-based poverty during the drafting of the treaty to gain a deeper appreciation of the structure of the treaty. This historical assessment of CEDAW in Chapter 2 is also used to chart the evolution in conceptualising gender-based poverty. This establishes the necessary base for constructing an evolutionary and persuasive interpretation of CEDAW that includes gender-based poverty in Chapters 3 and 4.

Before asking the central question—are equality and non-discrimination in CEDAW capable of being interpreted to address gender-based poverty?—it is helpful to pause and address a series of ancillary points that centre upon the interpretative process. How is CEDAW to be persuasively interpreted? What role does the Committee and other UN human rights bodies play in interpreting human rights treaties? And are there other interpretative options besides equality and non-discrimination which could address the gender-based poverty gap in CEDAW? Chapter 3 examines the principles and challenges raised by an evolutionary interpretation of international law, focusing specifically on the interpretative framework in the Vienna Convention on the Law of Treaties (VCLT).[123] It assesses the legal weight and authority of the work of UN human rights bodies who are advocating for a human

---

[121] Although states may still object to this interpretation and refuse to acknowledge it, this is investigated in Chapter 3.

[122] States routinely report on the efforts they have taken to address gender-based violence in the periodic reporting process. See, The Committee, 'General Recommendation No 35: on Gender-Based Violence Against Women' (2017) CEDAW/C/GC/35.

[123] Vienna Convention on the Law of Treaties (adopted 23 May 1969, entered into force 27 January 1980) 1155 UNTS 331.

rights-based approach to poverty in the process of interpreting CEDAW. Chapter 3 concludes by examining how comparatively situated actors use human rights to combat gender-based poverty to map out other potential approaches to interpreting CEDAW. Pausing and investigating these inter-related aspects of interpretation provides the necessary insights and tools to strengthen the interpretation of CEDAW proposed in Chapter 4.

The fourth chapter then approaches the central task of interpreting the text of CEDAW. The first step is to identify an interpretative methodology. The VCLT 'constitutes a single framework for treaty interpretation [and] can now be identified as generally applicable and that those rules should be understood and used by all engaged in treaty interpretation'.[124] The International Court of Justice has held these rules are applicable to the interpretation of all treaties.[125] Given the status of the VCLT rules, they are used to analyse how CEDAW can be interpreted to incorporate and remedy gender-based poverty. Article 31(1) of the VCLT holds that the terms of a treaty should be given their ordinary meaning in context and in light of the treaty's object and purpose. Seemingly, then, the first place to start would be with the text of CEDAW. However, although Chapters 2 and 3 do not start with the treaty this is not as problematic as it originally appears. Gardiner argues interpretation is not a purely mechanical application of the rules to the text.[126] Chapters 2 and 3 are useful contextual knowledge for understanding the root problem that a comprehensive interpretation is meant to remedy, the structure of the treaty and provide tools to construct a rigorous and persuasive interpretation of CEDAW. Building upon the insights from the analysis of the *travaux préparatoires* and similarly situated UN human rights bodies, Chapter 4 then applies the VCLT framework to assess how CEDAW can be interpreted to incorporate gender-based poverty. It argues for a comprehensive interpretation of CEDAW that uses equality and non-discrimination to incorporate the harms of gender-based poverty. All of these issues will be explored in greater detail in the proceeding chapters; at this stage this outline serves to map out the solution to the gender-based poverty gap in CEDAW.

The book then shifts to Part II and asks: how can this interpretation of CEDAW be successfully included in the Committee's accountability mechanisms? It is hoped that if the Committee becomes a strong advocate for approaching gender-based poverty as a human rights issue in CEDAW, this will spark a global dialogue and prompt other relevant actors to follow in the footsteps of the Committee. Chapter 5 investigates how the Committee currently approaches the issue of gender-based poverty. This analysis reveals that it is working towards understanding gender-based poverty as

---

[124] R Gardiner, *Treaty Interpretation*, 2nd edn (Oxford University Press, 2016) 6.
[125] *Avena and other Mexican Nationals (Mexico v United States of America)* [2004] ICJ Rep [83]; *Arbitration regarding the Iron Rhine Railway (Belgium/Netherlands)* Award of 24 May 2005 (2005) 27 RIAA 35 [45].
[126] R Gardiner (n 124) 40.

an issue of gender equality, but it has not yet fully embraced this approach. Chapter 6 explores how the working methods of the Committee contribute to the gender-based poverty blind spots identified in Chapter 5. The analysis in both of these chapters demonstrates the importance of drafting a General Recommendation on women and poverty to ensure that the Committee, the state and the larger global community understand the relationship between gender-based poverty and human rights. This is a significant evolution in international human rights law. It would be the first General Comment or Recommendation from any of the UN human rights treaty bodies that explicitly and exclusively focuses on poverty. To gain insight into how best to structure a General Recommendation on women and poverty, Chapter 7 analyses evolutionary General Recommendation and Comments. Finally, Chapter 8 brings all these threads together to demonstrate the effect of comprehensively interpreting gender-based poverty into CEDAW by proposing the content and structure of a General Recommendation on women and poverty.

VI. CONCLUSION

Poverty is not gender neutral. The reasons why men and women are poor can be drastically different. Gender plays a pivotal role in perpetuating and maintaining women's poverty. Gender-based poverty is defined as the redistribution wrongs of not having access to material resources connected with the recognition and participation harms that exclude and devalue women. Not only is poverty gender-based but it is also a major contributing factor to the non-enjoyment by women of their human rights. With the renewed interest in ending extreme poverty and achieving women's empowerment, as evidenced by the Sustainable Development Goals, it is an opportune moment to consider carefully how the international legal framework can best address gender-based poverty. Although ICESCR is designed to address poverty through the progressive realization of socioeconomic rights, it is argued that equality and non-discrimination in CEDAW offers a sophisticated legal framework to address gender-based poverty. Unlike other UN human rights treaties, CEDAW was specifically designed to remedy the gender-based nature of human rights violations. Surprisingly, there are no substantive references to gender-based poverty in the text of the treaty. Our central challenge to investigate is how to redress CEDAW's silence on gender-based poverty.

There are two possible solutions to this gap in CEDAW: an amendment or an interpretation of the existing provisions of CEDAW. As the procedure for an amendment can be very prolonged, an interpretation of CEDAW that includes gender-based poverty offers the most compelling approach. A comprehensive interpretation of CEDAW based on equality and non-discrimination ensures that all possible legal tools are used to require states to approach gender-based poverty as a serious human rights issue.

2

The Drafting of CEDAW

CEDAW IS THE pre-eminent legal instrument on women's human rights, but there are surprising omissions in the text. Although there is a reference to women's poverty in the preamble, there is, similar to gender-based violence, no substantive provision on gender-based poverty in the treaty. Given that women disproportionately live in poverty and the severe denial of human rights inherent in gender-based poverty, this is a striking omission. Why didn't the leading treaty on women's rights squarely address the gender aspects of poverty? Was there a principled opposition to the inclusion of gender-based poverty in CEDAW? Is there any implicit intention for CEDAW to redress gender-based poverty? Before turning to examine how we can now best overcome the gender-based poverty gap in CEDAW, it is enlightening to look at the history of drafting CEDAW and examine why there is no substantive provision in the treaty on gender-based poverty.

The drafting history of CEDAW has been preserved in the *travaux préparatoires*. By analysing these documents, it is possible to uncover and hypothesise on the intentions of the drafters. It is evident that there was no overt rejection of gender-based poverty in CEDAW. Rather, the historical record indicates that it was simply overlooked. Despite the lack of direct engagement with gender-based poverty, states' representatives were aware of women's disadvantaged socioeconomic position. States repeatedly emphasised the importance of socioeconomic rights and of addressing global economic inequalities. These past debates paint a complicated picture on gender equality, poverty, and human rights. Contemporary understandings of women's poverty and human rights, budgetary implications and the politics of the Cold War all help explain why there are no direct provisions on gender-based poverty in CEDAW. The debates at the drafting table also reveal that there is a latent and implicitly embedded commitment in the treaty to combat gender-based poverty.

The aim of this chapter is to put CEDAW in its historical context. It does not examine the *travaux préparatoires* to aid in the interpretation of the text—this issue is considered in Chapter 4. The focus here is more narrowly circumscribed to understanding why CEDAW did not address gender-based poverty. Section I canvasses different historical methodologies so as to equip us with tools to analyse the *travaux préparatoires* with sensitivity and rigour. Section II summarises the drafting history of CEDAW. Section III maps where in the drafting process the state representative engaged with gender-based poverty. Section IV argues that there are three overlapping explanations as to why gender-based poverty was not included in CEDAW: (i) gender-based poverty was not understood as an issue of discrimination against women or human rights; (ii) the politics of the Cold War made it impossible to have open and frank debates on gender-based poverty; and (iii) states were concerned that it would be too costly to use human rights to alleviate gender-based poverty. Placing the *travaux préparatoires* in their contemporary political, social and legal context, it is also possible to see an emerging understanding of the relationship between gender equality, poverty and human rights. Article 11 (employment) and Article 14 (rural women) reflect this new perspective and were designed to tackle women's socioeconomic disadvantage. Thus, rather than rejecting gender-based poverty, the drafters were using contemporary tools to ensure that CEDAW was attuned to gender-based poverty. This implicit commitment buttresses the arguments in Chapter 1: that the time has come for CEDAW explicitly to address the harms of gender-based poverty.

I. UNDERSTANDING THE PAST

How did the men and women at the drafting table conceptualise gender equality, poverty and human rights? This is a historical investigation aiming to 'explain why events transpired as they did and why they did not come out differently'.[1] Legal historians 'trace chains of causation, locat[e] the origins and impacts of legal rules and ideas'.[2] The *travaux préparatoires* offer a rich archive of the proposals and counterproposals on the text of the treaty that allows for a fruitful tracing of the drafting of CEDAW.

The UN has kept meticulous records of the numerous working group sessions involved in drafting CEDAW, but it is not a perfect insight into the past. There are inevitable challenges on relying on secondary sources to understand historical events. The 'historian's job is to map the deep structure of the linguistic system that provided the vocabulary and consequently organized the thoughts of the members of a culture ... in the past'.[3] Peller warns on the elusiveness of the drafter's intent because 'linguistic conventions

---

[1] W Fisher, 'Texts and Contexts: The Application to American Legal History of the Methodologies of Intellectual History' (1996–97) 49 *Stanford Law Review* 1065, 1088.
[2] ibid.
[3] ibid 1087, summarizing M Foucault, *The Archaeology of Knowledge* (Sheridan Smith, 1972).

constrain subjective intent into objective given forms'.[4] JGA Pocock further explains that: '[M]en [or women] cannot do what they have no means of saying they have done; and what they do must in part be what they can say and conceive that it is.'[5] State representatives were necessarily limited to expressing themselves in the words and concepts that existed at the time of drafting. As a result, Peller suggests that meaning can also be 'constructed in differential relations, in the blank spaces and silences of communications'.[6] The inability to perfectly capture intent through language means that what is not said is just as illuminating in a historical analysis as what is said. This is particularly true in the context of drafting international legal documents as politics and international relations can operate to stifle forthright expressions of intention. Rehof notes that due to the background political forces and compromises 'some of [the] real considerations could not be expressed openly ... some of them may therefore be cloaked in vague concepts and terms'.[7] It is crucial to take into account of and address, as far as possible, the methodological challenges in using the *travaux préparatoires* to ascertain why gender-based poverty was not referred to in CEDAW.

Intellectual history—'the history of what people have thought about and believed'[8]—offers helpful tools. Fisher classifies four different methodologies in intellectual history: structuralism, contextualism, textualism and new historicism. *Structuralism* is the study of continuities and discontinuities in the history of a particular idea.[9] It follows a certain idea and examines the moments of change on the timeline. *Contextualism* argues that the language used is 'radically dependent upon the systems of words and concepts in which the author moved when she was writing'.[10] The political, economic and social context of the community can influence and limit how an individual expresses an idea.[11] The aim of contextualism is to understand the motivations and assumptions that guided the drafter. This entails 'immersion in the world of one's subject, mastery of [her] vocabulary [and] sensitivity to the problem [she] was trying to solve'.[12] *Textualism* seeks to 'brush history against the grain'.[13] It asks questions that challenge the ideological

---

[4] G Peller, 'The Metaphysics of American Law' (1985) 73 *California Law Review* 1151, 1162.

[5] JGA Pocock quoted in J Appleby, 'Ideology and the History of Political Thought' (1980) 2 *Intellectual History Newsletter* 10, 15.

[6] Peller (n 4) 1167–68.

[7] L Rehof, *Guide to the Travaux Preparatoires of CEDAW* (Nijhoff, 1993) 3.

[8] Fisher (n 1) 1065.

[9] P Petit, *The Concept of Structuralism: A Critical Analysis* (University of California Press, 1975).

[10] Fisher (n 1) 1068.

[11] Appleby (n 5) 15.

[12] Fisher (n 1) 1095.

[13] D La Capra, 'Intellectual History and its Ways' (1992) 97 *American History Review* 425, 435–37.

context in which the text was written.[14] For instance, what can the Magna Carta, a document in which women were not even mentioned, tell us about the relationship between women and the neoliberal state? *New historicism* 'focus[es] on small events or anecdotes ... that ... are suggestive of the behavioural codes, logics and motive forces controlling a whole society'.[15]

The analysis of the *travaux préparatoires* of CEDAW in Sections III and IV uses all four methodologies, but primarily employs contextualism. It examines the wider sociopolitical context to understand how the drafters conceptualised gender equality, poverty and human rights to uncover the intentions behind CEDAW. No methodology is perfect and there have been critiques of contextualism which are particularly salient to take account of when analysing the drafting of CEDAW. Contextualism has been criticised as creating a hegemonic view of the past. The temptation is to apply a single context to a document. This does a disservice to the richness of the debates of the past. Fisher notes 'one should not expect to find in any society a "closed static, singular and homogenous ideology"'.[16] Similar to today, 'past world views would be "heterogeneous and unstable ..."'.[17] CEDAW was drafted by state representatives with widely different cultural, religious, economic and political ideologies. There were

> tiny island nations to the world's largest countries ... representing different levels of development and legal systems, manifesting a variety of religious, traditional and cultural systems; with political systems ranging from advanced liberal democracies through socialist States to countries in turmoil or seeking to find a transition from ... conflict and ... disruption.[18]

At the time of drafting, within the West there were intense debates among liberal,[19] radical,[20] black[21] and socialist feminists.[22] There would have been equally as pluralistic feminist perspectives from other regions in the world. State representatives would bring these diverse understandings to the drafting of CEDAW. It is a fallacy to seek for a definitive context in the *travaux préparatoires* and the documents must be read within a conflicting and chaotic contextual framework.

---

[14] ibid.

[15] Fisher (n 1) and HA Veeser, 'Introduction' in HA Veeser (ed), *The New Historicism* (Routledge, 1989) xi.

[16] Fisher (n 1) 1072, citing LA Montrose, 'Professing the Renaissance: The Poetics and Politics of Culture' in HA Veeser (ed), *The New Historicism* (Routledge, 1989) 22.

[17] ibid.

[18] A Byrnes, 'The CEDAW Committee' in A Hellum and HS Aasen (eds), *Women's Human Rights: CEDAW in International, Regional and National Law* (Cambridge University Press, 2013) 48.

[19] B Friedan, *The Feminine Mystique* (WW Norton & Co, 1963).

[20] K Millett, *Sexual Politics* (Doubleday, 1970).

[21] P Haden et al, 'A Historical and Critical Essay for Black Women' in L Tanner (ed), *Voices from Women's Liberation* (Signet, 1971).

[22] J Mitchell, 'Women: The Longest Revolution' (1966) 40 *New Left Review* 11.

Contextualism has also been criticised for conclusions that are based on meagre evidence. Fisher warns that: '[T]oo often [contextualists] content themselves with identifying similarities between the vocabularies employed during the same period in two discursive communities and then infer a causal connection between the two.'[23] This whitewashes the past and ignores the possibility that different communities may use the same language to express different meanings. It can also result in impermissible logical leaps. For instance, can we conclude that the United States was promoting a model of gender discrimination based on *The Feminine Mystique* by Betty Friedan simply because the USA representative used language similar to the book? Certain states may be associated with particular feminist beliefs or other political, religious or cultural ideologies. How much can the state representative be said to be promoting the state's ideology such that it is permissible to read the *travaux préparatoires* within a specific political, cultural or feminist context? There are conflicting perspectives on this question. There are those who strongly hold that the individual was a conduit for the state's ideology. Fraser goes so far as to hold that: '[I]ndividual people didn't speak at these conferences, governments spoke.'[24] Tinker observes that: '[S]ome women were convinced that the governments used women's conferences as a proxy for global debates, recognizing that many women delegated had no alternative to following the political line.'[25] Ghodsee, the USA representative at the second global conference on women's issues held in 1980 during the UN Decade of Women, noted that: '[O]f course, it must be acknowledged that the women sent to the official meetings to represent their governments were under the firm control of the male politicians back home.'[26]

On the other hand, Leticia Ramos Shahani, from the Philippines, who worked as an assistant secretary for the UN in the 1960s–70s, indicates in her reflections that she wrote the Filipino draft of CEDAW without consultation with her government.[27] She felt this was necessary to ensure that at the first meeting there was a draft to begin the process of refining the treaty. She believed that if she had gone through the usual government channels, this would have unduly delayed the drafting process. Shahani did receive

[23] Fisher (n 1) 1091.
[24] Avronne Fraser, personal communication with Kristen Ghodsee refered to in K Ghodsee, 'Revisiting the UN Decade for Women: Brief Reflections on Feminism, Capitalism and Cold War Politics in the Early Years of the International Women's Movement' (2010) 33(1) *Women's Studies International Forum* 3, 5.
[25] I Tinker, 'Introduction: Ideas into Action in Developing Power' in AS Fraser and I Tinker (eds), *Developing Power: How Women Transformed International Development* (Feminist Press, 2007) xxi.
[26] Ghodsee (n 24) 5.
[27] L Ramos Shahani, 'The UN, Women, and Development: The World Conference on Women' in AS Fraser and I Tinkers (eds), *Developing Power: How Women Transformed International Development* (Feminist Press, 2007) 32.

a telegram from the Philippines reprimanding her 'for not having sought the permission of the government to present the draft paper, which contained several topics not yet resolved nor reflected in ... national laws'.[28] In a similar vein, John P Humphries, the first Director of the UN Secretariat Division of Human Rights, noted that 'many governments had appointed as their representatives women who were militants in their own countries'.[29] Representatives involved in the international process could be progressive, and understanding the state's stance on women's human rights may not accurately reflect the context of the representative at the drafting table. With these conflicting viewpoints on the autonomy of the representatives, it is difficult to conclude decisively that, for example, when the Iranian state representative proposes an amendment she is following state ideology. The most that can be done is to detect overlaps, correlations and echoes within the drafting documents and the larger context to draw as far as legitimately possible an inference on what the drafters intended. It may never be possible to completely uncover the drafters' exact intentions and reasoning processes. The methodology of intellectual history, however, does provide guidance on how to assess the *travaux préparatoires* with a degree of sophistication.

II. THE HISTORY OF CEDAW

The impetus for CEDAW began in 1960s and it was drafted throughout the 1970s. The wider sociopolitical context was dominated by the USA and the USSR. States were pressured to align themselves with one of these superpowers.[30] This was also a period of rapid decolonisation and many new states were emerging. Feminism was an active and energised movement with numerous new organisations being established.[31] Groups in the West focused on a wide range of issues including sexuality, family, work and reproductive rights.

Against this backdrop, the UN Commission for the Status of Women (CSW) proposed a binding international human rights treaty that exclusively focused on women. The CSW was established in 1946 as a functional commission of the UN Economic and Social Council (EcoSoc) and was designed to promote women's human rights.[32] In the 1960s, there

---

[28] ibid.
[29] J Morsink, 'Women's Rights in the Universal Declaration' (1991) 13(2) *Human Rights Quarterly* 229.
[30] H Meiertöns, *The Doctrines of US Security Policy—An Evaluation under International Law* (Cambridge University Press, 2010).
[31] In the USA, for example, in 1966 Betty Friedan founded the National Organization for Women and in 1973 the National Black Feminist Organization emerged.
[32] UN Entity for Gender Equality and Empowerment of Women, 'Commission on the Status of Women', www.un.org/womenwatch/daw/csw/.

were numerous international treaties that touched upon women's human rights. The International Covenant on Economic, Social and Cultural Rights (ICESCR)[33] and the International Covenant on Civil and Political Rights (ICCPR)[34] guarantee women's equal enjoyment of civil, political, economic, social and cultural rights. There were also specific UN treaties on trafficking and exploitative prostitution,[35] political rights,[36] the nationality of married women[37] and consent, the minimum age for, and the registration of, marriages.[38] There were numerous International Labour Organization conventions on night work for women, equal pay and maternity.[39] Notwithstanding these protections, the CSW argued that there were gaps in protecting women's rights. There was concern 'that the general human rights regime was not, in fact, working as well as it might to protect and promote the rights of women';[40] a concern that still persists today.[41] Furthermore, the women-specific treaties in place at the time were fragmented and ad hoc and failed to comprehensively address discrimination against women.[42] Responding to these shortcomings, the CSW submitted the draft Declaration on the Elimination of Discrimination Against Women (DEDAW) to the UN General Assembly. This was adopted on 7 November 1967.[43] DEDAW, similar to CEDAW, calls upon states to end discrimination against women as such discrimination limits their equality with men and is an offence against human dignity.[44] It contained provisions on: eliminating discrimination in

---

[33] Art 3 International Convention on Economic, Social and Cultural Rights (adopted 16 December 1966, entered into force 3 January 1976) 999 UNTS 3.

[34] Art 3 International Convention on Civil and Political Rights (adopted 16 December 1966, entered into force 23 March 1976) 999 UNTS 171.

[35] Convention for the Suppression of the Traffic in Persons and of the Exploitation of the Prostitution of Others (adopted 2 December 1949, entered into force 25 July 1951) 96 UNTS 271.

[36] Convention on the Political Rights of Women (adopted 2 December 1952, entered into force 7 July 1954) 135 UNTS 193.

[37] Convention on the Nationality of Married Women (adopted 20 February 1957, entered into force 11 August 1958) 65 UNTS 309.

[38] Convention on Consent to Marriage, Minimum Age for Marriage and Registration of Marriages (adopted 7 November 1962, entered into force 9 December 1964) 521 UNTS 231.

[39] International Labour Organization (ILO) Convention No 3 (1919) concerning the Employment of Women before and after Childbirth; ILO Convention No 41(Revised 1934) concerning Employment of Women during the Night; ILO Convention No 100 (1951) concerning Equal Remuneration for Men and Women Workers for Work of Equal Value; ILO Convention No 103 (Revised 1952) Maternity Protection Convention; and ILO Convention No 111 (1958) concerning Discrimination in Respect of Employment and Occupation.

[40] Division for the Advancement of Women (DAW), 'Short History of CEDAW Convention', www.un.org/womenwatch/daw/cedaw/history.htm.

[41] H Charlesworth, 'Not Waving but Drowning: Gender Mainstreaming and Human Rights in the United Nations' (2005) 18 *Harvard Human Rights* 1.

[42] ibid.

[43] Declaration on the Elimination of Discrimination Against Women, A/Res 2199 (XXI); A/Res 2263 (XXII).

[44] Art 1 DEDAW.

laws and customs, enshrining equality in national constitutions, eradicating prejudice and customary practices, the right to vote, to hold public office, nationality, family life, removing discrimination in penal codes, trafficking and exploitative prostitution, education, and employment. DEDAW was not legally binding but 'merely a statement of moral and political intent'.[45] In practice, it suffered from weak accountability structures, reporting was voluntary and it was never successfully implemented.[46]

The CSW decided that 'a binding treaty [to] give normative force to the provisions' in DEDAW was necessary.[47] Capitalising on political momentum, in 1972 the CSW requested states to submit proposals on a binding Convention.[48] In 1974, the CSW set up a working group to consider these proposals.[49] Three different drafts, one from the Philippines, another from the USSR and a joint Philippines–USSR draft, were submitted to the working group.[50] For each of these drafts DEDAW served as an initial frame of reference.[51] All three drafts contain provisions on eliminating discrimination, modifying cultural attitudes and ensuring equality in political participation, nationality, criminal, civil and family law, legal capacity, prostitution and trafficking, education, and employment. These first drafts, however, were not duplicates. The USSR explained that its draft 'took account [of] certain changes which had taken place since the adoption of [DEDAW]'.[52] In its draft there were protections for working mothers, free or moderately priced childcare and restrictions on night work, heavy labour and working conditions that were physically harmful.[53]

The three initial drafts were synthesised into one document, which was distributed for review. After this process, in 1976, the CSW submitted a draft to EcoSoc.[54] At this stage, the provisions for rural women (Article 14) and temporary special measures (Article 4) had been included.[55] In 1977, a draft of CEDAW was submitted to the Third Committee of the UN General Assembly.[56] Three further working groups were established, which met forty-five times throughout 1977–79.[57] It was at this stage that provisions for health (Article 12) and economic and social life (Article 13) were added as stand-alone obligations, previously having been subsumed in

---

[45] N Burrows, 'The 1979 Convention on the Elimination of All Forms of Discrimination Against Women (1985) 32 *Netherlands International Law Review* 419, 419.
[46] Rehof (n 7) 7.
[47] DAW (n 40).
[48] E/CN.6/591.
[49] ibid.
[50] E/CN.6/573; E/CN.6/AC.1/L.2; E/CN.6/AC.1/L.4.
[51] E/CN.6/573 [39]; E/CN.6/574 [15].
[52] E/CN.6/574 [15].
[53] E/CN.6/AC.1/L.2, Arts 5, 11 and 12.
[54] E/CN.6/L.716; E/CN.6/591/Add.1.
[55] E.CN.6/L.687; E/CN.6/L.709.
[56] E/Res 2058 (LXII).
[57] A/C.3/33/WG.1/CRP.1; Rehof (n 7) 10–11.

employment (Article 11).[58] It was also at these later stages that the provision requiring states to amend penal codes was dropped.[59] In 1979, the UN General Assembly adopted the final draft and invited signatures and ratification. CEDAW came into force in 1981.[60]

III. MAPPING GENDER-BASED POVERTY IN THE *TRAVAUX PRÉPARATOIRES*

There were no open debates on the risks and rewards of including gender-based poverty in CEDAW. Neither did state representatives hold on the record that they were proposing provisions so that CEDAW would implicitly be able to address gender-based poverty. The term 'gender-based poverty' was not even part of the lexicon in the 1960–70s. To draw out the best possible evidence as to the aims and reasoning process of the drafters, the assessment of the *travaux préparatoires* takes a broad approach to the relationship between gender equality, poverty and human rights. When states refer to, inter alia, living conditions, the costs associated with enjoying human rights, income, global economic inequalities, economic structures and socioeconomic rights, it is mapped as a connection between human rights and gender-based poverty.

At the initial stages there were very limited references to using CEDAW to redress gender-based poverty. At the outset, the Federal Republic of Germany noted that: '[T]he strong emphasis the draft placed on economic, social and cultural rights corresponds to the need to make improvements in the conditions of life for women, the first priority.'[61] In the 1976 meetings of the CSW working group, Mexico suggested that the preamble include the phrase 'the elimination of the gap between developed and developing countries'.[62] This proposal was not included in the final draft of CEDAW. The *travaux préparatoires* does not preserve the reasons why this proposal or any of the other proposals that did not make the final text were rejected. Early in the drafting process, Guyana proposed that women should have the same basic wage as men, which hints at the obligation for a minimum wage.[63] Similar to Mexico's proposal, this was never included in any of the drafts of CEDAW. It was also at this stage of the drafting process that the provisions for rural women (Article 14) were introduced by Egypt, India, Indonesia, Iran, Pakistan, Thailand and the USA.[64] This becomes

---

[58] A/C.3/WG.1/CRP.1/Add.3; A/C.3/WG.1/CRP.5/Add.11.
[59] A/C.3/34/WG.1/CRP.6.
[60] A/Res 34/180.
[61] A/32/218 [9].
[62] ibid [8].
[63] E/CN.6/574 [86].
[64] E/CN.6/L.687.

an important obligation in relation to gender-based poverty as later in the drafting process states loaded this provision with crucial socioeconomic rights.

When the drafting process moved to the Third Committee of the UN General Assembly, more gender-based poverty-related measures were brought forward. A significant number of proposals focused on rural women and global inequalities. Bangladesh, Indonesia, Pakistan, Singapore and Somalia submitted a new paragraph on poverty for the preamble: 'concerned that in situations of poverty women have the least access to food, health, education, training and opportunities for employment and other needs'.[65] This proposal was included in CEDAW and is the only explicit mention of gender-based poverty in the treaty. Both Bangladesh and Kenya proposed additions to Article 14 (rural women) that were included in CEDAW. Bangladesh proposed a chapeau to the substantive provisions: '[S]tate parties shall take into account the significant roles women play in economic survival of their families in the rural areas by working in the non-monetized sectors of the economy.'[66] Bangladesh also proposed adding a clause to Article 14 (rural women) that the state should ensure that rural women 'receive adequate nutrition during pregnancy and lactation'.[67] This proposal ultimately became Article 12(2) (health) which guarantees that all women, not just rural women, receive adequate nutrition during pregnancy and lactation. Kenya proposed that: '[S]tate parties shall undertake all measures necessary to improve living conditions of rural women, particularly in fields of housing, water supply, health services, transport and communication.'[68] This proposal became Article 14(2)(h).

Several states proposed that the preamble mention or implicitly refer to the new international economic order. This concept was in vogue in the 1970s and 1980s. It recognised that the present international economic order perpetuated inequalities between developed and developing states and called for 'the active, full and equal participation of developing countries in the formulation and application of all decisions that concern the international community'.[69] Although this concept has fallen out of fashion, it was prevalent in the drafting of CEDAW. Accordingly, a number of preamble paragraphs were suggested. Bangladesh, Indonesia, Pakistan, Singapore and Somalia proposed:

> Convinced that full realization of equality between women and men is possible only if a new socio-economic order is created where women and men participate equally in development and decision making processes.[70]

[65] A/C.3/32/L.59.
[66] A/C.3/32/WG.1/CRP.6/Add.4.
[67] A/C.3/WG.1/CRP.1/Add.2.
[68] A/C.3/32/WG.1/CRP.6/Add.3.
[69] UN General Assembly, 'Declaration on the Establishment of a New International Economic Order' (1974) A/Res/S-6/3201 [2].
[70] A/C.3/32/WG.1/CRP.2.

Mexico proposed:

> Emphasizing that underdevelopment subjects women to a twofold burden of exploitation and that the full implementation of national development policies aimed at removing that burden is seriously hampered by the existing unjust system of international economic relations.[71]

Kenya proposed:

> Convinced that the establishment of a new international economic order will contribute significantly toward the promotion of equality between men and women, and in particular the elimination of the prevailing inequitable relationship between developed and developing countries which limits the latter's capacity to advance the position of women.[72]

These proposals were synthesised and became the paragraph 9 of the preamble: '[C]onvinced that the establishment of the new international economic order based on equity and justice will contribute significantly towards the promotion of equality between men and women.'

There were various proposals to enrich socioeconomic rights in CEDAW. With respect to employment (Article 11), Kenya proposed changing 'the right to work as an inalienable right of all human beings' to 'the right to work *and benefits accruing there from* as an inalienable right of all human beings'.[73] The precise meaning of this phrase is unclear. It could suggest that women are entitled to all social security benefits stemming from employment or that payment for employment should be given directly to the woman worker rather than to the man as customary head of the household. This proposal was not included in CEDAW. Sweden proposed that under the employment provision (Article 11) working women should be granted *free* medical services in connection with pregnancy, confinement and the postnatal period.[74] This proposal was rejected. However, in October 1978, Denmark and Norway proposed a separate article of general application for women's health (Article 12(1)) and access to maternal medical and family planning services (Article 12(2)). Prior to this point these provisions had been subsumed in employment (Article 11).[75] Guyana had originally proposed under employment (Article 11) the addition of a sub-clause guaranteeing women 'equal access to bank loans, mortgage and any other forms of financial credit' and 'the right to participate in and enjoy leisure and cultural activities'.[76] It was Denmark and Norway who proposed that Guyana's proposal form Article 13 (economic and social life).[77] Lastly, Denmark proposed including

---

[71] A/C.3/32/WG.1/CRP.2.
[72] A/C.3/32/WG.1/CRP.6.
[73] A/C.3/32/WG.1/CRP.6/Add.2.
[74] A/C.3/33/WG.1/CRP.5/Add.1.
[75] A/C.3/33/WG.1/CRP.5/Add.11.
[76] A/C.3/33/WG.1/CRP.5/Add.4.
[77] A/C.3/33/WG.1/CRP.5/Add.11.

in the chapeau to Article 14 (rural women) that rural women have the equal right 'to benefit from rural development'.[78] There is no record of any states contesting or modifying these amendments and the proposals became the final versions of Articles 12 (health), 13 (economic and social life) and 14 (rural women) of CEDAW.

There were also counterproposals and amendments that, if not outright limiting the ability of CEDAW to redress gender-based poverty, created ambiguity about the extent of the state's obligation. These proposals centred upon restricting the breadth and scope of socioeconomic rights. While the drafting process was still under the auspices of the CSW, the UK, Japan, Norway and Ethiopia complained that the 'text was overloaded with provisions on protection and welfare'.[79] The UK observed: '[T]he text imposes obligations in the field of social policies which are too rigid and sweeping and that the text in its present form would be unacceptable.'[80] Canada and the USA took issue with the obligation to provide *free* retraining for women under Article 11 (employment). The USA stated that free retraining and vocational training 'was unacceptable because it transferred to public expense programmes that were presently financed through private insurance'.[81] Canada proposed changing this provision to '*opportunity* for retraining'.[82] In the final version of CEDAW, the state only has to ensure that women have the right to receive retraining with no mention of who bears the cost of this training (Article 11(1)(c)).

There also was significant debate on the scope of maternity rights under CEDAW. An earlier draft held that the costs of maternity pay would be 'borne by social security systems or other public funds or collective systems'.[83] The USA proposed that this clause be deleted. Similarly, at another point in the drafting process maternity leave was defined as *paid* maternity leave, but Japan proposed that the word 'paid' be struck out.[84] Both the USA and Japan wanted to restrict the scope of pregnancy and childcare health services to a needs-based system under Article 12(2) (health). The USA wanted to insert the word 'needy' in respect to pregnancy and childcare services,[85] while Japan wanted to change 'free care during pregnancy' to 'adopt relief measures, including financial assistance, for confinement expenses'.[86] The UK proposed deleting the provision in

---

[78] A/C.3/33/WG.1/CRP.8
[79] E/CN.6/591.
[80] ibid.
[81] A/32/218.
[82] ibid.
[83] E/CN.6/AC.1/L.2.
[84] A/C.3/32/WG.1/CRP.8/Add.4.
[85] A/C.3/33/WG.1/CRP.3.
[86] A/32/218, Annex I.

maternity leave, treating the periods of leave as equivalent to periods of work actually performed.[87] The effect of this would be to give the state the discretion on the levels of benefits during maternity leave. In a similar vein, the Netherlands wanted to replace the words under Article 12(2)(health) 'and to grant *free* medical services' with the words 'and to ensure women's *access* to medical services'.[88] These objections had an impact on the final text. In CEDAW, the state has the discretion on funding and provision on maternity leave (Article 11(2)(b)) and states only have to provide free maternal health services where necessary (Article 12(2)).

In sum, while the drafters did not directly debate the merits of including gender-based poverty in CEDAW, they were alive to using the treaty to improve women's economic position. States from the global South and Scandinavia proposed many obligations that had strong potential to remedy gender-based poverty. On the other hand, proposals from states from the North, while not per se limiting the ability of CEDAW to redress gender-based poverty, gave the state discretion on how to fund crucial measures needed to comprehensively combat gender-based poverty.

IV. EXPLAINING CEDAW'S SILENCE

Why didn't the indirect discussions on gender-based poverty translate into a substantive obligation in CEDAW? The drafting documents do not give any direct answers. An analysis of the larger political and sociocultural context regarding gender equality, poverty and human rights in the text of CEDAW and a careful reading of the *travaux préparatoires* reveal that there is no single justification but rather several reasons operating together that offer the best explanation for this silence. First, at the time of drafting, gender-based poverty was predominantly seen as an issue of politics and development. The drafters simply would not have seen the relevance or appropriateness of placing gender-based poverty in a legal instrument. Gender-based poverty was only beginning to be understood as an obstacle to human rights and there was still uncertainty as to whether gender-based poverty was best remedied through a right to equality and non-discrimination or development. The nascent recognition of the relationship between gender equality, poverty, human rights and development does find expression in CEDAW, namely in Article 14 on rural women. Second, the politics of the Cold War meant an open discussion on gender-based poverty was impossible as both superpowers would deny that their respective economic systems perpetuated

---

[87] A/C.3/32/WG.1/CRP.6/Add.3.
[88] A/C.3/32/WG.1/CRP.4.

gender-based poverty. However, both the East and the West used Article 11 (employment) to improve women's economic status. These first two reasons reveal that CEDAW was implicitly designed to incorporate the harms of gender-based poverty. Moreover, with the passage of time the reasons for not explicitly dealing with gender-based poverty are no longer relevant. Gender-based poverty, as argued in Chapter 1, is not only a political or developmental issue but also a serious obstacle to women's human rights. The political constraints that muted discussions on gender-based poverty no longer exist. It is possible openly to examine the potential of CEDAW to combat gender-based poverty. The third reason relates to the cost to states of fulfilling their CEDAW obligations. This is still a highly relevant concern which is canvassed in Chapter 4. This section examines these explanations in greater detail and evaluates the implications for a modern interpretation of CEDAW.

A. Gender-Based Poverty Separate from Gender Equality

(i) Gender-Based Poverty as Politics

The most prominent reason that gender-based poverty was not included in CEDAW was that it was not conceived as a human rights issue. During the drafting process, when states referred to women's poverty and global inequalities these issues were never explicitly connected to gender equality or human rights. There is one exception to this trend: Bangladesh, Indonesia, Pakistan, Singapore, Somalia and Kenya wanted to include reference to a new economic order increasing *equality* between men and women.[89] The overall tendency was not to see gender-based poverty as a matter of human rights, but to conceptualise it as a multifaceted issue and one of those facets was political.

During the drafting of CEDAW, the UK stated that the text contained too many social policy issues, suggesting that there was concern that the treaty had strayed into the political arena.[90] The strongest evidence that the drafters conceived of gender-based poverty as a political issue comes from examining CEDAW's preamble. In the preamble, the states express concern that women in poverty do not have access to food, health, education and employment opportunities. At first glance, it might appear that the text establishes a loose relationship between gender equality, poverty and human rights. A closer examination of the preamble actually demonstrates the drafters' political understanding of gender-based poverty. Traditionally

---

[89] E/CN.6/591.
[90] Burrows (n 45) 424.

'the preamble to a convention should ... lay down the purposes and reasons behind [its] contents'.[91] The first few paragraphs of the CEDAW preamble follow this pattern and explain the motivation for creating a separate treaty for women's rights, namely that despite the existence of various UN instruments, discrimination against women still exists. CEDAW then breaks with drafting tradition and the remaining paragraphs in the preamble 'make[] "what are essentially political statements," some of its paragraphs [are] couched as political rhetoric, raising contemporaneous issues not immediately directed to the core goal of the Convention—to eliminate discrimination against women'.[92] The remaining nine paragraphs of the CEDAW preamble refer to poverty, the new international economic order, apartheid, racism, colonialism, neocolonialism, aggressive foreign occupation, domination and interference, international peace and security, disarmament, nuclear disarmament, self-determination, national and territorial sovereignty, social progress, development, peace, family, the social significance of maternity, parenthood, and the roles of men and women. At the time of drafting many of these issues were perceived as political, not legal or human rights issues.[93] During the drafting process, the UK observed that the preamble was too long and too political[94] and the representative stated that: '[S]ome of those paragraphs ... were unquestionably politically controversial and in some cases had little, if any, relevance to the Convention!'[95] Not long after CEDAW came into force, Meron observed that: '[T]he importance of the elimination of foreign domination may be clear, as is the desirability of achieving international agreement on disarmament, but the relevance of these matters to the efforts to end sexual discrimination cannot be assumed a priori.'[96] The inclusion of women's poverty in close proximity to other major contemporary geopolitical issues and in contravention of drafting traditions suggests that the state representatives perceived women's poverty to be a political issue. As such, from the drafters' standpoint, it would not be relevant to include any *legal* obligation on gender-based poverty in the substantive text of the treaty. This argument does not detract the legal status of the preamble as the reference to women's poverty in the preamble is used as an interpretative aid in Chapter 4.

---

[91] ibid 423.

[92] C Chinkin and B Rudolf, 'Preamble' in M Freeman, C Chinkin and B Rudolf (eds), *CEDAW: A Commentary* (Oxford University Press, 2013) 36; L Reanda, 'The Commission on the Status of Women' in P Alston (ed), *The United Nations and Human Rights: A Critical Appraisal* (Oxford University Press, 1992) 265.

[93] UN, 'Global Issues', www.un.org/en/globalissues/index.shtml.

[94] A/C.3/34/S.R.

[95] As cited in Burrows (n 45) 424.

[96] T Meron, 'The Convention on the Elimination of All Forms of Discrimination Against Women' in *Human Rights Law Making in the UN: A Critique of Instruments and Processes* (Oxford University Press, 1986) 58.

(ii) Gender-Based Poverty as Development

At the time of drafting, gender-based poverty was not only a political issue but also a matter of development. Similar to gender-based poverty and poverty, development is not easy to define. Development can focus on, inter alia, improving the country's economic growth or individual well-being.[97] Development is used here as an umbrella term to capture various measures aimed at both state and individual improvement that are not connected to human rights. Examining the sociopolitical context at the time of drafting, particularly the approach of the CSW, reveals a fluid, chaotic and tentative relationship between gender equality, poverty, human rights and development. On one hand, development was perceived as the best approach to reducing gender-based poverty and there was both uncertainty and scepticism on any links between equality, human rights and development. In part, this scepticism explains why there are no direct provisions on gender-based poverty in CEDAW. It is highly possible that a significant portion of the drafters would have exclusively connected gender-based poverty to development and would not have thought about including a development issue in a treaty on gender equality and human rights. On the other hand, there was also at this time a growing recognition that there were connections between gender equality, poverty and development. The debates on the interconnections between gender equality, poverty and development provide greater clarity on aims of Article 14 of CEDAW (rural women). To a certain extent Article 14 of CEDAW draws together these debates as it guarantees to women *equal* participation in *development* and basic socioeconomic *rights*. This indicates the latent potential of CEDAW to combat gender-based poverty.

There is limited evidence in the *travaux préparatoires* on the conflicting understandings of the connections between gender equality, poverty and development. States were concerned about economic inequalities. Hungary noted that 'the status of women is affected by the stage of development in different parts of the world.'[98] Mexico drew the most overt connection between gender equality, poverty, human rights and development. The state representative noted that 'under-development subjects women to exploitation, development policies hampered by existing unjust system of international economic relations'.[99] Denmark observed 'that rural women could benefit from rural development'.[100] This comment suggests the importance of development rather than human rights in improving rural women's lives.

---

[97] The World Bank, 'What Is Development?', www.worldbank.org/depweb/beyond/beyondco/beg_01.pdf.

[98] E/CN.6/591.

[99] A/C.3/32/WG.1/CRP.2.

[100] A/C.3/33/WG.1/CRP.8.

The varying perspectives come to the fore when examining the sociopolitical context outside of the drafting table. The CSW held three conferences during the UN Decade on Women: Mexico City in 1975, Copenhagen in 1980 and Nairobi in 1985. The meetings around these conferences demonstrate two very different perceptions on the connection between development, equality, poverty and human rights. First, there is ample evidence that some actors believed gender-based poverty was best solved through development. A joint meeting of the Commission for Social Development and the CSW in 1972 'stressed that the low status of women, especially in developing countries was a major factor in global concerns such as poverty, rapid populations growth, illiteracy, forced urbanization, poor nutrition and health'.[101] It is at a *development* meeting, rather than during discussions on equality or human rights, that the low status of women is connected to poverty. At a planning meeting for the Copenhagen conference held in 1976, some CSW members 'suggested that special place and emphasis should be placed on community *development*, on women in economic *development* and on methods for increasing employment opportunities for women'.[102] Shahani, the Philippines representative who had submitted the first draft of CEDAW, also stressed the importance of development. She argued that:

> [I]n order for human rights to be realised and exercised ... in developing countries, the proper economic and social conditions—such as rights to education, employment and freedom of expression—had to be created and put in place ... *development* would create these conditions. Women's issues began to evolve in the direction of *development*.[103]

These comments suggest that the solution to gender-based poverty was through development.

There is also evidence that the CSW was concerned that focusing on development would foreclose discussions on women's equality. The original perception was that 'too much attention to economic development would divert the commission from its primary goal of women's equal rights'.[104] The CSW was pitting gender equality and development against each other and ignored any potential for synergies. Ester Boserup, who in 1970 wrote the landmark book on women's role in economic development, remembers that in 1972 the CSW Secretariat saw development 'as a means ... to change their focus from the generally unpopular subject of abstract women's rights

---

[101] K Timothy, 'Walking on Eggshells at the UN' in AS Fraser and I Tinkers (eds), *Developing Power: How Women Transformed International Development* (Feminist Press, 2007) 53.
[102] E/CN.6/L.716/Add.4.
[103] Shahani (n 27) 29. Emphasis added.
[104] D Jain, *Women, Development, and The UN: A Sixty-year Quest for Equality and Justice* (Indiana University Press, 2005) 35.

to the popular one of economic development'.[105] Development and gender equality were perceived as mutually exclusive concepts.

The tension between gender equality and development is also evident in setting the agenda for global conferences on women. There was a perception that in the 1970s, women from the North saw gender as the main site of women's oppression.[106] Consequentially, they were focused primarily on male–female relations.[107] In contrast, 'for women from the South fresh from colonial domination, issues such as apartheid, the global economy ... were integral to improving the status and station of women'.[108] Tinker also observes a disagreement on the substantive content of women's issues. She remembers that at the conferences 'many women of the North preferred to separate "women's issues" from "global issues" and questioned the usefulness of spending time at women's meetings attempting to influence policy that would be decided by the [UN General Assembly]'.[109] Women from the developing world 'felt that poverty or powerlessness of women cannot be addressed by looking at gender alone but must be seen as a consequence of the Third World's economic dependency on the industrialized North'.[110] This perspective is reflected in Mexico's proposal for the CEDAW preamble: on the current unjust international economic system that hampers development policies.[111] Synder, reflecting on the Mexico City conference, felt that the women from the South were disillusioned with the international process as 'male–female issues could not be resolved while oppressions of whole societies prevailed'.[112] She pointed out that women from the South were asking: '[H]ow can women achieve equality when their nations are subject to global inequalities?'[113] One delegate from the South at Mexico City declared that: '[T]o be equal in poverty with men is no blessing, we need development.'[114] These statements are evidence that at the time of drafting women's poverty was conceptualised as an issue of development which was

---

[105] E Boserup, *My Professional Life and Publications 1929–1998* (Museum Tusculanum Press, 1999) 49.

[106] J Bond, 'Gender, Discourse and Customary Law in Africa' (2010) 83 *Southern California Law Review* 509, 529.

[107] M Synder, 'Walking My Own Road: How a Sabbatical Year Led to a United Nations Career' in AS Fraser and I Tinkers (eds), *Developing Power: How Women Transformed International Development* (Feminist Press, 2007) 42.

[108] ibid.

[109] Tinkers (n 25) xxi.

[110] ibid xxii.

[111] A/C.3/32/WG.1/CRP.2.

[112] M Synder, 'Unlikely Godmother: The UN and the Global Women's Movement' in MM Ferree and AM Tripp (eds), *Global Feminism: Transnational Women's Activism, Organizing and Human Rights* (New York University Press, 2006) 32.

[113] ibid 24.

[114] ibid 32.

disconnected from gender equality, thus helping explain why there are no provisions on gender-based poverty in CEDAW.

On the other hand, it is necessary to be attentive to the complexity and richness of contextual understandings. There is some limited evidence of a positive relationship between gender equality, human rights and development. The proposals for the preamble from Bangladesh, Indonesia, Pakistan, Singapore and Somalia did draw a tenuous relationship between development and equality: 'convinced that the *full realization of equality* between women and men *is possible only if* ... women and men participate equally in *development* and decision making process'. At a planning meeting for the Copenhagen conference where some representatives called for a greater emphasis on development, in contrast there were also CSW members who felt gender equality and development must be addressed concurrently. Some representatives 'felt that development could not be approached separately from equality and peace, for women though they participated in development were not equal to men and the possibility of continuation of conflict posed a threat to development'.[115] This suggests that there was increasing recognition that gender equality and development could be used together to improve women's lives.

The drafting of CEDAW was influenced by these debates and this can best be seen in Article 14 (rural women). Article 14 draws a tentative connection between poverty, development, gender equality and human rights. Article 14(1) recognises the importance of rural women's work to their families' survival in the non-monetized sector. The sub-provisions ensure rural women participate in development planning (Article 14(2)(a)); that they benefit directly from social security programmes (Article 14(2)(c)); can participate in self-help groups (Article 14(2)(e)); and enjoy adequate living conditions particularly in relation to housing, sanitation, electricity, water supply, transport and communications (Article 14(2)(h)). Notwithstanding Article 14's guarantee of equality for rural women, Pruitt interprets it as addressing development not equality. She has suggested that the fact that the rights to standard of living, housing and water are solely provided to rural women means that 'rural' should be read as 'developing'. She argues that the mention of development in Article 14 assumes that 'rural places are in need of development'.[116] Pruitt characterises the provisions as primarily programmatic and setting forth aspirational 'future policy for governments to follow in their *development* planning'.[117] She uses contextualism to argue that Article 14 was meant to address developing women as the UN

---

[115] E/CN.6/L.716/Add.4.

[116] L Pruitt, 'Deconstructing CEDAW's Article 14: Name and Explaining the Rural Difference (2011) 17 *William & Mary Journal of Woman and the Law* 347, 364.

[117] ibid 362, citing Burrows (n 45) 447 (emphasis added).

General Assembly Resolution on the 'Effective Mobilization of Women in Development'[118] echoes article 14(2)(d)–(g): inclusion in self-help groups, access to credit, loans, cooperative and community activities.[119] Similarly, Burrows believes Article 14 of CEDAW was meant to address women's poverty in the developing world. She writes that it is 'a manifestation of the impact of delegates of women from the Third World on the Commission on the Status of Women' and could be seen as 'perhaps an inevitable culmination of the work of the UN linking question of development with those women'.[120]

The conflicting perspectives on gender equality, poverty, human rights and development reflect the emergence of a new understanding on the relationship between these elements. As with any new idea there will be contradictory debates on it. What these remembrances add up to is that at the time of drafting there was uncertainty. Some actors thought that gender-based poverty was best tackled through development and development was something separate from gender equality. Other actors argued that both development and gender equality were needed to empower women. This tension is reflected in Article 14 (rural women). This provision tentatively joins together development, gender equality and human rights to combat gender-based poverty. This contextual analysis offers an explanation for why there is no explicit obligation in CEDAW on gender-based poverty and demonstrates how gender-based poverty was implicitly included in CEDAW.

B. The Politics of the Cold War

CEDAW was drafted in a period of *détente* during the Cold War, but there were still attendant tensions. These factors played out during the drafting process and affected the ability of states to openly discuss poverty as a gender-based phenomenon connected to human rights. Neither the capitalist nor communist system would admit that their economic system created or maintained gender-based poverty. However, both of these political and economic ideologies placed importance on formal employment in improving living conditions. Consequentially, at the drafting table it was also through Article 11 (employment) that key aspects of gender-based poverty were incorporated into CEDAW. The wider context supports this interpretation of Article 11 as states have a history of building consensus around women's employment and socioeconomic status as evidenced by the various International Labour Organization treaties, referred to above, on women's equality in the labour market.

---

[118] Resolution 31/75 (1976).
[119] Pruitt (n 116) 364.
[120] Burrows (n 45) 447.

Before proceeding, it is necessary to pause and note the difficulty of finding source material from the Eastern states detailing their involvement in the drafting of CEDAW, or more generally their participation in the UN during the 1960s and 1970s. Eastern women have not written memoirs that are easily accessible to English scholars. The socialist and materialist feminists who at the time of drafting were analysing Marx, Engels and Lenin were actually Western women.[121] Thus, it is impossible to truly paint the whole picture. All that is readily available are contemporaneous Western understandings of communism and socialism. Despite this limitation, the available material, especially the writings on Marx and Engels, permit a broad understanding of the ideological contexts at play during the drafting of CEDAW. These texts were highly influential, and Havelkova, writing on gender under state socialism in Czechoslovakia, identifies this as one of the main features of state socialist law.[122] Throughout the Cold War and particularly in the Stalinist period 'the canonic interpretation of Marxism by the socialist legal scholars and the Party was followed like a religion ... law was used to bring about various tenets of Marxism, including its response to the "woman question"'.[123] Although it is not contemporary evidence, using the foundational sources for communism does permit a contextual understanding on how the representatives from the Eastern bloc understood gender equality, poverty and human rights.

State representatives could not have explicitly included an obligation on gender-based poverty as neither of the powerful and dominant players, the USA and the USSR, would admit on the international stage that gender-based poverty was a problem. Both the capitalist and communist systems believed that their economic systems had or would ultimately solve the problem of poverty; therefore there was no need to discuss it in relation to women's equality.[124] Ghodsee noted that: '[T]he women's issues promoted by the USA government were those seen as being free of any discussion of comparative economic systems and focused narrowly on the inequalities between men and women.'[125] Representatives were to focus

---

[121] See Mitchell (n 22); H Hartmann, 'The Unhappy Marriage of Marxism and Feminism: Towards a More Progressive Union' in L Sargent (ed), *Women and the Revolution: A Discussion of the Unhappy Marriage of Marxism and Feminism* (Black Rose Books, 1981); I Young, 'Beyond the Unhappy Marriage: A Critique of the Dual Systems Theory' in L Sargent (ed), *Women and the Revolution: A Discussion of the Unhappy Marriage of Marxism and Feminism* (Black Rose Books, 1981).

[122] B Havelkova, *Gender Equality in Law: Uncovering the Legacies of State Socialism* (Hart, 2017).

[123] ibid. Citing J Přibáň, 'Na stráži jednoty světa: Marxismus a právní teorie' [Guarding the Unity of the World: Marxism and Legal Theory] in M Bobek, P Molek and V Šimíček (eds), *Komunistické právo v Československu, Kapitoly z dějin bezpráví. Mezinárodní politologický ústav* (Masarykova univerzita, 2009).

[124] See Hartmann (n 121).

[125] Ghodsee (n 24) 6.

on 'employment discrimination, inequalities in educational attainment or women's representation in political office'.[126] The USA's agenda for women at the UN specifically foreclosed any assessment of how economic structures discriminate against women. Trying to trace the role of capitalism in discriminating against women 'was characterized as irrelevant communist propaganda'.[127]

On the other side of the Iron Curtain there was also an unwillingness to engage with gender-based poverty. Rehof notes that the socialist countries took issue with including a paragraph in the preamble of CEDAW on the continuing existence of discrimination against women since they felt 'that discrimination against women had been eliminated in their countries'.[128] While the Eastern Bloc did not explicitly state that gender-based poverty did not exist under socialism or communism, this comment does suggest an unwillingness to engage in critical reflection on the status of women. Havelkova notes an institutional trend against self-examination. She writes: '[S]tate Socialist law often expressed achievement—whether or not the statements were in any way connected to reality.'[129] This dogmatic approach to equality filters into the states' understanding of women's economic status. According to Marxist theory, equality was conceived in terms of class and the primary method to achieve equality was the overthrow of capitalism.[130] In the Eastern Bloc 'as economic equality was considered already achieved— through the socialist ownership of means of production—much of the legal writing on equality was congratulatory'.[131] In 1964, Czech academics were arguing that the change from a market-based system to a planned economy 'guaranteed women actual real equal wages for equal work with men'.[132] At this time, however, women only earned 66% of men's wages.[133] Theoretically, under this new regime, all workers had an equal share in the means of production and thus none should be living in poverty. Consequentially, to raise questions on the gender wage gap, or more broadly on gender-based poverty, would be perceived as uncomfortable and problematic.

This ideologically enforced silence was even more pronounced on the international stage, as Rehof notes in his study on the *travaux préparatoires*

---

[126] ibid.

[127] ibid.

[128] Rehof (n 7) 35; A/C.3/32/L.59.

[129] Havelkova (n 122).

[130] Hartmann (n 121).

[131] Havelkova (n 122).

[132] ibid, citing J Jirásek, 'Některé otázky postavení žen v pracovněprávních vztazích' [Some Issues of Women's Standing in Labour Relations] [1964] *Právník* 177.

[133] ibid, citing A Křížková and M Vohlídalová, 'Czech labour market' in H Hašková and Z Uhde (eds), *Description of Legislation and Statistical Data on Childcare Leaves, Childcare Benefits, Childcare Facilities and Work–Life Balance Arrangements in the Czech Labor Market since WWII* (unpublished report for FEMCIT grant [2007] 6.RP EU, No 028746-2.

of CEDAW.[134] The CEDAW drafting processes and the UN conferences were an opportunity to showcase the best of each economic system. Ghodsee notes that 'championing the cause of women's rights was an integral part of the Soviet Union's strategy of winning nations to the communist cause in the developing world'.[135] Additionally, mentioning gender-based poverty might, as Ghodsee indicates, be perceived as comparing economic systems which easily could have lead into a political minefield and derailed the drafting of CEDAW. With these forces at play, it would have been a challenge to have gender-based poverty on the agenda for CEDAW and further explains why states were largely silent as to woman's poverty. A structuralist methodological lens supports this argument. Prior to the dissolution of the USSR, there were very limited references to poverty within the UN system. Almost immediately after the end of the Cold War, the UN began to focus more openly on poverty. The Human Development Index was developed in 1990 'to shift the focus of development economics from national income accounting to people centred policies'.[136] The Committee on Economic, Social and Cultural Rights (CESCR) began releasing General Comments on socioeconomic rights in 1989. In comparison, the Human Rights Committee and the CEDAW Committee began releasing General Comments/Recommendations in the early 1980s. There may be various reasons why CESCR did not release General Comments until the end of the Cold War, but this coinciding with a major geopolitical change does indicate at least the possibility that the end of USA–USSR tensions was beneficial to discussions on poverty and human rights.

While open discussion on gender-based poverty was foreclosed, both the East and West used their ideological understandings on the role of employment in improving the lives of women as a screen for discussing women's economic situation. Here I will briefly sketch the two regimes' understanding of women and formal employment and then trace how these perspectives were incorporated into Article 11 (employment) of CEDAW. From the Soviet perspective: '[M]ost Marxist analysis of women's position takes as their question the relationship of women to the economic system.'[137] Marx, Engels and Lenin argued that women's participation in the formal labour force was the key to their emancipation and a necessary prerequisite for them to participate in the proletarian revolution.[138] Hungary, a member of the Eastern Bloc, reflected this position during the drafting and observed that employment is a necessary condition of equality.[139] The liberal feminists

---

[134] Rehof (n 7).
[135] Ghodsee (n 24) 5.
[136] UNDP, 'About Human Development', http://hdr.undp.org/en/humandev/.
[137] Hartmann (n 121) 3.
[138] ibid.
[139] E/CN.6/591.

of the West also placed a premium on paid employment in improving women's status. They focused on expanding women's participation in public life, of opening up the male world to women, and this included formal employment.[140] Liberal feminists were arguing that economic independence would result in improved male–female relations, but this independence would consequentially have a positive impact on women's poverty. During the drafting of CEDAW, the USA wanted to emphasise the need for legislation to ensure equal employment opportunities and was concerned that protectionist legislation prevented women from getting high-paid jobs.[141]

Although the ideological underpinnings connecting formal employment with women's economic status were different, both the West and the East incorporated many poverty-related measures under Article 11 (employment). The final text reflects the USA's ideology. Article 11 opens up opportunities for women (Article 11 (1)(b) (the right to same employment opportunities); Article 11(1) (c) (the right to receive free vocational training) and strives for economic independence (Article 11 (1) (a) (the right to work) and Article 11(1)(d) (the right to equal work of equal value). In the USSR draft, submitted to the CSW in 1974, the preamble called for an expansion of women's participation in the formal labour force.[142] In this draft, it is under employment that working women have the right to free retraining, social security, pensions, free medical care during pregnancy, and free or low-cost childcare.[143] In a modified form these provision can be found in the final text of Articles 11 and 12 of CEDAW. Also in the USSR draft, there is an obligation for the state to treat part-time workers identically to full-time workers and an obligation to take all measures to allow women to work and fulfil their maternal care-giving role.[144] During the drafting process, other gender-based poverty-related measures were also originally proposed under the employment obligation. Access to medical services and pregnancy-related health services were originally sub-clauses of Article 11 (employment).[145] On the other hand, the USA was primarily focused on opposing the USSR's proposal to include protectionist provisions on night work and heavy lifting. With respect to the role of protectionist provisions, both sides were so intransigent that it was agreed that delegates from the USA and the USSR should meet separately to work out a compromise.[146] The glimmers of tensions that survive in the record indicate that an open discussion of gender-based poverty was simply not possible. However, both

---

[140] D Clare, 'Where We Stand: Observations on the Situation of Feminist Legal Thought' (1987–88) 3(1) *Berkeley Women's Law Journal* 1.
[141] E/CN.6/L.680.
[142] E/CN.6/AC.1/L.2.
[143] ibid.
[144] ibid.
[145] A/C.3/32/WG.1/CRP.4; A/C.3/32/WG.1/CRP.5/Add.1; A/C.3/33/WG.1/CRP.5/Add.6.
[146] E/CN.6/SR.647.

countries were using the Article 11 (employment) to further their own ideological understanding of women, equality and economic status.

C. The Expense of Gender-Based Poverty

The drafting record also indicates an apprehension regarding the costs of
alleviating gender-based poverty through the provision of human rights in
an international treaty. States from the developed world—USA, Canada,
UK, Japan, France and the Netherlands—in the latter stages of the drafting
process removed obligations to provide rights free of charge. Their proposed amendments made these rights either more narrowly tailored or created ambiguity. For example, the right to '*free* medical services' became the
right to '*access* medical services'.[147]

An analogy with poverty is helpful in explaining the concern about the
costs of using human rights to remedy gender-based poverty. The West's
uneasiness about human rights and public spending is well documented.[148]
It is reflected in the bifurcation between civil and political rights and socioeconomic rights in the two cornerstone UN human rights treaties: ICCPR
and ICESCR. Both ICCPR and ICESCR entered into force in the 1970s and
serve as contextual evidence on the perception of the costs associated with
using rights to address poverty and gender-based poverty. ICESCR contains
many rights that can improve the lives of people in poverty as it creates an
obligation to improve the standard of living, a right to be free from hunger
and a right to social security. However, it has been described as a 'promo-
tional covenant'.[149] States are only required under Article 2(1) of ICESCR
to use the maximum available resources to progressively achieve the full
right. Furthermore, Article 2(3) of ICESCR allows developing states, due to
their national economy, to limit the socioeconomic rights of non-nationals.
This is an acknowledgement that developing states may not be able to
afford to protect socioeconomic rights to the fullest extent. In comparison,
under ICCPR, rights are to be realised immediately and there is no mention
of developing states limiting civil and political rights. The different implementation standards, with the lower standard for rights more closely associated with poverty, is a 'recognition of ... the fact that resources may not be
immediately available to fulfil the right'.[150]

---

[147] A/C.3/32/WG.1/CRP.4.

[148] B Stark, 'The International Covenant on Economic, Social, and Cultural Rights and
Monitoring' [2009] Hofstra University School of Law Legal Studies Research Paper Series,
Research Paper No 08–18.

[149] E Schwelb, 'Some Aspects of the International Covenants on Human Rights of December
1966' in A Eide and A Schou (eds), *International Protection of Human Rights* (Nobel Sympo-
sium 7, 1968) 103.

[150] S Fredman, *Human Rights Transformed* (Oxford University Press, 2008) 80.

Turning back to CEDAW, there is a further complexity as the rights in CEDAW are premised on non-discrimination and equality. This means that they are immediately enforceable obligations.[151] Unlike ICESCR, in CEDAW there are no provisions allowing states to gradually realise their commitments to eliminate discrimination and achieve gender equality. Consequentially, states would be concerned about the costs of creating a full, immediate right to free health services or childcare facilities. These issues are explored in greater detail in Chapter 4 when analysing how interpreting gender-based poverty into CEDAW affects the nature of the state's obligations. At this stage, it is useful to note that the budgetary implications on using rights to combat poverty and gender-based poverty provides a further explanation on why there is no explicit obligation to remedy gender-based poverty in CEDAW.

V. CONCLUSION

At the drafting table, while states made proposals that implicitly referred to gender-based poverty, there were no proposals for a substantive provision. There was no outright rejection of including gender-based poverty in CEDAW, rather it appears this issue was overlooked. The *travaux préparatoires* do not preclude an evolutionary interpretation of CEDAW that includes gender-based poverty.

There are several reasons for the gender-based poverty gap in CEDAW. First, gender-based poverty was understood as an issue of politics and development and not of gender equality or human rights. Second, the tensions of the Cold War foreclosed any open discussion on gender equality, poverty and human rights. The Cold War is now over and there are no equivalent international geopolitical forces requiring states to ignore gender-based poverty. Moreover, as argued in Chapter 1, there is now a clearer understanding of the relationship between gender equality, poverty and human rights. Thus, it is an opportune moment to consider how CEDAW can respond to new obstacles to women's rights. The reasons for not discussing poverty when drafting CEDAW also indicate that states used Article 11 (employment) and Article 14 (rural women) to understand and remedy women's economic status. Third, states expressed concerns on the budgetary implications of ensuring gender equality and women's human rights. Concerns on the nature of state obligations and resource implications are still prevalent. This means that when interpreting CEDAW to understand the harms of gender-based poverty it is necessary to assess the impact this will have on

---

[151] Committee on Economic, Social and Cultural Rights, 'General Comment No 20: Non-discrimination in Economic, Social and Cultural Rights (2009) E/C.12/GC/20 [7].

the obligations of states. This is canvassed in Chapter 4. With the passage of 40 years, there has been recognition that gender-based poverty is an obstacle to women's rights, meaning it is time to explore openly how to use CEDAW to tackle this pressing issue. To gain further knowledge on how this can best be accomplished, the next chapter investigates methods and tools for constructing a persuasive interpretation of CEDAW.

3

Strategies for Interpreting CEDAW

S INCE THE DRAFTING of CEDAW, the relationship between gender equality, poverty and human rights has substantially shifted. There is an increasing momentum at the UN to use human rights to remedy gender-based poverty.[1] This advocacy has not been done within a *legal* context. The next step forward is to explore how CEDAW, the leading legal instrument on women's rights, can address gender-based poverty. Although there is no provision dealing expressly with gender-based poverty, the analysis in Chapter 2 demonstrates that several articles in CEDAW are capable of tackling gender-based poverty. To draw out this implicit commitment, I propose that equality and non-discrimination in CEDAW be interpreted to account for the harms of gender-based poverty. It is not sufficient merely to make this assertion. The strength of this proposal needs to be careful weighed. Before asking the central question—are equality and non-discrimination in CEDAW capable of being interpreted to include gender-based poverty?—it is helpful to pause and address a series of ancillary points that centre upon the interpretative process. How is CEDAW to be persuasively interpreted? What role does the CEDAW Committee (the Committee) and other UN human rights bodies play in interpreting human rights treaties? And are there other interpretative options besides equality and non-discrimination that could address the gender-based poverty gap in CEDAW? This chapter investigates these underlying questions so that Chapter 4 can use established legal methodology to propose an interpretation of CEDAW that is rigorous and authoritative.

Section I canvasses the established rules for interpreting international legal treaties. This framework is used in Chapter 4 when evaluating the different approaches to interpreting CEDAW to account for the harms of gender-based poverty. This section also addresses two further relevant aspects of interpretation. As there is no explicit obligation on gender-based poverty in CEDAW, any interpretation that addresses this problem inherently involves an evolutionary interpretation. It is necessary to understand the principles that govern this mode of interpretation. Furthermore, this chapter asks

---

[1] See, for example, UN Special Rapporteur on extreme poverty and human rights, 'Final Draft of the Guiding Principles on Extreme Poverty and Human Rights' (2012) A/HRC/21/39.

whether there are alternative methods for bringing gender-based poverty into CEDAW. To answer this question, it is illuminating to take a comparative approach and examine how different UN human rights entities are addressing gender-based poverty. Before undertaking this analysis in Section III of this chapter, it is useful to look at the benefits and pitfalls of comparative interpretation in Section I.

Section II asks which actors are empowered to interpret CEDAW. This question is not a straightforward as it would seem. Prima facie, the Committee, the body that has been tasked with monitoring compliance with CEDAW, would have a prominent role. It is an incredibly active treaty body and has generated a substantial body of material on the concept of equality and non-discrimination in CEDAW. Other treaty- and UN Charter-based bodies are also exploring the relationship between gender equality, poverty and human rights which can help shed light on the meaning of CEDAW. Due to the differences between domestic and international law, the output of the Committee and these other actors are not binding interpretations of CEDAW. This does not mean the Committee and other treaty- and UN Charter-based bodies are irrelevant. Section II investigates the precise legal weight and authority of the work of UN human rights bodies when interpreting treaties.

The final section examines how comparatively situated actors use human rights to combat gender-based poverty to map out other potential approaches to interpreting CEDAW. Although any interpretation of gender-based poverty in CEDAW must be faithful to the treaty, it is permissible under the rules of interpretation to 'take into account the broader normative environment'.[2] In this case, there are valuable insights to be gained from assessing how actors who are embedded in the same human rights system as CEDAW are grappling with gender-based poverty. The UN Charter-based bodies consistently advocate that *all* human rights be used in a comprehensive manner to remedy gender-based poverty. The treaty-based bodies often overlook the gender aspects of poverty but they more consistently address poverty. The Human Rights Committee (HRC) which monitors the implementation of the International Covenant on Civil and Political Rights (ICCPR) is interpreting *specific* rights in relation to poverty.[3] The Committee on Economic, Social and Cultural Rights (CESCR), which monitors the interpretation of the International Covenant on Economic, Social and

---

[2] Art 31(3)(c) of the Vienna Convention on the Law of Treaties (adopted 23 May 1969, entered into force 27 January 1980) 1155 UNTS 331; VP Tzevelekos, 'The Use of Article 31(3) (c) of the VCLT in the Case Law of the ECtHR' (2010) 31 *Michigan Journal of International Law* 621, 631.

[3] International Covenant on Civil and Political Rights (adopted 16 December 1966, entered into force 23 March 1976) 999 UNTS 171.

Culture Rights (ICESCR), has developed a comprehensive *framework* to interpret rights in relation to poverty and has established socioeconomic status as a *ground* of discrimination.[4] The potential of these three different approaches and the central hypothesis on the promise of equality and non-discrimination are evaluated in the next chapter. Pausing and investigating these interrelated aspects of interpretation provides valuable insights and tools to strengthen the interpretation of CEDAW proposed in Chapter 4.

I. THE ART OF INTERPRETATION

An interpretation rather than an amendment or an optional protocol offers the best route to address the gender-based poverty gap in CEDAW. While interpretation has significant potential to ensure that CEDAW is able to address the pressing problems facing women in the twenty-first century, it is also presents challenges. This section canvasses the rules of interpretation so as to be able to address these challenges. As mentioned above, it pays specific attention to the evolutionary and comparative interpretation of treaties as both modes of interpretation are highly relevant to using interpretation to incorporate gender-based poverty into CEDAW.

A. Articles 31–33 of the VCLT

There are conflicting approaches to interpretation. At the extreme end of the spectrum, interpretation can be solely guided by the interpreter's subjective intention. A good example of this is when Humpty Dumpty in *Through the Looking Glass* scornfully tells Alice: 'When *I* use a word ... it means just what *I* choose it to mean.'[5] However, it is widely recognised that some interpretative rules are necessary so that words and phrases cannot take on a meaning that is objectively unsupportable. With respect to legal interpretation, there are advocates for a strict adherence to the literal text[6] and those who support a dynamic approach that takes account of extra-legal socio-political factors.[7] Each extreme presents dangers: a narrow approach could ossify the law, while an expansive interpretation is vulnerable to political manipulation.

---

[4] International Covenant on Economic, Social and Culture Rights (adopted 16 December 1966, entered into force 3 January 1976) 993 UNTS 3.
[5] L Carroll, *Through the Looking Glass* (Hayes Barton Press, 1872) 72. Emphasis added.
[6] *Certain Expenses of the United Nations (Advisory Opinion)* [1962] ICJ Reports 151, 155.
[7] This approach has been criticised in the dissenting opinion of Judge Martens in *Brogan v United Kingdom* [1988] 11 EHRR 117.

In the domestic sphere, particularly in common law jurisdictions, there are often interpretation statutes or interpretative clauses in constitutions that set out the factors that an interpreter must consider and weigh. CEDAW and the other UN treaty bodies are silent as to interpretation. Beginning in the 1940s, the International Law Commission began drawing together disparate doctrines on the legal interpretation of treaties.[8] This culminated in the Vienna Convention on the Law of Treaties (VCLT)[9] which establishes a single framework for interpretation and has become the definitive methodology for the interpretation of international treaties.[10]

The touchstone of the VCLT rules is to establish the intention of the parties.[11] In domestic law relying on the intention of the drafters or legislature is often controversial and can be viewed with deep suspicion.[12] At the international level it is different. The intention of the parties is a fundamental principle due to the horizontal nature of the international legal system. Generally, although there are exceptions, states are bound by international law only to the extent that they have consented to be bound. Thus, it is crucial to ascertain the state's intentions in consenting to be bound by a treaty. Article 31(1) of the VCLT is designed to ascertain this intention. Article 31(1) holds that: '[A] treaty shall be interpreted in good faith in accordance with the *ordinary* meaning to be given to the terms of the treaty in their *context* and in the light of its *object and purpose*.'[13] The key elements are: (i) ordinary meaning; (ii) context; and (iii) object and purpose. The first element, ordinary meaning, holds that the words of the treaty should be read in their plain, obvious and natural meaning.[14] The second element, context, is defined in Article 31(2) and (3) of the VCLT as including the remaining text of the treaty, its preamble and annexes, any subsequent agreements and practice of the parties, and any relevant rules of international law. Context is designed to ensure the interpretation of a specific provision is coherent with the treaty and international law.[15] The third element, object and purpose, is used to arrive at an interpretation that achieves the treaty's goals while still being consistent with the ordinary meaning and context of the treaty.[16]

---

[8] R Gardiner, *Treaty Interpretation*, 2nd edn (Oxford University Press, 2016) 57–80.

[9] ibid.

[10] Vienna Convention on the Law of Treaties (adopted 23 May 1969, entered into force 27 January 1980) 1155 UNTS 331.

[11] E Bjorge, *The Evolutionary Interpretation of Treaties* (Oxford University Press, 2014) 58.

[12] See *Ashoka Kumar Thakur v Uniion of India* (2008) 6 SCC 1 (Indian Supreme Court).

[13] Emphasis added.

[14] A Orakhelashvili, *The Interpretation of Acts and Rules in Public International Law* (Oxford University Press, 2008) 318.

[15] ibid 339.

[16] ibid 395; Gardiner (n 8) 199; B Schlutter, 'Aspects of Human Rights Interpretation by the UN Treaty Bodies' in H Keller and G Ulfstein (eds), *UN Human Rights Treaty Bodies: Law and Legitimacy* (Cambridge University Press, 2012) 319.

The treaty needs to be interpreted effectively so that it 'provides an outcome that advances the aims of the treaty'.[17] The object and purpose or 'general sense and spirit' of the treaty[18] are derived from a holistic examination of the preamble, text, its general design and a comparison with other treaties.[19]

There is no hierarchy within these elements. Each is of equal weight and no conclusions can be drawn until the end of the interpretative process.[20] Although the general interpretative rule is to be applied simultaneously, 'logic might dictate a certain order'.[21] It is also important to note that 'the rules are not a set of simple precepts that can be applied to produce a scientifically verifiable result'.[22] Interpretation is an art not a science.

If the application of the general rule leaves the meaning ambiguous or results in a manifestly absurd or unreasonable interpretation, under Article 32 'recourse may be had to supplementary means of interpretation, including the preparatory work of the treaty'. Article 33 provides guidance on interpretation when the treaty is authenticated in two or more languages.

B. As Time Goes By: Evolutionary Interpretation

The general rule of interpretation is straightforward but in application can be controversial.[23] One pressing issue is: how does the passage of time effect the interpretation of treaties? This issue is salient here as gender-based poverty was not included in CEDAW or any other UN treaties. My central claim is that an evolutionary interpretation of CEDAW can address this gap. It is helpful to briefly consider this mode of interpretation. There are two diametrically opposed perspectives on the role of time in interpretation. The principle of contemporaneity holds that words in the treaty should be interpreted as they were defined at the time of drafting.[24] On the other hand, the evolutionary approach to interpretation recognises that words and phrases in the treaty should be interpreted in light of new developments in international law. The International Court of Justice (ICJ) explains that

---

[17] Gardiner (n 8) 211; *Territorial Dispute (Libyan Arab Jamahiriya/Chad)* [1994] ICJ Reports 6 [25]–[26], [51]–[52].

[18] W Hall, *A Treatise on International Law* (1895) (Kessinger Publishing, 2010) 353–54 as cited in Orakhelashvili (n 14) 344.

[19] ibid 339.

[20] Gardiner (n 8) 10.

[21] ibid 32.

[22] ibid 7.

[23] J Christofferesen, 'Impact on General Principles of Treaty Interpretation' in M Kamminga and M Scheinin (eds), *The Impact of Human Rights Law on General International Law* (Oxford University Press, 2009) 40.

[24] *Legal Consequences for States of the Continued Presence of South Africa in Namibia (South West-Africa) notwithstanding Security Council Resolution 276* (Advisory Opinion) [1971] ICJ Rep 16, 182 (Judge de Castro, Dissenting Opinion).

some words are 'by definition evolutionary ... and not static'.[25] Judge Jessup notes: 'The law can never be oblivious to changes in life, circumstance and community standards. ... Treaties—especially multi-partite treaties of an institutional or legislative character—cannot have an absolutely immutable character.'[26] A court must 'take into consideration the changes which have occurred [since drafting]'.[27] The challenge is in determining whether an evolutionary or contemporaneous approach should be taken to interpreting a specific treaty.

The VCLT framework gives very little explicit guidance[28] and international courts and tribunals have not consistently explained their interpretative approach.[29] Bjorge convincingly argues that the criterion for an evolutionary or contemporaneous interpretation is: was it the intention of the parties that the treaty should take account of the passage of time?[30] There are several criteria that can be used to determine the intention of the parties. It can be derived from the proper application of Article 31(1).[31] For instance, in *Gabčíkovo–Nagymaros Project (Hungary/Slovakia)*[32] the ordinary meaning 'of the treaty indicates that states have committed to a programme of progressive development'.[33] In *Award in the Arbitration regarding the Iron Rhine ('Ijzeren Rijn') (Belgium v Netherlands)*[34] 'an evolutionary interpretation was chosen as that would ensure that the intention of the parties was reflected by reference to the object and purpose'.[35] If the language, structure, object and purpose of the treaty do not reveal the intention of the parties, recourse can be had under Article 32 to the *travaux préparatoires*. The ICJ holds that there is a presumption in favour of an evolutionary interpretation when interpreting generic or open-textured terms.[36] A generic term is defined as 'a known legal term, whose content the parties expected would change over time'.[37] The ICJ also examines: (i) the nature

[25] ibid.

[26] *South West Africa (Ethiopia v South Africa; Liberia v South Africa)* [1966] ICJ Rep 6, 439 (Judge Jessup, Dissenting Opinion).

[27] ibid.

[28] Gardiner (n 8) 290–96.

[29] *Case Concerning the Dispute Regarding Navigational and Related Rights (Costa Rica v Nicaragua)* [2009] ICJ Rep 231 [10] (Judge ad hoc Guillaume, Declaration).

[30] *Namibia* (n 24) [53].

[31] C McLachlan, 'The Principle of Systemic Integration and Article 31(3)(c) of the Vienna Convention' (2005) 54 *International and Comparative Law Quarterly* 279, 317; Bjorge (n 11) 92.

[32] *Gabčíkovo–Nagymaros Project (Hungary/Slovakia)* [1997] ICJ Rep 14, 67–8.

[33] Bjorge (n 11) 119.

[34] *Award in the Arbitration regarding the Iron Rhine ('Ijzeren Rijn') (Belgium v Netherlands)* (2005) 27 RIAA 35.

[35] Bjorge (n 11) 119.

[36] *Aegean Sea Continental Shelf (Greece v Turkey)*, [1978] ICJ Rep 3 [77].

[37] *Kasikili/Sedudu Island (Botswana/Namibia)*, [1999] ICJ Rep 1045, 1113–14 (Judge Higgins, Declaration).

of the legal regime: is this a narrow, contract-like treaty between two states or a multilateral quasi-legislative treaty? and (ii) time: is the treaty fixed term or meant to endure throughout time?[38] The more enduring, legislative or institutional in nature the treaty, the more likely the presumption of an evolutionary interpretation will apply. This presumption is not without criticism.[39]

The use of evolutionary interpretation is firmly established in human rights treaties. Human rights are in constant change.[40] They are sensitive to external influences and are not meant to be read as frozen politics.[41] As a result, the terms in human rights treaties tend to be open-textured. Furthermore, human rights treaties are meant to withstand the test of time. Thus, on multiple criteria human rights treaties invoke the ICJ's presumption of an evolutionary interpretation. Judicial and quasi-judicial bodies routinely adopt an evolutionary approach to interpretation.[42] The European Convention on Human Rights (ECHR) is described as a 'living instrument which ... must be interpreted in light of present-day conditions'.[43] Similarly, the Committee holds that CEDAW is a dynamic legal instrument.[44] The HRC also embraces the evolutionary approach to deciding Individual Communications.[45]

C. Apples and Oranges: Comparative Interpretation

There is one further aspect of interpretation that needs to be canvassed. Comparative interpretation recognises that the international legal system is interconnected.[46] Treaties are not drafted in isolation of each other. With the explosion of international law, there is a concern that it is becoming fragmented. To ensure its legitimacy, stability, coherence and continued viability, there is a growing impetus to interpret one treaty with reference

---

[38] *Costa Rica v. Nicaragua* (n 29) [6] (Judge Skotnikov, Separate Opinion).
[39] ibid; M Dawidowicz 'The Effect of the Passage of Time on the Interpretation of Treaties: Some Reflections on *Costa Rica v Nicaragua*' (2011) 24(1) *Leiden Journal of International Law* 201, 221.
[40] K Vasak, *Towards a Specific International Human Rights Law* (Greenwood Press, 1982) 672.
[41] LD Eriksson, 'The Indeterminacy of Law or Law as a Deliberate Practice' in A Hirvonen (ed), *Polycentricity: The Multiple Scenes of Law* (Pluto Press, 1998) 46.
[42] Gardiner (n 8) 294.
[43] European Convention on Human Rights (entered into force 4 November 1950) ETS 5; *Tyrer v United Kingdom*, [1978] 2 EHRR 1 (European Court of Human Rights).
[44] The Committee, 'General Recommendation No 25: on Temporary Special Measures' (2004) CEDAW/C/GC/25.
[45] *Roger Judge v Canada*, (2003) CCPR/C/78/D/ 829/1998 [10.3]–[10.4].
[46] McLachlan (n 31).

to another.[47] Koskenniemi argues that the key point in comparative inter-pretation is that the interpreter should examine the wider normative frame-work in which the treaty operates.[48] The legal basis for this is Article 31(3)(c) of the VCLT (any relevant rules of international law).[49] Orakhelashvili is skeptical of this approach, fearing that it will only add further complications and confusion to the already difficult scientific-art of interpretation.[50] He does raise some important questions: what legal instruments should be compared? How is this to be systematically achieved? What conditions are necessary so as to interpretatively rely on an instrument that a state may not have consented to?[51] His concerns are particularly legitimate in the wider context of public international law. When, how and why should a treaty on depleting resources between the United Kingdom and Iceland be used as a comparative interpretative tool for a treaty regarding a maritime boundary dispute between El Salvador and Honduras?

These concerns are not so prominent in international human rights law for several reasons. First, human rights treaties are designed as universal declarations. They are not narrow treaties meant only to govern a particular issue between two or more specific parties. Human rights are indivisible, interdependent and interrelated, and meant to apply to all human beings for all time. This means human rights treaties do not operate in isolation; rather, they must be interpreted and understood in relation to each other.[52] This is particularly true when treaties are embedded in the same legal frame-work. CEDAW is part of the UN human rights system. Any interpretation of CEDAW is happening within a more formalized multilateral legal system that needs to be internally coherent rather than two or more independent sovereign states negotiating a discrete legal issue.[53] Furthermore, interna-tional human rights bodies are faced with similar legal questions to such an extent that it is not only self-evident, but in fact beneficial, to examine the reasoning process involved in answering similar questions. This is not to say that all international legal commitments must be interpreted consistently; but rather that drawing on the common pool of knowledge and assessing whether to accept or reject another similarly situated body's assessment of

---

[47] M Koskenniemi, 'Fragmentation of International Law: Difficulties Arising from the Diversification and Expansion of International Law Report of the Study Group of the Interna-tional Law Commission', A/CN.4./L.682 [416].

[48] ibid [415].

[49] McLachlan (n 31).

[50] Orakhelashvili (n 14) 382.

[51] ibid 367.

[52] C McCrudden, 'A Common Law of Human Rights?: Transnational Judicial Conversa-tions on Constitutional Rights' (2000) 20 *Oxford Journal of Legal Studies* 499, 504.

[53] See Office of the High Commissioner for Human Rights (OHCHR), 'Strengthening the UN Human Rights Treaty Bodies' (2012) 25, www2.ohchr.org/english/bodies/HRTD/docs/HCReportTBStrengthening.pdf.

the same human rights problem can immeasurably enhance the quality of legal reasoning.[54]

There are numerous precedents for a comparative approach to international human rights law. The European Court of Human Rights (ECtHR) referred to the Convention on Torture (CAT)[55] to clarify the meaning of the prohibition against torture and degrading treatment in the ECHR,[56] and it used the conventions of the International Labour Organization, ICCPR and ICESCR to conclude that municipal servants could form trade unions.[57] The ECtHR explains that: '[T]he Court has never considered the provisions of the [ECHR] as the sole framework of reference for the interpretation ... it must also take into account any relevant rules and principles of international law.'[58] The HRC explicitly relies on various forms of both binding and non-binding law when deciding Individual Communications.[59] Keller and Grover conducted a series of interviews with the members of the HRC which reveal that they try 'to reconcile the [ICCPR] in a principled manner with the content of hard and soft laws'.[60] Dr Eckart Klein, a previous member of the HRC, indicates that even if a General Comment does not explicitly cite another treaty body, the drafter might have taken a 'close look at the parallel provisions of other human rights instruments and the jurisprudence and literature related to them in order to enrich ... [her] own knowledge and to avoid contradictions'.[61] Dr Walter Kalin, another former HRC member, provided specific examples: in the General Comment on equality before the courts, the HRC harmonised its interpretation of how juveniles were protected with the reasoning of the Committee on the Rights of the Child (CCRC),[62] and with respect to admissibility of evidence obtained under torture, the General Comment 'broadly aligns itself with the reasoning of the [CAT] Committee'.[63] As a further example of the interpretative cross-harmonisation happening at the UN, due to their overlapping mandate the

---

[54] S Fredman, 'Foreign Fads or Fashions? The Role of Comparativism in Human Rights' (2015) 64 *International and Comparative Law Quarterly* 631.

[55] Convention on Torture (adopted 10 December 1984, entered into force 26 June 1987) 1465 UNTS 85.

[56] *Soering v UK*, (1989) 11 EHRR 439 (European Court of Human Rights); *Selomuni v France*, (2000) 29 EHRR 403 (European Court of Human Rights).

[57] *Demir and Bekyara v Turkey*, (2009) 48 EHRR 54 [98]–[104] (European Court of Human Rights).

[58] ibid [67].

[59] *Sarma v Sri Lanka*, (2003) CCPR/C/78/D/950.2000 [9.2]; *Sharma v Nepal*, (2008) CCPR/C/94/D/1496/2000 [7.4]; *Madoui v Algeria*, (2008) CCPR/C/94/D/1495/2006 [7.2].

[60] H Keller and L Grover, 'General Comments of the Human Rights Committee and Their Legitimacy' in H Keller and G Ulfstein (eds), *UN Human Rights Treaty Bodies: Law and Legitimacy* (Cambridge University Press, 2012) 157.

[61] ibid 157.

[62] ibid.

[63] ibid.

Committee and the CCRC released a joint General Recommendation on harmful practices.[64] The Committee, UN Women, the Office of the High Commissioner of Human Rights, and the Committee on the Protection of All Migrant Workers and Members of Their Families released a joint statement addressing the gender dimensions of large-scale movements of refugees and migrants.[65] There is also evidence of informal cross-fertilisation. In 2011, CESCR 'sought to coordinate its work with that of other bodies to the greatest extent possible and to draw as widely as it can on available expertise in the fields of competence',[66] and it consistently consults with UN bodies and Special Rapporteurs.[67] The UN Special Rapporteur on violence against women, its causes and consequences contributed to the Committee's updated General Recommendation on violence against women, General Recommendation No 35 on gender-based violence against women.[68] There is a joint Working Group for the Committee and the HRC which consists of members from each treaty body.[69] This all demonstrates that there is a strong commitment to harmonise the UN human rights framework, which, as Keller and Grover conclude, 'from a legal policy perspective … makes good sense'.[70]

II. THE INTERPRETATIVE ROLE OF UN HUMAN RIGHTS BODIES

There is authority under the VCLT and a strong de facto practice to interpret human rights in the UN system in an evolutionary, comparative and coherent manner. Using these rules, albeit not comprehensively or consistently, the Committee and other treaty- and UN Charter-based bodies routinely interpret the human rights obligations of states.[71] For instance, through its accountability mechanisms the Committee has 'contributed through progressive thinking to the clarification and understanding of the substantive content of the Convention … and the specific nature of discrimination against women'.[72] These sources are used extensively throughout this

---

[64] The Committee and Committee on the Rights of the Child (CCRC), 'General Recommendation No 31: on Harmful Practices' (2014) CEDAW/C/GC/31.

[65] Joint Statement, 'Addressing the Gender Dimensions in Large-Scale Movements of Refugees and Migrants', 19 September 2016, www.ohchr.org/Documents/HRBodies/CEDAW/JointStatement_CEDAW-CMW_AsAdopted19.09.pdf.

[66] Committee on Economic, Social and Cultural Rights (CESCR), 'Report on the 46th and 47th Session' (2011) E/2010/22/E/C.12/2011/3 [57].

[67] ibid.

[68] The Committee, 'General Recommendation No 35: on Gender-Based Violence Against Women' (2017) CEDAW/C/GC/35 [2].

[69] The Committee, 'Report on the Committee on the Elimination of Discrimination Against Women: 55th Session' (2013) A/69/38, Decision 55/VII.

[70] Keller and Grover (n 60) 158.

[71] K Mechlem, 'Treaty Bodies and the Interpretation of Human Rights' (2009) 42 *Vanderbilt Journal of Transnational Law* 905.

[72] 'General Recommendation No 25: on Temporary Special Measures' (n 44) [3].

chapter and the next. It is necessary to canvass the debates on the legal authority of UN human rights bodies. Although this material is highly useful and relevant to interpreting CEDAW, the Committee is not a court and does not issue binding interpretations. But there remains confusion on the precise legal weight to be given to treaty- and UN Charter-based bodies in the interpretative process.[73] This section canvasses these debates so as to understand the role of UN human rights bodies when interpreting CEDAW.

A. Treaty Bodies

At the outset it is important to distinguish between treaty- and UN Charter-based bodies. While both bodies are mandated to 'flesh out the meaning and implications of the relatively bare norms' in international human rights law,'[74] they have different legal origins and serve different purposes. The treaty bodies are established under the terms of the treaty to monitor the implementation of the treaty's obligations. In this quasi-judicial role, they consider state reports, make General Recommendations, decide Individual Communications and conduct Inquiry Procedures into systemic abuses.[75] Decision-making is done on the basis of consensus. This process has been criticised as resulting in 'compromise, the blunting of positions [and can result in] the failure to take the bolder step'.[76]

The treaty bodies have developed a multifaceted accountability structure. The focus here is on the General Comments. Alston explains that the General Comments are the means by which the treaty body 'distils its considered views on an issue … in the context of a formal statement of its understanding … the aim is to … make more accessible the "jurisprudence" emerging from its work'.[77] Since they consolidate the experience of the treaty bodies only the General Comments and not the Concluding Observations, Individual Communications and Inquiry Procedures are used here as an example to assess the legal weight of the work of the treaty bodies.[78] The General

---

[73] International Law Association, 'Final Report on the Impact of Findings of the United Nations Human Rights Treaty Bodies' (Berlin Conference, 2004) [25]–[26].

[74] P Alston and R Goodman, *International Human Rights: The Successor to International Human Rights in Context: Law, Politics and Morals* (Oxford University Press, 2013). See UN General Assembly Resolution 60/251 (2006); UN General Assembly Resolution 48/141 (1993).

[75] See Arts 17, 18, 21 CEDAW and Optional Protocol to the Convention on the Elimination of All Forms of Discrimination Against Women (adopted 16 October 1999, entered into force 22 December 2000) 2131 UNTS 83.

[76] Alston and Goodman (n 74) 765.

[77] ibid 764.

[78] P Alston, 'The Historical Origins of the Concept of "General Comments"' in L Boisson de Chazournes and V Gowland Debbas (eds) *The International Legal System in Quest of Equity and Universality: Liber Amicorum Georges Abi-Saab* (Martinus Nijhoff, 2001) 763.

Comments serve, inter alia, a legal analytical function, but are not binding interpretations of the treaty. The exact extent of the legal significance of General Comments is contested. On one hand, they have been described as 'indispensable sources of interpretation' and on the other, as 'broad, unsystematic statements which are not always well founded'.[79]

There are different theories explaining the legal weight of General Comments. Under the context element of the general rule of interpretation, it is permissible to take account of subsequent state practice.[80] One theory holds that unless a state contests the General Comment, it is evidence of subsequent state practice and can be used to interpret the original instrument.[81] Methodologically characterising General Comments as subsequent state practice under the context element of the VCLT interpretative rules requires the treaty body to assess if states have accepted or rejected the General Comment.[82] This is no easy feat. There are 189 state parties to CEDAW and it is unclear how many states would need to accept a General Recommendation for it to qualify as subsequent state practice. Moreover, states rarely, if ever, formally respond when a General Recommendation is released, so determining acceptance or rejection is not straightforward. There have been attempts to argue that subsequent state practice could be evidenced by the treaty body itself rather than by the state's conduct.[83] Under this approach, the practice of the treaty body could be sufficient so as to legitimately use the General Comment/Recommendation to interpret the treaty.[84] This position remains controversial.[85]

Another theory holds that General Comments, while not binding, are authoritative interpretations. The authority stems from the character of the treaty bodies. These are independent and impartial bodies of human rights experts[86] who have been 'entrusted and empowered ... to determine authoritatively whether the rights have been violated'.[87] Pragmatically, there is no other body mandated to monitor the implementation of the UN human rights treaties. States do not explain how they understand the nature and scope of their obligations.[88] Rather, treaty bodies have been delegated authority by the states to use their expertise to draft General Comments.[89]

---

[79] Keller and Grove (n 60) 118.
[80] Art 31(3)(b) VCLT.
[81] Keller and Grove (n 60) 131.
[82] ibid.
[83] *R v Secretary of State for the Home Department, ex parte Adan* [2001] 2 AC 477, 499–500; Gardiner (n 8) 239.
[84] International Law Association (n 73).
[85] ibid; Mechlem (n 71) 919–20.
[86] Art 28 ICCPR.
[87] Alston and Goodman (n 74) 792.
[88] Alston (n 78) 768.
[89] Art 40(4) ICCPR; Art 18 ICESCR.

This exclusive mandate 'enhances their persuasiveness'[90] and ensures 'international norms are "usable" within national legal systems'.[91] The ICJ adopts a non-binding authoritative approach to General Comments. When interpreting ICCPR the court notes that 'it is in no way obliged, in the exercise of its judicial function, to model its own interpretation of the Covenant on that of the [HRC, but] it believes that it should *ascribe great weight* to the interpretation adopted by this independent body'.[92] This position is less problematic and more persuasive and is adopted when interpreting CEDAW in Chapter 4.

B. Charter-Based Bodies

There are numerous Charter-based bodies, including the Security Council, the General Assembly, the Office of the High Commissioner of Human Rights (OHCHR) and Special Mandate Holders, who all derive their authority from the UN Charter. The OHCHR and Special Mandate Holders, such as the Special Rapporteurs and Working Groups, have investigated the connection between human rights and gender-based poverty, so only their role is explored further. The OHCHR and Special Mandate Holders have been described as political organs as they directly criticise specific governments on their human rights record.[93] They also 'have a much broader mandate to promote awareness, to foster respect and to respond to violations' of human rights.[94] For instance, Special Rapporteurs investigate alleged violations, undertake fact-finding missions, study a particular right and advocate human right issues to states.[95] The reports of the OHCHR and Special Mandate Holders are authored by one individual or a small group of people and can be adopted after a 'strongly contested majority voting'.[96] This can create factional and political battles, but it also allows them to take a stronger stance on human rights.

The OHCHR is the principal human rights organ of the UN. Its goal 'is to work for the protection of all human rights for all people ... and to assist those responsible for upholding such rights in ensuring that they are implemented'.[97] The OHCHR works with the entire UN system to 'develop

[90] Keller and Grover (n 60) 129.
[91] Alston (n 78) 768.
[92] *Case Concerning Ahmadou Sadio Diallo (Republic of Guinea v Democratic Republic of the Congo)*, [2010] ICJ Rep 693 (emphasis added).
[93] Alston and Goodman (n 74) 693.
[94] ibid.
[95] 'Manual of Operation of the Special Procedures of the Human Rights Council', www.ohchr.org/Documents/HRBodies/SP/Manual_Operations2008.pdf.
[96] Alston and Goodman (n 74) 693.
[97] OHCHR, 'Who We Are: Mission Statement', www.ohchr.org/EN/ABOUTUS/Pages/MissionStatement.aspx.

and strengthen capacity ... for the protection of human rights'.[98] It 'speaks out on virtually any significant human rights issue around the world'.[99] The High Commissioner for Human Rights, the head of the OHCHR, has been described as the champion and conscience of human rights.[100] The OHCHR is designed to act independently of states and respond quickly to human rights violations. It has been criticised as been overly political. The USA Ambassador said it 'was inappropriate and illegitimate for an international civil servant to second-guess' the USA's use of secret prisons.[101] The legal significance of the reports of the OHCHR is unclear and has not been the subject of much discussion. The High Commissioner's mandate does not indicate the legal authority of its findings.[102] However, similar to the treaty bodies, the High Commissioner is a person of high moral standing, and is an impartial, objective expert on human rights.[103] The OHCHR's interpretation on human rights should similarly be seen as persuasive and be given authoritative interpretative weight.

The same legal uncertainty is true of the work by the Special Rapporteurs. The Special Rapporteurs are appointed by the Human Rights Council (who operate under the authority of the UN Charter). Their mandate is either state specific or on a particular human rights issue—for example, extreme poverty and human rights or discrimination against women in law or practice. They are selected 'on the basis of their expertise, experience, independence, impartiality, integrity and objectivity'.[104] Special Rapporteurs are an attempt by the UN 'to pierce the veil of national sovereignty ... to handle serious cases of human rights violations'.[105] Subedi, the Special Rapporteur on the situation of human rights in Cambodia, notes that 'because they are not part of an intergovernmental body [Special Rapporteurs] have greater freedom of action, greater flexibility, and fewer political constraints on speaking their mind'.[106] Similar to the OHCHR, the Special Rapporteurs have been criticised on political grounds and states have 'challenged [their] professionalism, impartiality and objectivity'.[107] Notwithstanding this criticism, reports by Special Rapporteurs 'can make important contributions to the overall body of knowledge in the field and to the understanding of

[98] ibid.
[99] Alston and Goodman (n 74) 744.
[100] F Gaer, 'Book Review' (2004) 98 *American Journal of International Law* 391, 392.
[101] Alston and Goodman (n 74) 745.
[102] UN General Assembly Resolution 48/141 (1993).
[103] ibid.
[104] ibid.
[105] S Subedi, 'Protection of Human Rights through the Mechanism of UN Special Rapporteurs' (2011) 33(1) *Human Rights Quarterly* 201, 202.
[106] ibid 218.
[107] ibid 219.

complex problems and their possible solutions'.[108] Alston and Goodman
note that Special Rapporteurs can have 'a major impact when judged by
the ... uptake of their ideas by judges, governments, human rights groups
[and] scholars'.[109] When a report is based on high-quality and persuasive
legal reasoning it may become influential through an indirect process. The
same argument also holds true for General Comments: a higher quality of
argument can ensure a wider acceptance and use by numerous actors.[110]
Similar to the treaty bodies and the OHCHR, the Special Rapporteurs'
expertise and role at illuminating specific human rights issues implies that
their work could have persuasive interpretative weight.

It is not necessary to conclusively resolve the precise legal authority
of norm interpretation by UN human rights bodies. It is clear that these
sources are not legally binding for interpreting CEDAW. However, these are
impartial and independent experts grappling with gender equality, poverty
and human rights and are drawn on when interpreting CEDAW.

III. GENDER-BASED POVERTY AND THE UN HUMAN RIGHTS BODIES

The final preliminary investigation necessary to build a persuasive interpretation of CEDAW is to consider other interpretative routes to address the
gender-based poverty gap in CEDAW. Using the VCLT rules, this section
assesses how the treaty- and Charter-based bodies are interpreting human
rights to account for the harms of gender-based poverty. These other options
are then considered and evaluated alongside the central hypothesis on the
potential of equality and non-discrimination in the next chapter.

A. An Incomplete Approach: Treaty-Based Bodies

Similar to CEDAW, none of the treaties require states to combat gender-
based poverty. To varying degrees all of the treaty bodies are interpreting
human rights obligations to address this problem. As ICCPR and ICESCR
are the cornerstone treaties of the UN framework, the investigation here
centres on the bodies that monitor these treaties: the HRC and CESCR.
Although there is evidence that CESCR is attentive to gender-based poverty in its Concluding Observations, the analysis only draws upon the

---

[108] Alston and Goodman (n 74) 728.
[109] ibid.
[110] See *Vishaka v State of Rajasthan* (1997) 6 SCC 241 (Indian Supreme Court).

General Comments.[111] The General Comments are the culmination of the treaty bodies' experience and knowledge from reviewing state reports and individual communications. Examining these sources permits a focused and in-depth assessment.

(i) Gender-Based Poverty in ICCPR and ICESCR

There is only one instance where the HRC specifically assesses the role gender-based poverty plays in the realisation of human rights. In General Comment No 28 on the equal rights of men and women, the HRC explains that the right to life (Article 6 of ICCPR) requires states to assess when poverty jeopardises women's lives.[112] The HRC offers no explanation for this interpretation of Article 6 of ICCPR. Furthermore, this is an extreme example. The HRC overlooks numerous other instances where gender and poverty have intersected to deny women their civil and political rights. Women in poverty are often stereotyped as promiscuous and 'indifferent to the health and education of their children'.[113] In response to these gender stereotypes, states frequently attach intrusive conditions to social assistance that violates the right to privacy of women in poverty (Article 18 of ICCPR) and reinforces traditional gender roles (Article 3 of ICCPR).[114] The criminalisation of prostitution can significantly increase the risks of harm to women in poverty, jeopardising their right to security (Article 9 of ICCPR).[115] Girls in poverty are disproportionately forced into early marriage, which grossly undermines their rights to enter freely into marriage (Article 23 of ICCPR).[116] Despite these and many other violations, the HRC has not been attuned to the relationship between gender-based poverty and civil and political rights.

CESCR has a more complicated relationship with gender-based poverty and socioeconomic rights. CESCR specifically recognises that poor women are likely to experience intersectional discrimination in the context of the right to sexual and reproductive health.[117] This is a grounds-based approach.

[111] CESCR, 'Concluding Observations: Canada' (2016) E/C.12/CAN/CO/6 [9]; CESCR, 'Concluding Observations: Kenya' (2016) E/C.12/KEN/CO/2–5 [41]; CESCR, 'Concluding Observations: Namibia' (2016) E/C.12/NAM/CO/1 [54].
[112] Human Rights Committee (HRC), 'General Comment No 28: The Equal Rights of Men and Women' (2000) CCPR/C/21/Rev.1/Add.10 [10].
[113] UN Special Rapporteur on extreme poverty and human rights, 'Penalization of Poverty' (2011) A/66/265 [7].
[114] ibid [53], [62]; *Falkiner v Ontario (Minister of Community and Social Services)* (2002) 59 OR (3d) 481 (Ontario Court of Appeal).
[115] *Canada (Attorney-General) v Bedford* [2013] 3 SCR 1101 (Canadian Supreme Court).
[116] The Committee and CCRC, 'General Recommendation No 31: on Harmful Cultural Practices' (n 64) [20]–[22].
[117] CESCR, 'General Comment No 22: The Right to Sexual and Reproductive Health' (2016) E/C.12/GC/22 [30].

Gender and poverty are recognised as intersecting grounds of discrimination. The potential for establishing gender-based poverty as a ground of discrimination in CEDAW is considered in Chapter 4. CESCR often implicitly addresses aspects of socioeconomic rights that positively impact gender-based poverty, such as maternal mortality, affordable access to generic medicines and contraception, gender pay gaps, safe access to abortion and rights of informal workers.[118] However, this is an ad-hoc approach and there is no sustained or comprehensive engagement with gender-based poverty. As a result CESCR has significant gaps in its assessment of gender-based poverty and socioeconomic rights. In the General Comments on the right to housing, food and social assistance, CESCR ignores the unique synergy between redistribution, recognition and exclusion harms that underpin gender-based poverty and the lack of enjoyment of socioeconomic rights.[119] As a comparison, the UN Special Rapporteur on the right to food observes that due to patriarchal power relations women have limited control over access to household resources and suffer in the intra-household allocation of food.[120] He further explains that this situation is amplified in times of food crisis and financial austerity. Gender-based poverty issues such as these are completely overlooked by CESCR.

(ii) Poverty in ICCPR and ICESCR

Expanding the scope of the analysis to examine how the treaty bodies tackle poverty does provide greater insights into other methods for interpreting CEDAW. The HRC has sporadically developed the relationship between poverty and civil and political rights. It recognises that the requirement of an address may negatively impact the right to vote for homeless people (Article 25(b) of ICCPR)[121] and the imposition of costs in litigation, court fees and a lack of legal aid can undermine the right to equality before the courts (Article 14 of ICCPR).[122] This patchwork or specific-right approach reflects the fact that there is no framework to comprehensively interpret

---

[118] ibid; CESCR, 'General Comment No 23: The Right to Just and Fair Working Conditions' (2016) E/C.12/GC/23.

[119] CESCR 'General Comment No 4: The Right to Adequate Housing' (1992) E/1992/23 [8]; CESCR, 'General Comment No 12: The Right to Adequate Food' (1999) E/C.12/1999/5 [6]–[13]; CESCR, 'General Comment No 19: On the Right to Social Security' (2008) E/C.12/GC/19.

[120] UN Special Rapporteur on the right to food, 'Gender Equality and Food Security: Women's Empowerment as a Tool Against Hunger' (2013) 11–16, www.srfood.org/images/stories/pdf/otherdocuments/20130724_genderfoodsec_en.pdf.

[121] HRC, 'General Comment No 25: The Right to Participate in Public Affairs, Voting Rights and the Right of Equal Access to Public Service' (1996) CCPR/C/21/Rev.1/Add.7 [11].

[122] HRC, 'General Comment No 32: The Right to Equality before the Courts and Tribunals and a Fair Trial' (2007) CCPR/C/GC/32 [11].

ICCPR to incorporate poverty. Examining the language of the HRC in the General Comments is also revealing. It describes poverty as an impediment and a factor preventing access to rights.[123] Obstacles and accessibility are linked to effectiveness and the object and purpose element of the VCLT framework. The HRC is in essence holding that to achieve the aims of ICCPR the barriers to enjoyment of rights, such as poverty, must be accounted for when interpreting the normative content of the right.

CESCR has taken a different approach than the HRC. It consistently applies an interpretative framework to account for poverty. It interprets the obligations in ICESCR with respect to accessibility, availability, acceptability and quality (AAAQ).[124] While this framework has not yet been calibrated to take account of the gender-specific harms of poverty, it can tackle the redistribution and recognition ills of poverty and theoretically also gender-based poverty. The accessibility dimension specifically interprets rights in light of their affordability, which addresses the redistribution harms of poverty. CESCR explains that the cost of rent or buying a home cannot undermine other basic rights, such as food and water;[125] a right to food includes economic access to food;[126] and the state must provide sexual and reproductive health services 'at no cost or based on the principle of equality to ensure that individuals and families are not disproportionately burdened with health expenses'.[127] The remaining elements of the AAAQ framework can address the recognition harms of poverty, although CESCR has not always used the framework in this way. Availability holds that socioeconomic rights should not be interpreted or reduced to the science of survival.[128] Rights to food and water should not be equated to daily intake of calories or litres of water as these ignore the social and power relations inherent in eating and drinking.[129] Acceptability requires that rights be interpreted in their social and cultural context.[130] To alleviate poverty among the nomadic Roma, for example, it would be culturally unacceptable to interpret the right to housing as a requirement for permanent homes. The final element, quality, upholds the dignity and equality of people in poverty. Health clinics in areas of poverty cannot be stocked with pharmaceuticals that are out of date, and low-fee-paying schools should not be staffed with unqualified teachers.

---

[123] ibid; HRC, 'General Comment No 25: The Right to Participate' (n 121).
[124] CESCR, 'General Comment No 12: Adequate Food" (n 119) [6]–[13].
[125] ibid [13]. Also see CESCR 'General Comment No 4: The Right to Adequate Housing' (1992) E/1992/23 [8].
[126] CESCR, 'General Comment No 12: Adequate Food' (n 119) [6].
[127] CESCR, 'General Comment No 22: Sexual and Reproductive Health' (n 117) [17].
[128] CESCR, 'General Comment No 4: Adequate Housing' (n 125) [7].
[129] S Fredman, 'The Potential and Limits of an Equal Rights Paradigm in Addressing Poverty' (2011) 22 *Stellenbosch Law Review* 566, 569–70.
[130] CESCR, 'General Comment No 12: Adequate Food' (n 119) [6].

While CESCR has never justified its use of the AAAQ framework, it does draw on the object and purpose, context and the *travaux préparatoires* to explain its evolutionary interpretation of socioeconomic rights. One of the foundational aims of ICESCR, as evidenced in the treaty's preamble, is to ensure 'the inherent dignity of the human person'. CESCR explains that rights to housing, food, social security and water 'should not be interpreted in a narrow or restrictive sense ... rather it should be seen as the right to live in security, peace and *dignity*'.[131] It elaborates that the 'inherent *dignity* of the human person ... requires the term "housing" to be interpreted to take account of a variety of other considerations, most importantly that the right to housing should be ensured to all persons irrespective of income or access to economic resources'.[132] CESCR also uses the context element of the VCLT framework. It stresses the indivisibility of the socioeconomic rights in ICESCR to justify expansive interpretations of rights to an adequate standard of living, food and health.[133] There is also evidence of CESCR relying on the *travaux préparatoires* and the presumption in favour of evolutionary interpretation for generic, open-textured terms. CESCR notes that the drafting records on the right to health indicate that the states intended a wide understanding of health.[134] CESCR further explains that the notion of health has substantially changed since ICESCR was drafted.[135] States intended an evolutionary interpretation:

> [T]he express wording [of the provision] acknowledge[s] that the right to health embraces a wide range of socio-economic factors ... and extends to the underlying determinants of health such as food and nutrition, housing, access to safe and potable water and adequate sanitation.[136]

Along with the AAAQ framework, CESCR is exploring the relationship between poverty and discrimination. Article 2(2) of ICESCR contains a non-exhaustive list of prohibited grounds of discrimination. CESCR is a pioneer in arguing that socioeconomic status discrimination is an analogous ground because individuals in poverty are 'vulnerable and have suffered and continue to suffer marginalisation'.[137] It notes that 'living in poverty or being homeless may result in pervasive discrimination, stigmatisation and negative stereotyping which can lead to the refusal of, or unequal

---

[131] CESCR, 'General Comment No 4: Adequate Housing' (n 125) [7]; CESCR, 'General Comment No 12: Adequate Food' (n 119) [4]; CESCR, 'General Comment No 19: The Right to Social Security' (n 119).

[132] CESCR, 'General Comment No 12: Adequate Food' (n 119) [4].

[133] ibid [1].

[134] CESCR, 'General Comment No 14: The Right to the Highest Attainable Standard of Health' (2000) E/C.12/2000/4 [10].

[135] ibid [10].

[136] ibid [11].

[137] CESCR, 'General Comment No 20: Non Discrimination in Economic, Social and Cultural Rights' (2009) E/C.12/GC/20 [27], [35].

access to' socioeconomic rights.[138] This again reflects an object and purpose interpretation as CESCR is drawing on the normative aims of ICESCR to justify including socioeconomic status as a ground of discrimination. This 'is an immediate and cross-cutting obligation'[139] and requires states to pay sufficient attention to the de facto situation, to adopt necessary measures and devote greater resources to people who suffer socioeconomic discrimination.[140] Recognising socioeconomic discrimination is a powerful tool to assess how the state has ensured the socioeconomic rights of people living in poverty.

In sum, both treaty bodies have not comprehensively addressed gender-based poverty nor have they justified the legal basis in the limited instances where they engage with gender-based poverty. Expanding the scope of the comparative analysis to include poverty does provide useful insights to the primary task of interpreting CEDAW. The HRC interprets a few *specific* rights in relation to poverty. CESCR, on the other hand, consistently pays attention to the relationship between socioeconomic rights and poverty. It has a multifaceted approach: (i) it employs a comprehensive interpretative *framework* to account for poverty; and (ii) it establishes socioeconomic status as a *ground* of discrimination. Both treaty bodies implicitly draw on the VCLT rules to justify including poverty in their interpretation of ICCPR and ICESCR.

B. The Indivisibility of Rights: Gender-Based Poverty and the UN Charter Bodies

The Charter-based bodies have paid significant attention to gender-based poverty. The Special Rapporteur on extreme poverty and human rights emphasises that 'women are disproportionately represented among the poor owing to the multifaceted and cumulative forms of discrimination that they endure'.[141] She then highlights facets of the relationship between gender and poverty: patriarchal attitudes; gender-based violence; limited access to economic opportunities; lack of control of resources and decision-making power; inequality in marriage and family life; and disproportionate responsibility for unpaid care work.[142] The UN Special Rapporteur on the right

---

[138] ibid.
[139] ibid [7].
[140] ibid [5]–[6], [39].
[141] UN Special Rapporteur on extreme poverty and human rights, 'Guiding Principles' (n 1) [23].
[142] ibid; UN Special Rapporteur on extreme poverty and human rights, 'Unpaid Care Work, Poverty and Women's Human Rights' (2013) A/68/293; UN Special Rapporteur on extreme poverty and human rights, 'Conditional Cash Transfers Programmes' (2009) A/HRC/11/9.

to food analyses the complex relationship between gender discrimination, poverty and the right to food,[143] and the UN Special Rapporteur on the right to health has investigated the connection between poverty and maternal mortality.[144] The Working Group on Discrimination Against Women in Law and Practice has extensively assessed discrimination against women in economic and social life with a focus on the recent economic crisis.[145] These sources, as argued above in Section II, have authoritative interpretative weight and are useful in understanding the relationship between equality, non-discrimination, human rights and poverty in CEDAW and are relied upon in Chapter 4.

If the UN Charter bodies are advocating for a greater understanding of gender-based poverty, is there any need to locate it in CEDAW? The output of the Charter-based bodies is informed by and draws significantly on the legal obligations in CEDAW but it is not a direct interpretation of the text of treaty. While the Working Group and various UN Special Rapporteurs make important contributions to the understanding of gender-based poverty, this does not make the proposed interpretation of CEDAW redundant. CEDAW is a legal instrument and contains legal obligations, and it is imperative to understand how international legal rights and duties can be used to combat gender-based poverty. Moreover, while these bodies pursue similar aims they have different accountability mechanisms. The Special Mandate Holders, through country missions and thematic reports, study how states can eliminate discrimination against women and make recommendations to improve legal responses to women's disadvantage.[146] The CEDAW Committee's mandate is to monitor the progress made in the implementation of CEDAW.[147] The Committee has developed a multifaceted and sophisticated review process. It is breaking new ground to unlock the potential of the periodic review process, Individual Communications and Inquiry Procedures so that the CEDAW Committee can dialogue with states on how to best address the harms of gender-based poverty. The treaty- and Charter-based bodies are not in competition with each other for legal or normative force; they should be seen as complimentary and part of a multivalent, holistic and comprehensive human rights framework intended to engage the state and other relevant actors on gender-based poverty.

---

[143] UN Special Rapporteur on the right to food, 'Women's Rights and the Right to Food' (2012) A/HRC/22/50.

[144] UN Special Rapporteur on the right to health, 'The Right to the Highest Standard of Health: Reduction of Maternal Mortality' (2006) A/61/338.

[145] Working Group on Discrimination Against Women in Law and Practice, 'Discrimination against Women in Economic and Social Life, with a Focus on Economic Crisis' (2014) A/C/26/39.

[146] Human Rights Council, 'Elimination of Discrimination Against Women' (2010) A/HRC/RES/15/23.

[147] Art 17 CEDAW.

While the Charter-based bodies acknowledge the role of gender in per-petuating poverty and women's human rights violations, it is also revealing to assess their approach to poverty and human rights. First, they emphasise that poverty is a cross-cutting obstacle that affects all human rights. The UN Special Rapporteur on extreme poverty and human rights argues that poverty cannot be equated to a violation of one single right, rather 'poverty is a denial of *all* human rights'.[148] For people living in poverty there are 'multiple [and] reinforcing violations of civil, political, economic, social and cultural rights'.[149] The interrelatedness, interdependence and indivisibility of human rights mean that the entire spectrum of rights is engaged in a human rights-based approach to poverty.[150] The UN Special Rapporteur on minorities explains how 'extreme poverty involves the denial, not of a single right or a given category of rights, but of human rights as a whole'.[151] Therefore, all rights should have evaluative reference to poverty.[152] The OHCHR draws a helpful analogy with other human rights strategies to explain the relationship between poverty and human rights. It notes 'a strat-egy to combat torture, sexual stereotyping or unfair trials would have to address a much wider range of rights than those by which these phenomena are defined'.[153] The right to fair trial would include not only the presump-tion of innocence (Article 14 of ICCPR) but also just and favourable work-ing conditions for judges (Article 7 of ICESCR). As explained in Chapter 1, although it is appealing, gender-based poverty cannot be reduced solely to socioeconomic rights.[154] A woman living on the street is vulnerable to gender-based violence. She may not seek help due to strained relationships with law enforcement, especially if she belongs to a racial or ethnic minor-ity, and without a fixed address she faces longer pretrial detention if she is arrested.[155] This violates her rights to life, physical integrity, access to justice, equal protection before the law and an adequate standard of liv-ing. This approach points towards adopting a comprehensive interpretation of CEDAW that engages all of the substantive obligations in the text. The viability of this is considered in detail in Chapter 4.

[148] UN Special Rapporteur on extreme poverty and human rights, 'Economic, Social and Cultural Rights: Human Rights and Extreme Poverty Report' (1999) E/CN.4/1999/48 [116] (emphasis added).
[149] UN Special Rapporteur on extreme poverty and human rights, 'Guiding Principles' (n 1) [3].
[150] OHCHR, 'Human Rights and Poverty Reduction: A Conceptual Framework' (2004) HR/PUB/04/1 11.
[151] ibid.
[152] ibid.
[153] ibid.
[154] OHCHR, 'A Concpetual Framework' (n 150) 10.
[155] The Committee, 'Report of the Inquiry Concerning Canada of the Committee on the Elimination of Discrimination Against Women under Article 8 of OP-CEDAW' (2015) CEDAW/C/OP.8/CAN/1.

The Charter-based bodies also frame poverty as an obstacle to and cause of human rights violations. This draws on the object and purpose element of the VCLT framework. The UN Special Rapporteur on minorities observes that: '[A] consensus emerged that extreme poverty and social exclusion ... stood in the way of the full and *effective* enjoyment of human rights.'[156] The Special Rapporteur on extreme poverty and human rights explains that poverty was 'the principal *cause* of human rights violations in the world' and describes poverty as inhibiting human rights.[157] Similarly, the OHCHR also holds that poverty leads to the *non-fulfilment* of human rights.[158] The UN Charter-based bodies echo the approach of CESCR, and point towards a comprehensive approach to interpreting CEDAW that engages with the civil, political and socioeconomic rights in the treaty.

IV. CONCLUSION

This chapter has analysed the interpretative process to develop strategies for constructing a persuasive and compelling interpretation of CEDAW that includes gender-based poverty. It has set out the interpretative methodology that is used in Chapter 4 when interpreting CEDAW and determined that although the work of Committee and other UN human rights bodies is not binding, it is authoritative and should be given weight in the interpretative process. This chapter also analysed how the treaty- and UN Charter-based bodies have understood the connection between gender equality, poverty and human rights. The different approaches these bodies take raises questions on how best to interpret CEDAW: through an individual right in CEDAW; or by using a framework that comprehensively that engages all substantive provisions of CEDAW; or through establishing gender-based poverty as a ground of discrimination. All of these possibilities are explored in the next chapter.

---

[156] UN Special Rapporteur on minorities, 'The Realization of Economic, Social and Cultural Rights: Final Report on Human Rights and Extreme Poverty' (1996) E/CN.4/Sub.2/1996/13 [14].
[157] UN Special Rapporteur on extreme poverty and human rights, 'Report' (n 148); UN Special Rapporteur on extreme poverty and human rights, 'Guiding Principles' (n 1) [3].
[158] OHCHR, 'A Conceptual Framework'(n 150).

4

Interpreting Gender-Based Poverty into CEDAW

GENDER-BASED POVERTY ACTS as a significant obstacle preventing women from enjoying their human rights. Although CEDAW addresses women's civil, political and socioeconomic rights and patriarchal sociocultural norms, it contains no obligations on gender-based poverty. A new interpretation can ensure that CEDAW is responsive to one of the most pressing challenges of the twenty-first century. Having canvassed the drafting history of CEDAW and the elements that strengthen the interpretation of international treaties, the focus here is on evaluating if equality and non-discrimination, two norms that permeate the entire text of CEDAW, are able to account for the harms of gender-based poverty.

The starting place is to carefully consider the different interpretative options mapped out in the previous chapter. Following in the footsteps of the Human Rights Committee (HRC), is it possible to interpret a *specific* right in CEDAW to encompass gender-based poverty? Examining equal access to healthcare (Article 12 of CEDAW) and equality in economic and social life (Article 13 of CEDAW) demonstrates that this is a limited approach. A specific right is simply not able to address all of the interlocking redistribution, recognition and participation ills of gender-based poverty. This limitation points towards developing a *comprehensive framework* echoing the approach of the Committee on Economic, Social and Cultural Rights (CESCR) and the UN Special Rapporteurs. The example of gender-based violence in CEDAW helps further illustrate the need for a comprehensive approach and the potential role of equality and non-discrimination. Like gender-based poverty, there is no reference to violence in CEDAW. In the early 1990s, the Committee faced a similar question: how should gender-based violence be interpreted into CEDAW? Rather than interpreting a specific right to address gender-based violence, the Committee strongly held that gender-based violence is a facet of equality and non-discrimination. This sets a precedent and marks a path for understanding gender-based poverty as another facet of equality and non-discrimination.

Using the interpretative framework of the Vienna Convention on the Law of Treaties (VCLT),[1] Section II argues that equality and non-discrimination offers the best route to account for gender-based poverty within CEDAW. This proposed interpretation is faithful to the text, context, and object and purpose of CEDAW. An equality and non-discrimination interpretation ensures that the complexity of gender-based poverty can be incorporated into the treaty. Moreover, it offers a comprehensive framework so that all of the obligations in CEDAW can be used to account for how gender-based poverty limits women's human rights. It is also at this stage that the potential of establishing gender-based poverty as a *ground* of discrimination in CEDAW is considered.

This proposed interpretation is novel, in that it is the first time any of the UN treaties would be explicitly addressing gender-based poverty. Section III asks: what does this interpretation mean for the nature of the state's obligations? Is the state in violation of CEDAW if there are women living in poverty within its jurisdiction? Interpreting gender-based poverty as an aspect of equality and non-discrimination seemingly links together conceptions that are in tension with each other. Gender equality is an immediate obligation[2] while the human rights most closely associated with poverty are often framed in terms of progressive realisation.[3] Does interpreting gender-based poverty into CEDAW also import concepts such as the minimum core or progressive realisation into the treaty? A comparison with the state's obligations under the International Covenant on Economic, Social and Cultural Rights[4] (ICESCR) and an assessment of the text of CEDAW clarifies how the proposed interpretation affects the state's obligations. Under the interpretation posed in this chapter, the state is not obligated to immediately end gender-based poverty but it must immediately demonstrate against a non-discrimination and equality framework that its laws, policies and programmes take account of and address the gender-related aspects of poverty.

I. POTENTIAL INTERPRETATIONS OF CEDAW

A. The Limits of the Specific Right Approach

Rather than approaching the gender-based poverty gap in CEDAW through equality and non-discrimination, perhaps it is feasible to interpret

---

[1] Vienna Convention on the Law of Treaties (adopted 23 May 1969, entered into force 27 January 1980) 1155 UNTS 331.

[2] Committee on Economic, Social and Rights (CESCR), 'General Comment No 16: The Equal Rights of Men and Women to the Equal Enjoyment of Economic, Social and Cultural Rights' (2005) E/C.12/2005/4.

[3] See, CESCR, 'General Comment No 3: The Nature of the State's Obligation' (1990) Fifth Session.

[4] International Covenant on Economic, Social and Cultural Rights (adopted 16 December 1966, entered into force 3 January 1976) 999 UNTS 171.

a specific right. There are several obligations in CEDAW that hold promise. The drafting history of CEDAW shows that the obligations on employment (Article 11) and rural women (Article 14) were designed to improve women's socioeconomic status.[5] However, the structure of these obligations restricts their ability to comprehensively redress gender-based poverty. Under article 11 there needs to be an employment relationship, and article 14 is only applicable to rural areas. Equal access to healthcare (Article 12) and equality in economic and social life (Article 13) hold the most potential, but upon closer examination these specific rights are also not able to fully combat the complex way in which gender-based poverty undermines women's human rights.

Equal access to healthcare (Article 12) can be interpreted to address some of the most pressing harms of gender-based poverty. The lack of economic resources can have profoundly negative effects on physical and psychological health. For instance, women and girls represent 60% of the world's malnourished and as a result can suffer severe health consequences including maternal mortality.[6] The right to health is also evolving to include the underlying determinants of health, such as 'food and nutrition, housing, access to safe and potable water and adequate sanitation, safe and healthy working conditions and a healthy environment'.[7] This expansive understanding of health could capture many of the problems women in poverty experience. As one example, equal access to healthcare can be interpreted to ensure appropriate and culturally sensitive sanitation services in schools. This in turn can have a multiplying and empowering effect of increasing the likelihood of girls completing their education and securing decent, well-paid employment.[8] Or requiring employers to have health and safety plans can prevent incidents similar to the fire in 2012 in Bangladesh that killed over 100 garment workers, most of whom were women.[9] Attention to these and other health-related factors could improve both the health and well-being of women who live in poverty.

Another interpretative option, and perhaps the most natural place to situate an understanding of gender-based poverty in CEDAW, is Article 13 (equality in economic and social life). Rudolf argues the text of Article 13— '*other* areas of economic and social life'—means it should be interpreted

[5] See Chapter 2.
[6] Hunger Notes, 'Women and Hunger Facts', www.worldhunger.org/women-and-hunger-facts/.
[7] Office of the High Commissioner of Human Rights (OHCHR), 'Human Rights and Gender Equality in Health Sector Strategies: How to Assess Policy Coherence' (2011) 15, www.ohchr.org/Documents/Publications/HRandGenderEqualityinHealthSectorStrategies.pdf.
[8] *Environment & Consumer Protection Foundation v Delhi Administration* [2012] INSC 584 [4] (Indian Supreme Court).
[9] P Paul-Majumder and A Begum, 'The Gender Imbalance in the Export Oriented Garment Industry in Bangladesh' (2000) http://siteresources.worldbank.org/INTGENDER/Resources/trademajumder.pdf.

to include 'all rights not explicitly mentioned in [CEDAW] which are relevant in economic and social life'.[10] She holds that at its heart Article 13 requires the state to 'take account of the denial of access to resources and opportunities'.[11] Specifically, she argues that under Article 13 of CEDAW the state has an obligation to ensure equality in food, housing, clothing, social services, water, sanitation, healthy environment and participation in cultural activities.

While these rights can be expansively interpreted, there are several interrelated reasons why exclusively situating gender-based poverty in a specific right falls short. First, interpreting a specific right to encompass all the redistribution, recognition and participation wrongs of gender-based poverty strains the logic of interpretation. Due to unequal pay and gender job segregation, women are often unable to afford to access justice. The structure of legal aid programmes can further compound this problem as income testing for legal aid eligibility may not account for women's limited de facto control of household resources.[12] Can a right to health grasp how gender-based poverty impacts on a right to access justice? Intuitively equal access to healthcare brings to mind physical and mental diseases, healthcare systems and pharmaceuticals. It is not the natural tool to analyse how women's lack of decision-making power, unequal pay, job segregation and the structure of legal aid programmes negatively impacts their ability to access the court system. Equal access to healthcare, even including underlying determinants of health, has not been so expansively interpreted to include access to justice or other civil and political rights. There are similar concerns on the applicability of Article 13 (equality in economic and social life) to all aspects of gender-based poverty. Women have greater difficulty accessing forms of financial credit and can be denied their share of an inheritance due to patriarchal social norms and traditional customs.[13] At the most extreme end, this can result in homelessness.[14] Without a fixed address women are more likely to be denied bail when arrested.[15] Gender-based poverty in this example is acting as an obstacle to women's right to inherit, right to housing and right to access justice. Interpreting equality in economic and social life to capture all of these interconnected wrongs possibly stretches the normative content beyond its limits. Gender-based poverty is a

---

[10] B Rudolf, 'Article 13' in M Freeman, C Chinkin and B Rudolf (eds), *CEDAW: A Commentary* (Oxford University Press, 2012) 339.

[11] ibid.

[12] The Committee, 'General Recommendation No 33: on Women's Access to Justice' (2015) CEDAW/C/GC/33 [36].

[13] World Bank, 'Voice and Agency: Empowering Women and Girls for Shared Prosperity' (2014) 125–26, https://openknowledge.worldbank.org/handle/10986/19036.

[14] OHCHR and UN Habitat, 'The Right to Adequate Housing' (Fact Sheet No 21) 16–8, www.ohchr.org/Documents/Publications/FS21_rev_1_Housing_en.pdf.

[15] UN Special Rapporteur on extreme poverty and human rights, 'Access to Justice' (2012) A/67/278 [49].

cross-cutting problem that affects all areas of women's lives. Trying to subsume all aspects of it into one right would involve overly expansive interpretations of rights. Human rights are interrelated and interdependent, but they have not been collapsed into one all-encompassing right.

Second, on the other side of the coin, when the boundaries of each right are respected, there are significant gaps in situating the relationship between gender-based poverty and human rights in one specific right. Girls may be pulled out of school to help with domestic responsibilities, such as childcare, fetching water and firewood, and in times of household austerity, girls are more likely to be taken out of school than boys.[16] Can equality in economic and social life be interpreted so as to grasp the role that gender-based poverty plays in limiting a girl's right to education? Although Rudolf is correct that Article 13 should be expansively interpreted, it is not clear that it could be interpreted this far. Thus, there is a real risk that a specific right could result in an incomplete approach to using human rights law to address gender-based poverty.

Third, trying to collapse gender-based poverty into a specific right, in the context of CEDAW, is counterintuitive. The lack of accessible and high-quality public services and household poverty deny a girl her right to *education*, not her enjoyment of economic and social life. A right to education must also be able to account for the constraints of gender-based poverty. CEDAW has provisions on education (Article 10) and numerous other civil, political and socioeconomic rights. There is no need to exclusively understand the impact of gender-based poverty on women's rights through the lens of one, specific right. This is not to argue that each specific right should not be given a rich interpretation, but rather that all the substantive provisions in CEDAW should be used to combat the myriad of ways that gender-based poverty undermines women's rights. Certain aspects of gender-based poverty, namely inadequate funding for maternal health or social assistance schemes that perpetuate gender power imbalances, should be tackled through a right to health (Article 12) and a right to economic and social life (Article 13). Women in poverty experience a reinforcing web of violations of their political, civil, economic, social and cultural rights. A single-right approach forecloses a nuanced understanding of this web and the multifaceted role that gender-based poverty plays in obstructing the enjoyment of rights.

B. Gender-Based Violence and CEDAW

The Committee's approach to gender-based violence further supports the argument that a comprehensive framework on gender-based poverty

---

[16] Working Group on Discrimination Against Women in Law and Practice 'Discrimination Against Women in Economic and Social Life, with a Focus on Economic Crisis' (2014) A/C/26/39 [36].

is needed. Similar to gender-based poverty, there is no reference to gender-based violence, one of the most pernicious forms of discrimination against women, in CEDAW. In the early 1990s, the Committee faced a choice between locating violence in a specific right or adopting a comprehensive interpretative approach. In General Recommendation No 19 on violence against women the Committee unequivocally adopted the later and identified violence as a matter of gender inequality and discrimination and have reaffirmed this interpretation in General Recommendation No 35 on gender-based violence against women.[17] Examining the Committee's past and current approach to gender-based violence offers an analogy for interpreting gender-based poverty into CEDAW.

There was no meaningful discussion of gender-based violence in the *travaux préparatoires* of CEDAW. This is because up until the 1990s, violence was perceived as a matter for criminal law or health, not of gender equality. In 1982, the UN Committee on Crime Prevention and Control identified violence against family members as an important issue of *crime* prevention and control.[18] The UN Economic and Social Council, acting on a recommendation from the Commission on the Status of Women, described violence against women and children as blatant and inhumane abuses which cause serious physical and mental *health* problems.[19] The UN General Assembly, in 1985, adopted a resolution that noted 'abuse and battery in the family are critical problems that have *serious physical and psychological effects* on individual family members'.[20] The resolution called for research 'on domestic violence from a *criminological* perspective'.[21] The three UN Conferences on Women, held from 1975 to 1985, also failed to explicitly address the connection between violence and gender equality. At Mexico City in 1975, violence was once again situated within family conflicts.[22] Five years later in Copenhagen, violence was located within health policies and was to be remedied by protecting women from physical and mental abuse.[23] In Nairobi in 1985, violence was understood as a social problem and an obstacle to peace but separate from gender equality.[24] What is striking is that none of these statements reflect any meaningful understanding of the

---

[17] The Committee, 'General Recommendation No 19: on Violence Against Women' (1992) CEDAW/C/GC/19; The Committee, 'General Recommendation No 35: on Gender-Based Violence Against Women' (2017) CEDAW/C/GC/35.

[18] See C Chinkin, 'Violence Against Women' in M Freeman, C Chinkin and B Rudolf (eds), *CEDAW: A Commentary* (Oxford University Press, 2012) 445.

[19] Economic and Social Council, Resolution 1988/2 on efforts to eradicate violence against women within the family and society.

[20] UN General Assembly, Resolution 40/36 (29 November 1985) A/RES/40/36.

[21] ibid.

[22] Secretariat of the United Nations, 'Ending Violence Against Women: From Words to Action' (2006) 7, www.un.org/womenwatch/daw/public/VAW_Study/VAWstudyE.pdf.

[23] Chinkin, 'Violence Against Women' (n 18) 445.

[24] Secretariat (n 21) 8.

role that gender power imbalances play in perpetuating violence. Connecting violence to the family localises it within the private sphere, while linking it to peace portrays it as a violation of the social order.[25] Violence against women is then framed as the result of deviant behaviour of an individual, thereby obscuring the role of patriarchy.

The CEDAW Committee originally had a patchwork approach to gender-based violence. In 1989, drawing upon the state's core obligations (Article 2), cultural attitudes (Article 5), employment (Article 11), health (Article 12) and family life (Article 16), the Committee called upon states to protect women against violence in the family, workplace and social life.[26] In the periodic reporting process, Committee members regularly asked states about the measures they had taken to prevent violence against women.[27] However, the Committee was not consistent in where it interpreted violence into CEDAW in the Concluding Observations.[28] There is also evidence of a right-to-health approach. General Recommendation No 14 on female circumcision identifies female genital mutilation as harmful to women's *health* without also identifying the role of patriarchy.[29] At this stage, the Committee is still not truly identifying gender-based violence as an aspect of discrimination against women.

Beginning in the 1980s, there was increasing recognition that the right to health and criminal law were not accurately capturing the harms of gender-based violence. This shift was the result of a number of factors, most strikingly a global grassroots campaign to bring attention to the pervasiveness and seriousness of violence against women.[30] The central argument was that 'violence against women was not the result of individual acts of misconduct, but was deeply rooted in structural relationships of inequality between women and men'.[31] The UN study on violence against women, from 1989, which was an exception to the general trend at the UN, concluded that violence is 'a function of the belief that men are superior and that the women they live with are their possessions or chattels that they can treat as they wish and as they consider appropriate'.[32] That same year, Bunch wrote a seminal article connecting gender-based violence to human rights. She forcefully challenged the myths that violence

---

[25] Chinkin, 'Violence Against Women' (n 18) 445.
[26] The Committee, 'General Recommendation No 12: on Violence Against Women' (1989) CEDAW/C/GC/12.
[27] Elizabeth Evatt, 'Finding a Voice for Women's Rights: The Early Days of CEDAW' (2002–03) 34 *George Washington International Law Review* 515, 545.
[28] ibid.
[29] The Committee, 'General Recommendation No 14: on Female Circumcision' (1990) CEDAW/C/GC/14.
[30] Secretariat (n 22) 8.
[31] ibid 9.
[32] *Violence Against Women in the Family* (1989) UN Sales No E/89/IV/5.

was an individualised problem. Instead she demonstrated that gender-based violence is the result of the structural relationships of power and domination between men and women.[33] Recognising that violence against women is linked to gender power relations consequentially links violence to discrimination against women, gender equality and human rights.[34]

The Committee, when revisiting this issue in 1992, was faced with a choice: should gender-based violence be interpreted into a specific right in CEDAW or as a matter of non-discrimination and equality? There are indications that the Committee preferred the specific right approach. The Secretariat of the Working Group that was convened to draft General Recommendation No 19 circulated 'an analysis of article 6 [prostitution and trafficking] under which states had reported on violence against women'.[35] Unfortunately, there is no summary record of the Working Group's discussion to explain the Committee's shift to conceptualising gender-based violence as discrimination against women.[36] Nevertheless, with the available evidence it is possible to infer an explanation for the Committee's decision. At the time of drafting General Recommendation No 19, the Commission for the Status of Women was advocating for a separate legally binding instrument to address violence against women. The Committee may have wanted to retain its position as the foremost legal instrument for women's human rights and therefore favoured an interpretation that engages all of the provisions in CEDAW. Furthermore, for the first time in its history, the Committee invited civil society organisations to contribute background information.[37] It is possible that the Committee was aware and persuaded by the growing movement connecting violence to non-discrimination and equality. General Recommendation No 19 explains that there is a 'close relationship between discrimination against women, gender-based violence, and violations of human rights and fundamental freedoms'.[38] Most significantly the role of gender is emphasised: gender-based violence is 'violence that is directed against a woman because she is a woman or that affects women disproportionately'.[39]

It is now firmly accepted that gender-based violence is a matter of gender equality and non-discrimination in CEDAW. In 2017, the Committee returned to violence against women in General Recommendation No 35 on gender-based violence against women. It forcefully holds 'that gender-based violence against women is one of the fundamental social, political and

---

[33] C Bunch, 'Women's Rights as Human Rights: Towards a Re-vision of Human Rights' (1990) 12 *Human Rights Quarterly* 486, 489.
[34] ibid 491.
[35] Evatt (n 27) 547.
[36] ibid 546–47.
[37] ibid 546.
[38] 'General Recommendation No 19: on Violence Against Women' (n 17) [4].
[39] ibid [6].

economic means by which the subordinate position of women with respect to men ... are perpetuated'.[40] States are asked to include information on legislation prohibiting violence against women;[41] in all of its accountability mechanisms the Committee assesses the states measures to eliminate gender-based violence;[42] and the efforts it is taking to prevent and protect women from violence and the steps it taking to prosecute and punish perpetrators.[43] States have not objected to this interpretation of CEDAW but provide statistics, data and evidence on how their laws and national machinery protect women.[44] It is also interesting to note how the Committee structures its concerns and recommendations on violence as it is a good example of how a comprehensive interpretation works in practice. In the Concluding Observations, the Committee has a sub-heading dealing with violence against women and integrates the analysis on violence into many of the substantive provisions of CEDAW: education (Article 10), employment (Article 11), health (Article 12) and access to justice (Article 15).[45]

The Committee's interpretation of gender-based violence as a facet of non-discrimination and equality establishes an interpretative route for gender-based poverty and provides further impetus for connecting gender-based poverty to equality and non-discrimination. Similar to gender-based violence, connecting gender-based poverty to equality and non-discrimination throws the spotlight on the role that gender plays in women's poverty. Furthermore, both violence and poverty have been portrayed as private moral failings of the individual.[46] An equality and non-discrimination approach emphasises the structural and entrenched nature of these problems. There are crucial differences between violence and poverty—there are underlying prohibitions against violence that do not exist in the case of poverty and it is comparatively easier to identify the perpetrators of gender-based violence.[47]

---

[40] 'General Recommendation No 35: on Gender-Based Violence Against Women' (n 17) [10].

[41] OHCHR, 'Complication of Guidelines on the Form and Content of Reports to be Submitted by States Parties to the International Human Rights Treaties: Report of the Secretary-General' (2009) HRI/GEN/2/Rev. 6, 66.

[42] See *Yildirim v Austria*, (2007) CEDAW/C/D/39/6/2005; The Committee, 'Report of the Inquiry Concerning Canada of the Committee on the Elimination of Discrimination Against Women under Article 8 of OP-CEDAW' (2015) CEDAW/C/OP.8/CAN/1; The Committee, 'Concluding Observations: Argentina' (2016) CEDAW/C/ARG/7 [20]–[21].

[43] 'General Recommendation No 35: on Gender-Based Violence Against Women' (n 17) [40]–[45].

[44] See 'Seventh Periodic State Report: Italy' (2016) CEDAW/C/ITA/7; 'Information Received from the Government of Canada's on the Measures Taken in Response to the Inquiry Concerning Canada of the Committee on the Elimination of Discrimination against Women under Article 8 to the Optional Protocol to CEDAW'(2016) CEDAW/C/OP.8/CAN/3.

[45] The Committee, 'Concluding Observations: UK' (2013) CEDAW/C/GBR/CO/7 [23], [26], [34], [45], [56], [58].

[46] G Brodsky et al, 'Gosselin v Canada' (2006) 18 *Canadian Journal of Women and the Law* 189, 193.

[47] There is growing awareness that gender-based violence also transcends state boundaries, particularly in relation to trafficking. See 'General Recommendation No 35: on Gender

The challenge that these differences raise are explored in Section III when evaluating the nature of the state's obligations.

II. A COMPREHENSIVE INTERPRETATION: EQUALITY AND NON-DISCRIMINATION IN CEDAW

Gender-based poverty is a complex phenomenon that cannot be adequately addressed through a specific human right. A comprehensive interpretation of CEDAW is necessary if human rights are going to take seriously gender-based poverty. The gendered and entrenched nature of poverty and the structure of the treaty suggest that equality and non-discrimination can fulfil this task. Applying the VCLT interpretative rules, I demonstrate how these two norms can be coherently and persuasively interpreted to unlock the potential of CEDAW to tackle gender-based poverty.

A. The Role of Equality and Non-Discrimination in CEDAW

Before examining the ordinary meaning of equality and non-discrimination in light of the context and object and purpose of CEDAW, it is helpful to understand the role that equality and non-discrimination play in CEDAW. There are no free-standing rights to equality and non-discrimination in the treaty, but rather states are required to eliminate non-discrimination and secure women's equality in broad areas of life. Both are central and intertwined concepts and together form the core of the state's obligations.[48] The Committee makes a similar observation. It holds that states 'must ... take concrete steps to formulate and implement a policy that is targeted ... towards ... fully eliminating all forms of *discrimination* against women and achieving women's substantive *equality* with men'.[49]

Article 12 exemplifies the function of these norms in CEDAW:

> States Parties shall take all appropriate measures to eliminate *discrimination* against women in the field of health in order to ensure on a basis of *equality* of men and women, access to health care services.[50]

Based Violence Against Women' (n 17); '15 Years of the UN Special Rapporteur on Violence Against Women, its Causes and Consequences (1994–2009): A Critical Review', www.ohchr.org/Documents/Issues/Women/15YearReviewofVAWMandate.pdf, 28.

[48] A Byrnes, 'Article 1' in M Freeman, C Chinkin and B Rudolf (eds), *CEDAW: A Commentary* (Oxford University Press, 2012) 52.
[49] The Committee, 'General Recommendation No 28: on the Core Obligations' (2010) CEDAW/C/GC/28 [4].
[50] Emphasis added.

Under CEDAW, states are obligated to eliminate discrimination so that women can enjoy their rights on the basis of equality. The goal of eliminating discrimination is to achieve equality.

The definition of discrimination in Article 1 reveals that equality serves an additional function:

> Any distinction, exclusion or restriction made on the basis of sex which has the effect or purpose of impairing or nullifying the recognition, enjoyment or exercise by women, irrespective of their marital status, *on a basis of equality* of men and women, of human rights and fundamental freedoms in the political, economic, social, cultural, civil or any other field.[51]

When the state is obligated to eliminate discrimination, by the definition in the treaty, it is required to ensure that any distinction, exclusion or restriction does not impede equality. If a distinction does not uphold or further equality, there has been discrimination against women. Thus, equality is both the goal of CEDAW *and* the analytical frame for evaluating the state's laws, policies and programmes.

There are four obligations that are based solely on equality and they also reflect the dual purpose of equality in CEDAW. Under Article 3 states must take all measures to ensure the full advancement and development of women 'for the purpose of guaranteeing them the exercise and enjoyment of human rights and fundamental freedoms *on a basis of equality* of men'.[52] Equality is the standard to assess if women have achieved full development and advancement. Article 4(1) requires states to 'adopt temporary special measures aimed at accelerating *de facto equality* between men and women' and 'these measures shall be discontinued when the objectives of *equality of opportunity and treatment* have been achieved'.[53] Again equality is the goal to be achieved and the benchmark to determine when temporary special measures can be discontinued. There are two further provisions that are premised solely on equality. Article 9 requires states to 'grant women equal rights with men to acquire, change or retain their nationality', while Article 15 ensures 'women equality with men before the law'.

B. Applying the VCLT Framework to Equality and Non-Discrimination in CEDAW

Under Article 31 of the VCLT rules, the interpreter is to simultaneously apply the ordinary meaning, context and objective and purpose to derive

---

[51] Emphasis added.
[52] Emphasis added.
[53] Emphasis added.

the meaning of the words and phrases in the treaty.[54] The analysis here begins with the ordinary meaning and then proceeds to the two remaining elements. This is not to imply that ordinary meaning takes precedence. Each element is of equal weight and is used harmoniously to ascertain the meaning of the text. The choice to start with ordinary meaning simply reflects the reality that 'one has to start somewhere'.[55]

This analysis does not draw on the *travaux préparatoires* to clarify the meaning of equality and non-discrimination (Article 32 of the VCLT). This is for a very practical reason that the drafters did not spend any significant time debating the meaning of equality and non-discrimination. Rehof notes that during the drafting the main issues were (i) whether the treaty should only protect women or both men and women; and (ii) whether positive measures to empower women would be considered discrimination.[56] Given the various ideologies at the drafting table as described in Chapter 2, this is not surprising. Generating consensus on the precise meaning of these terms could have indefinitely delayed the drafting of CEDAW and the drafters probably wanted to avoid these legal and political pitfalls.

(i) The Ordinary Meaning

Equality and non-discrimination are elusive concepts and defy attempts to be pinned down to a definitive meaning. There are multiple and often conflicting definitions. The aim here is not to reconcile different theories but rather to map out the key definitions that have been prominent in legal discourses and evaluate how these different understandings can capture the harms of gender-based poverty.

There are two primary understandings of equality: formal and substantive. Formal equality is the strict application of treating likes alike and treating differences differently. It requires consistent treatment, prohibits arbitrary distinctions and aims to treat everyone on the basis of her merits.[57] It is an important step in diagnosing and remedying how gender-based poverty limits the enjoyment of human rights. It can address the blatant wrongs of gender-based poverty such as requiring a husband's permission to work, restrictions on women working at night, prohibitions on inheritance or the exclusion of married or pregnant girls from school.[58]

---

[54] R Gardiner, *Treaty Interpretation*, 2nd edn (Oxford University Press, 2016) 10.

[55] ibid 181.

[56] L Rehof, *Guide to the Travaux Préparatoires of CEDAW* (Nijhoff, 1993) 44–71. See also Byrnes, 'Article 1' (n 48) 57–8.

[57] S Fredman, *Discrimination Law*, 2nd edn (Clarendon Press, 2011) 8.

[58] The World Bank, 'Gender at Work: A Companion to the World Development Report on Jobs' (2014) 41, 43, http://documents.worldbank.org/curated/en/884131468332686103/pdf/8 92730WP0Box3800report0Feb-02002014.pdf.

The limitations of formal equality have been thoroughly canvassed and this serves as a brief summary. First, formal equality offers no moral framework for identifying when people are similar and when they are different. As Westen observes, equality 'contains no standards for distinguishing "good" reasons from "bad" reasons'.[59] For centuries women were seen as different from men. This supposed difference was used to justify depriving women of property, rights over their own children and even rights over their own bodies.[60] Second, formal equality only requires that the two similarly-situated individuals being compared be treated consistently. Formal equality is indifferent to whether the individuals are treated equally badly or equally well. If the gender wage gap is narrowed due to a decrease or stagnation in men's wage rather than an increase in women's wages, formal equality is satisfied as both men and women are earning the same amount.[61] Third, formal equality requires a comparator. If there is no comparator it is difficult to identify and remedy the wrong. This became apparent in the battle for pregnancy rights. Without a male comparator maternity benefits were characterised as violating equality.[62] Similarly, in female-dominated sectors it has been difficult to successfully argue for equal pay as there is no equivalent higher-earning male comparator.[63] Moreover, feminists argue that there is no neutral comparator. Comparisons when linked to consistent equal treatment actually require conformity to the comparator, which in the case of women requires conformity to the male norm.[64] This in turn devalues difference, can result in exclusion, and does little to address the misrecognition harms associated with gender-based poverty. In practice, formal equality is a limited tool to break cycles of economic deprivation, social marginalisation and exclusion.

Substantive equality seeks to transcend these problems and infuses equality with a normative underpinning.[65] It recognises that, for historical, biological, social and cultural reasons, men and women are not the same and to achieve equality different treatment may be required.[66] Substantive equality is a contested term for which various meanings have been proposed. The four

---

[59] P Westen, 'The Empty Idea of Equality' (1982) 95 *Harvard Law Review* 537, 575.

[60] Fredman, *Discrimination Law* (n 57); S Fredman, *Woman and the Law* (Oxford University Press, 1998) chs 1 and 2.

[61] M Redden, 'Global Gag Rule Reinstated by Trump, Curbing NGO Abortion Services Abroad', *The Guardian*, 23 January 2017, www.theguardian.com/world/2017/jan/23/trump-abortion-gag-rule-international-ngo-funding.

[62] *Bliss v Canada (Attorney General)*, [1979] 1 SCR 183 (Canadian Supreme Court).

[63] *Dumfries and Galloway Council v North*, [2009] ICR 1363 (UK Employment Appeals Tribunal).

[64] C MacKinnon, *Feminism Unmodified* (Harvard University Press, 1987) 34.

[65] See, *Minority Schools in Albania*, Advisory Opinion, PCIJ 1935, Ser A/B No 64 (Permanent Court of International Justice).

[66] The Committee, 'General Recommendation No 25: on Temporary Special Measures' (2004) CEDAW/C/GC/28 [8].

that have dominated in law are: equality of results, equality of opportunity, dignity and transformative equality.

Equality of results examines the end-point. It is 'primarily concerned with achieving a fair distribution of benefits'.[67] Equality of results ensures that socially valuable goods, jobs or places in academic institutions are shared equally among all groups, including women. As an example, it requires an equal percentage of women in decision-making bodies to reflect 'their proportion in the population as a whole'.[68] There are a various methods that can be used to achieve equality of results such as removing explicit restrictions, providing training and most controversially by establishing quotas.[69] Equality of results raises several concerns. As Young observes, it does little to challenge oppressive structures and institutions.[70] To achieve equality of results in public decision-making bodies women may be forced to assimilate to male values and working patterns. As a result, high-earning women often delegate childcare responsibility to 'other women, who remain under-paid and under-valued'.[71] This only masks rather than gets to the root of gender-based poverty. Furthermore, equality of results is easiest to apply in areas which are quantifiable: representation in government or education. The recognition harms that women in poverty experience—lazy, promiscuous, unfit mothers—are difficult to capture under this model of equality.

In contrast, equality of opportunity examines the starting point. Once this has been equalised everyone can be treated on the basis of individual merit and personal responsibility. Equality of opportunities has the potential for radical redistribution if applied substantively. To facilitate genuine opportunity, the state can be required to take positive measures to address access and quality of education, to reconfigure working days, to provide childcare, and to examine norms and structures that perpetuate exclusion such as the bias and stereotypes that can infiltrate the definition of merit.[72] However, as Fredman notes, equality of opportunity has only been applied procedurally. It has removed word-of-mouth job recruitment but it has not guaranteed that women, who remain saddled and trapped with a disproportionate amount of unpaid care work, 'will in fact be in a position to take advantage of those opportunities'.[73]

---

[67] Fredman, *Discrimination Law* (n 57) 14.
[68] ibid.
[69] C-450/93 *Kalanke* [1995] ECR I-3051; C-407/28 *Abrahamsson v Fogelqvist* [2000] ECR 1-5539 (Court of Justice of the European Union).
[70] I Young, *Justice and the Politics of Difference* (Princeton University Press, 1990) 31–2.
[71] S Fredman, 'Beyond the Dichotomy of Formal and Substantive Equality: Towards a New Definition of Equal Rights' in I Boerefijn et al (eds), *Temporary Special Measures: Accelerating de facto Equality of Women under Article 4(1) CEDAW* (Intersentia, 2003) 114.
[72] Fredman, *Discrimination Law* (n 57) 18.
[73] ibid.

Equating equality with dignity requires that the law demonstrate equal concern and respect for the moral worth of the individual. It is a powerful concept in advancing the recognition of women. Dignity responds to the levelling-down critiques of formal equality. Equality 'based on dignity must enhance rather than diminish the status of individuals'.[74] Social assistance benefits that are only provided to the male as head of the home; that are based on assumptions that women need financial incentives to take care of their children; or have conditions that are deeply intrusive into a woman's private life connote lesser moral worth. The problem is that dignity is a malleable concept. McCrudden argues that it is 'culturally relative, deeply contingent on local politics and values, resulting in diverging, even conflicting conceptions'.[75] Due to its elusive nature, collapsing equality into dignity has been questioned.[76] One pressing concern in the context of gender-based poverty is the relationship between dignity and economic resources. Can the state be said to uphold the inherent moral worth of the individual when it restricts access to or cuts back social assistance?[77] There are those who argue that economic resources are vital to dignity and those who disagree.[78] Thus, its use as a sole normative underpinning for equality and its ability to redress gender-based poverty is perhaps inherently limited.

The final model of equality is transformative. There are also different definitions, but most agree that transformative equality entails fundamental structural changes. Cusack and Pusey argue for a two-pronged approach to transformative equality: first, the transformation of 'institutions, systems and structures that cause or perpetuate discrimination and inequality'; and second, 'the modification or transformations of harmful, norms, prejudices and stereotypes'.[79] Fredman argues that transformative equality pursues four overlapping aims: (i) to break the cycle of disadvantage; (ii) to promote respect for dignity and worth; (iii) to accommodate difference by achieving structural change; and (iv) to promote political and social inclusion.[80] Looking at each dimension in turn, breaking the cycle of disadvantage recognises that individuals and groups have suffered because of their personal characteristics. To redress this imbalance, positive and targeted

---

[74] ibid 21.
[75] C McCrudden, 'Human Dignity and Judicial Interpretations of Human Rights' (2008) *European Journal of International Law* 655, 698.
[76] *R v Kapp*, [2008] 2 SCR 483 (Canadian Supreme Court).
[77] *Gosselin v Quebec (Attorney-General)*, [2002] 4 SCR 429 (Canadian Supreme Court); *Khosa and Others v Minister of Social Development* (CCT 13/03, CCT 12/03) [2004] ZACC 11 (South African Supreme Court).
[78] D Reaume, 'Discrimination and Dignity' (2003) 63 *Louisiana Law Review* 645 in support of dignity requiring a redistribution of goods. For the contrary view, see Christopher Essert, 'Dignity, Equality and Membership' (2006) 19 *Canadian Journal of Law Jurisprudence* 407.
[79] S Cusack and L Pusey, '*CEDAW* and the Rights to Equality and Non-Discrimination' (2013) 14 *Melbourne Journal of International Law* 54, 64.
[80] Fredman, *Discrimination Law* (n 57) 25.

measures are required. Second, the inclusion of recognition harms in equality addresses harassment, prejudice, stereotypes, stigmas, negative cultural attitudes, indignity and humiliation.[81] Third, with respect to structural change, rather than requiring individual conformity, equality requires institutions and structures to change. As an example, the formal labour market is based on male working patterns and is divorced from childcare responsibilities. Equality demands: (i) that the formal labour market be reformed to account for women's disproportionate role in childcare; and (ii) that male employees be encouraged and supported to be active parents. Fourth, the participation dimension requires the meaningful inclusion of women in all public, private, political and social decision-making processes. It recognises that women are not homogeneous and may have different and competing perspectives.

Placing these four dimensions together highlights the connection between the redistribution, recognition and exclusion harms of gender-based poverty. A transformative equality analysis can capture how social benefits that are based on a male breadwinner model deny women access to financial resources, perpetuate relationships of powerlessness and dependency, and exclude women from decision-making within and beyond the household unit. Achieving gender equality is a complex and often difficult task. Measures designed to promote equality can in effect perpetuate stereotypes or re-entrench disadvantage. Conditional cash transfers can redress women's economic disadvantage but perpetuate misrecognition harms that women in poverty need incentives to provide education and healthcare to their children and that women are primary care-givers.[82] At-home prenatal care may improve women's health but reinforce women's exclusion from public life, particularly in societies that are highly gender segregated.[83] The four-dimensional model of equality provides a rubric so that these tensions become apparent. Fredman explains:

> [W]here there are conflicts between different dimensions, the tension might be resolved by referring to the framework as a whole, the aim being, not so much to insist that one has priority but to create a synthesis which takes account of all dimensions.'[84]

Turning to discrimination, unlike equality, the text does define this concept. The contextual element of the VCLT interpretative analysis looks at the nuances of discrimination in CEDAW. At the ordinary meaning stage,

---

[81] ibid 29.

[82] S Fredman, 'Women and Poverty: A Human Rights Approach' (2016) 24(4) *African Journal of International and Comparative Law* 479.

[83] 'Sixth Periodic Report of State Parties: Turkey' (2008) CEDAW/C/TUR/6 [91].

[84] S Fredman, 'Substantive Equality Revisited' (2016) 14(3) *International Journal of Constitutional Law* 712, 728.

the aim is to understand the regular, normal or customary meaning of discrimination.[85] There are also two models of discrimination: direct and indirect. Direct discrimination is explicit differential treatment that perpetuates disadvantage—for example, laws that explicitly prohibit women from inheriting property.[86] Discrimination is deeply invidious, and often-invisible institutional structures perpetuate disadvantage. In response to this, the law has developed the concept of indirect discrimination. This is when differential treatment is based on an apparently neutral rule but when applied disproportionately disadvantages a group that shares a protected characteristic.[87] For example, women are disproportionately employed as part-time workers and legislation that does not protect these workers from unfair dismissal is indirectly discriminatory against women unless it can be justified for reasons unrelated to sex.[88]

Discrimination law has had a substantial impact in addressing recognition harms. In the case of direct discrimination, when an individual is treated less favourably on the basis of a protected group characteristic, there is an attribution of negative worth and inferiority to the individual because of that characteristic.[89] This in turn can create humiliation, stigma and indignity. By prohibiting less favourable treatment on certain grounds, non-discrimination forces the decision-maker to examine the individual merit of the person and not assume they possess the stereotype because of their membership in the group.[90] This ensures that the individual's identity is properly recognised and gains respect for the protected characteristic—for example, removing prohibitions against night work for women dispels stereotypes that women are weak. This is also true when there is a finding of indirect discrimination. For example, requiring the seemingly neutral physical fitness qualifications for firefighters to be recalibrated to take account of women's different physiology ensures they are not excluded from firefighting because they do not meet the standard based on the male norm.[91] This aids in the recognition of women as physically strong, capable and courageous.

However, discrimination is not a complete solution to all the recognition harms associated with gender. Similar to formal equality, direct discrimination only requires removing the distinction and ensuring consistency

---

[85] Gardiner (n 54) 183.

[86] The Committee, 'General Recommendation No 21: on Equality in Marriage and Family Relations' (1994) CEDAW/C/GC/21.

[87] Equality Act 2010 (UK) s 19; *Griggs v Duke Power* (1971) 401 US 424 (US Supreme Court).

[88] *R v Secretary of State for Employment, ex p Equal Opportunities Commission* [1994] IRLR 176 (UK House of Lords).

[89] Reaume (n 78) 35–40.

[90] *R (European Roma Rights Centre) v Immigration Officer at Prague Airport*, [2004] UKHL 55 [82] (UK House of Lords).

[91] *British Columbia Public Service Employees Relations Commission v BCGSEU*, [1999] 3 SCR 3 (Canadian Supreme Court).

of treatment.[92] In practice, the concept of direct discrimination has not been used to challenge the gender-based structures and institutions that perpetuate and contribute to economic, misrecognition and exclusion harms women in poverty experience. Removing the direct prohibitions against women entering the formal labour market has not resulted in revaluing the work traditionally assigned to women nor has it been able to address gender job segregation that sees women concentrated in low-status and low-paid jobs.[93] Drawing on the firefighter example, removing any direct prohibitions and reconceptualising the fitness standards removes some, but not all, of the barriers preventing a woman from becoming a firefighter. It does not address how the structure of the working day, the lack of formal childcare outside regular working hours and 'the underlying division of power within the family which leaves women with the primary responsibility for childcare'.[94] The almost exclusive responsibility for childcare means many women have no choice but to accept low-paid and precarious informal and part-time work.[95]

Discrimination has not had a significant impact on redistribution harms. The ability of women to work at night, to become firefighters, to inherit land and property, to be able to access credit in their own name and better protection for part-time workers all break cycles of exploitation and positively impact a woman's access to economic resources. The challenge arises when resources are required to remedy the wrongs of discrimination.[96] As childcare workers are predominantly women, discrimination law cannot address their low pay because there is no male comparison with which to demonstrate less favourable treatment. Women are often foreclosed from taking high-paid positions because of their childcare responsibilities and discrimination law cannot mandate the creation of childcare facilities.[97]

In sum, equality and discrimination are complex and contested. There is no ordinary meaning of either term. The conceptions prominent in human rights law, albeit to varying degrees, can be interpreted to incorporate the redistribution, recognition and exclusion harms associated with gender-based poverty. The first stage of the VCLT interpretative analysis suggests

---

[92] Fredman, *Discrimination Law* (n 57) 168.
[93] See Statistics Canada 'Women in Canada: A Gender Based Statistical Report: Paid Work', www.statcan.gc.ca/pub/75-001-x/2011001/pdf/11394-eng.pdf; K Sankaran and R Madhav, 'Gender Equality and Social Dialogue in India' (Working Paper 1/2011, ILO).
[94] Fredman, *Discrimination Law* (n 57) 183.
[95] S Fredman, 'Engendering Socio-Economic Rights' (2009) 25 *South African Journal on Human Rights* 517.
[96] S Fredman, 'Redistribution and Recognition: Reconciling Inequality' (2007) 23 *South African Journal on Human Rights* 214, 221.
[97] ibid.

that in CEDAW these terms should be understood as open-textured and capable of adapting to new situations.[98]

(ii) Context

The contextual element of the VCLT interpretative rules examines how the remaining provisions in CEDAW shape the definition of equality and discrimination. The analysis here uses the interpretation of CEDAW advanced by the Committee in the General Recommendations as significant and persuasive legal authority.[99] Article 31(3) also directs the interpreter to examine under the contextual element any subsequent agreements, subsequent state practice and any other relevant rules of international law, which, as discussed in Chapter 3, permits a comparative interpretation. This subsection considers each of these aspects of context in turn. It is also at this stage that the potential of establishing gender-based poverty as a ground of discrimination in CEDAW is evaluated.

(a) The Text of CEDAW

An analysis of the substantive provisions reveals that formal equality and several of the different models of substantive equality—results, opportunities and transformative—are all found within CEDAW.[100] This echoes the ordinary meaning assessment and also supports a multifaceted interpretation of equality that incorporates gender-based poverty. This pluralism is not as surprising as it first might appear. CEDAW has been ratified by 187 countries at various stages of achieving gender equality and with a wide range of political, legal, social and cultural institutions, traditions and practices. A flexible approach to equality allows the Committee to use the model of equality that can most effectively and accurately diagnosis and remedy the harms of gender inequality and gender-based poverty.[101]

Formal equality is evident in numerous provisions in CEDAW. Women are guaranteed *identical* legal capacity to that of men in civil matters, contracts, the administration of property, freedom of movement, residence, and in courts and tribunals (Article 15). Every provision in Article 16 begins with the term 'the *same* right to ...' and guarantees formal equality in numerous aspects of marriage and family life. Similarly, girls have the right to: access

---

[98] See *Convention concerning Employment of Women during the Night* PCIJ (1932) Series A/B No 50, 377; E Bjorge, *The Evolutionary Interpretation of Treaties* (Oxford University Press, 2014).

[99] See Chapter 3.

[100] Byrnes, 'Article 1' (n 48) 62.

[101] ibid.

the *same* curricula and exams; to the *same* conditions for career guidance and access to continuing education; the *same* opportunities to benefit from scholarships; and the *same* access to sports as boys.[102] Article 11(1)(d) guarantees women equal remuneration for work. Even when the obligations in CEDAW are not explicitly framed in terms of identical treatment or sameness, the Committee explains that removing all de jure barriers are 'essential prerequisites to true equality'.[103] Drawing on formal equality, the Committee holds that CEDAW requires inter alia states to repeal marital exemptions to sexual assault[104] to amend legislation that strips women of their legal status when they marry a non-national[105] and to decriminalise health services that only women require.[106]

CEDAW has been criticised as only guaranteeing women formal equality.[107] This is a misreading. It does not merely guarantee to women 'what men already have'.[108] Formal equality is merely the first step and needs be supplemented by substantive equality.[109] Substantive equality is central to the treaty. CEDAW is committed to achieving equality of results, equality of opportunity and transformative equality.

Equality of results is not easily detected in the text of CEDAW. The treaty does not stipulate precise quotas in public office or educational facilities. Nevertheless, the Committee has relied on equality of results to explain the state's obligations, particularly in relation to women's participation in public life (Article 7). It holds that 'equality of results is the logical corollary of de facto or substantive equality' and notes that the CEDAW requires 'that women ... be empowered by an enabling environment to achieve equality of results'.[110] The Committee recommends the 'adoption of a rule that neither sex should constitute less than 40 per cent of the members of the public body'.[111] It advocates setting numerical goals and quotas for women in all public positions and other essential professional groups.[112] Increasing women's participation in public life can open up sites of power so as to empower women's voice and promote reform of laws, policies and practices that perpetuate gender-based poverty.

---

[102] Art 10(a), (b), (d) and (e) CEDAW.
[103] The Committee, 'General Recommendation No 23: on Women in Political and Public Life' (1997) CEDAW/C/GC/1997 [15].
[104] The Committee, 'Concluding Observations: Haiti' (2016) CEDAW/C/HTI/CO/8–9 [21].
[105] The Committee, 'Concluding Observations: Jordan' (2012) CEDAW/C/JOR/CO/5/ [33].
[106] The Committee, 'Concluding Observations: Tanzania' (2016) CEDAW/C/CO/TZA/7–8 [43].
[107] See D Otto, 'Holding Up Half the Sky, but for Whose Benefit? A Critical Analysis of the Fourth Conference on Women' (1996) 6 *Australian Feminist Law Journal* 7.
[108] Byrnes, 'Article 1' (n 48) 61.
[109] See, 'General Recommendation No 23: on Women in Political Life' (n 103).
[110] 'General Recommendation No 25: on Temporary Special Measures' (n 66) [9].
[111] ibid [16], [29].
[112] ibid [15].

Unlike equality of results, equality of opportunity is expressly referred to in the treaty. Article 4(1) requires temporary special measures to be discontinued when 'equality of *opportunity* and treatment have been achieved'.[113] Equality of opportunity is at the forefront on education. Article 10 repeatedly stresses the girl should have same *opportunities* to benefit from scholarships, career guidance and education.[114] Equality of opportunity is also evident in employment (Article 11). Women have the right to have the same *opportunities* and access to jobs, benefits, vocational training and promotions.[115] The Committee explains that 'the Convention requires that women be given an equal start'[116] and highlights the 'Convention's emphasis on ... equality of opportunity [in] participation in public life and decision making'.[117] Ensuring women's equal opportunities in education and employment can have a multiplying effect and is crucial for breaking cycles of gender-based poverty.

Dignity does not play a crucial role in CEDAW and the Committee has not relied on it in any significant way. There is no reference to dignity in the substantive text of CEDAW. There are references to it in the preamble, but these are so brief that arguably it is not a fully fleshed-out normative concept. So far as the Committee is concerned, its nods to dignity tend to be superficial. It observes that prostitution and trafficking are incompatible with women's rights and dignity.[118] Similarly, the right to informed consent to healthcare,[119] to choose a spouse, and to choose the number and spacing of children is described as central to a woman's dignity and equality.[120]

The transformative model of equality is prominent in CEDAW.[121] Although there are several different understandings of this concept, Fredman's has been particularly influential in the UN human rights framework. It has been adopted by UN Women in their latest flagship report[122] and various UN treaty bodies are implicitly relying on transformative equality.[123] For ease of analysis, I use this model to demonstrate CEDAW's commitment to transformative equality. The four dimensions of transformative equality

---

[113] Emphasis added.

[114] Art 10(a), (d), (g) and (e) CEDAW.

[115] Art 11(1)(b) and (c) CEDAW.

[116] 'General Recommendation No 25: on Temporary Special Measures' (n 66) [8].

[117] 'General Recommendation No 23: on Women in Political Life' (n 103) [7].

[118] 'General Recommendation No 19: on Violence Against Women' (n 17) [14].

[119] The Committee, 'General Recommendation No 24: Women and Health' (1999) CEDAW/C/GC/24 [22], [25].

[120] 'General Recommendation No 21: On Equality in Marriage' (n 86) [16].

[121] Cusack and Pusey (n 79) 64.

[122] UN Women, 'Transforming Economies, Realizing Rights' (2015) 42, http://progress.unwomen.org/en/2015/pdf/UNW_progressreport.pdf.

[123] S Fredman and B Goldblatt, 'Discussion Paper: Gender Equality and Human Rights for Progress of the World's Women 2015–2016' (2015) 12, www.unwomen.org/-/media/headquarters/attachments/sections/library/publications/2015/goldblatt-fin.pdf?vs=1627.

are evident in many of the provisions. The first dimension, breaking the cycle of disadvantage, means that treating women as identical to men is not sufficient and differential treatment is required. Temporary special measures play a pivotal role in redressing disadvantage (Article 4(1)).[124] The Committee explains that temporary special measures require the state to take positive measures to accelerate gender equality. This can include creating support programmes, targeting recruitment and reallocating resources.[125] In a similar vein, Article 10(f) recognises that girls are more likely than boys not to finish school and requires the creation of special programmes for girls and women who have dropped out. In response to women's unique role in reproduction, CEDAW requires states to provide maternity leave benefits, appropriate maternal healthcare services and access to family planning.[126] Rural women, who on every indicator fare worse than rural men, and urban women and men, are specifically protected under Article 14.[127] This provision ensures that rural women benefit directly from social security programmes and have adequate living conditions, such as housing, sanitation, electricity and water supply.[128]

The strongest evidence of the recognition dimension is Article 5(a). States are 'to modify the social and cultural patterns of conduct of men and women ... based on the idea of inferiority or the superiority of either sex or on stereotyped roles of men and women'. This is a powerful tool to address stigma, prejudice, stereotypes and the devaluation of all women including women in poverty.[129] Chinkin explains that this provision is meant to ensure 'a positive appreciation of women's contribution to society'.[130] Both the preamble and Article 5(b) require the state to ensure 'family education includes a proper understanding of maternity as a social function ... and the recognition of the common responsibility of men and women in the upbringing and development of their children'. This stresses seeing maternity as a positive value and challenges social norms which dictate that women have sole responsibility for childcare.[131] Equal pay for work of equal value (Article 11(1)(d)) can increase the pay of female jobs and also contribute to the proper recognition of work traditionally assigned to women. Article 14(1) on rural women notes the 'significant roles which rural women play in the economic survival of their families'. In education, states are

---

[124] 'General Recommendation No 25: on Temporary Special Measures' (n 66) [8].
[125] ibid.
[126] Arts 10(h), 11(2)(b), 12(2), 14(2)(b) and 16(1)(e) CEDAW.
[127] The Committee, 'General Recommendation No 34: on the Rights of Rural Women' (2016) CEDAW/C/GC/34 [5].
[128] Art 14(2)(c) and (h) CEDAW.
[129] C Chinkin, 'Article 5' in M Freeman, C Chinkin and B Rudolf (eds), *CEDAW: A Commentary* (Oxford University Press, 2012) 142.
[130] ibid.
[131] ibid.

required to revise textbooks, school programmes and teaching methods to eliminate stereotypes on the role of men and women.[132]

The structural component seeks to value difference and requires institutions rather than individuals to change. The Committee advocates that states adopt measures 'towards a real transformation of opportunities, institutions and systems so that they are no longer grounded in historically determined male paradigms of power and life patterns'.[133] There are numerous examples of the structural dimension of transformative equality in CEDAW. It is a strong advocate for restructuring parenting.[134] Under Article 11(2)(c) states are 'to encourage the provision of the necessary supporting social services to enable parents to combine family obligations with work responsibilities and participation in public life, in particular through promoting the establishment and development of a network of child-care facilities'. This could require states to modify working hours to accommodate parenting obligations and to establish childcare centres. The preamble also calls for 'a change in the traditional role of men as well as the role of women in society and the family ... to achieve full equality between men and women'. Other provisions also have the potential to transform oppressive structures. Equal remuneration for work of equal value, in Article 11(1)(d), is a potentially revolutionary concept. It can challenge women's low wages, gender-based job segregation and require a re-evaluation of the 'tasks performed predominantly by women' on objective gender-neutral criteria.[135] Evaluating equal pay for work of equal value reconceptualises traditional definitions of qualification and merit. The Committee recommends the concept of merit be 'reviewed carefully for gender bias as they are normatively and culturally determined'.[136] Article 14(2)(c) gives rural women the right to directly benefit from social security models which could be used to challenge head of household models of social benefits.

The participation dimension of transformative equality is apparent in Articles 7 and 8 which require states to ensure women participate in the formulation of government policy, and in non-governmental and international organisations. The Committee recommends that states 'achieve a balance between women and men holding publicly elected positions' and 'equality of representation of women in the formulation of government policy'.[137] Under Article 14(2)(a) women have the equal right to participate in the implementation and development of all planning and all community

---

[132] Art 10(c) CEDAW.
[133] 'General Recommendation No 25: on Temporary Special Measures' (n 66) [9].
[134] See, Art 5(b) CEDAW.
[135] F Raday, 'Article 11' in M Freeman, C Chinkin and B Rudolf (eds), *CEDAW: A Commentary* (Oxford University Press, 2012) 293.
[136] 'General Recommendation No 25: on Temporary Special Measures' (n 66) [23].
[137] 'General Recommendation No 23: on Women in Political Life' (n 103) [46]–[47].

activities. States are required to guarantee equal participation in recreation, sports and cultural life[138] and to reduce the female student drop-out rate at all levels of education.[139]

Article 3 brings together all four dimensions of transformative equality. Article 3 requires states to take 'in all fields ... all appropriate measures to ensure the *full development and advancement* of women for the purpose of guaranteeing them the exercise and enjoyment of human rights and fundamental freedoms on a basis of equality with men'.[140] Article 3 has not yet been developed by the Committee.[141] Full development and advancement captures the idea of being able to freely develop and pursue choices and abilities; and to 'form mutually supporting human relationships in the home, community, workplace and society'.[142] Raday observes that Article 3 'locates women as rights-holders, not just as object or prospective beneficiaries of development policy'.[143] Whatever precise meaning is given to this term, what is clear is that to achieve the full development and advancement of women in poverty all aspects of transformative equality must be applied. To 'develop, participate and flourish as human beings'[144] requires breaking cycles of disadvantage, ensuring proper respect and recognition of the women, modifying structures which exclude, oppress and demean, and ensuring the participation of women in all aspects of life.

Thus, equality in the context of CEDAW is a rich and varied concept. This also steers towards a conclusion that equality in CEDAW includes formal equality as well as a multifaceted substantive equality.

(b) Gender-Based Poverty as a Ground of Discrimination

Every jurisdiction has a unique approach to discrimination that springs from its own context. The US Supreme Court has developed different standards of scrutiny in relation to different grounds of discrimination.[145] In the UK direct discrimination cannot be justified,[146] while in Canada the courts

---

[138] Art 13 CEDAW.

[139] Art 10(e) CEDAW.

[140] Emphasis added.

[141] C Chinkin, 'Article 3' in M Freeman, C Chinkin and B Rudolf (eds), *CEDAW: A Commentary* (Oxford University Press, 2012) 103.

[142] C Albertyn and B Goldblatt, 'Facing the Challenge of Transformation: Difficulties in the Development of Indigenous Jurisprudence' (1998) 14 *South African Journal on Human Rights* 248, 254; 'General Recommendation No 28: on Core Obligations' (n 49) [22]; B Hepple, *Equality: The New Legal Framework* (Hart, 2011) 12.

[143] F Raday, 'Gender and Democratic Citizenship: The Impact of CEDAW' (2012) 10(2) *International Journal of Constitutional Law* 512, 525.

[144] S Liebenberg and B Goldblatt, 'The Interrelationship between Equality and Socio-Economic Rights Under South Africa's Transformation Constitution' (2007) 23 *South African Journal on Human Rights* 335, 343.

[145] *United States v Virginia* 518 US 515 (1996) 116 S Ct 2264 (US Supreme Court).

[146] *R (on the application of E) v Governing Body of JFS and the Admissions Appeal Panel of JFS* [2009] UKSC 15 (UK Supreme Court).

are moving towards collapsing the distinction between direct and indirect discrimination so that both types of discrimination are justifiable.[147] The South African Constitutional Court has embraced the concept of dignity in determining if discrimination is unfair.[148] The Canadian Supreme Court, on the other hand, recently jettisoned the concept and now assesses if the law perpetuates prejudice and stereotypes.[149] It is crucial to understand CEDAW's distinctive conception to determine if and how gender-based poverty should be established as a ground of discrimination.

To reiterate, discrimination is defined in Article 1 of CEDAW as

> Any *distinction, exclusion or restriction* made on the *basis of sex* which has the effect or purpose of *impairing or nullifying the recognition, enjoyment or exercise* by women, irrespective of their marital status, *on a basis of equality* of men and women, of human rights and fundamental freedoms in the political, economic, social, cultural, civil or any other field.[150]

From this definition, there are three elements to discrimination in CEDAW. First, there must be a distinction, exclusion or restriction. The use of multiple terms suggests that differential treatment is to be broadly defined, recognising that at times equality requires identical treatment, and at others, differential treatment.[151] The words 'which has the effect or purpose of' indicates that both direct discrimination (explicit differential treatment)[152] and indirect discrimination (where identical or neutral laws, policies or programmes that in application disadvantage women)[153] are included in CEDAW.

Second, as discussed above, a distinction only amounts to discrimination when it impairs women's rights on the basis of equality. Equality is the evaluative framework under CEDAW. The challenge of using equality as an analytical tool is canvassed in Section III when delineating the nature of the state's obligations when interpreting gender-based poverty into CEDAW.

Third, the distinction must be made on the basis of sex. The Committee has clarified that this also includes gender.[154] It might appear that CEDAW only protects the monolithic category of women and that intersectional claims, such as those based on the synergistic interaction between gender

---

[147] *British Columbia (Public Service Employee Relations Commission) v BCGEU* (1999), 3 SCR 3 (Canadian Supreme Court).

[148] *Harksen v Lane NO and Others* (1998) 1 SA 300 (South African Constitutional Court).

[149] *Kapp* (n 76); *Quebec (Attorney-General) v A*, [2013] 1 SCR 161 (Canadian Supreme Court).

[150] Emphasis added.

[151] R Cook and S Cusak, *Gender Stereotyping: Transnational Legal Perspectives* (Princeton University Press, 2010) 111; Byrnes, 'Article 1' (n 48) 59.

[152] 'General Recommendation No 28: on Core Obligations' (n 49) [16].

[153] ibid [5].

[154] Although Art 1 of CEDAW only refers to sex, the Committee has interpreted this to include both sex and gender. See ibid [5].

and poverty, fall outside of the treaty's ambit.[155] Although the text of the treaty references different identities that women experience such as race, poverty, marital status, pregnancy, nationality and it specifically protects rights of women living in rural areas,[156] there is no fully formed concept of intersectionality in CEDAW.[157] However, in practice, the Committee has 'identified many groups of women to whom [CEDAW] extends protection to on the basis of their sex in combination with another status'.[158] In General Recommendation No 35 on gender-based violence against women the Committee comprehensively recognises that due to ethnicity, race, indigenous or minority status, caste, language, religion or belief, political opinion, marital status, age, urban/rural location, disability, health status, property ownership, being lesbian, bisexual, transgender or intersex, illiteracy, trafficking, conflict, migration and asylum seeking, heading households, prisoner status, prostitution and geographical remoteness can result in different and often times aggravated experiences of gender-based violence.[159] This raises questions on the role that identity grounds play in CEDAW and the potential of establishing gender-based poverty as a ground of discrimination.

In comparison, CESCR has interpreted socioeconomic status as a ground of discrimination in ICESCR.[160] CEDAW does not operate in the same manner since there is no open list of grounds for discrimination as in ICESCR. CEDAW has chosen one specific ground: women. Instead of looking at the intersection between the grounds the Committee has taken an expansive understanding of sex/gender discrimination to account for women's different identities and experiences.[161] This fluid approach is based on the core obligations in Articles 2 and 3 of the treaty. CEDAW 'condemns discrimination in *all its forms*' (Article 2) and aims to achieve equality so that women can enjoy 'their human rights and fundamental freedoms *in all fields of life*' (Article 3). These provisions 'establish a comprehensive obligation to eliminate discrimination in all its forms'.[162] This inherently includes intersectional discrimination as it is a unique form of discrimination.[163] Thus, there is actually a strong textual basis for requiring states to appreciate and account for all identities, experiences and

---

[155] JE Bond, 'International Intersectionality: A Theoretical and Pragmatic Exploration of Women's International Human Rights Violations (2003) *Emory Law Journal* 71, 95.

[156] Preamble, Arts 1, 4(2), 11(2), 9 and 14 CEDAW.

[157] Cusack and Pusey (n 79) 59–60.

[158] Byrnes, 'Article 1' (n 48) 68; Raday, 'Article 11' (n 135) 146.

[159] 'General Recommendation No 35: on Gender-Based Violence Against Women' (n 17) [12].

[160] CESCR, 'General Comment No 20: Non-Discrimination in Economic, Social and Cultural Rights' (2009) E/C.12/GC/20 [35].

[161] M Campbell 'CEDAW and Women's Intersecting Identities: A Pioneering Approach to Intersectionality' (2015) *Revista Diretio GV* 479.

[162] 'General Recommendation No 19: On Violence Against Women' (n 17) [10].

[163] K Crenshaw, 'Demarginalising the Intersection of Race and Sex' (1989) *University of Chicago Legal Forum* 139.

factors that contribute to gender discrimination and inequality. According to the Committee, 'the discrimination of women based on sex and gender is *inextricably linked* with other [identity characteristics] that affect[] women'.[164] Raday similarly explains that intersectionality is 'an off-shoot of the core right to equality'.[165] If women experience discrimination that is rooted in their sex and/or gender and this intersects with other aspects of their identity or experiences and results in a denial of human rights, it can be addressed through CEDAW.[166]

This novel approach to intersectional discrimination means that CEDAW is not wedded to the traditional canon of identity grounds. As evidenced in General Recommendation No 35, the Committee refers to many forms of intersectional discrimination not typically recognized in other domestic and international human rights instruments.[167] CEDAW takes a much wider viewpoint and can examine how women experience discrimination in relation to cross-cutting themes—violence, conflict, climate change or poverty—or in relation to certain identities or experiences—migrant status, prison or age. It is because women experience these forms of discrimination in a unique way intrinsically linked to their sex and gender that they are protected under CEDAW. For example, in *Teixeira*, a poor, rural Afro-Brazilian woman died in childbirth due to delays in receiving medical treatment.[168] To properly assess gender discrimination and inequality in the healthcare system it is vital to understand how not only her gender but her poverty, race and living in a rural community contributed to her death. The Committee has used this fluid approach to inter alia address migrant status,[169] age,[170] ethnic minorities,[171] disabilities,[172] women in prisons,[173] women with HIV,[174] refugees,[175] albinos,[176] girls living on the street[177] violence[178] and armed conflict.[179]

---

[164] 'General Recommendation No 28: on Core Obligations' (n 49) [18] (emphasis added).
[165] Raday, 'The Impact of CEDAW' (n 143) 516.
[166] Campbell, 'A Pioneering Approach' (n 161).
[167] 'General Recommendaiton No 35: on Gender-Based Violence Against Women' (n 17) [12].
[168] *Alyne da Silva Pimentel Teixeira v Brazil* (2011) CEDAW/C/49/D/17/2008.
[169] The Committee, 'General Recommendation No 26: on Women Migrant Workers' (2008) CEDAW/C/GC/26.
[170] The Committee, 'General Recommendation No 27: on Older Women and the Protection of their Human Rights' (2010) CEDAW/C/GC/27.
[171] 'Concluding Observations: UK' (n 45) [34].
[172] ibid [42], [46]–[47].
[173] ibid [54].
[174] The Committee, 'Concluding Observations: Democratic Republic of the Congo' (2013) CEDAW/C/COD/CO/6–7 [9(h)].
[175] ibid [35(c)].
[176] ibid.
[177] ibid.
[178] 'General Recommendation No 19: On Violence Against Women' (n 17).
[179] The Committee, 'General Recommendation No 30: on Women in Conflict Prevention, Conflict and Post-Conflict Situations' (2013) CEDAW/C/GC/30.

Thus, gender-based poverty is not a ground of discrimination in CEDAW. This helpfully avoids the debate on this contentious issue.[180] The text of CEDAW and the Committee's interpretation protects both women's identity characteristics and their experiences as these are inextricably linked to gender discrimination.[181] Recognising gender-based poverty as an issue of gender discrimination and equality in CEDAW acknowledges that that poverty is part of the spectrum of women's identities and experiences.

(c) Subsequent Agreements

After examining the text of CEDAW to ascertain an initial contextual understanding of equality and non-discrimination, the VCLT framework proceeds to assess how any subsequent agreements on the interpretation and application of the treaty assists in a contextual interpretation (Article 31(3) (a) of the VCLT). There is an Optional Protocol to CEDAW which empowers the Committee to decide Individual Communications where the state has failed to fulfil CEDAW and to undertake Inquiry Procedures into grave and systemic abuses of gender equality.[182] The text of the Optional Protocol is focused on establishing procedural rules for these new accountability mechanisms and does not provide any insights into the interpretation of equality and non-discrimination.[183]

(d) Subsequent State Practice

This is a crucial factor in the interpretation process. As discussed in Chapter 3, the touchstone for treaty interpretation is: what did the parties intend? The entire VCLT process is directed towards answering this question. However, the subsequent practice element of the contextual factor is an opportunity to assess how states through their practice in implementing the treaty have interpreted CEDAW (Article 31(3)(b) of the VCLT). Gardiner goes so far as to explain that subsequent practice 'constitutes objective evidence of the understanding of the parties as to the meaning of the treaty'.[184]

In bilateral or even small multilateral treaties on discrete issues, it may be relatively straightforward to ascertain subsequent state practice and its role

---

[180] See S Fredman 'The Potential and Limits of an Equal Rights Paradigm in Addressing Poverty' (2011) 22(3) *Stellenbosch Law Review* 566, 581–87.

[181] 'General Recommendation No 28: on Core Obligations' (n 49) [18].

[182] Optional Protocol to the Convention on the Elimination of All Forms of Discrimination Against Women (adopted 18 October 1999, entered into force 22 December 2000) 2131 UNTS 83.

[183] M Campbell, 'Women's Rights and the Convention on the Elimination of Discrimination Against Women: Unlocking the Potential of the Optional Protocol' (2016) 34(4) *Nordic Journal of Human Rights* 247.

[184] *Kasikili/Sedudu Island (Botswana/Namibia)* [1999] ICJ Report 1045 [49] quoting from (1966) II *Yearbook of the ILC* [15].

in the interpretative process. CEDAW is different from the 'presumed ideal type of multilateral treaty'.[185] It has been ratified by 187 states, its obligations are owed to individuals, not to other states, and the treaty touches upon almost every aspect of public and private life. States may adopt laws, policies and programmes that are explicitly or implicitly directed towards ameliorating gender-based poverty. However, it is by no means clear that when the state passes laws, policies or programmes on gender-based poverty that it does so to discharge its obligations under CEDAW and that these measures can be considered as subsequent state practice implementing the treaty. It may take a stance on women's poverty in fulfilment of domestic or regional human rights instruments or out of a commitment to a certain moral or political ideology. This makes it difficult to locate, collate and assess the evidence of subsequent state practice on the meaning of equality and non-discrimination in the CEDAW in relation to gender-based poverty.[186]

While it may be complicated to assess subsequent state practice under CEDAW, it is not impossible. Although there have been some attempts to argue that the practice of the Committee could qualify as subsequent state practice under the VCLT, this position is unorthodox as it undermines the horizontal and voluntary nature of international law.[187] The summary records of the oral dialogue session between the state representative and the Committee during the periodic reporting process and the follow-up reports states submit to the Committee provides a chance to assess how the state interprets and implements CEDAW. Unlike domestic legislation or court judgments, the summary records and follow-up reports are exclusively focused on the meaning of CEDAW. Although the state report which details the efforts the state has taken over a four-year period to implement CEDAW also interprets the treaty, the summary records and follow-up procedure are where the state is most likely to accept or reject an interpretation of equality and non-discrimination that incorporates gender-based poverty into the treaty. These sources offer the best objective evidence of subsequent state practice of CEDAW.

Using the summary records and follow-up reports raises its own set of hurdles. The Committee has held thousands of dialogue sessions with state representatives. With this impressive volume of primary material, some selection must be made to fruitfully evaluate subsequent state practice. Gardiner observes that it is not necessary that every party to CEDAW undertake such practice but 'it is sufficient if there is practice of one or

---

[185] International Law Association, 'Final Report on the Impact of Findings of the United Nations Human Rights Treaty Bodies' (Berlin Conference, 2004) [25]–[26].

[186] Gardiner (n 54) 270.

[187] *Japan—Alcoholic Beverages Case* AB-1996-2, Report of 4 October 1996, WT/DS8/AB/R, WT/DS10/AB/R, WT/DS11/AB/R.

more parties and good evidence that other parties have endorsed the practice'.[188] The natural place to turn for assistance in selecting summary records and follow-up reports is previous studies on CEDAW. There are two types of studies on CEDAW. The first focuses on how a specific state has implemented CEDAW.[189] These studies only use the source material from one state, so there is no requirement for any selection process. The remaining studies on CEDAW do draw upon on multiple states. However, either the number of states analysed is very small[190] or it is not always clear how the states were chosen for assessment.[191] The former type of study does not provide a sufficient basis of material for a comprehensive analysis necessary for assessing subsequent state practice. The latter type of study is vulnerable to criticism of cherry-picking states to further a particular theory rather than an objective assessment of the primary material. To ensure the assessment is not open to allegations of selection bias, it is necessary to have a methodological framework for choosing summary records and follow-up reports.

Ideally, any analysis of subsequent state practice should have geographic breadth and include states at different stages of development with respect to gender equality and discrimination as gender-based poverty is a global phenomenon and not confined to the developing world. To achieve these aims, three criteria are used to select summary records and follow-up procedures: (i) the UN Development Programme (UNDP) Gender Inequality Index (GII); and the World Bank's (ii) gross national income scale and (iii) geographic locations classification. Before applying these criteria, it is helpful to briefly examine the GII and World Bank categorization systems.

The GII arose out of the failure of the Human Development Index (HDI) to capture gender inequality.[192] The HDI was pioneered in the 1990s and is a multidimensional poverty index derived from Sen's capabilities approach.[193]

---

[188] Gardiner (n 54) 270.

[189] For example, see M Bydoon, 'Reservations on the Convention of Elimination of All Forms of Discrimination Against Women Based on Islam and its Practical Application in Jordan: Legal Perspectives' (2011) 25(1) *Arab Law Quarterly* 51; C Shinohara, 'Global Pressure, Local Results: The Impact of CEDAW on Working Women in Japan' (2008) 13(4) *Journal of Workplace Rights* 449.

[190] L Pruitt and MR Vanegas, 'CEDAW and Rural Development: Empowering Women with Law form the Top Down, Activism from the Bottom Up' (2012) 41 *Baltimore Law Review* 264.

[191] See M Freeman, C Chinkin and B Rudolf (eds), *CEDAW: A Commentary* (Oxford University Press, 2012).

[192] S Klasen and D Schuler, 'Reforming the Gender Related Development Index and Gender Empowerment Measure: Implementing Some Specific Proposals' (2011) 17(1) *Feminist Economics* 1. See also S Alkrie and ME Santos, 'A Multidimensional Approach: Poverty Measurement and Beyond' (2013) 112(2) *Social Indicators Research* 239 for the development of a multidimensional approach to poverty.

[193] Klasen and Schuler (n 192).

It examines three dimensions: (i) life expectancy at birth; (ii) years of education; and (iii) the gross national income per capita. The HDI has been criticised for assuming that individuals have reached the average achievement level, which whitewashes gender inequalities.[194] In 1995, the UNDP introduced the Gender Development Index (GDI) and Gender Empowerment Measurement (GEM). Both of these were limited tools[195] and in application both were skewed in favour of developed countries.[196] The UNDP discarded these measurements in 2010 and now uses the GII.[197] It measures gender inequality on three dimensions: reproductive health, empowerment and the labour market; and five indicators: maternal mortality, adolescent fertility, women's representation in parliament, levels of education, and participation in the formal labour force.[198] There are still notable gaps in the GII. It does not take into account the informal labour market or caring work.[199] Every two years the UNDP releases states' rankings for gender equality using the GII. Somewhat counter intuitively, countries that have a very high GII are those that have high levels of gender equality.

The World Bank has two axes of classifications: gross national income per capita (GNI) and geography.[200] GNI is calculated in US dollars. The classifications are: low income, $1,025 or less; lower middle income, $1,026–4,035; upper middle income, $4,036–12,475; and high income, $12,476 or more. Only those countries ranked below higher incomes are further classified by geographic region. The regional breakdown is: Latin American & Caribbean, Europe & Central Asia, Middle East & North Africa, Sub-Saharan Africa, South Asia and East Asia & Pacific.

Using the GII rankings from 2014[201] and the World Bank's two classifications from 2016 the states in Table 1 were selected for further study. This method is not purely mathematical and in some instances a choice had to be made between two equally 'qualified' states. Notwithstanding this, the sample size provides a range of states with different levels of gender equality, GNI and geographic location.

---

[194] ibid.
[195] L Beneria and I Permanyer, 'The Measurement of Socio-Economic Gender Equality Revisited' (2010) 41(3) *Development and Change* 375, 376–77.
[196] Klasen and Schuler (n 192) 2.
[197] UNDP, 'Gender Inequality Index', http://hdr.undp.org/en/statistics/gii/.
[198] ibid.
[199] ibid.
[200] The World Bank, 'How We Classify Countries', http://data.worldbank.org/about/country-classifications.
[201] UN Data, 'Gender Inequality Index', http://data.un.org/DocumentData.aspx?q=HDi&id=332.

Table 1: Selection of states for analysis of subsequent state practice

Country	2014 GII Rank	GNI	Geographic region
Norway	9	high income	Western Europe
Canada	25	high income	North America
Jordan	50	upper middle income	Middle East & North Africa
Romania	64	upper middle income	Europe & Central Asia
Argentina	69	upper middle income	Latin American and Caribbean
Turkey	71	upper middle income	Europe and Central Asia
Mexico	74	upper middle income	Latin America & Caribbean
Philippines	89	low middle income	East Asia & Pacific
Bangladesh	111	low middle income	South Asia
Kenya	126	low middle income	Sub-Saharan Africa
Ethiopia	129	low income	Sub-Saharan Africa
Egypt	131	low middle income	Middle East & North Africa

The states in Table 1 have a GII ranging from 9 to 131. There are two high-income states, five upper-middle-income states, four lower-middle-income states and one low-income state. There is one state from Western Europe, one from North America, two from Europe & Central Asia, two from Latin American & Caribbean, one from East Asia & Pacific, two from Middle East & North Africa, one from South Asia and two states from Sub-Saharan Africa. This analysis relies on summary records and follow-up reports from the periodic reporting sessions from 2001 to 2016. The three selection criteria and the sample size of states address both the need for concurrence and the consistency required for subsequent state practice under the VCLT framework,[202] and provide a basis for an objective understanding of how states have understood gender equality, non-discrimination and gender-based poverty in CEDAW.

There is strong evidence from the summary records and the follow-up reports that states are interpreting equality and non-discrimination in CEDAW to include gender-based poverty. Bangladesh's opening statement to the Committee is compelling evidence of this: '[T]he Government

---

[202] Gardiner (n 54) 270.

of Bangladesh firmly believed that gender equality was a precondition for meeting the challenge of reducing poverty'.[203] In a similar vein, Argentina in their opening statement to the Committee in 2016 states that in efforts to achieve substantive equality it is developing special economic empowerment programmes.[204] The Philippines also draws a connection between women's poverty and gender equality; according to its state representative, 'progress in women's rights and gender equality need to be examined in the context of other circumstances in the Philippines, such as poverty'.[205] Egypt also identifies poverty as an obstacle to women's advancement.[206]

While these states are interpreting gender equality in CEDAW to include gender-based poverty, it is essential under the VCLT framework that subsequent state practice be reflected not only in statements but in actual acts. Argentina, Bangladesh, Canada, Ethiopia, the Philippines and Kenya provide substantial information on the steps they have taken to reduce gender-based poverty. Bangladesh explains that 'women's economic empowerment had ... gained momentum' and the 'government had taken concrete action to reduce poverty'.[207] It has 'launched a number of poverty-alleviation programmes',[208] such as collateral-free loans, targeted social assistance programmes to improve rural women's maternal nutritional, special welfare payments for Dalit women, and daycare centres for low- and middle-income working mothers.[209] The Philippines has created targeted financial assistance for girls in poor, indigenous and Muslim communities, 'to help them make the transition from school to the labour market',[210] as well as conditional cash transfer programmes.[211] Similarly, Canada 'endeavoured to address specific gender related economic gaps ... such as the National Child Benefit Supplement for low income families'.[212] Going forward, Canada explained it would be taking an 'intersectional approach to tackling poverty among women and includ[ing] a gender perspective in poverty reduction strategies'.[213] Ethiopia's national poverty reduction strategy also 'recognised women's stake in the country's development'.[214] The fact that so many states present evidence of the efforts they have taken to reduce gender-based poverty when discussing the implementation of CEDAW with

---

[203] The Committee, 'Summary Record of the 969th Meeting' (2011) CEDAW/C/SR.969 [1].
[204] The Committee, 'Summary Record of the 1443rd Meeting' (2016) CEDAW/C/SR.1443 [5].
[205] The Committee, 'Summary Record of the 747th Meeting' (2006) CEDAW/C/SR.747(A) [7].
[206] The Committee, 'Summary Record of the 492nd Meeting' (2001) CEDAW/C/SR.492 [1].
[207] The Committee, 'Summary Record of the 1453rd Meeting (2016) CEDAW/C/SR.1453 [4]–[5].
[208] 'Summary Record of the 969th Meeting' (n 203) [8].
[209] 'Summary Record of the 1443rd Meeting' (n 204) [4]–[5].
[210] The Committee, 'Summary Record of the 1406th Meeting' (2016) CEDAW/C/SR.1406 [21].
[211] The Committee, 'Summary Record of the 1405th Meeting' (2016) CEDAW/C/SR.1406 [43].
[212] The Committee, 'Summary Record of the 854th Meeting' (2008) CEDAW/C/SR.854 [6].
[213] The Committee, 'Summary Record of the 1434th Meeting' (2016) CEDAW/C/SR.1434 [43].
[214] The Committee, 'Summary Record of the 954th Meeting' (2010) CEDAW/C/SR.954 [3].

the Committee suggests an emerging practice connecting gender, equality, poverty and human rights.

Gender-based poverty is a cross-cutting problem. States often provide information on many facets of gender-based poverty without directly referring to gender-based poverty. Almost all of the states provide information on violence, equal pay, legal aid and on the allocation of property on divorce or widowhood. For example, Argentina explains efforts to decentralise health services and increase the availability of generic pharmaceuticals.[215] In Bangladesh poor women 'regularly receive support from the Government' to access justice.[216] After the devastating fire in a Bangladeshi garment factory, the state has adopted health and safety policies.[217] Norway's action plan focuses on equality in education, parenting and family-friendly work life, gender segregation in employment, and the distribution of economic power.[218] Egypt notes that its tax laws have been reformed so that women are counted as the head of the household, and it has removed the need for a woman to obtain her husband's permission to apply for a passport.[219] As evidence of the constructive relationship between the Committee and the state, Argentina notes that in light of the Committee's recommendations, it has adopted policies and programmes to encourage and train women to enter non-traditional areas of work.[220] Again, this implies that states understand the complex ways poverty and gender inequality act to undermine women's human rights.

There were a few instances where the Committee asked questions during the dialogue session on gender-based poverty. There was no evidence of the state objecting to the appropriateness of the question or arguing that gender-based poverty was not within the mandate of CEDAW. Instead the state representative responded with further information on gender-based poverty. The best example of this is Canada. The state representative provided detailed information on the social assistance rates and minimum wage.[221] In response to questions on poverty-reduction policies essentialising women as mothers, the Canadian representative explained that: '[E]fforts to advance gender equality and gender-based analysis of policies[] were guided by three goals: improving women's economic independence, ensuring that women's human rights were protected and combating violence against women.'[222] When asked about its development programmes, the Ethiopian

---

[215] The Committee, 'Summary Record of the 584th Meeting' (2002) CEDAW/C/SR.584 [8].
[216] 'Summary Record of the 1443rd Meeting' (n 206) [18].
[217] ibid [20].
[218] The Committee, 'Summary Record of the 1024th Meeting' (2012) CEDAW/C/SR.1024 [5].
[219] The Committee, 'Summary Record of the 918th Meeting' (2010) CEDAW/C/SR.918 [31]; 'Summary Record of the 492nd meeting' (n 206) [6], [27].
[220] The Committee, 'Summary Record of the 1444th meeting' (2016) CEDAW/C/SR.1444 [29].
[221] 'Summary Record of the 854th Meeting' (n 212) [31], [39].
[222] The Committee, 'Summary Record of the 603th Meeting' (2003) CEDAW/C/SR.603 [51].

representative explained that: '[W]omen's issues were part and parcel of Ethiopia's national strategy to promote rural development and, more broadly, its sustainable development and poverty reduction programme'.[223] Similarly after numerous questions on the depth and extent of poverty in Mexico, the representative explained the state's free trade policies, national welfare laws and food programmes.[224] With respect to Bangladesh, the Committee asked for more information on women's participation in development programmes and for statistics on women's access to health, education, income-generating projects and rights of inheritance. The state representative responded with information on the programmes designed to bring economic and social benefits to women.[225]

The Committee, along with other treaty bodies, is developing follow-up procedures so that constructive dialogue can continue outside the formalised periodic reporting procedure. In the follow-up report the state can express its views about the Concluding Observations and any further steps it is taking to address the Committee's recommendations. States have used this forum to provide additional evidence of the measures they are employing to remedy gender-based poverty. Canada spent over forty paragraphs detailing the structure of social assistance.[226] Argentina explained the increased efforts to combat poverty among girls under seventeen and provides information on free legal assistance to women.[227] Norway provided extensive explanations on how it is regulating part-time work and transforming cultural norms on parenting.[228] There are no examples of the state rejecting gender-based poverty within CEDAW. Interestingly, the Philippines, in a follow-up statement to the Concluding Observations from 2016, objected to some of the Committee's concerns and recommendations but it did not object in relation to gender-based poverty.[229]

This is only a sample of subsequent state practice in relation to CEDAW and gender-based poverty, but it does strongly indicate that subsequent state practice reflects an interpretation of equality and non-discrimination in CEDAW that includes gender-based poverty.

---

[223] The Committee, 'Summary Record of the 646th Meeting' (2004) CEDAW/C/SR.646 [19].

[224] The Committee, 'Summary of Record of the 752th Meeting' (2006) CEDAW/C/SR.752 [33]–[37].

[225] The Committee, 'Summary Record of the 1454th Meeting' (2016) CEDAW/C/SR.1454 [40]–[42].

[226] 'Information Provided by Canada on the Follow-up to the Concluding Observations of the Committee' (2010) CEDAW/C/CAN/CO/7/Add.1.

[227] Information Provided by Argentina on the Follow-up to the Concluding Observations of the Committee' (2010) (2010) CEDAW/C/ARG/CO/6/Add.1 [10], [20].

[228] 'Information Provided by Norway on the Follow-up to the Concluding Observations of the Committee' (2012) CEDAW/C/NOR/CO/8/Add.1.

[229] 'Comments of the Philippines on the Concluding Observations of the CEDAW Committee', http://tbinternet.ohchr.org/Treaties/CEDAW/Shared%20Documents/PHL/INT_CEDAW_COB_PHL_25000_E.pdf.

(e) Relevant Rules of International Law

Under Article 31(3)(c) of the VCLT, the interpreter can consider other relevant rules of international law, including comparative legal material.[230] In the case of gender-based poverty and CEDAW, this contextual element points towards examining how other UN treaty bodies, the Human Rights Committee (HRC), CESCR and the other treaty bodies, have defined equality and non-discrimination. Surprisingly, given that the rights in these treaties are guaranteed on the basis of equality, the treaty bodies shed very little additional light on the meaning of equality and non-discrimination in CEDAW in relation to gender-based poverty. Similar to the Committee, the HRC and CESCR define formal equality as neutrality between men and women.[231] With respect to substantive equality, these bodies reiterate and draw upon the definition of discrimination in Article 1 of CEDAW.[232] CESCR explains that substantive equality 'is concerned with the effects of laws, policies and practices and with ensuring that they do not maintain, but rather alleviate, the inherent disadvantage that particular groups' experience'.[233] The HRC holds that substantive equality requires the state to adopt positive measures in 'all areas so as to achieve [women's] effective and equal empowerment'.[234] This echoes much of the work the Committee has done to develop these norms. As canvassed in Chapter 3, both the HRC and CESCR have only drawn a minimal connection between gender equality, poverty and human rights. Thus, a comparative approach under the relevant rules of international law, Article 31(3)(c) of the VCLT, does not provide any substantial guidance on gender-based poverty and the meaning of equality and non-discrimination in CEDAW.

(iii) The Object and Purpose

The final element of the VCLT framework investigates how the object and purpose of the treaty shed light on the meaning of equality and discrimination in CEDAW. While the preamble may be the 'principal and natural source' of the treaty's object and purpose,[235] Gardiner advocates caution 'because preambles are not always drafted with care and a preamble

---

[230] M Koskenniemi, 'Fragmentation of International Law: Difficulties Arising from the Diversification and Expansion of International Law Report of the Study Group of the International Law Commission' A/CN.4./L.682 [416].

[231] 'General Comment No 16: The Equal Rights Between Men and Women' (n 1) [7].

[232] ibid [11]; Human Rights Committee (HRC), 'General Comment No 28: The Equality of Rights between Men and Women' (1999) CCPR/C/21/Rev.1/Add.10

[233] CESCR, 'General Comment No 16: The Equal Rights Between Men and Women' (n 1) [7].

[234] HRC, 'General Comment No 28: The Equality of Rights' (n 227) [3].

[235] *US—Import Prohibition of Certain Shrimp and Shrimp Products* WT/DS58/AB/R (1998) [17].

itself may need interpreting'.[236] This is particularly salient in the context of CEDAW, for as discussed in Chapter 2, CEDAW's preamble is unique among international human rights treaties. It is crucial to examine the entire text of the treaty to ascertain its object and purpose. A careful reading of CEDAW reveals that there are three mutually supportive goals: (i) the elimination of discrimination; (ii) achieving gender equality; and (iii) women's exercise and enjoyment of human rights.

The purpose of CEDAW is seemingly emblazoned in the title: eliminating all forms of *discrimination* against women. The substantive provisions of CEDAW also require states to eliminate *discrimination* in political, economic, social, cultural and civil life. The preamble also reaffirms the treaty's commitment to eradicating discrimination against women. It notes that the Universal Declaration of Human Rights is grounded on the 'principle of the inadmissibility of *discrimination*', expresses concern that despite repeated efforts 'extensive *discrimination* against women continues to exist', and explains that to address this problem states will 'adopt measures required for the elimination of such *discrimination* in all its forms and manifestations'.[237] The Committee also identifies eliminating discrimination as the goal of CEDAW. It states that the 'Convention focuses on *discrimination* against women, emphasizing that women have suffered and continue to suffer from various forms of *discrimination* because they are women'.[238]

However, Gardiner's advice on treaty interpretation is again pertinent. He warns that ascertaining the object and purpose of the treaty can be difficult and that a treaty might pursue several aims.[239] Discrimination is central to CEDAW but it is interconnected to two further harmonious goals. First, as discussed above, *equality* is also a cornerstone objective of CEDAW. States are to eliminate discrimination so that women can enjoy their rights in broad fields of life on the basis of *equality*.[240] In a similar vein, the preamble stresses that 'promoting social progress and development' through, inter alia, nuclear disarmament, self-determination and strengthening international peace and security will 'contribute to the attainment of full *equality* between men and women'.[241]

CEDAW aims to eliminate discrimination so that women can not only achieve equality but also enjoy their *human rights*. Article 1 defines discrimination as 'any ... restriction ... made on the basis of sex which has the

---

[236] Gardiner (n 54) 205–06.

[237] Emphasis added.

[238] 'General Recommendation No 25: on Temporary Special Measures' (n 66) [5] (emphasis added).

[239] *Case concerning the Arbitral Award of 31 July 1989 (Guinea-Bissau v Senegal)*, Dissenting Opinion [1991] ICJ Reports 53, 142.

[240] See, Arts 10–16 CEDAW.

[241] Emphasis added.

effect or purpose of impairing ... the enjoyment by women, ... on the basis of equality ... of *human rights* and fundamental freedoms'.[242] Discrimination limits women's rights and thus by eliminating discrimination against women the state is directed to protect women's rights. The substantive provisions also seek to uphold women's rights to participation in public life (Article 7), education (Article 10), employment (Article 11), healthcare (Article 12), economic and social life (Article 13), before the law (Article 15), family life (Article 16) and the rights of rural women (Article 14. Article 3 requires the full advancement and development of women so that they can enjoy their *human rights*. The preamble also expresses concern about the lack of human rights protection for women. Intriguingly it notes that women in poverty are denied 'food, health, education, training and opportunities for employment'. It also emphasises that the International Covenant on Civil and Political Rights[243] (ICCPR) and ICESCR 'ensure the equal *rights* of men and women to enjoy all economic, social, cultural, civil and political *rights*' and that the eradication of racism, colonialism and aggressions 'is essential to the full enjoyment of *rights* of men and women'.[244] Again, the work of the Committee supports this understanding of the purpose of CEDAW. It observes that CEDAW 'guarantees women the equal recognition, enjoyment and exercise of all *human rights*'.[245] It further describes CEDAW as 'part of a comprehensive international human rights framework directed at ensuring the enjoyment of all *human rights*'.[246]

Drawing these insights together, there are numerous of ways that human rights can be violated. CEDAW investigates one specific way that rights are undermined. It examines how gender inequality and discrimination limit women's human rights. The treaty pursues three overlapping and complementary goals. It seeks to (i) eliminate *discrimination* against women with a view to achieving women's (ii) de jure and de facto *equality* in (iii) the enjoyment of their *human rights*.[247]

Understanding the purpose of CEDAW further illuminates the meaning of equality and non-discrimination in the treaty. Gardiner observes that the terms of the treaty need to be interpreted in a way that effectively advances the aims of the treaty.[248] This means the concept of equality and discrimination in CEDAW must be responsive to the de jure and de facto ways that sex and gender discrimination and inequality create obstacles to women's human rights. This returns to the central challenge of this chapter.

---

[242] Emphasis added.
[243] International Covenant on Civil and Political Rights (adopted 16 December 1966, entered into force 23 March 1976) 999 UNTS 171.
[244] Emphasis added.
[245] 'General Recommendation No 28: on Core Obligations' (n 49) [4].
[246] ibid [1].
[247] 'General Recommendation No 25: on Temporary Special Measures' (n 66) [4].
[248] Gardiner (n 54) 217.

Does an effective interpretation of CEDAW include gender-based obstacles, such as poverty, which are not explicitly articulated in the treaty but still limit women's human rights?[249] This question raises the potential of an effective and evolutionary interpretation of CEDAW. As canvassed in Chapter 3, an evolutionary interpretation of a text recognises that certain words through the passage of time are meant to be continually reinterpreted.[250] This interpretative approach is becoming increasingly standard in human rights treaties.[251] The legitimacy of an evolutionary interpretation is rooted in the intention of the parties. The intention can be determined by examining the language, structure and goals of the treaty.[252]

There is a strong textual basis for an evolutionary interpretation of CEDAW that includes gender-based poverty. The definition of discrimination in Article 1 requires states to take all appropriate measures to ensure that women enjoy their 'human rights and fundamental freedoms in political, economic, social, cultural, civil or *any other field*'. Byrnes argues that due to this provision CEDAW must be interpreted dynamically so as to respond to new or newly recognised obstacles to women's human rights.[253] Article 2 also requires states to eliminate discrimination in '*all forms*' and Article 3 refers to women's full advancement and development in '*all fields*'. Under Article 4(1) on temporary special measures, the Committee recognises 'women's needs may change' and thus to be effective it calls on states to be vigilant to new forms of discrimination.[254] The preamble also directs states to adopt appropriate measures to eliminate discrimination 'in *all* of its forms and manifestations'. The text of CEDAW frames equality and discrimination in open terms. Thus, these norms are meant to anticipate 'the emergence of new forms of discrimination that had not been identified at the time of drafting'.[255] CEDAW is a living instrument.[256]

An effective and evolutionary interpretation 'has been at the heart of the Committee's approach' to monitoring CEDAW. It is the basis for its seminal General Recommendation on violence against women.[257] In General Recommendation No 19 the Committee notes that CEDAW 'covers other rights that are not explicitly mentioned in the Convention but have an impact on the achievement of equality ... which impact represents a form

[249] Chinkin, 'Article 3' (n 141) 102.
[250] A Orakhelashvili, *The Interpretation of Acts and Rules in Public International Law* (Oxford University Press, 2008) 291.
[251] Gardiner (n 54) 221.
[252] C McLachlan, 'The Principle of Systemic Integration and Article 31(3)(c) of the Vienna Convention' (2005) 54 *International and Comparative Law Quarterly* 279, 317. Also see Bjorge (n 98) 92.
[253] Byrnes, 'Article 1' (n 48) 67.
[254] 'General Recommendation No 25: on Temporary Special Measures' (n 66) [11].
[255] 'General Recommendation No 28: on Core Obligations' (n 49) [8].
[256] 'General Recommednation No 25: on Temporary Special Measures' (n 66) [3].
[257] ibid.

of discrimination against women'.[258] This echoes the understanding of the Office of the High Commissioner of Human Rights of the relationship between human rights and poverty discussed in Chapter 1, namely that all rights have instrumental relevance to poverty. The Committee has addressed numerous other gender-based obstacles to women's rights that are not referred to in the treaty, including women's rights in time of conflict, and post-conflict and gender-related dimensions of refugee status, asylum, nationality and statelessness of women.[259] The Committee is currently working on a General Recommendation on gender and the effects of climate change.[260] The treaty is meant to be responsive to changes in the nature of discrimination against women and gender inequality. As the understanding develops on how different social wrongs, such as conflict, migration, climate change and poverty, are connected to gender and human rights, the ideas of equality and non-discrimination in CEDAW can be interpreted to account for this change.

In sum, the object and purpose of CEDAW is to eliminate discrimination against women to achieve gender equality and to uphold women's human rights. An effective and evolutionary interpretation of CEDAW, as mandated by the text, means equality and discrimination can be interpreted to account for new obstacles. Poverty, as argued in Chapter 1, is a gender-based experience. Women's unequal share of care work, their lower levels of education, their inability to seek financial independence, their limited to access sexual and reproductive health services, their marginalisation in home and society, and negative prejudices and stereotypes creates a vicious cycle of social and economic disempowerment and results in women being unable to exercise and enjoy their human rights.[261] For CEDAW to effectively achieve its aims, discrimination and equality need to be interpreted in an evolutionary manner to incorporate the interaction between poverty and gender as an obstacle to women's human rights.

(iv) A New Interpretation of CEDAW

Using the VCLT framework, the ordinary meaning, the context, and the object and purpose of CEDAW all point toward interpreting equality and

---

[258] 'General Recommendation No 28: on Core Obligations' (n 49) [7].

[259] 'General Recommendation No 30: on Conflict Prevention, Conflict, Post-Conflict' (n 179); The Committee, 'General Recommendation No 32: on Gender-Related Dimensions of Refugee Status, Asylum, Nationality and Statelessness of Women' (2014) CEDAW/C/GC/32.

[260] The Committee, 'Half Day Discussions on Gender-Related Dimensions of Disaster Risk Reduction and Climate Change', www.ohchr.org/EN/HRBodies/CEDAW/Pages/ClimateChange.aspx.

[261] S Fredman, 'Anti-Discrimination Laws and Work in the Developing World: A Thematic Overview' (Background Paper for World Development Report, 2013) 1, http://siteresources.worldbank.org/EXTNWDR2013/Resources/8258024-1320950747192/8260293-1320956712276/8261091-1348683883703/WDR2013_bp_Anti-Discrimination_Laws.pdf.

discrimination as dynamic concepts that include gender-based poverty. Equality is a multifaceted concept in CEDAW that captures the role gender plays in perpetuating poverty. The concept of discrimination in the treaty incorporates women's experiences, identities and cross-cutting experiences, including gender-based poverty. States are beginning to understand the role that gender inequality and poverty play in limiting women's rights. The interpretation proposed here draws these connections together. Moreover, interpreting gender-based poverty as a facet of equality and non-discrimination is a comprehensive approach. The substantive provisions in CEDAW are all based on equality and non-discrimination. Under this proposed interpretation each of the substantive obligations can be examined from the perspective of gender-based poverty. How this interpretation could be integrated in the Committee's accountability mechanisms is explored throughout Part II and culminates in a proposed General Recommendation on women and poverty in Chapter 8.

An equality and non-discrimination approach is a powerful way forward to address the gender-based poverty gap in CEDAW and it directs the international human rights regime towards taking women's poverty as a legal human rights issue. However, this new interpretation raises questions on how gender-based poverty in CEDAW impacts the nature of the state's obligations. It is to this issue that we now turn.

III. NATURE OF THE STATE'S OBLIGATIONS

The resistance to interpreting and using CEDAW and other human rights instruments to address the gender-based aspects of poverty is often based on the perceived runaway financial costs to the state. In fact, as assessed in Chapter 2, at the drafting stage states were concerned that including robust socioeconomic rights in CEDAW would be too costly. Conceptualising gender-based poverty as a facet of equality and discrimination in CEDAW raises very challenging questions on how this new interpretation impacts the nature of the state's obligations under the treaty. Is the state in violation of CEDAW if there are women living in poverty? Is the state required to prioritise gender-based poverty and consequentially shift its allocation of resources? Or does the state now have an obligation to raise revenue, such as through taxes or international assistance and cooperation, so as to have the necessary resources to address gender-based poverty? Is the state's duty to redress gender-based poverty under CEDAW an immediate obligation or can the obligation be realised over a period of time? If the obligation can be progressively realised, is there a minimum core obligation that has to be immediately fulfilled?

In the monitoring of socioeconomic rights under ICESCR, CESCR has had to consider these questions. This section begins by analysing the state's obligations under ICESCR and CESCR's approach to monitoring these obligations. It then proceeds to assess if and how these approaches could be transplanted into CEDAW. While the nature of the state's obligations under ICESCR does offer some insights, there is a fundamental difference between socioeconomic rights and the right to gender equality. Unlike the socioeconomic rights in ICESCR, which are subject to progressive realisation, the obligations in CEDAW to eliminate discrimination and achieve gender equality are immediate. Thus, the state's socioeconomic obligations are not applicable to gender-based poverty in CEDAW. Instead, it must demonstrate against a non-discrimination and equality framework that its laws, policies and programmes take account of and address the gender-related aspects of poverty.

A. The Obligation to Realise Socioeconomic Rights

Before turning to CEDAW, it is illuminating to consider some of the challenges that arise with socioeconomic rights. Many of the difficulties of interpreting gender-based poverty into CEDAW have arisen in relation to socioeconomic rights. This is in part due to the different framing of civil and political rights and socioeconomic rights in international law. The civil and political rights in ICCPR are 'unqualified and of immediate effect. A failure to comply with this obligation cannot be justified by reference to political, social, cultural or economic considerations within the State.'[262] On the other hand, under Article 2(1) of ICESCR a state is only obligated to 'take steps ... to the *maximum of its available resources*, with a view to achieving *progressively the full realization*' of economic, social and cultural rights.[263] This is a bifurcated and complicated obligation. First, under the 'maximum available resources' element the state must assess its entire pool of resources. It must then determine the maximum amount of these resources that should be devoted to the realisation of socioeconomic rights.[264] Second, under the 'progressive realisation' element the state needs to set benchmarks and indicators to assess if it has moved sufficiently fast to fully realize socioeconomic rights. The difference between the immediate obligation to realise civil and political rights and the progressive realisation of socioeconomic rights recognises 'the fact that the full realization of all economic, social and cultural rights will generally not be able to be achieved in a short period of time'.[265]

---

[262] HRC, 'General Comment No 31: Nature of the General Legal Obligation Imposed on State Parties to the Convenant' (2004) CCPR/C/21/Rev.1/Add.13 [14].

[263] Art 2(1) ICESCR. Emphasis added.

[264] The calculation of maximum available resources is highly contested, particularly in relation to the normative content of the right. See D Bilchitz, *Poverty and Fundamental Rights* (Cambridge University Press, 2008).

[265] CESCR, 'General Comment No 3: Nature of the State's Obligations' (n 3) [9].

Initially, there was a fear that the obligation in ICESCR was too flexible and that states would continue to treat socioeconomic rights as policy aspirations rather than as legally enforceable human rights. In response, CESCR explained that the 'the fact that realization is over time ... should not be misinterpreted as depriving the obligation of all meaningful content'.[266] 'Maximum available resources' and 'progressive realization' are necessary 'flexibility devices',[267] but ICESCR still imposes an obligation to take concrete steps towards realising socioeconomic rights immediately or within a reasonably short time.[268] CESCR pioneered the concept of the immediately realisable minimum core of socioeconomic rights.[269] It holds that states are under a 'minimum core obligation to ensure the satisfaction of, at the very least, minimum essential levels of each of the right'.[270] When a significant number of individuals are deprived of food, primary healthcare, shelter, housing and basic education, then the state is in violation of the minimum core obligation of ICESCR.[271] Under ICESCR the state is obligated to: (i) ensure the *minimum core* of socioeconomic rights and (ii) devote the *maximum available resources* to *progressively realising* the full implementation of socioeconomic rights.

This multifaceted obligation is contentious. Beginning first with the minimum core, advocates of this concept argue that it gives a necessary determinacy to the state's obligations. Bilchitz points out that if socioeconomic rights are to be treated as rights, it is imperative that the state not be left with an 'amorphous standard by which to judge its own conduct'.[272] To concretise the state's obligation to fulfil socioeconomic rights, there must be a coherent articulation of the 'minimum' standard. Although CESCR has been at the vanguard of the minimum core, in practice it is not currently engaging with this doctrine. There is no reference to the minimum core in the Concluding Observations, and in the General Comments CESCR only holds that 'state parties have a core obligation to ensure, at the very least, minimum essential levels of satisfaction of the right'.[273] This omits defining the minimum core or connecting it to any normative standard.

To fill this lacuna, there have been academic proposals on how to give meaning to the minimum core. These include equating the minimum core

---

[266] ibid.

[267] ibid.

[268] ibid.

[269] C Scott and P Mecklem, 'Constitutional Ropes of Sand or Justiciable Guaratnees? Social Rights in a New South African Constitution' (1992) 141 *University of Pennsylvania Law Review* 1; S Fredman, *Human Rights Transformed* (Oxford University Press, 2008) 84.

[270] CESCR, 'General Comment No 3: Nature of the State's Obligations' (n 3) [10].

[271] ibid.

[272] Bilchitz (n 264) 162.

[273] CESCR, 'General Comment No 22: The Right to Sexual and Reproductive Health' (2016) E/C.12/GC/22 [49]; CESCR, 'General Comment No 23: The Right to Just and Fair Working Conditions' (2016) E/C.12/GC/23 [65].

to survival, dignity and consensus-based definitions. Young analyses all of these and convincingly concludes that these are all imperfect attempts to flesh out the minimum core.[274] Focusing on the minimum socioeconomic rights necessary for survival conceptualises a very narrow understanding of life and 'misses the connection between dignity and human flourishing'.[275] However, equating the minimum core to dignity is equally problematic as dignity is an elusive concept that cannot be easily defined, making it difficult to determine the minimum level of socioeconomic rights necessary for a dignified life.[276] In respect to consensus-based definitions, aside from the methodological concerns on determining if and when consensus exists, it connects the minimum core to the lowest common denominator.[277] Thus, attempts to substantiate the minimum core have only lead to further confusion.

This dissatisfaction has resulted in a subtle shift to core obligations. Rather than attempting to pin down the concept of the minimum core, CESCR lists central or core obligations which operationalise the state's obligations and 'signal "violations" under [ICESCR]'.[278] The core obligations approach has also been criticised as being ad hoc and following 'a meandering course of logic'.[279] The core obligations in the General Comment on the right to fair and just working conditions include: minimum wages, health and safety policies, and working standards,[280] while for the General Comment on the right to sexual and reproductive health, the core obligations focus on the equal provision of health services and medicines.[281] When comparing the core obligations between these socioeconomic rights it is difficult to ascertain a unifying principle that underpins these obligations.

The other component of the state's obligations—maximum available resources and progressive realisation—have also not been fully developed by CESCR. It has never provided guidance on how to calculate the state's maximum resources or how budgets can be utilised to fulfil socioeconomic rights. In a recent round of Concluding Observations, CESCR expressed concerns under the heading 'maximum available resources' about stagnating levels of social spending, low corporate tax rates, corruption, illicit financial flows and tax avoidance.[282] A fully developed maximum available resources test would involve a detailed analysis of the resources and budget of the state to

---

[274] K Young, 'The Minimum Core of Economic and Social Rights: A Concept in Search of Content' (2008) 33 *Yale Journal of International Law* 113.
[275] ibid 121.
[276] ibid 130.
[277] ibid 135.
[278] ibid 152.
[279] ibid. 154.
[280] CESCR, 'General Comment No 23: Fair and Just Working Conditions' (n 273) [65].
[281] CESCR, 'General Comment No 22: Sexual and Reproductive Health' (n 273) [49].
[282] CESCR, 'Concluding Observations: Canada' (2016) E/C.12/CAN/CO/6 [9]–[10]; CESCR, 'Concluding Observations: Kenya' (2016) E/C.12/KEN/CO/2-5 [17]–[18].

determine if the maximum portion of its resources were directed towards socioeconomic rights, not merely flagging areas of underspending or corruption. There is a similar problem with respect to progressive realisation. CESCR only recommends that the state 'take steps to progressively develop and apply appropriate indicators on the implementation of economic, social and cultural rights'.[283] This falls far short of robust analysis of the state's obligations under ICESCR.

There are two potential explanations for CESCR's lack of attention to the nature of the state's obligation as articulated in Article 2(1) of ICESCR. First, maximum available resources and progressive realisation are highly contextual and individualised. Assessing the available resources and determining the speed of progress for each of the 164 state parties to ICESCR is beyond the capacity of CESCR.[284] Second, echoing the conflicting perspectives on the minimum core, there are competing proposals for how to calculate resources and measure progress.[285] The UN Special Rapporteur on the right to health identifies fifteen potential types of indicators and benchmarks to assess progressive realisation.[286] There is a growing momentum to examine the state's tax structures,[287] the availability of resources through international cooperation and assistance,[288] and even non-financial resources[289] under the maximum available resources element of the state's obligation. These new approaches are still in their infancy and remain contested.

B. The Obligation to Eliminate Discrimination and Achieve Gender Equality in CEDAW

The duties in ICESCR are so context specific that deriving at coherent, comprehensive and universally accepted understanding of the state's obligations

---

[283] See, for example, CESCR, 'Concluding Observations: Kenya' (n 282) [65]; CESCR, 'Concluding Observations: Canada' (n 282) [62]; CESCR, 'Concluding Observations: Namibia' (2016) E/C.12/NAM/CO/1 [78].

[284] O de Schutter, *International Human Rights Law: Cases, Materials, Commentary* (Cambridge University Press, 2010) 462; AR Chapman, 'A "Violations Approach" for Monitoring ICESCR' (1996) 18 *Human Rights Quarterly* 23.

[285] See O de Schutter (ed), *Economic, Social and Cultural Rights as Human Rights* (Edward Elgar, 2013).

[286] UN Special Rapporteur on the right to health, 'Right to Health Indicators' (2003) A/58/427[14].

[287] UN Special Rapporteur on extreme poverty and human rights, 'Fiscal and Tax Policy' (2014) A/HRC/26/28.

[288] MS Carmona, 'The Obligations of "International Assistance and Cooperation" under ICESCR: A Possible Entry Point to a Human Rights Based Approach to Millennium Development Goal 8' (2009) 13 *International Journal of Human Rights* 86.

[289] S Skogly, 'The Requirement of Using the Maximum Available Resources for Human Rights Realisation: A Question of Quality as Well as Quantity?' (2012) 12(3) *Human Rights Law Review* 393.

has proven difficult in both theory and practice. The minimum core and maximum available resources/progressive realisation obligations may be flawed, but perhaps they retain a utility, particularly at addressing the budgetary implications of using human rights to redress gender-based poverty? A close reading of CEDAW indicates that it is simply not possible to transplant these concepts. The fundamentally different nature of socioeconomic rights and the right to equality means a new understanding of the state's obligations in relation to gender-based poverty must be formed. The nature of gender-based poverty and the structure of CEDAW mean that the state is required to prove against an equality and non-discrimination standard that it has taken all appropriate measures to redress gender-based poverty.

At first glance, importing the minimum core and maximum available resources/progressive realisation into CEDAW is an attractive option. This would address the financial and budgetary concerns of using human rights to alleviate gender-based poverty. However, the UN human rights community characterises eliminating discrimination and achieving gender equality as an immediate obligation. The UN Working Group on Discrimination Against Women in Law and Practice states that: '[W]omen's right to equality … is substantive, *immediate* and enforceable.'[290] Similarly, the HRC, CESCR and the UN Special Rapporteur on extreme poverty and human rights explain that: '[E]quality and non-discrimination are *immediate* and cross-cutting obligations.'[291] In fact, Article 2 of CEDAW requires states to pursue a policy of gender equality without delay.[292] Thus, there is a deep conceptual impasse in bringing the obligations in ICESCR which occur over a period of time into CEDAW.[293] There have been attempts to work through this impasse by holding that only certain aspects of equality are immediately enforceable. Drawing on the respect, protect and fulfil model, it has been argued that the state has an immediate obligation to respect and protect the right to non-discrimination and only has to progressively realise the obligation to fulfil equality.[294] However, these arguments were developed in the context of ICESCR and are not applicable in CEDAW. As discussed in Section II, the definition of discrimination in Article 1 of CEDAW intertwines non-discrimination and equality to such an extent that it is impossible to fracture non-discrimination and equality into different obligations. More dangerously, splitting the obligations in CEDAW between immediate and progressive components unravels the multifaceted

---

[290] Working Group (n 16) [8].
[291] CESCR, 'General Comment No 16: The Equal Rights of Men and Women' (n 2) [16].
[292] Art 2 CEDAW.
[293] Working Group (n 16) [8].
[294] B Porter, 'Re-thinking Progressive Realization: How Should it be Implemented in Canada?' (2015) Social Rights Advocacy Centre, 2, www.socialrights.ca/documents/publications/Porter%20Progressive%20Implementation.pdf.

concept of equality in the treaty. Connecting immediacy to obligations of respect strongly implies that the state only has an immediate obligation to achieve formal equality. In turn, substantive and transformative equality, which are closely associated with the obligation to fulfil, only has to be progressively realised. This characterises substantive gender equality as some distance, quasi-unattainable goal that women must wait to enjoy, which runs counter to the central aims of CEDAW.

The substantive provisions of CEDAW delineate how to operationalise the state's obligations. A majority of the substantive provisions in CEDAW begin with the: '[S]tate parties shall take all *appropriate measures* to eliminate discrimination against women ... in order to ensure [women's human rights in various fields of life] on the basis of equality.'[295] This is a broad term and requires the state 'to adopt a comprehensive range of measures'.[296] Article 2 of CEDAW clarifies that 'appropriate measures' include, inter alia, enshrining gender equality in the national constitution; adopting legislation that prohibits discrimination; pursuing without delay a policy for eliminating discrimination; and establishing public institutions for effective protection against discrimination. The Committee further elaborates that states need 'to adopt measures to ensure the practical realization of the elimination of discrimination against women and women's equality'.[297] This can include legislative, executive and administrative instruments, outreach and support programmes, the relocation of resources, and temporary special measures.[298] This requires the state to adopt action plans that apply to public, private, economic and domestic spheres; to establish monitoring, implementation, accountability and remedial mechanisms; and to provide 'adequate administrative and financial support to ensure that the measures adopted make a real difference in women's lives in practice'.[299]

With respect to the timing of the obligations, under CEDAW the state is obligated to immediately take all appropriate measures to eliminate discrimination and achieve gender equality. The Committee explains that the state is required: (i) to *immediately* assess the de jure and de facto situation of women; and (ii) to *immediately* take concrete steps to formulate and implement a policy that 'is targeted as clearly as possible towards' achieving substantive equality.[300] The language in the treaty—without delay—'is unqualified, and does not allow for any delayed or purposely chosen incremental implementation'.[301] States cannot justify failing to immediately assess

---

[295] Arts 7–16 CEDAW.
[296] A Byrnes, 'Article 2' in M Freeman, C Chinkin and B Rudolf (eds), *CEDAW: A Commentary* (Oxford University Press, 2012) 77.
[297] 'General Recommendation No 28: on Core Obligations' (n 49) [10].
[298] 'General Recommendation No 25: on Temporary Special Measures' (n 66) [22].
[299] 'General Recommendation No 28: on Core Obligations' (n 49) [10].
[300] ibid [24].
[301] ibid [23]–[25].

and implement a comprehensive policy on gender equality 'on any grounds including political, social, cultural, religious, economic or resource'.[302] At the same time, the Committee speaks of establishing indicators and benchmarks.[303] Rather than taking this as an indication of reverting to a maximum available resources/progressive realisation model, it should be seen as an acknowledgement that the obligation to eliminate discrimination and achieve gender equality is 'continuing and includes the responsibility to monitor progress and adjust the policy as time passes'.[304] Under CEDAW 'the emphasis is on movement forward ... to build on [appropriate] measures continuously in the light of their effectiveness and new or emerging issues, in order to achieve the treaty's goals'.[305]

Having broadly established the nature of the state's obligations under CEDAW, the question becomes: what does it mean to have an immediate and continuous obligation to take all appropriate measures to address gender-based poverty as a matter of a comprehensive policy to eliminate discrimination and achieve gender equality under CEDAW? To answer this question it is necessary to appreciate the unique dimensions of both gender-based poverty and of CEDAW. Gender-based poverty is not solved simply through the reallocation of resources and in these types of cases the state has an immediate obligation. When funding or a reallocation of resources is required to address how gender-based poverty limits women's rights, the state must immediately demonstrate that its budgetary decisions fulfil its commitment under CEDAW to eliminate discrimination and achieve gender equality. Non-discrimination and equality are the benchmark against which to evaluate the state's law, policies and programmes.

To begin with, it is important to clarify that the state is not obligated to eliminate poverty. Living in poverty entails material disadvantage, powerlessness, exclusion and 'the failure to achieve a basic level of capabilities'.[306] Gender-based poverty goes beyond this understanding and captures how one of the causes of poverty—gender power relations—shapes the economic disadvantage, recognition and exclusion harms of poverty. Gender-based poverty is the combination both of material disadvantage and gendered sociocultural norms that limit the ability of women in poverty to create a meaningful life. This mirrors the asymmetrical nature of CEDAW. While most human rights instruments protect both men and women, CEDAW is exclusively focused on women.[307] Thus, the state is not obligated to address

---

[302] ibid [29].
[303] ibid [28].
[304] Byrnes, 'Article 2' (n 296) 76–78.
[305] 'General Recommendation No 28: on Core Obligations' (n 49) [24].
[306] D Narayan et al, *Voices of the Poor: Crying out for Change* (Oxford University Press and World Bank, 2000).
[307] 'General Recommendation No 28: on Core Obligations' (n 49) [5].

all the ways that poverty acts as obstacle to human rights. Its obligations under CEDAW are more narrowly tailored on how the gender dimensions of poverty impact the human rights already recognised in CEDAW. This means that if women are living in poverty due to non-gender-based causes, this would fall outside of the state's obligations under CEDAW. The state only has to take appropriate measures to address how gender-based poverty negatively impacts women's human rights.

Appreciating the role of gender in CEDAW and poverty also makes clear that the state's obligations are not fulfilled only through the provision of resources. Under the umbrella of appropriate measures, the Committee holds that states must 'respect, protect and fulfil women's right to non-discrimination and to the enjoyment of equality'.[308] The duties to respect, protect and fulfil sheds light on the nature of the state's obligations. The obligation to respect requires the state to refrain from contributing to gender-based poverty. There are still numerous instances where the law acts to perpetuate and maintain gender-based poverty. In 2016, the World Bank found that in over 100 economies women face gender-based job restrictions, and in eighteen of these economies, husbands can legally prevent women from working.[309] Under the interpretation of CEDAW proposed in this chapter, the state needs, inter alia, to amend titling policies that systematically overlook women in informal unions, revise family laws that vest control of joint property solely in the husband and remove all restrictions on the type of work women can perform.[310] None of these measures require a significant expenditure of resources but could have a positive impact by improving women's agency and access to resources, and increasing their participation in public and private life. The state has an obligation to identify these types of restrictions that exist within its national law, programmes and institutions and immediately remove these barriers.

The obligation to protect and fulfil is more complex as these duties can require the state to reallocate and generate resources. The obligation to protect requires states to prevent third parties from perpetuating gender-based poverty. The state needs, inter alia, to develop implementation and monitoring mechanisms to ensure equal pay for work of equal value in the private sector; to increase efforts to ensure girls' security when travelling to and from school; to hold private actors who are involved in the delivery of public services—schools, prisons, social security—to account for human rights violations; and to enact legislation and provide training programmes to ensure that non-state justice officials uphold women's rights

---

[308] ibid [9].

[309] World Bank, 'Women, Business and the Law 2016: Getting to Equal' (2016) 2, http://wbl.worldbank.org/~/media/WBG/WBL/Documents/Reports/2016/Women-Business-and-the-Law-2016.pdf.

[310] ibid 7–16.

to land and property.[311] The obligation to fulfil requires the state to take positive steps to fulfil the human rights of women who live in poverty. This can include providing free sexual and reproductive health services; developing programmes to reduce the amount of time rural girls spend in unpaid care work; providing training programmes in information communication technology; and providing legal aid services.[312] These types of obligations will almost invariably require various levels of resources. When the state has blatantly ignored or underestimated the human rights needs of women who live in poverty—say, for example, by not funding maternal health policies—it will be relatively straightforward to conclude that the state has failed to uphold CEDAW. The greater challenge is when the state has allocated a certain level of funding to protect and fulfil women's human rights and the Committee has to determine if this level of funding is sufficient to discharge the state's obligations under CEDAW. In this situation, the state has to justify with evidence the appropriateness of the measures it is taking to redress gender-based poverty to eliminate discrimination against women and uphold gender equality. Rather than evaluating whether the state has achieved a minimum core or is devoting the maximum level of resources to progressively realise women's human rights, under CEDAW, non-discrimination and equality act as the benchmark and analytical matrix.

An example illustrates how interpreting gender-based poverty as a facet of equality and non-discrimination shapes the state's obligations under CEDAW. Alyde da Silva Pimentel Teixeira, a poor, rural Afro-Brazilian woman, died in childbirth. The central issue in her mother's claim to the Committee under the Optional Protocol to CEDAW was whether her daughter's death was due to medical negligence or to systemic discrimination in the Brazilian healthcare system. This is a good case to explore interpreting gender-based poverty into CEDAW as maternal mortality is disproportionate among women in poverty.[313] Under Article 12 of CEDAW: '[S]tates Parties shall take all appropriate measures to eliminate discrimination in the field of health care in order to ensure, *on a basis of equality* of men and women, access to health care services.'[314] To fulfil its obligations under CEDAW, Brazil must prove it has eliminated discrimination and upheld gender equality in its maternal healthcare policies so that all women, including

---

[311] 'General Recommendation No 34: on Rural Women' (n 127) [50]; UN, *The Millennium Development Report: 2015* (2015) 29, www.un.org/millenniumgoals/2015_MDG_Report/pdf/MDG%202015%20rev%20(July%201).pdf; M Campbell and G Swenson, 'Legal Pluralism and Women's Rights After Conflict: The Role of CEDAW' (2016) 48(1) *Columbia Human Rights Law Review* 111.

[312] 'General Recommendation No 34: on Rural Women' (n 127) [82].

[313] UN Special Rapporteur on the right to health, 'The Right to the Highest Standard of Health: Reduction of Maternal Mortality' (2006) A/61/338 [7].

[314] Emphasis added.

poor, Afro-Brazilian women, are able to enjoy their right to health. The Committee concluded that Brazil violated Article 12 of CEDAW.

Although the conclusions in the decision mark an important development in women's rights, the Committee has not developed non-discrimination and equality as evaluative tools to assess a state's acts and omissions.[315] This is unfortunate as the Committee misses fully fleshing out a state's obligations. Since equality and non-discrimination are multifaceted concepts in CEDAW, when evaluating this claim the Committee has a choice and must justify using a specific model of equality. In *Teixeira*, the central issue was whether the design, delivery and funding of maternal health programmes was discriminatory.[316] Given the institutional nature of this claim, the four-dimensional transformative equality model, which is designed to uncover unequal structures and is able to capture the interaction between recognition, redistribution and participation harms of gender-based poverty, is the best evaluative model.

The first dimension, redressing disadvantage, requires the state to demonstrate that it has properly understood the unique maternal health needs of women in poverty and has put in place policies to meet these needs. The UN Special Rapporteur on the right to health notes that women living in poverty or in rural areas and women belonging to ethnic minorities or indigenous populations are most at risk of maternal mortality. Physical access, cost of care, and delay in seeking and receiving care have been identified as key factors contributing to maternal mortality in developing countries. Brazil needs to provide evidence on the availability of high-quality and well-equipped medical centres in rural areas; demonstrate that there is speedy and affordable access to emergency medical services; and assess the impact of any access fees on women in poverty. In essence, the state should be able to identify concrete steps it has taken to fulfil the right to maternal health of poor, Afro-Brazilian women.

The recognition dimension evaluates if negative stereotypes and prejudices affect the location, funding and quality of maternal health facilities where ethnic, indigenous and poor women live. The state must demonstrate that its policies treat women in poverty as empowered and autonomous agents and that staff are sensitive to the lives of women in poverty. As to the participation dimension, this requires Brazil to meaningfully consult with poor, indigenous and rural women on their maternal health needs and any proposed policies and programmes.

The final dimension examines if the maternal health policies will transform institutional structures. This requires the state 'to treat men and women by

---

[315] Campbell, 'Unlocking the Potential' (n 183) 242.
[316] D Elson, 'Budgeting for Women's Rights: Monitoring Government Budgets for Compliance with CEDAW' (UNIFEM, 2008) 7.

reference to their relative incidence levels of conditions of ill-health diseases in their population'.[317] Thus, Brazil must prove that it has made an accurate assessment of the maternal health needs of women and has allocated a sufficient level of resources to meet those needs. Yamin helpfully notes that lack of funding may not be the only reason for failures in the health system. It may be due to 'lack of capacity to absorb resources, ineffective investment of funds, weak financial management, poor procurement practices, limited oversight and poor district level management in decentralized health systems'.[318] The state must provide evidence that all elements of the health system are functioning to meet the needs of women in poverty. It is here that the state may argue that an imposition to fund or implement maternal health policies to a greater degree could preclude spending on other socially valuable endeavours, such as funding other human rights. This is not an easy calculation but an equality framework provides guidance in analyzing this complex factual matrix. Equality requires that healthcare budgets and policies pay attention to the most 'poor and marginalized groups'[319] such as poor, rural Afro-Brazilian women.[320] Maternal mortality is a matter of extreme urgency. There is 'no single cause of death and disability for men between the ages of 15 and 44 that is close to the magnitude of maternal death and disability'.[321] Tragic consequences can ensue when women are not able to access timely healthcare while giving birth. Moreover, maternal mortality is easily preventable given adequate funding. Determining if the state is in violation of CEDAW, particularly in relation to the structural dimension, is not a scientific evaluation; it is a highly contextual analysis.[322] Given the prevalence of maternal death and the ease with which it can be prevented, the state must provide significantly weighty reasons for why its budget and its delivery of maternal health policies do not meet the needs of women in poverty.[323]

In the case of *Teixeira*, to fulfil its obligations under CEDAW in relation to gender-based poverty, the state must provide evidence of all the appropriate measures it has taken to eliminate discrimination in the healthcare system. This includes presenting information on the depth and extent of maternal mortality and morbidity and the positive steps it has taken to redress these

[317] R Cook and V Undurraga, 'Article 12' in M Freeman, C Chinkin and B Rudolf (eds), *CEDAW: A Commentary* (Oxford University Press, 2012) 325.
[318] A Yamin, 'Toward Transformative Accountability: A Proposal for Rights-based Approaches to Fulfilling Maternal Health Obligations' (2012) 7 (12) *Sur: International Journal on Human Rights* 95.
[319] ibid 324.
[320] A Yamin, 'From Ideals to Tools: Applying Human Rights to Maternal Health (2013) 10(11) *PLoS Medicine* e1001546.
[321] UN Special Rapporteur on the right to health, 'Maternal Mortality' (n 313) [9].
[322] Elson (n 316).
[323] ibid.

issues (the disadvantage dimension); demonstrating attention to the ways women with intersecting identities experience childbirth and that all maternal health policies uphold women's agency (the recognition dimension); providing evidence that women have participated in the design of maternal health policies (the participation dimension); and showing that the design, funding and delivery are tailored to meet the needs of women in poverty (the structural dimension). If the Committee finds that Brazil's justifications for the limited funding are unsupportable against an equality framework, its task is to advocate for a stronger implementation of CEDAW. It can also remind the state that its obligations under CEDAW are both immediate and continuous. Changing demographic patterns, technological advances, and shifts in the political, social, economic and environmental landscape may mean that what was once sufficient against a transformative equality standard may not be adequate in the future. The Committee can encourage the state to understand that its obligations are sensitive to these changing and varying factors. This does not mean it is necessary to set indicators to monitor the progressive realisation of gender equality. An equality and non-discrimination framework is able to capture changes over a period of time.

C. A Duty to Cooperate to Tackle Gender-Based Poverty?

One further issue that needs to be considered are the extraterritorial realities of gender-based poverty. In a globalised world, gender-based poverty is not always captured by a state-centred lens.[324] Raday observes that global neoliberalism 'has exacerbated inequality globally, between countries and within countries ... these extreme inequalities are often born disproportionately by women'.[325] Transnational labour practices, international lending policies and debit agreements between states are factors contributing to gender-based poverty. International assistance programmes can exacerbate gender-based poverty. A good example of this is the Trump administration's recent withdrawal of funding to development programmes that support women's reproductive rights.[326] Or the funding by developed countries of private, low-fee-paying schools, which has been shown to negatively impact girls' access to education.[327] These types of issues are coming to the attention of the Committee. As one example, the Committee is concerned that

[324] N Fraser, 'Social Exclusion, Global Poverty, and Scales of (In)Justice: Rethinking Law and Poverty in a Globalising World' (2011) 22 *Stellenbosch Law Review* 452.
[325] Raday, 'The Impact of CEDAW' (n 143) 528.
[326] Redden (n 61).
[327] The Global Initiative for Socio-Economic Rights et al, 'Privatization and its Impact on the Right to Education of Women and Girls' (2014) 5, http://cme-espana.org/media/publicaciones/3/GCE_Submission_Privatisation_CEDAW_2014.pdf.

in Ethiopia foreign companies are displacing local communities, effectively perpetuating women's food insecurity and the feminisation of poverty.[328]

Does the interpretation of CEDAW proposed in this chapter require the state to respond to the extraterritorial realities of gender-based poverty? Increasing attention is being paid to how the duty of cooperation in ICESCR, the Convention on the Rights of the Child[329] and the Convention on the Rights of Persons with Disabilities[330] can be used to hold states to account for their laws, policies and practices that have extraterritorial human rights impact.[331] There is no explicit obligation requiring states to cooperate to eliminate discrimination against women in CEDAW. However, there are indications that the Committee is interpreting a duty of cooperation into CEDAW. The Committee explains that the obligation to eliminate discrimination 'without delay' (Article 2) requires that 'when a state party is facing resource constraints or needs expertise to facilitate the implementation of [CEDAW], it may be incumbent upon it to seek *international cooperation* in order to overcome these difficulties'.[332] It has begun to unpack what international cooperation entails. The Committee recommends that international trade policies be gender sensitive;[333] that states enter into multilateral agreements to protect the rights of migrant women workers;[334] that states should cooperate with UN agencies supporting women asylum-seekers and refugees and on issues of gender-based violence against women;[335] and that states should share best practices on encouraging girls to choose non-traditional career paths, reforming family law and women's nutrition.[336] It has called on states to regulate multinational corporations acting abroad

---

[328] The Committee, 'Concluding Observations: Ethiopia' (2011) CEDAW/C/ETH/CO/6–7 [36].

[329] Art 41 Convention on the Rights of the Child (adopted 20 November 1989, entered into force 2 1990) 1577 UNTS 3.

[330] Arts 4(2), 32, Convention on the Rights of Persons with Disabilities A/RES/61/106 (entered into force 3 May 2008).

[331] Carmona (n 288); O de Schutter et al, 'Commentary to the Maastricht Principles on Extraterritorial Obligations of States in the Area of Economic, Social and Cultural Rights', (2012) 34 *Human Rights Quarterly* 1084; S Skogly, *Beyond National Borders: States' Human Rights Obligations in International Cooperation* (Intersentia, 2006); Malcolm Langford et al (eds), *Global Justice, State Duties: The Extraterritorial Scope of Economic, Social and Cultural Rights in International Law* (Cambridge University Press, 2013).

[332] 'General Recommendation No 28: on Core Obligations' (n 49) [29].

[333] The Committee, 'Procedural Decision of the Committee on the Elimination of Discrimination Against Women, Gender and Sustainable Development (2002) UN Doc A/57/38 (Part I) [424].

[334] 'General Recommendation No 26: on Women Migrant Workers' (n 169) [27(a)].

[335] 'General Recommendation No 32: on Refugee Status' (n 259) [41].

[336] The Committee, 'Concluding Observations: Solomon Islands' (2014) CEDAW/C/SLB/CO/1–3 [33(d)]; The Committee, 'Concluding Observations: Brunei Darussalam' (2014) CEDAW/C/BRN/CO/1–2 [39(a)]; The Committee, 'Concluding Observations: Eretria' (2015) CEDAW/C/ERI/CO/5 [35(b)].

to prevent and protect women living outside of the state from gender-based violence.[337] There is no evidence of the Committee encouraging states to cooperate through the provision of economic assistance. Alston notes that: '[N]o UN body ... has accepted the proposition that any given country is obligated to provide specific assistance to any other country.'[338] The role of inter-state cooperation in redressing human rights violations and extraterritorial realities of poverty and gender-based poverty is underdeveloped and ripe for further academic study.

At this early stage in the evolution of an obligation to cooperation in CEDAW, it is difficult to definitively pin down how CEDAW requires states to cooperate to redress gender-based poverty. Through its obligation to eliminate discrimination without delay (Article 2) the Committee can encourage the state to seek international assistance and cooperation. The Committee can urge states to cooperate with international agencies on gender-based poverty; to refrain from undertaking policies and programmes that undermine the human rights of women in poverty; to regulate multinational corporations when they act in other states; and to apply a gender-sensitive approach to international agreements and the provision of aid.[339] This tentative approach to the extra-territorial realities of gender-based poverty and human rights allows scope for further development as the relationship between cooperation, gender equality and CEDAW is further refined.

IV. CONCLUSION

To ensure CEDAW responds to the lived experiences of women and girls, it is vital to address the gender-based poverty gap in CEDAW. Given the extent and complexity of the human rights violations that are inherent in gender-based poverty, a comprehensive interpretation that engages all of the rights in CEDAW is required if human rights law is to seriously tackle gender-based poverty. Applying the VCLT interpretative framework, an evolutionary interpretation of equality and non-discrimination, two norms that permeate all of CEDAW, can be interpreted to comprehensively bring gender-based poverty into the treaty. This proposed interpretation both draws together nascent state practice and highlights the entrenched and gender-based nature of women's poverty. Recognising gender-based poverty

---

[337] 'General Recommendation No 35: on Gender-Based Violence Against Women' (n 17) 24(b).
[338] P Alston, 'Ships in the Night: The Current State of Human Rights and Development Debate Seen through the Lens of Millennium Development Goals' (2005) 27 *Human Rights Quarterly* 755, 777.
[339] Carmona (n 288).

as a facet of equality and non-discrimination does not fundamentally alter the nature of the state's obligations. The state is not required to realise a minimum core or to devote maximum resources to progressively realise the human rights of women in poverty. It must demonstrate against an equality and non-discrimination framework that its laws, policies and programmes are geared towards redressing gender-based poverty. An equality-based understanding of the state's obligations for gender-based poverty allows the state flexibility and creativity in taking measures to ensure women in poverty enjoy their human rights. At the same time, this provides meaningful guidance to the state and to the Committee, which has to monitor the state's implementation of CEDAW.

It is not enough to interpret gender-based poverty into CEDAW.[340] The next step is to investigate how this interpretation can be incorporated into the Committee's accountability mechanisms. It is hoped that integrating gender-based poverty into CEDAW will promote a stronger understanding that gender-based poverty is an issue of equality and non-discrimination and an obstacle to human rights. We can now transition to consider how to move this interpretation forward into the work of the Committee so that the proposed interpretation can have de facto legal significance.

---

[340] G Ulfstein, 'Individual Communications' in H Keller and G Ulfstein (eds), *UN Human Rights Treaty Bodies: Law and Legitimacy* (Cambridge University Press, 2012) 74.

Part II

5

The Committee
and Gender-Based Poverty

THE GENDER-BASED POVERTY gap in CEDAW can be overcome with an evolutionary interpretation of equality and non-discrimination. To fulfil its commitment to eliminate discrimination and achieve equality, the state needs to take all appropriate measures to tackle how the interaction between gender and poverty limits women's human rights. Through an interpretation that connects gender-based poverty to equality, non-discrimination and human rights, CEDAW could become a political, legal and cultural focal point for international and national debates on women's poverty.[1] The treaty could act as a catalyst to shift perceptions of gender-based poverty from being the result of private individual failings to being the result of structural power relations between men and women. To achieve these aims it is necessary to consider how the interpretation proposed in Chapter 4 can be applied by the Committee in its accountability structures.

The Committee has no power to issue binding judgments or remedial orders. It is tasked with monitoring the implementation of CEDAW[2] and now, under the Optional Protocol to CEDAW, it can communicate views and recommendations on Individual Communications and can determine gross and systemic violations of CEDAW via the Inquiry Procedure.[3] The formal mandate of the Committee belies the practical reality that it can be a highly persuasive authority and is of 'considerable practical importance for the interpretation and application of the rights ... in CEDAW'.[4]

---

[1] M Nussbaum, 'Women's Progress and Women's Human Rights' (2016) 38(3) *Human Rights Quarterly* 589; SE Merry, *Human Rights and Gender Violence: Translating International Law into Local Justice* (University of Chicago Press, 2006) 16.

[2] Art 17 CEDAW.

[3] Arts 7 and 8 Optional Protocol to the Convention on the Elimination of Discrimination Against Women (adopted 6 October 1999, entered into force 22 December 2000) 1213 UNTS 81.

[4] S Cusack and L Pusey, 'CEDAW and the Rights to Non-Discrimination and Equality' (2013) 14 *Melbourne Journal of International Law* 54, 58; P Alston and R Goodman, *International Human Rights: The Successor to International Human Rights in Context: Law, Politics and Morals* (Oxford University Press, 2013) 691.

The treaty's accountability mechanisms are designed to highlight areas of under-implementation and encourage states to adopt best practices on gender equality. A good example of this is General Recommendation No 19 on violence against women, which has been drawn upon by many apex domestic and regional courts.[5] It also forms the backbone of the Indian Sexual Harassment of Women at Workplace (Prevention, Prohibition and Redressal) Act, 2013. Building on this positive history, the Committee can be a strong voice and shine a spotlight on the relationship between gender equality, poverty and human rights. By understanding how CEDAW's accountability mechanisms can be sensitive to gender-based poverty, the proposed interpretation of CEDAW can potentially filter into the state's domestic law, policies and programmes. Even if the state remains resistant or inattentive to gender-based poverty, the work of the Committee can act as a rallying point and empower civil society organisations and grassroots campaigns by opening up new lines of argument. While there is no guaranteed method to ensure the impact of CEDAW, a crucial step in this process is to reflect on how the treaty's accountability mechanisms can capture the connection between equality, non-discrimination and gender-based poverty.

To begin with it is necessary to understand how the Committee currently grapples with gender-based poverty. The aim of this chapter is to analyse the extent to which the Committee is drawing on equality and non-discrimination to diagnose how gender-based poverty acts as an obstacle to women's rights and how it uses equality and non-discrimination to propose tailored recommendations. Notwithstanding the fact that the only reference to poverty is in the preamble in the CEDAW, the Committee repeatedly expresses concern that women in poverty are denied their human rights. Analysing the output of the Committee against an equality and non-discrimination framework reveals that it is implicitly using these norms to ground its assessment of gender-based poverty. Thus, the interpretation of CEDAW proposed in Chapter 4 both brings together and builds upon the work the Committee is already doing. At the same time, without explicitly interpreting gender-based poverty as a facet of equality and non-discrimination in CEDAW, there are gaps in the Committee's reasoning process. Most striking is the Committee's lack of consistency in understanding how gender-based poverty impacts the enjoyment of human rights. Even more dangerously, the Committee, at times, overlooks the harms of gender-based poverty. The analysis in this chapter marks a path forward for considering how to ensure the Committee takes a consistent

---

[5] *Vishakav State of Rajasthan* AIR 1997 SC3 011(India Supreme Court); *Carmichele v Minister of Safety and Security and Another* 2001 (1) BCLR 995 (South African Constitutional Court); and *R v Ewanchuk* [1999] 1 SCR 330 (Canadian Supreme Court); *Opuz v Turkey* App No 33401/02 (European Court of Human Rights, 9 June 2009).

and comprehensive approach to gender-based poverty as a facet of equality and non-discrimination in CEDAW.

Section I outlines the different accountability mechanisms that exist under CEDAW and the Optional Protocol to CEDAW. Using the four-dimensional model of transformative equality, Section II maps how the Committee conceptualises gender-based poverty. The final section evaluates where the Committee has approached gender-based poverty with sophistication and nuance and highlights the gaps and inconsistencies that exist. The analysis in this chapter serves as a springboard for exploring how to address these inconsistencies to ensure that CEDAW and the work of the Committee remains at the forefront of achieving gender equality for women in poverty.

I. CEDAW'S ACCOUNTABILITY STRUCTURE

Before analysing the Committee's approach to gender-based poverty, it is helpful to sketch out CEDAW's accountability structures. Through its mandate to monitor the implementation of CEDAW, the Committee has developed diverse accountability mechanisms. The bedrock of accountability under CEDAW is the periodic reporting process. Under the terms of the treaty, every four years states are required to submit a report to the Committee detailing all the measures the state has taken to eliminate discrimination against women.[6] Through a written and oral dialogue session with the state and along with input from civil society organisations, the Committee releases *Concluding Observations* which highlight areas of concern and provide recommendations on how the state can further implement CEDAW. The *General Recommendations* synthesise the Committee's insights from the periodic reporting process and provide a focused assessment of different aspects of women's human rights. The Optional Protocol to CEDAW establishes two further accountability mechanisms: the *Individual Communications* and the *Inquiry Procedure*. Under the Individual Communications, an individual can commence a claim arguing that the state has failed to uphold CEDAW. The Committee evaluates this claim and releases a decision. If it finds the state has not upheld CEDAW it provides specific recommendations to remedy the individual situation and general recommendations to protect the rights of similarly situated women. With the Inquiry Procedure, the Committee can investigate serious, grave or systematic violations of CEDAW. This involves fact-finding country visits where the Committee undertakes dialogues with state officials, civil society organisations and individuals. To date, it has investigated the abduction, rape and murder of women in Ciduad Juárez, Chihuahua, Mexico; murdered

---

[6] Art 18 CEDAW.

and missing indigenous women in Canada; and access to contraception in the Philippines.

Between these four forums the Committee has generated a large volume of material. As of 2017, there are thirty-five General Recommendations, over a thousand Concluding Observations, fifty-one Individual Communications and three Inquiry Procedures. All of the General Recommendations, Individual Communications and Inquiry Procedure are used in the analysis below. Only a select number of Concluding Observations are relied upon. This chapter uses the same states relied upon in Chapter 4 when analysing subsequent state practice under the interpretative rules of the Vienna Convention on the Law of Treaties: Norway, Canada, Romania, Turkey, Argentina, Mexico, the Philippines, Jordan, Kenya, Egypt, Bangladesh and Ethiopia. As will be recalled, these states were selected based on their 2014 Gender Inequality Index and World Bank gross national income and geographic classification. The Concluding Observations examined here span from 1984 to 2017, which also makes it possible to chart any evolution in the Committee's reasoning on gender-based poverty.

II. MAPPING THE COMMITTEE'S APPROACH TO GENDER-BASED POVERTY

The human rights violations inherent in gender-based poverty are so overwhelmingly apparent that throughout the Committee's history it has made repeated references to gender-based poverty. The point of this analysis is not simply to point out that the Committee engages with gender-based poverty, but to grasp how the Committee conceptualises gender-based poverty. Has the Committee embraced the interpretation proposed in Chapter 4 or has it instead adopted other interpretative routes? Has it interpreted a specific obligation, such as equality in healthcare (Article 12) or economic and social life (Article 13) to account for gender-based poverty? Or has it in fact approached gender-based poverty as a facet of equality and non-discrimination? If it does adopt an equality and non-discrimination approach which engages all of the obligations in CEDAW, does it in practice favour certain provisions in CEDAW at the expense of others? Applying equality and non-discrimination as an analytical mapping tool to the General Recommendations, Concluding Observations, Individual Communications and Inquiry Procedure uncovers the steps the Committee is taking towards adopting the interpretation of CEDAW proposed in Chapter 4. It also reveals where the Committee's reasoning is underdeveloped and marks out areas for further refinement, particularly in relation to the connections between gender-based poverty and civil and political rights.

Using an equality and non-discrimination framework to understand the Committee's current approach to gender equality is challenging as the

Committee has not yet translated these norms into evaluative tools.[7] This was discussed in Chapter 4 when using *Teixeira* to illustrate how interpreting gender-based poverty affects the nature of the state's obligations. Equality and non-discrimination are intermeshed and rich concepts in CEDAW. The definition of discrimination against women in Article 1 holds that any distinctions which impair women's rights on the basis of equality are discriminatory. Equality is at the heart of CEDAW. For the analysis in this chapter the focus is on deriving an equality framework. CEDAW speaks in many tongues when it refers to equality. Both formal and substantive equality can be found within the text. Formal equality is where likes are treated alike[8] while substantive equality recognises that to achieve equality different treatment may be required.[9] There are multiple versions of substantive equality in CEDAW: equality of results, equality of opportunity and the four-dimensional model of transformative equality. The Committee embraces all three of these models under its conception of substantive equality. Since the different dimensions of transformative equality—disadvantage, recognition, structure and participation—feature so prominently in the text of CEDAW and this equality model is designed as a nuanced analytical tool, only it is used to map the Committee's understanding of gender-based poverty.[10] The different dimensions are not 'watertight compartments', and there is a fluidity and shading between them, but it is 'useful to keep them separate' so as to see more clearly how the Committee approaches gender-based poverty.[11] The strength of Fredman's four-dimensional transformative model of equality is the dimensions' ability to mutually support each other and mediate tensions between competing visions of equality. To evaluate the Committee's approach to using and synthesizing all of the dimensions, I compare and contrast how it uses the intersecting dimensions in relation to rural women (Article 14), where it is particularly attentive to the links between equality and gender-based poverty, and equal access to healthcare (Article 12), where it fails to fully assess the impact of gender-based poverty.

As a second layer of analysis, I also make a further classification and assess how under each dimension of the transformative equality framework the Committee approaches gender-based poverty in relation to the different substantive provisions in CEDAW. Paying careful attention to the human rights context where the Committee is attentive to the impact of gender-based poverty reveals unseen patterns and provides a detailed

---

[7] M Campbell, 'Women's Rights and CEDAW: Unlocking the Potential of the Optional Protocol' (2016) 34(4) *Nordic Journal of Human Rights* 247.

[8] S Fredman, *Discrimination Law*, 2nd edn (Clarendon Press, 2011) 2.

[9] The Committee, 'General Recommendation No 25: on Temporary Special Measures' (2004) CEDAW/C/GC/25 [8].

[10] S Fredman, 'Substantive Equality Revisited' (2016) 14(3) *International Journal of Constitutional Law* 712.

[11] ibid 713.

picture of how the human rights commitments in CEDAW are currently being used to address gender-based poverty. One further point is that the Committee sometimes refers to core aspects of gender-based poverty under Article 13 (economic and social life) but more frequently it does not anchor its concerns and recommendations on gender-based poverty to any specific provisions of the treaty. At times, it appears the Committee is analysing gender-based poverty as if there is an explicit provision in the text of the treaty requiring states to redress women's poverty. This is not as surprising as it may initially appear. Recognising that CEDAW is a living instrument, the Committee often addresses issues that are not explicitly mentioned in CEDAW, such as refugee status, the impact of federalism, climate change and most notably gender-based violence. In the Concluding Observations, the Committee routinely addresses gender-based violence under a specific heading and also incorporates discussions on violence into its assessment of other substantive provisions in CEDAW. As a point of clarity, when gender-based poverty is referred to either under Article 13 (economic and social life) or independently of any articulated obligations in CEDAW, it will be classified as 'gender-based poverty & economic and social life'.

A. The Disadvantage Dimension

Disadvantage is disproportionately concentrated onto personal character-istics. Instead of treating everyone the same, the disadvantage dimension of equality recognises that groups have experienced disadvantage and tar-geted measures are required to redress this disadvantage. Gender-based poverty disadvantages women in all areas of life. Gender stereotypes in education cause women to opt for traditional occupations, which in effect segregate women into low-paid jobs. There is also evidence that women simply cannot afford to access contraception, education or the courts. Dif-ferential treatment—temporary special measures (Article 4) or programmes targeted to keeping girls in school (Article 10(f))—are necessary to break cycles of disadvantage. As the Committee points out, the basic yardstick of equality is not whether the same standards and procedures have been applied but whether the state has 'systematically strengthened its institu-tional response commensurate with the vulnerabilities identified and the seriousness of the situation'.[12] The question here is: to what extent has the Committee been cognisant of the need for measures targeted towards gender-based poverty?

---

[12] The Committee, 'Report of the Inquiry Concerning Canada of the Committee on the Elimination of Discrimination Against Women under Article 8 of OP-CEDAW' (2015) CEDAW/C/OP.8/CAN/1 [202].

(i) *Gender-Based Poverty & Economic and Social Life*

At the beginning of its history, the Committee appeared to be unsure how to respond to gender-based poverty. In the initial General Recommendations there are allusions to gender-based poverty: economic pressures to undergo harmful cultural practices, unpaid workers in family enterprises and including unpaid care work in gross national income.[13] These early General Recommendations are extremely brief and do not significantly engage with gender-based poverty. A similar hesitancy can be seen in the periodic reporting process. In numerous early Concluding Observations the state identifies gender-based poverty as a major obstacle to implementing CEDAW. In 1987, Bangladesh explained that it 'faced the obvious problems of a developing country that had a large population, widespread poverty and a high level of illiteracy'.[14] In a similar vein, in 1990, Egypt noted that 'with numerous economic and social problems, women were not able to exercise their full rights'.[15] Ethiopia argued, in 1996, that 'poverty constituted the root cause of many problems faced by women'.[16] In 1984, Mexico tried to explain and justify that discrimination against women was caused by poverty: 'As a developing country Mexico had short comings in its social and economic structure ... inevitably [this] affected the situation of women, particularly the more disadvantaged urban and rural women.'[17] Romania, in 1993, argued that 'the economic means were still inadequate to bring women into political life on an equal footing with men'.[18] States in the developed world also used economic conditions to justify violations of women's rights. In 1990, Canada noted that 'progress was stalled in social services for the poor ... owing to the economic conditions faced by the country'.[19] Surprisingly, in these early days the Committee did not comment on the appropriateness of using gender-based poverty as a justification for failing to implement CEDAW. In fact, the Committee made no substantive comments on gender-based poverty. While it is only possible to speculate on the reasons for this silence, it does suggest that initially the Committee may have only had a tentative understanding on how gender-based poverty fits within the CEDAW framework.

---

[13] The Committee, 'General Recommendation No 14: on Female Circumcision' (1990) CEDAW/C/GC/14; The Committee, 'General Recommendation No 16: on Unpaid Women Workers in Rural and Urban Family Enterprises' (1991) CEDAW/C/GC/16; The Committee, 'General Recommendation No 17: on Measurement and Quantification of the Unremunerated Domestic Activities of Women and their Recognition in the GNP' (1991) CEDAW/GC/17.

[14] The Committee, 'Concluding Observations: Bangladesh' (1987) A/42/38 [515].

[15] The Committee, 'Concluding Observations: Egypt' (1990) A/45/38 [399].

[16] The Committee 'Concluding Observations: Ethiopia' (1996) A/51/38 [137].

[17] The Committee 'Concluding Observations: Mexico' (1984) CEDAW/A/39/45 [69].

[18] The Committee 'Concluding Observations: Romania' (1993) CEDAW/A/48/38 [146].

[19] The Committee, 'Concluding Observations: Canada' (1990) CEDAW/A/45/38 [433].

This uncertainty has now given way to a relatively comprehensive under-standing of how women are disadvantaged by gender-based poverty. The Committee now emphasises that women are disproportionately disadvan-taged by poverty in both developed and developing countries. As a sign of how far the Committee has come, in General Recommendation No 26 on women migrant workers it boldly acknowledges the worldwide feminisa-tion of poverty,[20] and in General Recommendation No 29 on the economic consequences of marriage, family relations and their dissolution holds that women's status is inevitably affected 'above all [by] the persistence of wom-en's poverty'.[21] With respect to Canada, the Committee consistently draws attention to the disadvantage of gender-based poverty. In 1997, the Commit-tee noted that 'the restructuring of the economy ... appeared to have had a disproportionate impact on women' and is concerned 'about the deepening poverty among women'.[22] In 2008, cuts to social assistance in Canada were identified as having 'a negative impact on the rights of vulnerable groups of women ... who rely on social assistance for an adequate standard of living'.[23] And in the latest Concluding Observations from 2016, the Com-mittee expressed concern that Canadian women 'continue to experience significant levels of poverty'.[24] Similarly in Kenya in 2011, the Committee observed 'that female headed households are disproportionately represented among the chronically poor and households moving into poverty'.[25] In response to the 2000–01 economic collapse in Argentina, the Committee drew to the state's attention 'the situation of women resulting from the growing increase in poverty and extreme poverty ... which can have a dis-proportionately heavy impact on the female population'.[26] On the other hand, in relation to Egypt, Ethiopia, Norway and Romania, the Committee made no statement that women are disproportionately poor.

The disadvantage element of transformative equality is also implicitly used as the basis for the Committee's recommendations on how to redress gender-based poverty. For Canada, the Committee recommended 'that social assistance programmes directed at women be restored to an adequate level'[27] and that 'funding decisions [on social assistance] meet the needs

---

[20] The Committee, 'General Recommendation No 26: on Women Migrant Workers' (2008) CEDAW/C/GC/26 [5].

[21] The Committee, 'General Recommendation No 29: on Economic Consequences of Marriage, Family Relations and their Dissolution' (2013) CEDAW/C/GC/29 [4].

[22] The Committee, 'Concluding Observations: Canada' (1997) CEDAW A/52/38 [321], [331].

[23] The Committee, 'Concluding Observations: Canada' (2008) CEDAW/C/CAN/CO/7 [13].

[24] The Committee, 'Concluding Observations: Canada' (2016) CEDAW/C/CAN/CO/8–9 [46].

[25] The Committee, 'Concluding Observations: Kenya' (2011) CEDAW/C/KEN/CO/7 [35].

[26] The Committee, 'Concluding Observations: Argentina' (2002) CEDAW/A/57/38 part III [342].

[27] The Committee, 'Concluding Observations: Canada' (2003) A/58/38 (Part I) [342].

of the most vulnerable groups'.[28] Similarly, Canada was encouraged to
'assess the gender impact of anti-poverty measures and increase its efforts
to combat poverty among women'.[29] Canada was also specifically directed
to ensure that the National Poverty Reduction Strategy protected the rights
of all women with a focus on the most disadvantaged and vulnerable by
integrating a human rights- and gender-based approach.[30] Including a gender perspective is a powerful tool to open up sites of power for women to
hopefully redress disadvantage.[31] With respect to Kenya, the Committee
recommended targeted measures: the state should 'continue to intensify the
implementation of gender sensitive poverty reduction and development programmes ... and continue to develop target policies and support services
for women aimed at alleviating and reducing poverty among women'.[32]
The Committee recommended that Mexico 'give priority to women in its
poverty eradication strategy'.[33] Argentina was also urged to incorporate a
gender perspective into the design and implementation of income transfer
programmes aimed at poverty reduction[34] and take targeted measures such
as microcredit and low-interest credit schemes.[35]

(ii) Trafficking and Prostitution

States are obligated to suppress human trafficking and exploitative prostitution (Article 6). This provision is not premised on equality or non-
discrimination yet the Committee, at times, uses the disadvantage element
of transformative equality to understand the relationship between poverty,
gender, trafficking and exploitative prostitution. In times of conflict and
post-conflict reconstruction, the Committee noted that 'dire poverty and
inequality can lead [women] to exchange sexual favours for money, shelter,
food or other goods'.[36] Rural women face a similar plight: 'economic hard-
ships of rural life ... make [women] especially vulnerable' to trafficking.[37]

---

[28] 'Concluding Observations: Canada' (n 23) [26].
[29] The Committee, 'Concluding Observations: Canada' (2003) CEDAW/A/56/38 Part I
[358].
[30] 'Concluding Observations: Canada' (n 24) [47(a)].
[31] RR Marin, 'A New European Parity–Democracy Sex Equality Model and Why it Won't
Fly in the United States' (2012) 60 *American Journal of Comparative Law* 99, 101–03.
[32] 'Concluding Observations: Kenya' (n 25) [36].
[33] The Committee, 'Concluding Observations: Mexico' (2002) CEDAW/A/57/38 part III
[434].
[34] The Committee, 'Concluding Observations: Argentina' (2006) CEDAW/C/ARG/6
[19]–[20].
[35] The Committee, 'Concluding Observations: Argentina' (2016) CEDAW/C/ARG/7 [37].
[36] The Committee, 'General Recommendation No 30: on Women in Conflict Prevention,
Conflict and Post-Conflict Situations' (2013) CEDAW/C/GC/30 [54].
[37] The Committee, 'General Recommendation No 34: on the Rights of Rural Women'
(2016) CEDAW/C/GC/34 [26].

The Committee recommended that states address the root causes of trafficking by economically empowering women and that anti-trafficking legislation address social and economic challenges.[38] In Ethiopia, in 2004, the Committee observed that the state had undertaken 'limited measures to address poverty as the root causes of trafficking' and recommended that to overcome this disadvantage of vulnerable women that the state 'enhance the economic potential of women'.[39] Similarly, in the Philippines and Kenya, the Committee was concerned 'about the trafficking and sexual exploitation of girls stemming from poverty and from their need to provide support for their families'.[40] In Romania, in 2006, the Committee required the state to address women's 'economic insecurity and improve women's social and economic situation so as to eliminate their vulnerability' to trafficking and exploitative prostitution.[41] In 2016, the Committee was worried that Argentina had not put in place measures to promote the economic empowerment of women so as to prevent them from engaging in exploitative prostitution and recommended that the state strengthen income-generating opportunities.[42] In 2017, the Committee expressed concern that refugees in Jordan were living in precarious and insecure conditions and were at a heightened risk of sexual exploitation.[43] It directed the state to increase their access to livelihood opportunities and take measures to ensure they are not compelled into prostitution. Trafficking and exploitative prostitution also occurs in the developed world.[44] In 2012, the Committee noted that the au pair scheme in Norway has the potential to be a guise for trafficking and recommended that the state ensure these women have access to financial support.[45] In *Zhen Zhen v The Netherlands* the dissenting members of the Committee held that immigration officials must exercise due diligence when presented with evidence that the individual had been trafficked and inform her of her human rights and the availability of special protection schemes.[46] This is critical to ensure women who have been already been exploited are not revictimized by the state.[47]

---

[38] ibid [27].

[39] The Committee, 'Concluding Observations: Ethiopia' (2011) CEDAW/C/ETH/6–7 [25(c)].

[40] The Committee, 'Concluding Observations: Philippines' (2006) CEDAW/C/PHI/CO/6 [19]; 'Concluding Observations: Kenya' (n 25) [27].

[41] The Committee, 'Concluding Observations: Romania' (2006) CEDAW/C/ROM/CO/6 [23].

[42] 'Concluding Observations: Argentina' (n 35) [24]–[25].

[43] The Committee, 'Concluding Observations: Jordan' (2017) CEDAW/C//JOR/CO/6 [11].

[44] ibid [12(a)].

[45] The Committee, 'Concluding Observations: Norway' (2012) CEDAW/C/NOR/CO/8 [25]–[26].

[46] Individual opinion by Committee members Mary Shanthi Dairiam, Violeta Neubauer and Silvia Pimentel (dissenting) (2009) CEDAW/C/42/D/15/2007.

[47] K Finklea, 'Juvenile Victims of Domestic Sex Trafficking: Juvenile Justice Issues' (Congressional Research Services, 2014).

The Committee's treatment of the relationship between gender-based poverty and prostitution is, however, inconsistent. In Bangladesh's second periodic report, the representative for Bangladesh identified women's poverty as the main reason for both trafficking and prostitution.[48] Yet, in the next reporting cycle the Committee ignored the state's insights and required Bangladesh to conduct research on the causes of prostitution.[49] Even more problematic, the Committee is silent on any connection between disadvantage, gender-based poverty and prostitution and trafficking in Egypt, Turkey and Mexico.

(iii) Civil and Political Rights

The Committee is not attentive to the role that gender-based poverty plays in limiting women's participation in public life (Articles 7 and 8). In General Recommendation No 23 the Committee does recognise that financial constraints and women's economic dependence on men limits their opportunity to follow electoral campaigns, to freely exercise their right to vote and to actively participate in public life.[50] Unfortunately, the Committee's recommendations do not possess a high degree of detail. It only encourages states to 'ensure that barriers to equality are overcome, including those resulting from illiteracy, language and poverty'.[51] Even more disappointing, the Committee has not applied the insights into gender-based poverty and public life (Articles 7 and 8) from the General Recommendations in any of the Concluding Observations.

Nationality (Article 9) plays a crucial part in perpetuating women's poverty. Social welfare benefits are often tied to citizenship.[52] Particularly, as the Committee notes, in times of resource constraints the state will often restrict socioeconomic services to nationals.[53] In General Recommendation No 26 on migrant women workers, the Committee provides a detailed assessment of the disadvantages that poor migrant women face. Before departure, employment agencies may charge exploitative fees that cause greater financial hardship for women 'who generally have fewer assets than men' and 'makes them more dependent, if they need to borrow from family, friends or

---

[48] The Committee, 'Concluding Observations: Bangladesh' (1993) CEDAW/48/38 [261], [292].

[49] The Committee, 'Concluding Observations: Bangladesh' (1997) CEDAW/A/52/38/Rev.1 [462].

[50] The Committee, 'General Recommendation No 23: on Women in Political and Public Life' (1997) CEDAW/C/GC/23 [20(b)].

[51] ibid [45(c)].

[52] *Khosa v Minister of Social Development*, 2004(6) BCLR 569 (CC) [59] (South African Constitutional Court).

[53] 'General Recommendation No 30: on Conflict Prevent, Conflict and Post-Conflict' (n 36) [60].

moneylenders at usurious rates'.[54] In the country of destination, women are directed towards traditional gendered occupations, such as domestic work. In these types of jobs women 'have trouble obtaining binding contracts … causing them sometimes to work long hours without overtime payment'.[55] It urges states to put in place monitoring mechanisms so that employers uphold the rights of migrant women. The Committee is also concerned that 'women migrant workers may be unable to transmit savings through regular channels due to … high transaction costs'.[56] As part of comprehensive recommendation, it encourages states to establish remittance safeguards and assist women to participate in saving schemes.[57]

Again, the understanding of gender-based poverty and nationality evident in the General Recommendations has not completely filtered into the periodic reporting process. Migrant women in Canada, Ethiopia and Norway are included in larger discussions on disadvantaged women in relation to education, employment and health but no focused attention is given to the nexus between nationality and gender-based poverty.[58] An exception to this trend is Jordan, the Philippines and Argentina, where the Committee specifically focuses on domestic migrant workers. In Jordan, the Committee was alarmed about evidence of employers confiscating passports and ineffective application of the labour code to migrant domestic workers. It called on the state to establish regular workplace inspections and enforcement mechanisms.[59] In the Philippines, there is 'widespread exploitation and abuse' of Filipina migrant domestic workers and the protection policies the government has put in place do not cover unskilled labour.[60] The Committee recommended that the state strengthen the regulation of recruitment agencies and raise awareness among migrant women workers of their human rights. In Argentina, the Committee noted that there are no programmes aimed at economic integration of migrant, refugee and asylum-seeking women and recommended that the state develop comprehensive programmes to address this problem.[61]

(iv) Economic and Social Rights

The Committee is keenly aware as to how gender-based poverty disadvantages women in respect of the economic and social rights. The Committee

---

[54] 'General Recommendation No 26: on Women Migrant Workers' (n 20) [10].

[55] ibid [14].

[56] ibid [16].

[57] ibid [24(g)].

[58] 'Concluding Observations: Norway' (n 45) [35]–[36]; 'Concluding Observations: Ethiopia' (n 39) [35(h)]'.

[59] 'Concluding Observations: Jordan' (n 43) [45]–[46].

[60] The Committee, 'Concluding Observations: The Philippines' (2016) CEDAW/C/CO/PHI/7–8 [37].

[61] 'Concluding Observations: Argentina' (n 35) [42]–[43].

does propose tailored recommendations in respect of employment. On the other hand, the insight into gender-based poverty and education it demonstrates in the General Recommendation is not translating into proposing tailored recommendations in the Concluding Observations.

The Committee is sensitive to how poverty disadvantages women and girl's education (Article 10). In General Recommendation No 34 on rural women, it notes that unpaid care work, such as 'cooking, childcare, farm work and fetching water and firewood', are obstacles to girls attending school, and directs states to implement programmes to reduce this type of work.[62] The long distance to schools, which increases the risk of violence, and the lack of adequate water and sanitation facilities to meet the needs of menstruating girls, also deny rural girls their right to education.[63] With respect to Argentina in 2002, the Committee was concerned that the economic crisis had affected access for women and girls 'to public education because they lack the resources needed to either begin or continue their education'.[64] In Bangladesh 'girls leave school to work from home or in the fields at 8 or 10 years of age ... [and that] the distance of schools from home ... were considered negative factors in attendance of girls at school'.[65] In 1990, Egypt identified economic factors and early marriage, which they connected to poverty, as two reasons for women's higher drop-out rates.[66] Indirect schooling costs such as clothing, transportation and food and long distance to schools were identified as obstacles to girl's education in Kenya, Ethiopia and the Philippines.[67]

While being attuned to the de facto barriers created by gender-based poverty in accessing education, the Committee is not consistently proposing recommendations in the Concluding Observations to overcome these barriers. On the positive side, in General Recommendation No 31 on harmful practices, the Committee holds that universal, free and compulsory education is necessary to empower women to make autonomous and informed decisions.[68] It further encourages states to offer economic incentives through scholarships, microcredit programmes and saving schemes to encourage girls to postpone marriage and stay in school.[69] In 2009, the Committee drew on the disadvantage dimension of transformative equality to recommend that Ethiopia 'strengthen support services, including

---

[62] 'General Recommendation No 34: on Rights of Rural Women' (n 37) [42]–[43(d)].
[63] ibid.
[64] 'Concluding Observations: Argentina' (n 26) [362].
[65] 'Concluding Observations: Bangladesh' (n 14) [553].
[66] The Committee, 'Concluding Observations: Egypt' (1990) A/45/38 (1990) [395].
[67] 'Concluding Observations: Ethiopia' (n 39) [30]; The Committee, 'Concluding Observations: Philippines' (1991) CEDAW/A/46/38 [209].
[68] The Committee and the Committee on the Rights of the Child, 'General Recommendation No 31: on Harmful Practices' (2014) CEDAW/C/GC/31 [62].
[69] ibid [65].

scholarships, transport and tutorial support ... as well as incentives and subsidies' to encourage parents to send their daughters to school.[70] In Jordan, the Committee reiterated its position in the General Recommendations and urged the state to amend the regulations to allow 'young women's access to compulsory and free education without discrimination'.[71] Jordan and Ethiopia, while models of best practice, were outliers and it is unfortunate that there is no consistent recommendation to reduce the costs associated with education, to improve transport or to subsidise girl's education to ensure she is not taken out of school to support her family.[72] For the most part, the Committee's recommendations are inattentive to gender-based poverty. Bangladesh and Argentina best exemplify this tendency. In Bangladesh girls are dropping out of school due to gender-based poverty, pregnancy and the low value placed on girls' education, but the Committee recommendations remain broad: the state should 'retain girls in schools and adopt re-entry policies enabling young mothers who have dropped out to return to school'.[73] After expressing concern that women and girls in Argentina lack the economic resources to attend school, the Committee only recommended the state take all efforts to guarantee girls' access to education was equal to that of boys.[74] Similarly general recommendations can be found for Kenya, Turkey and the Philippines.[75]

The Committee is using its assessment of women's employment (Article 11) to draw the attention of states to how the labour market significantly disadvantages women and contributes to the material and social disadvantage of gender-based poverty. It is even attentive to women's employment in post-conflict settings and calls for 'reconstruction programmes to value and support women's contributions in the informal and productive areas of the economy'.[76] Across the twelve states evaluated in this analysis, there is a marked uniformity in understanding how employment disadvantages women. For almost every state the Committee routinely observes that: there is a gender pay gap; women are segregated into low-paid, underpaid and

---

[70] 'Concluding Observations: Ethiopia' (n 39) [21].

[71] The Committee, 'Concluding Observations: Jordan' (2012) CEDAW/C/JOR/CO/5 [36(a)].

[72] The Working Group on Discrimination Against Women in Law and Practice, 'Discrimination against Women in Economic and Social Life, with a Focus on Economic Crisis' (2014) A/C/26/39 [36].

[73] The Committee, 'Concluding Observations: Bangladesh' (2016) CEDAW/C/BDG/CO/8 [28]–[29].

[74] The Committee, 'Concluding Observations: Argentina' (1997) CEDAW/A/52/38/Rev.1 [362].

[75] The Committee, 'Concluding Observations: Bangladesh' (2011) CEDAW/C/BGD/CO/7 [28]; The Committee, 'Concluding Observations: Kenya' (2007) CEDAW/C/KEN/CO/6 [34]; The Committee, 'Concluding Observations: Turkey' (2010) CEDAW/C/TUR/CO/6 [31]; 'Concluding Observations: Philippines' (n 40) [18].

[76] 'General Recommendation No 30: on Conflict Prevention, Conflict and Post-Conflict' (n 36) [49].

unpaid jobs; the work traditionally assigned to women is not regulated by law; and women in the informal labour market are often denied social security benefits. It consistently notes that inadequate maternity leave, the lack of childcare facilities and the double burden of family care and employment negatively impact women's performance in the labour market. The best example of the Committee drawing all of these observations together is from Ethiopia in 2009. The Committee noted with concern

> the disproportionately high unemployment rate among women; the high proportion of women engaged in unpaid family work ... and in low paid jobs, owing to family responsibilities, lack of resources necessary to acquire skills, limited access to land, credit and information and traditional attitudes; the high percentage of women working in the informal sector without access to social protection; unequal pay and benefits, discriminatory hiring and promotion practices and unfair dismissals based on gender, marital status, family responsibility or pregnancy.[77]

This demonstrates a nuanced use of the disadvantage dimension of transformative equality to diagnose how employment practices contribute to gender-based poverty. Women predominate in domestic work,[78] part-time work,[79] in the informal labour market,[80] in unpaid work in the family business or family-owned subsistence farms,[81] and as unpaid caregivers for children and the elderly.[82] While these observations may at first appear to only be retreading well-established ground, emphasising women are disproportionately in low-paid, underpaid or unpaid work is important as states continue to deny that the labour market is gendered. In their latest periodic report from 2012, Norway argues that most women voluntarily choose part-time work.[83]

Breaking the cycle of disadvantage of poverty through employment requires specific measures. The Committee tends to employ all dimensions of transformative equality to use the employment obligation to remedy gender-based poverty. Three examples highlight how the Committee specifically uses the disadvantage element. Ethiopia was encouraged to create income-generating opportunities and economic empowerment programmes for women and to take temporary special measures such as priority to women in public sector recruitment.[84] The Committee recommended that Canada use temporary special measures to encourage women to enter traditional

---

[77] 'Concluding Observations: Ethiopia' (n 39) [32].
[78] The Committee, 'Concluding Observations: Egypt' (2010) CEDAW/C/EGY/7 [34].
[79] 'Concluding Observations: Canada' (n 23) [37].
[80] UN Special Rapporteur on extreme poverty and human rights, 'Unpaid Work, Poverty and Women's Human Rights' (2013) A/68/293.
[81] ibid.
[82] 'Concluding Observations: Canada' (n 23) [37].
[83] 'Concluding Observations: Norway' (n 45) [29].
[84] 'Concluding Observations: Ethiopia' (n 39) [38].

male occupations[85] and that the Philippines use temporary special measures to accelerate efforts to facilitate women moving from the informal to formal labour market.[86]

(v) Family Life

Marriage and family relations (article 16) are also a significant contributing source of gender-based poverty.[87] The evidence indicates that women, in both the developed and developing world, are worse 'off economically than men in family relationships and following the dissolution of those relationships' and that in some countries widowhood may leave a woman destitute.[88] The vast majority of the recommendations the Committee makes with respect to family law and gender-based poverty draw on a formal equality framework. It holds that the 'guiding principle should be that the economic advantages and disadvantages related to the relationships and its dissolution should be borne equally by both parties'.[89] For instance, in the Philippines, the Committee declared its concern that the Family Code still 'grants a husband's decision supremacy over that of wife with regard to community property'.[90] The Committee routinely calls for the same rights to inherit property and to equally divide joint property.[91]

In General Recommendation No 29 on the economic consequences of marriage, family relations and their dissolution, the Committee uses the disadvantage element of transformative equality to understand the social and economic consequences of family relationships. Women's interrupted education and employment histories and childcare responsibilities limit their opportunities in the labour market and leave them unable to support themselves upon the dissolution of relationships. In turn, the lack of resources means women may not be able to pay for court costs and have to 'forgo [their] economic rights to obtain a divorce'.[92] The Committee calls on states to provide free legal aid and for courts to recognise non-financial contributions including home and childcare, lost economic opportunity, and contributions to the partner's career development and human capital.[93] Unlike in relation to participation in public life (Articles 7 and 8) or nationality (Article 9), the Committee is attentive to these issues of family life in both the General Recommendations and Concluding Observations. When reviewing

---

[85] 'Concluding Observations: Canada' (n 23) [38].
[86] 'Concluding Observations: The Philippines' (n 60) [36(a)].
[87] Working Group (n 72) [14].
[88] 'General recommendation No 29: on Economic Consequences' (n 21) [5].
[89] ibid 45.
[90] 'Concluding Observations: The Philippines' (n 60) [49(a)].
[91] 'Concluding Observations: Ethiopia' (n 39) [40]–[41].
[92] 'General Recommendation No 29: on Economic Consequences' (n 21) [42].
[93] ibid [42], [47].

Egypt and Kenya, the Committee noted that non-financial contributions, such as unpaid care work, are not properly calculated in the division of matrimonial property.[94] Similarly, in Norway, the Committee expressed concern that the 'current law on property distribution upon divorce ... does not adequately address gender-based economic disparities between spouses resulting from traditional work and family life patterns' and that matrimonial property division does not accurately capture the complexity of gender and pensions.[95] To break the cycle of economic disadvantage caused by divorce, the Committee urged Norway to amend divorce laws to account for intangible properties, such as pensions, and that all joint property should be divided equally regardless of the spouse's contributions.[96]

In the General Recommendations, the Committee repeatedly acknowledges that poverty forces women into early marriage and family relationships.[97] In Egypt, the Committee noted that there are a high number of early marriages of poor girls to wealthy men in neighbouring countries.[98] This grossly undermines Article 16(b) of CEDAW, the right to freely choose a spouse. However the recommendations in the Concluding Observations tend to be focused on criminal law or awareness-raising of the negative implications of early marriages.[99] There is no consistent and targeted recommendation to remedy one of the root causes of girl's early marriage: gender-based poverty. The only instance where the Committee has recommended that a state address gender-based poverty to eliminate early forced marriage is the Philippines.[100]

B. The Recognition Dimension

The preceding subsection examined the disadvantage dimension; this one looks more closely at the recognition dimension. This dimension promotes respect and dignity and removes stigma, violence, humiliation, prejudice, stereotypes and oppression. The crucial insight from recognising gender-based poverty as distinct from poverty is attention to how the interaction between stereotypes on gender and on poverty contributes to women's material and social disadvantage. In Chapter 1, the treaty's mandate to

---

[94] 'Concluding Observations: Egypt' (n 78) [50].
[95] 'Concluding Observations: Norway' (n 45) [37].
[96] ibid [38].
[97] The Committee, 'General Recommendation No 21: on Equality in Marriage and Family Relations' (1994) CEDAW/C/GC/21 [16]; 'General Recommendation No 30: on Conflict Prevention, Conflict and Post-Conflict' (n 36) [62]; 'Concluding Observations: Jordan' (n 43) [11(d)].
[98] 'Concluding Observations: Egypt' (n 78) [28].
[99] ibid.
[100] 'Concluding Observations: The Philippines' (n 60) [50(d)].

address gender stereotypes (Article 5) was one of the central arguments for beginning with CEDAW, as opposed to any other treaty, in assessing how international human rights law can best respond to gender-based poverty. The evidence from this analysis further justifies using CEDAW as a starting place. In practice, the Committee has a strong, albeit not perfect, grasp of how traditional attitudes are linked to gender-based poverty.

(i) Gender-Based Poverty & Economic and Social Life

The Committee is very conscious of the intersectional dimensions of gender-based poverty. It repeatedly draws attention to the fact that women's poverty tracks onto other identity groups. In Argentina, rural women are described as living in a state of extreme poverty and marginalisation.[101] Over the course of several Concluding Observations, the Committee has highlighted that certain identity groups in Canada live in deep and persistent poverty: elderly women, female lone parents, Afro-Canadian women, immigrant women and women with disabilities.[102] The Committee has been especially attentive to the interaction of indigenous status, gender equality and poverty in Canada, pointing out that First Nation, Inuit and Métis women have high poverty rates, poor health, inadequate housing, lack of access to safe water, low school completion rates and high unemployment rates.[103] The Committee also noted its alarm about the situation of disadvantaged groups of women in Turkey who are disproportionately living in poverty: including 'Kurdish women and women of ethnic and minority communities, migrant women and women asylum-seekers, elderly women, as well as women with disabilities'.[104] In the Philippines, it noted that Muslim and indigenous women are 'subject to forced evictions and relocations as a result of large development projects and extractive industries'.[105] An outlier and point of disjuncture is *AS v Hungary*. The Committee, in analysing a claim under the Optional Protocol to CEDAW for forced sterilisation, where the individual was pressured into signing a sterilisation form in Latin, missed the fact that Roma women in Hungary are among the most illiterate and poor.[106]

While displaying attention to the interaction between gender equality, other identity grounds and poverty, the Committee is contradictory in proposing recommendations. Drawing on the disadvantage dimension, it

---

[101] 'Concluding Observations: Argentina' (n 34) [41].
[102] 'Concluding Observations: Canada' (n 29) [357]; 'Concluding Observations: Canada' (n 24) [46].
[103] 'Concluding Observations: Canada' (n 24) [28].
[104] 'Concluding Observations: Turkey' (n 75) [38].
[105] 'Concluding Observations: The Philippines' (n 60) [45(b)].
[106] (2006) CEDAW/C/36/D/4/2004.

recommended that poverty eradication strategies in Mexico and Canada pay special attention to the unique needs of women with multiple identities.[107] At other times, the Committee seems unclear on how to incorporate its concerns on intersectional gender-based poverty. In *Teixeira*, the Committee concluded that the fact that she was Afro-Brazilian, rural and poor contributed to her death in childbirth.[108] However, the Committee did not explore the implications of this conclusion. It did not ask how combined negative stereotypes on race, rural status, gender and poverty affect the location and funding of treatment centres and explain the severe delays in receiving maternal healthcare. As a result, the decision makes no recommendations to address the recognition dimension at stake in discrimination in women's healthcare.[109]

Poverty reduction programmes, while targeting the material aspect of poverty, can actually re-entrench and perpetuate the recognition harms of gender. The Committee has demonstrated remarkable perception into these tensions. Early in the Committee's reporting history, it noted when reviewing Bangladesh that 'it appeared that policies were directed more towards improving the welfare of women and towards women in connection with children than to the development of equality of women as individuals'.[110] When Argentina restructured its economic and social programmes after the collapse of the economy in the early 2000s, the Committee was concerned that the structure of these benefits actually reinforced discriminatory gender roles. Under these new programmes women were 'mainly beneficiaries of these measures rather than being equal participants and actors in their design and implementation'.[111] The Committee was worried that these approaches would perpetuate stereotypical views on the role of women and men rather than effectively support women's empowerment.[112] In a similar vein, it expressed concern that efforts to promote social protection in Ciudad Juárez, Mexico to protect women in poverty from rampant violence 'emphasize assistance rather than the empowerment of women'.[113] At the same time, another aspect of the recognition dimension that is underdeveloped concerns the stigmas that uniquely attach to gender-based poverty. Poor women are stereotyped as unloving mothers, lazy, undisciplined,

---

[107] 'Concluding Observations: Mexico' (n 33) [434]; 'Concluding Observations: Canada (n 24) [47(a)].

[108] (2011) CEDAW/C/49/D/17/2008.

[109] ibid [7.6]–[7.7].

[110] 'Concluding Observations: Bangladesh' (n 14) [511].

[111] The Committee, 'Follow-up Report to the Fifth Concluding Observations: Argentina' (2004) CEDAW/A/59/38 part II [372].

[112] ibid.

[113] The Committee, 'Report of the Inquiry Concerning Mexico of the Committee on Elimination of Discrimination Against Women under Article 8 OP-CEDAW' (2005) CEDAW/C/OP.8/MEX/1 [206].

undeserving, promiscuous, scheming, and as parasites leaching on limited state resources.[114] To date, there is no evidence of the Committee significantly engaging with this aspect of gender-based poverty.

(ii) Gender-Based Violence

Gender-based violence is one of the grossest and most pernicious denials of women's dignity. The UN Special Rapporteur on violence against women repeatedly identifies poverty as a contributing factor to gender-based violence.[115] The Committee's attention to these links is most evident in the Inquiry Procedure. In Mexico, it has noted that the victims of extreme sexual violence are young women living in poverty, mostly workers in *maquilas* who disappear 'while on their way to or from their homes since they have to cross deserted unlit areas at night or in the early morning'.[116] The Committee goes so far to conclude that these women are 'murdered because they are women and because they are poor'.[117] Authorities do not seriously investigate these deaths and the victims are often blamed for putting themselves in dangerous circumstances. The Committee's recommendations, however, are almost exclusively focused on remedying the gross failings of the criminal justice system and, for the most part, ignore the role of gender-based poverty.[118]

On the other hand, when assessing murdered and missing indigenous women in Canada, the Committee has provided guidance on how the state could improve the socioeconomic conditions of indigenous women to protect them from violence. As with Mexico, the Committee recognizes that the poverty indigenous women experience makes them susceptible to violence. For instance, rural, indigenous women are unable to afford the cost of transport and are forced to hitchhike, which dramatically increases their risk of abduction and murder.[119] The Committee is critical of the fact that Canada's efforts to address poverty are neutral to indigenous women's intersecting identities and experiences.[120] It urges the state to improve the

---

[114] G Brodsky et al, 'Gosselin v Canada' (2006) 18 *Canadian Journal of Women and the Law* 189, 193; J Mosher, 'Intimate Intrusions: Welfare Regulations and Women's Personal Lives' in S Gavigan and D Chunn (eds), *The Legal Tender of Gender: Welfare, Law and the Regulations of Women's Poverty* (Hart, 2010).

[115] 'Special Rapporteur on Violence against Women Finalizes Country Mission to the United Kingdom and Northern Ireland' (2014) www.ohchr.org/EN/NewsEvents/Pages/DisplayNews.aspx?newsid=14514&; 'Special Rapporteur on Violence against Women Finalizes Country Mission to Sudan' (2015) www.ohchr.org/EN/NewsEvents/Pages/DisplayNews.aspx?NewsID=16009; 'Concluding Observations: The Philippines' (n 60) [26(e)].

[116] 'Inquiry Procedure: Mexico' (n 113) [63].

[117] ibid [66].

[118] ibid [206].

[119] 'Inquiry Procedure: Canada' (n 12) [106]

[120] ibid [118].

socioeconomic conditions by developing anti-poverty, food security, housing, education, employment and transport strategies focusing on women in indigenous communities.[121]

(iii) Cultural Attitudes and Stereotypes

The Committee does demonstrate a firm appreciation of how negative cultural attitudes and stereotypes on gender more broadly contribute to women's poverty. This is largely done through Article 5(a), the requirement to modify cultural stereotypes and attitudes. Article 5(a) of CEDAW is also not premised on equality or non-discrimination. Notwithstanding this, the Committee seems implicitly to have used the recognition dimension of transformative equality when analysing the relationship between gender cultural stereotypes and poverty. This is most evident in the recent General Recommendations and Concluding Observations, suggesting a growing awareness of the gender-based aspects of women's poverty. The Committee notes that migrant women often face substantive pressure to send remittances back to their home country to support their families.[122] Young girls can face economic marginalisation if they do not conform to harmful social practices and norms.[123] Negative cultural attitudes can hinder women's inheritance and ownership of property.[124] The Committee specifically calls on states to 'address negative traditional practices which affect rural women's right to land', including through launching awareness-raising campaigns directed towards traditional leaders on women's right to ownership and inheritance.[125] In relation to Bangladesh, Egypt, Ethiopia and the Philippines, the Committee observes that: '[P]atriarchal attitudes and deep-rooted stereotypes regarding the roles and responsibilities of women and men ... are reflected in their disadvantageous and unequal status in many areas, including employment, decision-making, marriage and family relations and the persistence of violence against women.'[126]

Despite recognising the role that gender norms can play in perpetuating gender-based poverty, the Committee still has a tendency to lapse into broad and generic recommendations. In relation to the Inquiry Procedure into Mexico, rather than providing advice on how to best structure socioeconomic programmes, the Committee only encourages the state to 'restore the

---

[121] ibid [218].
[122] 'General Recommendation No 26: on Women Migrant Workers' (n 20) [16].
[123] 'General Recommendation No 31: on Harmful Practices' (n 68) [57].
[124] 'General Recommendation No 34: on Rights of Rural Women' (n 37) [22].
[125] ibid [23].
[126] 'Concluding Observations: Bangladesh' (n 75) [17]; 'Concluding Observations: Egypt' (n 78) [21], 'Concluding Observations: Ethiopia' (n 39) [18]; 'Concluding Observations: Philippines' (n 40) [17].

social fabric and create conditions' to guarantee women's human rights.[127] The Concluding Observations contain examples where the state is simply asked to 'continue to accelerate efforts to eliminate discriminatory and stereotypical attitudes'.[128]

(iv) Prostitution

The recognition dimension of prostitution is a matter of serious debate among feminist scholars reflected in the entrenched terminological dispute between prostitute and sex-worker.[129] To a certain extent, Article 6 transcends this discussion as it only requires states to eliminate exploitative prostitution. Therefore, the analysis of the Committee's approach to gender-based poverty and the recognition harms of prostitution are not meant to be an exhaustive discussion on these issues but are confined only to exploitative situations. Prominent scholars have argued that under certain exploitative conditions prostitution 'can only credibly be explained as devaluing women qua women and disrespecting women's humanity'.[130] Victims of trafficking are similarly dehumanised and treated without dignity. Yet on the basis of the material reviewed, the Committee is strangely silent as to sociocultural attitudes that demean and objectify women and girls in prostitution and human trafficking. For example, while the Committee urged a holistic approach to prostitution and trafficking in the Philippines, in fact its recommendations are primarily centred on economic empowerment.[131] This falls short of a true appreciation of how gender norms that devalue women make them more vulnerable to the poverty inherent in exploitative prostitution and trafficking.

(v) Economic and Social Rights

The Committee exhibits a good understanding of how cultural norms negatively impact education and how this contributes to gender-based poverty. For instance, it notes that there is a perception that it is not profitable to invest in skills training for older women.[132] But again, there is a disconnection between the Committee's concern and its proposed recommendation.

---

[127] ibid [290].

[128] 'Concluding Observations: Bangladesh' (n 75) [18].

[129] B Havelkova, 'Using Gender Equality Analysis to Improve the Well Being of Prostitutes' (2011) 18(1) *Cardozo Journal of Law & Gender* 55.

[130] MM Dempsey and J Herring, 'Why Sexual Penetration Requires Justification' (2007) 27 *Oxford Journal of Legal Studies* 467, 485.

[131] 'Concluding Observations: Philippines' (n 40) [19]–[20]; 'Concluding Observations: The Philippines' (n 60) [30].

[132] The Committee, 'General Recommendation No 27: on Older Women and the Protection of their Rights' (2010) CEDAW/C/GC/27 [19].

The Committee only holds that states should ensure older women have access to adult education without explicitly directing states towards addressing the perception that older women are an unworthy educational investment.[133] In the Concluding Observations, the Committee is more attentive to the need to propose recommendations that are targeted towards remedying gender norms in education that buttress gender-based poverty. In Turkey, cultural norms result in girls not enrolling or dropping out of school as families prioritise the education of boys and the state are called to address these factors.[134] The Committee has directed Egypt to take steps to address traditional attitudes that result in gender segregation in students' choice of education. It drew upon the disadvantage dimension and further recommended that Egypt use temporary special measures to 'offer incentives for young women to enter traditionally male dominated fields of study'.[135] In respect of Kenya, the Committee has expressed concern 'that gender stereotype may have an impact on women opting for traditional social occupations and on their limited comparative advantage in the labour market'.[136] Kenya and Argentina are called to take steps to address these attitudes, to encourage women to study in non-traditional fields and to 'eradicate gender stereotypes from both official and unofficial curricula'.[137]

In multiple and intersecting ways recognition harms also underlie women's low position in the labour market. Gender stereotypes explain, at least in part, the gender job segregation and gender pay gap. Women tend to be segregated into traditional female occupations—cleaning, caring and secretarial work—and the skills, effort and responsibility expanded in these types of jobs tend to be undervalued and underpaid.[138] Even in corporate structures women may be segregated into positions with less responsibility or prestige.[139] Pay structures may be infiltrated with gender biases.[140] Social norms on the performance of care work can severely limit the time and energy women have to achieve success in the labour market.[141] These stereotypes are deeply engrained in the social fabric. The Committee notes that in Canada, despite the availability of paternal leave, this is still not being used by fathers.[142]

---

[133] ibid [40].
[134] 'Concluding Observations: Turkey' (n 75) [30].
[135] 'Concluding Observations: Egypt' (n 78) [32].
[136] 'Concluding Observations: (n 25) [32].
[137] ibid [32]; 'Concluding Observations: Argentina' (n 34) [34].
[138] The Committee, 'Concluding Observations: Norway' (2007) CEDAW/NOR/CO/7 [17]; The Committee, 'Concluding Observations: Norway' (2003) CEDAW/A/58/38 part 1 (2003) [411].
[139] 'Concluding Observations: Jordan' (n 43) [43(c)].
[140] 'General Recommendation No 25: on Temporary Special Measures' (n 9) [23].
[141] 'Concluding Observations: Norway' (n 138) [397].
[142] 'Concluding Observations: Canada' (n 24) [38(c)].

The Committee proposes a series of recommendations. It repeatedly calls on states to take efforts to increase the number of women in non-traditional trades and professions[143] and to provide gender sensitivity training to employers to challenge stereotypes and encourage them to hire women.[144] To fully close the pay gap, it has recommended that Norway, Romania, Jordan and Kenya apply gender-neutral job evaluation.[145] This is an important method for uncovering gender bias in the concept of merit and ensuring that the skill, effort and responsibility women expend in the labour force is properly recognised and valued. Echoing the approach of the Working Group on Discrimination Against Women in Law and Practice (Working Group), the Committee advocates a redistribution of care work. The Committee has directed Canada and Jordan to adopt a 'rights-based national childcare framework in order to provide ... adequate childcare, and strengthen incentives for men to exercise their right to parental leave', including through compulsory leave.[146] To go a step further, it is crucial that states, as required under Article 5(b) of CEDAW, also conduct awareness-raising campaigns that both men and women have equal responsibility for care work so as to ensure men take their parenting roles seriously and actually use parental leave. There is no evidence in the material analysed of the Committee explicitly encouraging states to take this step. It is also important to note that the Working Group goes further and argues that care work also needs to be properly recognised by inter alia allowing care expenses as deductible for income tax purposes.[147] Initially, the Committee did discuss unpaid care work and gross national income in General Recommendation No 17 from the early 1990s, but in its more recent outputs it has not discussed this aspect of unpaid care work, recognition harms and gender-based poverty.

(vi) Access to Justice

There is only one example where the Committee discusses the recognition harms associated with access to justice from the perspective of gender-based poverty (Article 15). In General Recommendation No 21 on equality in marriage and family life it is troubled that women's evidence in court proceedings may carry less weight, hampering their ability to protect their

---

[143] 'Concluding Observations: Canada' (n 23) [38].

[144] 'Concluding Observations: Jordan' (n 71) [38].

[145] 'Concluding Observations: Romania' (n 41) [29]; 'Concluding Observations: Kenya' (n 25) [34]; 'Concluding Observations: Norway' (n 138) [397]; 'Concluding Observations: Jordan' (n 43) [44(d)].

[146] 'Concluding Observations: Canada' (n 24) [39(c)]; 'Concluding Observations: Jordan' (n 43) [44(a)].

[147] Working Group (n 72) [92].

property ownership, which in turn can undermine their livelihood and financial independence.[148] However, this is an outlier and there is no sustained engagement with this aspect of gender-based poverty.

(vii) Family Life

The role of custom in respect of divorce and inheritance and its impact on gender-based poverty cannot be understated.[149] In the General Recommendations, the Committee warns that any laws or customs concerning property division that rests on assumptions that the 'man alone is responsible for the support of women and children ... and that he can and will honourably discharge this responsibility is clearly unrealistic'.[150] Not only does this not reflect the reality of property division, but it also perpetuates stereotypes of female dependency and limits women's economic freedom. In *ES and SC v Tanzania*, under customary inheritance law, two widows were evicted from their homes by their husband's family and denied any rights of inheritance. In the decision upholding the rights of ES and SC, the Committee noted that the law forces women 'to perpetually depend on male relatives ... and therefore [they] do not enjoy economic opportunities'.[151] Drawing on the participation dimension, it called on Tanzania to, inter alia, encourage dialogue between women's organisations and traditional leaders on removing discriminatory customary law provisions.[152] A similar situation exists in Ethiopia. The Committee noted that in Ethiopia sons 'inherit land because it is assumed that daughters will move to the homes of their husbands, that the family of a deceased husband often claims the land from his widow [and] that women frequently lose their property to their husbands upon divorce'.[153] In this situation, the Committee only encourages Ethiopia to protect women from property-grabbing and to effectively enforce equal rights of women to inherit property. The Committee's recommendations are an important step but they lack the specificity required to offer meaningful guidance. There is no recommendation to address the sociocultural norms that assume that a woman's property will be subsumed within her spouse's or that upon death property should revert back to the husband's family.

---

[148] 'General Recommendation No 21: on Equality in Marriage' (n 97) [8].
[149] World Bank, 'Voice and Agency: Empowering Women and Girls for Shared Prosperity' (2014) ch 5, https://openknowledge.worldbank.org/handle/10986/19036.
[150] 'General Recommendation No 21: on Equality in Marriage' (n 97) [27]; 'General Recommendation No 29: on Economic Consequences' (n 21) [49]–[50].
[151] (2015) CEDAW/C/60/D/48/2013 [7.8].
[152] ibid [9(b)(iv)]; also see 'General Recommendation No 34: on Rights of Rural Women' (n 37) [58].
[153] 'Concluding Observations: Ethiopia' (n 39) [40].

C. The Structural Dimension

Having examined the disadvantage and recognition dimension, this sub-section analyses how the Committee has drawn on the structural element of transformative equality to address gender-based poverty. The structural element of transformative equality challenges oppressive legal, political, social, economic and cultural structures that perpetuate gender-based poverty. Similar to both the disadvantage and recognition dimensions, in certain instances the Committee forcefully challenges institutions that operate to oppress women and contribute to gender-based poverty and at other times, particularly in relation to participation in public life, this dimension of transformative equality is overlooked.

(i) Gender-Based Poverty & Economic and Social Life

As discussed under the recognition element, not only can poverty eradication programmes paint woman as passive recipients rather than empowered agents, but the structure of these programmes can also contribute to gender-based poverty. Poverty reduction programmes may be premised on a male breadwinner model; may deposit funds in only one bank account which 'can exacerbate potential vulnerability to abuse or economic deprivation;'[154] and may be connected to deeply intrusive conditions, such as the changes to the law in the UK only allowing women to receive child benefits for a third child when she can prove the third child is the consequence of sexual violence.[155] The only evidence of the Committee truly engaging with these oppressive structures comes from Canada. The Canadian federal government provides funds to the provinces for social assistance programmes for women. The current legislation transfers these funds without any conditions. Without any criteria, the provinces have drastically cut social assistance rates.[156] The Committee has recommended that Canada both increase the federal transfer payments to the provinces and make this transfer conditional on the provinces setting their social assistance rates at levels to ensure an adequate standard of living for women.[157] When investigating murdered and missing indigenous women in Canada, the Committee has observed that indigenous women in violent situations are reluctant to seek

---

[154] 'Concluding Observations: The Philippines' (n 60) [41(a)], [41(b)]; *Falkiner v Ontario (Minister of Community and Social Services, Income Maintenance Branch)* [2002] OJ No 1771 (Ontario Court of Appeal).

[155] The Child Tax Credit (Amendment) Regulations 2017 No 387.

[156] See Feminist Alliance for International Action, 'A Failing Grade on Women's Equality: Canada's Human Rights Record on Women' (2008) [8], tbinternet.ohchr.org/Treaties/CEDAW/Shared%20Documents/CAN/INT_CEDAW_NGO_CAN_42_8224_E.pdf.

[157] 'Concluding Observations: Canada' (n 23) [14]; 'Concluding Observations: Canada' (n 24) [46(c)].

help from the criminal justice system as they are afraid, due to systemic discrimination in the childcare system, that their children will be placed in foster care, which in turns reduces the amount of income assistance they receive.[158] Thus, due to the structure of social assistance legislation and discriminatory biases in the childcare system, indigenous women face a choice of staying in an abusive relationship or turning to the authorities and risk losing their children and being plunged into deeper poverty. The Committee urges Canada to address the disproportionate number of indigenous children institutionalised in the child welfare system but ignores the structure of the child benefit system.[159]

(ii) Civil and Political Rights

There is no discussion on how the structures of political life may exclude women in poverty, such as needing significant financial funding to run a campaign. The Committee's focus on gender-based poverty and oppressive structures is focused solely on nationality. Migrant women face numerous formal legal restrictions that undermine their ability to fully participate in public life and can trap them in cycles of gender-based poverty. General Recommendation No 26 on migrant women workers provides a thorough assessment of the unequal structures embedded in the law and community. The Committee expresses concern that states impose restrictions or bans on migrant women's being employed in particular sectors and exclude certain occupations, such as domestic work, from legal definitions of work which deny women protection from minimum wage and working time laws.[160] A woman may automatically become an undocumented worker if she leaves her employment which can trap her in exploitative and abusive working conditions.[161] Family reunification schemes may not be extended to female-dominated sectors and migrant women may be excluded from legal aid and national health schemes.[162] The Committee provides detailed recommendations to modify these structures.

In the latest Concluding Observations from Canada, Jordan and Bangladesh, the Committee addresses these aspects of gender-based poverty and structural inequality. It urges Bangladesh to ensure effective implementation of nationality legislation for unregistered Rohingya women so that they can access legal and social services.[163] The Committee calls on Canada to discontinue the Temporary Foreign Workers Program and for Jordan to

---

[158] 'Inquiry Procedure: Canada' (n 12) [115].
[159] ibid [218(d)].
[160] 'General Recommendation No 26: on Women Migrant Workers' (n 20) [14], [15].
[161] ibid [17].
[162] ibid [19], [21].
[163] 'Concluding Observations: Bangladesh' (n 73) [26]–[27].

suspend the *kafala* system so that migrant domestic workers can change their employers without losing their migration status.[164] Only after five years of residence can children of Jordanian mothers and foreign fathers' access services in education, health and employment. There is also evidence that these services have not been implemented after the five-year wait period. While expressing concern at this situation, the Committee's recommendations, in contrast to its approach in the General Recommendation, are tepid: consider lifting the five-year residency requirement.[165]

(iii) Economic and Social Rights

There are multiple and reinforcing ways that the structure of employment contributes to gender-based poverty and the Committee consistently draws this to the attention of states. For example, the type of work that women traditionally and disproportionately perform, as domestic workers, part-time workers, on family farms or in the informal labour market, is regularly excluded from legal protection, making women vulnerable to abuse and exploitation.[166] The criteria used for hiring and promotions do not capture the breadth and depth of women's qualifications. This in turn partially explains women's unequal pay.[167] Inadequate maternity leave and benefits and the lack of affordable childcare facilities are significant obstacles to women's full participation in employment.[168] The age limit in place on some microcredit schemes excludes older women.[169] Pensions are often linked to wages in the formal labour market. This results in older women who have earned less and performed a significant amount of unpaid care work receiving lower pensions.[170] The dissenting Committee members in *Ngyuen v The Netherlands* found that an anti-accumulation clause in the legislation prevented women who were both self-employed and worked part time from receiving maternity benefits that matched the amount of hours. They noted that this is a structural inequality because women are disproportionately employed in part-time work and within the family business.[171]

The Committee is a strong advocate for restructuring the labour market. It consistently recommends that states improve working conditions in the

---

[164] 'Concluding Observations: Jordan' (n 43) [45(c)]; 'Concluding Observations: Canada' (n 24) [39(f)].
[165] 'Concluding Observations: Jordan' (n 43) [40(c)].
[166] 'Concluding Observations: Egypt' (n 78) [33]; 'Concluding Observations: Philippines' (n 60) [40]; 'General Recommendation No 16: Unpaid Women Workers' (n 13); 'General Recommendation No 26: on Women Migrant Workers' (n 20) [14].
[167] The Committee, 'Concluding Observations: Argentina' (1988) CEDAW/A/43/38 [394].
[168] 'Concluding Observations: Canada' (n 19) [415].
[169] 'General Recommendation No 27: on Older Women' (n 132) [23].
[170] ibid [20].
[171] Individual opinion of Committee members, Ms Naela Mohamed Gabr, Ms Hanna Beate Schopp-Schilling and Ms Heisoo Shin (dissenting) CEDAW/C/D/36/3/2004.

private and informal sector,[172] implement a social protection scheme to cover the informal sector,[173] effectively enforce equal pay,[174] implement sanction and labour inspections,[175] provide gender sensitivity training to employers to dismantle stereotypes and encourage them to hire women,[176] and regulate the conditions of domestic workers.[177] The Committee also proposes recommendations in relation to women, motherhood and employment. States are encouraged to promote paternity leave, to develop and to challenge employment structures to enable women to balance work and family,[178] while at the same time states need to take steps to reduce women's double burden of employment and unpaid care work by creating childcare facilities.[179] To be truly effective, as discussed above under the recognition dimension, it is, however, crucial that these structural changes be linked to measures to redress sociocultural norms that require women to perform the bulk of unpaid care work.

(iv) Access to Justice

The Committee is increasingly drawing connections between the structure of the justice system and gender-based poverty. In General Recommendation No 33 on women's access to justice it calls on the state to refrain from 'jailing women for petty offenses and/or inability to pay bail' and using the disadvantage dimensions encourages states to 'remove economic barriers to justice by providing legal aid and ensuring that ... court costs are reduced for women with low incomes and waived for women living in poverty'.[180] Income tests for legal aid eligibility are often premised on the household unit's income and do not account for women's limited de facto control of assets. The Committee recommends that 'means testing to determine eligibility for legal aid ... should be based on the *real* income of women'.[181]

In Canada, the Committee notes that due to cuts in the legal aid system, low-income women are being denied access to justice. The Committee

---

[172] 'Concluding Observations: Canada' (n 29) [374].
[173] The Committee, 'Concluding Observations: Mexico' (2012) CEDAW/C/MEX/CO/7–8 [29]; 'Concluding Observations: The Philippines' (n 60) [41]; 'General Recommendation No 34: on Rights of Rural Women' (n 37) [52(f)].
[174] 'Concluding Observations: Canada' (n 23) [37].
[175] The Committee, 'Concluding Observations: Mexico' (2006) CEDAW/C/MEX/CO/6 [31].
[176] 'Concluding Observations: Jordan' (n 71) [38].
[177] 'Concluding Observations: Ethiopia' (n 39) [33].
[178] 'Concluding Observations: Argentina' (n 34) [36].
[179] 'Concluding Observations: Norway' (n 138) [430].
[180] (2015) CEDAW/C/GC/33 [17(a)].
[181] ibid [37(d)] (emphasis added).

draws on both the structural and disadvantage dimensions of transformative equality by recommending that Canada ensure vulnerable women have access to legal representation and remedies, particularly in the areas of family and poverty law.[182] It is concerned that income testing for civil legal aid is 'well below the poverty line, consequently denying low-income women access to legal representation'.[183] The Canadian Court Challenges Programme (CCP), a federally funded programme that provides assistance to cases that advance equality rights, has recently been reinstated. The Committee advises that the CCP should undertake claims that develop the relationship between the right to security under the Canadian Charter of Rights and Freedoms, socioeconomic inequality and poverty.[184] This is a bold recommendation as the Committee is in essence directing the future development of Canadian jurisprudence. Regarding the Philippines, the Committee notes that women in poverty cannot access justice and calls on the state to make sure that the justice system is affordable.[185] Similarly, in Kenya, women are unable to bring discrimination claims in courts due to the costs of filing an action and illiteracy.[186] The Committee draws on the structural element by requiring Kenya to 'speedily adopt national legal aid ... and ... institutionalize legal aid throughout the country'.[187] Although, in relation to Kenya, there is no specific requirement to target low-income women as there is in Canada.

(v) Family Life

There are a few examples of the Committee challenging the structures of family relationships. In General Recommendation No 29 on the economic consequences of marriage, family relations and their dissolution, the Committee explains that fault-based divorce systems tend to disadvantage women more than men as women are more financially dependent.[188] It is also concerned that customary and personal laws are exempt from constitutional guarantees of equality.[189] In Norway, women living in de facto cohabitation relationships have no economic rights or legal protection when these relationships dissolve. These women are vulnerable to poverty because structural legal barriers deny them their economic and property rights in de facto relationships.[190] The Committee advocates that Norway 'adopt legal

---

[182] 'Concluding Observations: Canada' (n 23) [21]–[22].
[183] 'Concluding Observations: Canada' (n 24) [14(b)].
[184] ibid [14(d)].
[185] 'Concluding Observations: The Philippines' (n 60) [14(b)], [16(a)].
[186] 'Concluding Observations: Kenya' (n 25) [13].
[187] ibid [14].
[188] 'General Recommendation No. 29: on Economic Consequences' (n 21) [39].
[189] ibid [10].
[190] See the dissent of Justice Abella in *Québec (Attorney General) v A*, [2013] 1 SCR 61 (Canadian Supreme Court).

measures necessary to guarantee women living in de facto relationships economic protection equal to married women, in the form of recognizing their right to property accumulated during the relationship'.[191]

In the individual decisions there are two examples of the Committee addressing the structural inequalities in family law, although one of the examples is a dissenting opinion. The dissenting Committee members in *BJ v Germany* noted that delays in finalising the divorce proceedings had a disproportionate negative economic affect on women.[192] The individual in this case had 'devoted her whole adult life to unpaid work in the family'.[193] She now had an uncertain financial future and required spousal maintenance. The domestic court's inability to resolve these issues speedily created a precarious situation for divorced women. The dissent recommends that the state have effective legal remedies to protect women from slipping into poverty because of divorce.[194] The majority dismissed the case because it occurred before the coming into force of the Optional Protocol to CEDAW. In *Kell v Canada* a majority of the Committee found that the failure by public housing authorities to notify Kell that her common law partner had illegally taken her name off the registry of their communal home was in violation of CEDAW.[195] Unfortunately, the Committee makes no recommendations on how to improve the structure of property registration to ensure other women do not lose their property rights.

D. The Participation Dimension

The participation dimension requires that the voices of women who live in poverty be meaningfully heard. To achieve gender equality, it is imperative that women in poverty participate in both political processes and within the social community. The Committee has made strides towards using this dimension of transformative equality in relation to gender-based poverty, but there is room for further development.

(i) Gender-Based Poverty & Economic and Social Life

The Committee recommends that any solution to gender-based poverty requires the participation of women. For example, Kenya has been encouraged to 'ensure the participation of women in the development programmes ... aimed at alleviating and reducing poverty among women'.[196]

---

[191] 'Concluding Observations: Norway' (n 45) [38(c)].
[192] *BJ v Germany* (2004) CEDAW/C/36/D/1/2003.
[193] ibid, see Individual Opinions of Committee members Krisztina Morvai and Meriem Belmihoub-Zerdani (dissenting).
[194] ibid.
[195] *Kell v Canada* (2012) CEDAW/C/51/D/19/2008 [10.1]–[10.11].
[196] ibid [36].

Argentina has been urged to 'include and involve women in the process of economic, financial, political and social reconstruction'.[197] As a further example, which also emphasises the recognition dimension, the Committee has recommended that Mexico include 'women's participation not only as beneficiaries but also as agents of change in the development process'.[198]

(ii) Civil and Political Rights

In the General Recommendation on women's participation in public life the Committee identifies gender-based poverty as a barrier to greater participation.[199] Yet as mentioned above, in the Concluding Observations, the Committee has only a limited understanding of how gender-based poverty is an obstacle to women's civil and political rights. When reviewing Mexico, the Committee identified indigenous women as disproportionately poor but when recommending the state increase the participation of indigenous women in public life made no reference to financial barriers.[200] Two outliers are from Ethiopia and Jordan. In Ethiopia, in 2009, Committee was concerned that limited financial resources impede women's participation in public life (Article 7) and recommended that the state allocate a higher budget for women's candidates to support their voices in the political process.[201] In Jordan, the Committee recommended free childcare so that neither care work nor the cost of childcare would prevent women from being able to become involved in political life.[202]

(iii) Economic and Social Rights

Participation in employment and improving women's position in the labour market necessarily draws on the participation dimension of transformative equality. In post-conflict rebuilding the Committee advocates that women be included in designing new economic opportunities.[203] In Canada, poor water and sanitation conditions are major barriers to indigenous women's economic empowerment, and the Committee has called on the state to actively engage with indigenous women in water systems management (Article 13).[204] The Committee routinely calls upon states to ensure women participate in the design of rural development programmes (Article 14).

---

[197] 'Concluding Observations: Argentina' (n 26) [368].
[198] 'Concluding Observations: Mexico' (n 33) [434].
[199] 'General Recommendation No 23: on Women in Political Life' (n 50) [45(c)].
[200] 'Concluding Observations: Mexico' (n 175) [22]–[23], [34].
[201] 'Concluding Observations: Ethiopia' (n 39) [26]–[27].
[202] 'Concluding Observations: Jordan' (n 71) [32].
[203] 'General Recommendation No 30: on Conflict Prevention, Conflict and Post-Conflict' (n 36) [52(b)].
[204] 'Concluding Observations: Canada' (n 24) [47(b)].

This is explained below in greater detail when assessing how the Committee approaches the interaction between the four dimensions of transformative equality. For the other substantive economic and social provisions, the Committee is not developing the participation dimension. In respect of education, the Committee is not requiring states to ensure the participation of women and girls. For example, there are no requirements that states consult with women, girls or parents in understanding why girls drop out of school, the design and placement of schools, the school curriculum, safety or infrastructure, or how best to structure financial incentives to ensure girls complete their education.

E. The Interaction between the Four Dimensions of Transformative Equality

One of the strengths of the four-dimensional model of equality is that the dimensions can be 'used to buttress one another and better address the weakness of each'.[205] Repeatedly, the Committee draws on multiple dimensions to diagnose and remedy the harms of gender-based poverty. As highlighted above, the Committee recommends that poverty reduction programmes targeted towards material disadvantage must also recognise women as empowered agents and not re-entrench gender recognition harms. Migrant women often do not possess identify documents due to discriminatory power structures in their state of origin, and drawing on the recognition dimension, the Committee warns that the state officials in the state of destination should not presume migrant women are less credible because of their lack of documentation.[206] To redress customary social laws and norms that limit women's ability to inherit and own land, using the participation element the Committee has encouraged Tanzania to foster dialogue between women's organisations and traditional leaders to reform the law.[207] In Canada, the Committee has noted that it is the interaction between disadvantaged socioeconomic conditions and prejudice in the criminal justice system that increases indigenous women's risk of violence. Its recommendations to Canada are a synthesis of the four dimensions: poverty reduction programmes (structural) that target indigenous women (disadvantage), awareness training for police and justice officials (recognition), and the full participation of indigenous women in all efforts to combat violence (participation).[208]

---

[205] Fredman, 'Revisited' (n 10) 734.
[206] The Committee, 'General Recommendation No 32: on Gender-Related Dimensions of Refugee Status, Asylum, Nationality and Statelessness of Women' (2014) CEDAW/C/GC/32 [43].
[207] *ES and SC* (n 151).
[208] 'Inquiry Procedure: Canada' (n 12) [218].

The problem with the Committee's approach, however, is that it does not consistently draw upon the interaction between all four dimensions of transformative equality when assessing how gender-based poverty acts as an obstacle to the obligations in CEDAW. For instance, it could make a stronger link between the recognition and structural dimensions in respect of unpaid care work. A comparative examination of the Committee's assessment of rural women (Article 14) and equal access to healthcare (Article 12) highlights these inconsistencies. It also showcases the Committee's use of an equality framework to understand the impact of gender-based poverty and at the same time, the work still to be done to fully conceptualise gender-based poverty as a facet of equality and non-discrimination in CEDAW.

(i) Rural Women

The Committee repeatedly draws on all of the dimensions of the transformative equality framework to understand how gender-based poverty impacts the human rights of rural women. Article 14 of CEDAW requires states to ensure to rural women the right to participate in planning, to healthcare, to benefit for social security, to obtain training and education, to organise cooperatives, to participate in community activities, to access agricultural credit, equal treatment in land reforms, and to enjoy an adequate living conditions, particularly in relation to housing, sanitation, electricity, water, transport and communications. One of the reasons for not including an explicit substantive provision on gender-based poverty, as argued in Chapter 2, was that at the time of drafting gender-based poverty was equated with rural women in the global South. As a consequence, crucial elements necessary to tackle gender-based poverty were only guaranteed to rural women. The legacy of this original conception is seen in two ways: first, in the Concluding Observations there is no connection drawn between gender-based poverty and rural women in developed countries. Second, in General Recommendation No 34 on the rights of rural women the Committee predominantly focuses on rural women in the developing world, although it does acknowledge that indigenous and migrant rural women in developed countries face similar challenges as their counterparts in developing countries.[209]

The Committee notes that rural women are among the most disadvantaged and are disproportionately poor.[210] The Committee carefully analyses the many areas of public and private life where rural women are disadvantaged. It notes that the state often fails to acknowledge the role of rural women and their contribution to sustainable development. As a result,

---

[209] 'General Recommendation No 34: on Rights of Rural Women' (n 37) [88]–[92].
[210] ibid [5]; 'Concluding Observations: Romania' (n 41) [30].

'bilateral and multilateral agreements on trade, tax and other economic and fiscal policies can have a significant negative impact on the lives of rural women'.[211] The type of work rural women perform is usually low skilled and low or unpaid and is regularly excluded from labour codes and social security legislation.[212] Rural women face increased health risks by being exposed to fertilisers and pesticides.[213] The impact of sociocultural norms and limited access to financial credit can be seen in the small number of rural women who own land.[214] The lack of services, such as clean drinking water and adequate sanitation, exposes women to violence and prevents them from going to school.[215] The disadvantage, recognition and structural dimensions of transformative equality are also used to highlight the obstacles poor rural women face throughout their lives. Due to limited household budgets, families may not invest in girls' education, condemning women to illiteracy. Being illiterate significantly reduces women's ability to own land.[216] A similar structural impediment is that land registers often only allow for one name, reducing the chance of women being landowners.[217] Lastly, the participation element is used to draw to the state's attention that women are routinely excluded from the design of development policies and are underrepresented in agricultural and land organisations.[218]

Transformative equality is also used to remedy gender-based poverty for rural women. Mexico is encouraged to use targeted temporary special measures with regard to land, property and basic social services.[219] Similarly, both Ethiopia and Argentina have been encouraged to provide training and credit facilities for women farmers.[220] States also need to develop programmes to increase rural women's financial literacy.[221] The Committee has encouraged the Philippines to eliminate income discrimination against rural women by setting a living wage and paying attention to the informal sector.[222] Jordan has been urged to address negative attitudes that

---

[211] 'General Recommendation No 34: on Rights of Rural Women' (n 37) [10].

[212] ibid [40].

[213] ibid [46].

[214] 'Concluding Observations: Ethiopia' (n 39) [36]; 'Concluding Observations: Kenya' (n 25) [41].

[215] 'General Recommendation No 34: on Rights of Rural Women' (n 37) [42].

[216] T Hanstad et al, 'Land and Livelihoods Making Land Rights Real for India's Rural Poor' (UN Food and Agricultural Organisation, 2004) ch 3.4.

[217] The World Bank, 'Rural Land Certification in Ethiopia Empowers Women', web.worldbank.org/WBSITE/EXTERNAL/TOPICS/EXTGENDER/0,contentMDK:22836986~pagePK:210058~piPK:210062~theSitePK:336868,00.html.

[218] 'General Recommendation No 34: on Rights of Rural Women' (n 37) [53].

[219] 'Concluding Observations: Mexico' (n 175) [35].

[220] 'Concluding Observations: Ethiopia' (n 39) [37(b)]; 'Concluding Observations: Argentina' (n 34) [42]; 'General Recommendation No 34: on Rights of Rural Women' (n 37) [52].

[221] 'General Recommendation No 34: on Rights of Rural Women' (n 37) [68].

[222] 'Concluding Observations: The Philippines' (n 60) [44(b)].

impact rural women's ability to own land. Applying the recognition and structural dimensions of transformative equality, the Committee recommended that Turkey adopt gender-sensitive development strategies for rural development.[223] To change patriarchal land structures, Kenya has been urged to increase women's access to fertile land and income-generating projects and to 'establish a clear legislative framework to protect women's rights to inheritance and ownership of land'.[224] Both Argentina and Kenya have been called upon to strengthen and encourage rural women's participation in decision-making processes.[225] In General Recommendation No 34 on the rights of rural women, drawing on the disadvantage and structural dimensions, the Committee recommends that the informal rural sector have access to non-contributory social protection, and that macroeconomic policies, trade agreements and management of natural resources should be targeted towards improving the lives of rural women.[226] To promote the active participation of women in rural life, the Committee, using the recognition dimension, recommends that states address unequal gender power relations in decision-making processes[227] and support rural women's collective bargaining power.[228]

(ii) Health

In comparison, the Committee is erratic in its approach to gender-based poverty and equal access to healthcare (Article 12). The one exception to this trend is the Committee's approach to affordable contraception, which it consistently advocates for.[229] In the Inquiry Procedure into the ban on accessing modern contraception in Manila, the Philippines, the Committee has repeatedly stressed that the ban disproportionately impacts economically disadvantaged women and drives them further into poverty.[230] It further notes that banning modern contraception can have grievous implications for poor women's health and increases their risk to maternal mortality and sexually transmitted infections. Using the disadvantage dimension, the Committee recommends that the Philippines address women's need for contraception, focusing on economically disadvantaged women, by ensuring affordable sexual and reproductive health services. It further encourages the

---

[223] 'Concluding Observations: Turkey' (n 75) [37].
[224] 'Concluding Observations: Kenya' (n 25) [42].
[225] ibid; 'Concluding Observations: Argentina' (n 34) [42].
[226] 'General Recommendation No. 34: on Rights of Rural Women' (n 37) [11]; [41].
[227] ibid [54(c)].
[228] ibid [46]; [52(d)]
[229] ibid [38]; 'Concluding Observations: Romania' (n 18) [181].
[230] The Committee, 'Report of the Inquiry Concerning the Philippines of the Committee on the Elimination of Discrimination Against Women under Article 8 of OP-CEDAW' (2015) CEDAW/C/OP.8/PHI/1 [13].

state to 'consider expanding the public health insurance system to cover the costs of modern contraceptive methods'.[231]

Beyond affordable access to contraception, there is no sustained assessment of how gender-based poverty can undermine women's right to health. In Argentina, the Committee has noted that low-income women have limited access to mental health services, but its recommendations are broad: adopt a strategy on mental health and it makes no reference to the link between gender-based poverty and healthcare.[232] It notes that women have limited access to health services and that there are unacceptably high rates of maternal mortality, but it only recommends that states improve access and reduce maternal mortality.[233] No connection is drawn between maternal mortality and gender-based poverty despite the fact that poverty is a significant contributing factor to maternal mortality.[234] This is also exemplified in the case of *Teixeira*, mentioned above and discussed in Chapter 4, concerning a poor, rural Afro-Brazilian woman who died in childbirth. The Committee has not fully integrated gender-based poverty into its analysis of the claim.

More recently, in General Recommendation No 34 on the rights of rural women, from 2016, the Committee assesses how rural health systems may have insufficient budgets, prevailing social norms may restrict rural women's access to health services, and health centres may lack infrastructure, trained personnel and transport.[235] This is further evidence that the Committee is still equating gender-based poverty with rural women in the developing world. It urges states to improve the quality of care and ensure adequate financing of healthcare.[236] However, without explicitly articulating and using an equality framework, the Committee still overlooks aspects of the relationship between gender-based poverty and health. The recognition dimension directs the Committee to urge states to improve negative stereotypes on gender-based poverty that affect the location, funding and staffing of healthcare services for women. It also requires states to investigate how household poverty may result in family resources not being used to ensure women and girls' health.[237] The participation dimension can be used to recommend that states consult with all relevant stakeholders. Incorporating women's voices in the structure of health policies will also ensure that they are responsive to women's actual needs and contribute to more effective implementation.

---

[231] ibid [52(a)].

[232] 'Concluding Observations: Argentina' (n 35) [35]–[36].

[233] 'Concluding Observations: Canada' (n 23) [41]–[42]; 'Concluding Observations: Ethiopia' (n 39) [32(a)].

[234] UN Special Rapporteur on the right to health, 'The Right to the Highest Standard of Health: Reduction of Maternal Mortality' (2006) A/61/338 [10], [28(b)].

[235] 'General Recommendation No 34: on Rights of Rural Women' (n 37) [37].

[236] ibid [38(a)]–[38(b)].

[237] 'Sixth and Seventh Periodic Reports State Parties: Ethiopia' (2009) CEDAW/C/ETH/6–7 [140].

III. EVALUATIVE DISCUSSION

There is a marked evolution in the Committee's engagement with gender-based poverty. After an initial uncertainty, the Committee now routinely analyses how gender-based poverty limits women's human rights and proposes recommendations to address this obstacle. Using the four-dimensional model as an analytical mapping tool also provides strong evidence that the Committee is embracing the interpretation of CEDAW proposed in Chapter 4. This multilevel framework allows a critical and in-depth insight into the extent that the Committee has understood the intricate web between gender-based poverty, equality and human rights. Rather than approaching gender-based poverty as a ground of discrimination or interpreting a specific right in CEDAW to account for gender-based poverty, the Committee is implicitly using an equality and non-discrimination framework to understand the complex human rights challenges intrinsic in gender-based poverty. It repeatedly, albeit not as consistently as would be desired, uses the different dimensions of equality to diagnose the harms of gender-based poverty and draws on the dimensions to craft recommendations.

This mapping exercise also shows that there are multiple levels of inconsistency. First, the analysis and insights the Committee demonstrates in the General Recommendations are not always drawn upon and applied to states in CEDAW's other accountability mechanisms. For instance, the Committee does identify how gender-based poverty limits women's participation in public life and the role of nationality in the General Recommendations, but a similar analysis is often absent from the Concluding Observations, Inquiry Procedure and Individual Communications. Second, there are also inconsistencies in the Committee's approach to different states. A good example is the Committee's irregular treatment of diagnosing how gender-based poverty forces women into exploitative prostitution. While recognising these links in the Philippines, Jordan, Kenya and Romania, it completely ignores them in Bangladesh, Egypt, Turkey and Mexico. Third, the Committee's understanding of gender-based poverty as an issue of equality and non-discrimination is not sustained across all of the obligations in CEDAW. It draws on all four elements of transformative equality to remedy rural gender-based poverty: states are recommended to use temporary special measures to train women's farmers, to improve cultural attitudes on women owning land, protect women's inheritance and ownership, and to encourage women's participation in all aspects of rural life. On the other hand, the Committee does not meaningfully engage with how women in poverty experience denials of healthcare.

Turning to each of the four dimensions, the Committee expresses concern that women are disproportionately disadvantaged by poverty; it demonstrates an acute awareness of the gender pay gap, gender job segregation, and unregulated domestic and informal work that disadvantages women and perpetuates gender-based poverty; and that excluding care work from the calculation of resources in the dissolution of family relations economically disadvantages women. Using temporary special measures and targeted recommendations, the Committee draws upon the disadvantage dimension of transformative equality to urge states to remedy gender-based poverty. However, without explicitly articulating gender-based poverty as a facet of equality and non-discrimination, the Committee falls into remedial pitfalls. Its recommendations on gender-based poverty and education are broad and it does not recommend that states address the role of gender-based poverty in contributing to early forced marriage.

With respect to the recognition dimension, the Committee highlights how negative cultural stereotypes result in women predominating in traditionally female areas of education and that these attitudes impact on women's disadvantage in employment and decision-making in public and private life. It habitually identifies how the nexus of gender and other identity characteristics exacerbates gender-based poverty but it is not consistent in proposing recommendations to address intersectional gender-based poverty. A similar irregular pattern emerges in the Committee's treatment of gender-based poverty and gender-based violence. The Committee does assess the impact of gender-based poverty in the murder and forced disappearance of women in Mexico and Canada, but only in relation to Canada does it propose recommendations to address the abhorrent poverty of indigenous women. The Committee is alert to how poverty reduction programmes can perpetuate stereotypes of female dependency but it fails to assess how gender norms limit poor women's ability to access justice, underpin exploitative prostitution and trafficking, and dictate that women perform a disproportionate amount of unpaid care work. Further, it completely ignores the unique set of recognition harms that are associated with gender-based poverty.

There is no sustained engagement with the structural dimension of transformative equality from a gender-based poverty perspective. As an encouraging trend, it does recognise and advocate that the state regulate domestic and informal work and recognise de facto relationships to protect women from the negative economic consequences of relationship breakdown. While the Committee is demonstrating greater attention to the structural barriers in the justice system that act against women in poverty, it is only in relation to Canada that the Committee analyses the structure of social assistance benefits or poverty reduction programmes. The Committee is similarly inconsistent in advocating for women's participation to ameliorate poverty. The Committee does encourage states to guarantee the participation of women in the design of poverty alleviation strategies but makes no recommendation on the participation of women in education or on assessing the role of gender-based poverty in limiting women's participation in public life.

IV. CONCLUSION

In the absence of substantive provisions, the Committee is implicitly using an equality and non-discrimination framework to interpret gender-based poverty into CEDAW. While this is not binding authority for the interpretation in Chapter 4, the Committee's interpretation of CEDAW does have significant practical importance. At the same time, mapping the Committee's approach to gender-based poverty reveals that there are also gaps and inconsistencies in how it engages with gender-based poverty. This indicates that the Committee is still grappling to explicitly articulate a coherent approach to gender-based poverty. To unlock the potential of CEDAW and the Committee so that they can act as legal, political and cultural focal points on human rights approaches to gender-based poverty, it is necessary to explore these gaps. Chapter 6 seeks to identify how the blockages in the Committee's working methods can be corrected to ensure a more consistent approach, while Chapters 7 and 8 considers how to draw together and expand the Committee's understanding of gender-based poverty.

6

The Working Methods of the Committee

THE HUMAN RIGHTS abuses in gender-based poverty are so innate that the Committee, despite CEDAW's silence, has a respectable record of using the substantive provisions in the treaty to engage states on gender-based poverty. Without articulating the legal basis for using CEDAW to address gender-based poverty, however, the Committee is not able to consistently grasp the complex nuances of gender-based poverty. A careful analysis of the Committee's work in Chapter 5 demonstrates that it has not yet fully addressed the connections between gender-based poverty and civil and political rights. Nor has it comprehensively approached the recognition and structural harms that underpin gender-based poverty. As a further layer of inconsistency, the Committee engages in a sustained assessment of gender-based poverty when reviewing certain states, individual claims, and inquiries into grave and systemic abuses of CEDAW, but is practically silent when reviewing others. The first part of the book, using the established rules of international interpretation, provides a firm foundation for bringing gender-based poverty into the treaty regime. By providing a clear understanding of the interpretative basis for gender-based poverty in CEDAW, it is hoped that the Committee can approach this issue in a more coherent and consistent manner. Furthermore, interpreting gender-based poverty as a facet of equality and non-discrimination in CEDAW provides a rich analytical framework for the Committee to use when assessing the polycentric web of human rights violations experienced by women in poverty.

This is only the first step. It is also crucial to consider how the treaty's accountability mechanism can be calibrated and used to account for the harms of gender-based poverty. After all, one of the strongest arguments in favour for using human rights law to address gender-based poverty is that states are accountable for their laws, policies and programmes that perpetuate gender-based poverty. It is evident, from the analysis in Chapter 5, that there are gaps in using CEDAW's accountability mechanisms to address gender-based poverty that have to be overcome. There are many potential factors that explain the Committee's multiple points of inconsistency towards gender-based poverty. For instance, the Committee may be engaging with gender-based poverty in response to the overwhelming scale of gender-based poverty in the state. A good example of this is the Committee's prolonged discussion on gender-based poverty in Argentina after the collapse of the economy in the early 2000s.[1] A desire to keep good relations and encourage the state to continue to participate in the international system could also explain why the Committee vigorously presses one state on gender-based poverty and only gives it passing treatment with another state. International comity may also explain why the Committee often uses broad language in relation to gender-based poverty or why it identifies gender-based poverty as an obstacle to a substantive provision of CEDAW but then fails to propose a targeted recommendation. Since the membership of the Committee changes over time, the differences may also be the result of the influence of individual Committee members who could be focused on other issues or could be acting as passionate advocates on gender-based poverty.[2] The intention in this chapter is not to investigate how *realpolitik* influences the development of international human rights law. International relations and the politics of the international human rights system are highly transient and can shift depending on global events and even the personalities of international policy-makers. Thus, an investigation into *realpolitik* is not helpful for proposing solutions for the evolution of CEDAW. The focus here is to isolate one vital factor: the Committee's working methods and procedures. How does the Committee's engagement with states, civil society organisations (CSOs) and individuals impact its assessment of gender-based poverty? And how can the Committee best respond to any gender-based poverty blind spots that exist in its working methods? In contrast to other factors influencing the development of CEDAW, examining the Committee's working methods and procedures highlights where reforms are needed and leads to forward looking proposals that can more strongly tap into the potential of CEDAW to tackle gender-based poverty.

The aim of the chapter is to identify how the submissions and evidence before the Committee can influence its assessment of gender-based poverty. Ideally the case study in this chapter would investigate the process for each of the Committee's accountability mechanisms: the Concluding Observations, Individual Communications, Inquiry Procedure and General Recommendations. For pragmatic reasons, it only examines the periodic reporting process. The process for drafting General Recommendations,

---

[1] The Committee, 'Concluding Observations: Argentina' (2002) A/57/38 [340]–[345].

[2] See E Evatt, 'Finding a Voice for Women's Rights: The Early Days of CEDAW' (2002–03) 34 *George Washington International Law Review* 515, 524 for a historical assessment of the influence of individual Committee members.

Individual Communications and the Inquiry Procedure are not as transparent as would be desired. This makes it extremely difficult to trace how the Committee's working methods influence its treatment of gender-based poverty in these forums and it is near impossible to draw any meaningful conclusions. For the periodic reporting process, however, multiple stages of the process are publicly available so it is possible to pinpoint the role that the working methods and different actors play in influencing the Committee's discussions on gender-based poverty in the Concluding Observations. The conclusions from the assessment of the periodic reporting process have positive spillover effects and point towards reforms that could ensure the Committee fully engages with gender-based poverty in all of its accountability structures.

A case study of the periodic reporting process given in Sections I and II of this chapter demonstrates that the Committee is highly reactive to the submissions of states and CSOs. Although there are various instances where the Committee can ask questions on gender-based poverty, there is very little evidence that it takes a probing approach when states or CSOs have not first raised the issue. To ensure a more consistent and coherent approach, it is crucial for the Committee to signal to states and CSOs the importance of providing information on gender-based poverty. This is slightly paradoxical. The Committee needs to indicate the significance of gender-based poverty, so that states and CSOs provide critical evidence on the human rights impact of gender-based poverty, which in turn will ensure that the Committee remains alive to this issue throughout the accountability process. Over the course of this chapter and the next two chapters, I propose how best to engage states and CSOs so as to sharpen the Committee's approach and improve CEDAW's ability to hold states to account for gender-based poverty. The results of the case study point towards: (i) reforming the state reporting guidelines and (ii) releasing a General Recommendation on women and poverty. Section III of this chapter focuses on reforms to the periodic reporting process to ensure that the Committee consistently approaches gender-based poverty as an aspect of equality and non-discrimination. As the General Recommendation is CEDAW's high-profile accountability mechanism, the final two chapters consider the purpose of this forum and best practices for structuring an authoritative General Recommendation. While reforming the periodic reporting guidelines can influence the discussion on gender-based poverty in the Concluding Observations, a General Recommendation that exclusively focuses on gender-based poverty can positively feed into the Concluding Observations as well as the Individual Communications and Inquiry Procedure. These combined proposals signal to individuals, CSOs and states that gender-based poverty is a facet of equality and non-discrimination in CEDAW and prompts these actors to take a critical perspective on the human rights of women in poverty.

I. MAPPING GENDER-BASED POVERTY AND THE COMMITTEE

A case study is the optimal diagnostic tool to uncover the role that the Committee's working methods in the periodic reporting process play in its understanding of gender-based poverty in the Concluding Observations.[3] By comparing select outputs with diverging approaches to gender-based poverty, a case study allows us to focus on the intricacies of the Committee's process and shed light on where blockages exist. The aim is to build a theory on how the working methods of the periodic reporting process explain the layers of inconsistencies in the Concluding Observations identified in Chapter 5. While a case study this small does not permit sweeping generalisations on the role of the working methods it does give a clear sense of the steps the Committee needs to adopt to comprehensively use CEDAW's commitment to non-discrimination and equality to combat gender-based poverty.[4] The material used in the case study captures the Committee's disparate assessment of gender-based poverty. It looks at the periodic reporting process for Canada[5] and Ethiopia,[6] where gender-based poverty is frequently referred to in the Concluding Observations, and Jordan[7] and Turkey,[8] where there are comparatively limited references. The brief assessment below of how these Concluding Observations approach gender-based poverty serves as the basis for analysis in Section II.

The Committee has repeatedly called to Canada and Ethiopia's attention how gender-based poverty prevents women from enjoying their rights. There is a marked degree of similarity on the aspects of gender-based poverty that are highlighted in the Concluding Observations for Canada and Ethiopia. The Committees has noted that the cost of tertiary education in Canada prevents indigenous, Afro-Canadian and rural women from attending,[9] and in Ethiopia, the Committee has observed that poor girls have limited access to primary and secondary school due to 'the economic and socio-cultural barriers, such as indirect costs of schooling'.[10] In both Canada and Ethiopia, the Committee has investigated the connection between gender-based poverty and employment, noting that there is persistent gender wage gap in Canada that affects women's careers and pensions; the concentration of

---

[3] W Schramm, 'Notes on Case Studies of Instructional Media Projects', Working Paper for the Academy for Educational Development, Washington DC (1971), quoted in R Yin, *Case Study Research: Design and Methods*, 4th edn (Sage, 2013) 15.

[4] J Gerring, *Case Study Research: Principles and Practice* (Cambridge University Press, 2007) 76.

[5] The Committee, 'Concluding Observations: Canada' (2016) CEDAW/C/CAN/CO/8–9.

[6] The Committee, 'Concluding Observations: Ethiopia' (2011) CEDA/C/ETH/CO/6–7.

[7] The Committee, 'Concluding Observations: Jordan' (2017) CEDAW/C/JOR/CO/6.

[8] The Committee, 'Concluding Observations: Turkey' (2010) CEDAW/C/TUR/CO/6.

[9] 'Concluding Observations: Canada' (n 5) [36(b)].

[10] 'Concluding Observations: Ethiopia' (n 6) [30].

women in part-time and low-paid jobs; and working permits for migrant women that chain them to their employers.[11] The Committee has expressed concern that Ethiopian women are engaged in unpaid family work; segregated in low-paying jobs often without access to social protection; and have limited access to land and credit.[12] In both Concluding Observations the Committee has discussed the extraterritorial aspects of gender-based poverty, which is likely evidence of nascent evolution of CEDAW as there is no reference to extraterritoriality in the treaty. Foreign companies in Ethiopia are leasing vast areas of arable land which displaces the rural population and 'further contributes to women's food insecurity and the feminisation of poverty'.[13] Canadian foreign companies when operating abroad violate the rights of local women.[14] For both states, the Committee has pinpointed aspects of family life that perpetuate gender-based poverty. In Ethiopia, women often do not inherit because it is assumed they will move to their husband's home and that upon widowhood or divorce a woman loses any rights in property,[15] and in Canada child support 'does not accurately reflect the reality of time and cost allocation between parents'.[16]

There is not perfect congruence in the Concluding Observations for Canada and Ethiopia. There is a sustained discussion on access to justice and gender-based poverty in Canada. Financial assistance for legal aid has been drastically reduced; income testing for civil legal aid is limited to only the poorest women and denies justice to low-income women; and the newly reinstated federal programme that develops the Canadian constitution does not focus on the links between poverty and civil, political and socioeconomic rights.[17] There is no assessment on access to justice from a gender-based poverty perspective for Ethiopia. The Committee has drawn to Canada's attention that indigenous women live in poverty and have limited access to education, healthcare, employment opportunities, affordable housing and clean water.[18] It has also expressed concern that women, especially single mothers and indigenous, Afro-Canadian, migrant, disabled and elderly women, experience high levels of poverty.[19] It calls on Canada to incorporate an intersectional gender perspective into its national poverty plan. The Committee has not investigated the intersectional aspects of gender-based poverty in Ethiopia. In Canada, there is a lack of affordable childcare and

---

[11] 'Concluding Observations: Canada' (n 5) [38].
[12] 'Concluding Observations: Ethiopia' (n 6) [32].
[13] ibid [36].
[14] 'Concluding Observations: Canada' (n 5) [18]
[15] 'Concluding Observations: Ethiopia' (n 6) [40].
[16] 'Concluding Observations: Canada' (n 5) [52].
[17] ibid [14].
[18] ibid [46].
[19] ibid.

the high cost of housing impacts low-income women; again, neither of these issues has been discussed with respect to Ethiopia.[20] However, the Committee has expressed concern that Ethiopia has taken 'limited measures to address poverty as the root cause of trafficking'.[21] The Committee is also concerned that Ethiopian

> rural women depend on men for economic support, that only 19 per cent of women own land and that the number of women borrowers from microfinance institutions is decreasing ... that the majority of the rural population has no sustainable access to safe drinking water ... forcing many women and girls to walk long distances to collect water ... preventing girls from attending school.[22]

No similar assessment of gender-based poverty, trafficking, prostitution and rural women exists for Canada.

In comparison to Canada and Ethiopia, references to gender-based poverty in Jordan and Turkey are in passing and tend to focus on a narrow subset of issues. For both Turkey and Jordan, the Committee has touched upon systemic issues: unequal pay, women's segregation in low-paid work and high rates of unemployment.[23] In Turkey, there are only two direct references to gender-based poverty. The Committee notes that women's economic dependence contributes to their poor health[24] and that disadvantaged women—Kurdish, ethnic, minority, migrant, elderly and disabled women—are more vulnerable to poverty.[25] In Jordan, the Committee's concerns on gender-based poverty almost exclusively focus on issues related to nationality and rural women. It has expressed concern that women in refugee camps live in insecure conditions and are deprived of education, economic opportunities and healthcare.[26] Refugee women in Jordan are entering into prostitution and early forced marriages for socioeconomic reasons. The Committee has expressed concern that migrant domestic workers are exploited at work,[27] and has highlighted that children of Jordanian women and foreign fathers are not able to access social services.[28] It has further noted that rural women face poverty, lack of access to health and social services and are often prevented from inheriting land due to discriminatory sociocultural attitudes.[29] A good example highlighting the Committee's

---

[20] ibid.

[21] 'Concluding Observations: Ethiopia' (n 6) [24].

[22] ibid [36].

[23] 'Concluding Observations: Turkey' (n 8) [32]; 'Concluding Observations: Jordan' (n 7) [43].

[24] 'Concluding Observations: Turkey (n 8) [34].

[25] ibid [38].

[26] 'Concluding Observations: Jordan' (n 7) [11].

[27] ibid [45].

[28] ibid [39].

[29] ibid [49].

diverging approaches to gender-based poverty in the Concluding Observations are its discussions on legal aid. It briefly observes in Jordan that there are inadequate legal aid services.[30] This is striking contrast to the robust assessment of the relationship between gender-based poverty and access to justice in Canada where the Committee looked at eligibility criteria and the remit of federally funded programmes.

II. A CASE STUDY ON THE COMMITTEE'S WORKING METHODS AND GENDER-BASED POVERTY

The detailed mapping of a small sample of the Committee's outputs in Section I is further evidence that the Committee has not yet adopted a consistent understanding of gender-based poverty. In the Concluding Observations for Canada and Ethiopia, the Committee grapples with the role of gender-based poverty in undermining women's rights, while for the Concluding Observations for Jordan and Turkey, the Committee either ignores gender-based poverty or only minimally engages with it. Even when the Committee is sensitive to gender-based poverty, there is limited consistency on the aspects it assesses. When reviewing Canada, it primarily examines gender-based poverty from an intersectional perspective, while with Ethiopia it draws out the connection between gender-based poverty and rural women, and with Jordan it focuses on the nexus between gender-based poverty and refugees.

Beginning with a brief description of the Committee's working methods for the periodic reporting process this section analyses the publically available material submitted for the latest periodic review for Canada, Ethiopia, Jordan and Turkey. These four states were reviewed in 2016, 2011, 2017 and 2010, respectively. This assessment reveals that the key factors for shaping the Committee's engagement with gender-based poverty in the Concluding Observations are state and CSO reports. The Committee can ask questions to gather information in the periodic reporting process, but the evidence indicates that it does not appear to substantially engage with gender-based poverty when it is not first raised by either states or CSOs. This is disconcerting as the Committee's silence can act as a powerful disincentive. To avoid criticisms from the Committee, a state may avoid reporting on gender-based poverty and there is no guarantee that CSOs will fill this knowledge gap. Thus, the findings of this case study are also a call to action. The Committee needs to take a stronger stance on gender-based poverty and ask more explicit questions even if state and CSO reports are silent.

---

[30] ibid [23].

A. Working Methods of the Periodic Reporting Process

Under Article 18 of CEDAW states are obligated to submit a report every four years detailing the measures the state has taken to implement CEDAW. The treaty gives the Committee complete discretion to develop its procedures.[31] Over the course of time, the Committee has developed a multilayered review process. The starting point is the *state report*, which is meant to paint 'a complete picture' of the situation of women in the state.[32] Alongside the state report, the state also submits a *common core document*. This document 'should contain information of a general and factual nature relating to the implementation of the treaties to which the reporting state is party and which may be of relevance to all or several treaty bodies'.[33] The Office of the High Commissioner of Human Rights and all of the UN treaty bodies, including the Committee, has provided reporting guidelines to assist the state in preparing these documents.

In order to enhance the effectiveness of the reporting process, 'the Committee designates from among its members a country rapporteur for the report of each state'.[34] The country rapporteur provides a briefing note, which is not publically available, pinpointing the key gender equality issues in the state. The template for the briefing note, however, is available on the Committee's website and does make reference to gender-based poverty. Under Article 13 (equality in economic and social life) the briefing note template directs the country rapporteur to ask: (i) whether 'development and anti-poverty strategies integrate a gender perspective and address specific needs of women'; (ii) what types of measures are in place to ensure women can access various forms of credit; (iii) and to explain the discrimination women face in accessing social benefits and pensions.[35] A sub-group of the Committee, the pre-session working group, drawing on the briefing note, then reviews the state and CSO reports.[36] This group draws up a *list of issues*, which is a series of targeted questions and not a comprehensive engagement with the state report.[37] The state is given an opportunity to provide a written response to these questions in the *state reply*.

---

[31] Art 19 CEDAW.
[32] Office of the High Commissioner of Human Rights (OHCHR), 'Compilation of Guidelines on the Form and Content of Report to be Submitted by State Parties to the International Human Rights Treaties, Report of the Secretary General' (2009) HRI/GEN/2/Rev.6 [3].
[33] ibid [27].
[34] ibid [5].
[35] The Committee, 'Report of the Committee on the Elimination of Discrimination against Women: 52nd, 53rd, and 54th Session—Annex II' (2013) A/68/38.
[36] ibid.
[37] The Committee, 'Overview of the Current Working Methods of the Committee on CEDAW' (2004) CEDAW/C/2004/1/4/Add.1 [6].

To offset any biases, factual inaccuracies or omissions in the state report, CSOs are encouraged to submit state-specific information to the pre-session working group.[38] There is no official recognition of CSOs in CEDAW, but there is now a well-established practice of drawing on *CSO reports* in the periodic reporting process. These reports serve as a counterweight to the state report and provide a critical perspective on the state's efforts to eliminate discrimination against women.[39] Given that the Committee has no fact-finding ability in the periodic reporting process, CSO reports have been described as an essential element to obtain an 'accurate picture of the human rights situation'.[40] Treaty bodies have explained that they could not 'function effectively if they were to disregard information that emanated from reliable and official sources'.[41] Unlike CSOs, there is formal recognition of the role of UN agencies in the reporting process. By Article 22 of CEDAW and the working methods of the Committee, other *UN agencies* are given the opportunity to contribute to the work of the Committee.[42] UN agencies can also submit material during closed sessions of the Committee.[43]

The last step is the oral dialogue session between the state representatives and the Committee. This is meant to be a constructive interaction. The session will try 'to focus on issues identified by the pre-session working group'[44] because only issues 'raised during the constructive dialogue are included in the Concluding Observations'.[45] Thus, it is vital at this last stage in the periodic reporting process that the Committee be cognisant of gender-based poverty and interrogate the state on this issue. The session is recorded in the *summary records* of the Committee. In closed session the Committee drafts the Concluding Observations.

As the Committee draws on numerous sources before releasing Concluding Observations, there are multiple instances where gender-based poverty can feed into the reporting process. Are there elements of this process that are more influential than others in directing the Committee towards evaluating

---

[38] ibid [30].

[39] J Whiteman, 'Lessons from Supervisory Mechanisms in International Regional Law' (2013) 26(3) *Journal of Refugee Studies* 360.

[40] L Theytaz-Bergman 'State Reporting and the Role of Non-Government Organisation' in A Bayesky (ed), *The UN Human Rights Treaty System in the 21st Century* (Kluwer Law International Publishers, 2000) cited in F Gaer, 'Implementing International Human Rights Norms: UN Human Rights Treaty Bodies and NGOs' (2002) 2(3) *Journal of Human Rights* 339, 348.

[41] C Medina, past Chair of the Human Rights Committee, 'UN Press Release' (26 March 2001) as cited in Gaer (n 40) 340.

[42] The Committee, 'Ways and Means of Expediting the Work of the Committee on the Elimination of Discrimination against Women' (2007) CEDAW/C/2007/I/4/Add.1 [34]–[37].

[43] The Committee, 'Report on the Committee on the Elimination of Discrimination Against Women: 55th Session' (2013) A/69/38, Decision 55/VII.

[44] 'Overview of Working Methods' (n 37) [12].

[45] ibid [18].

the impact of gender-based poverty? The next subsection analyses all these sources from the latest periodic reviews for Canada, Ethiopia, Jordan and Turkey and concludes that state and CSO reports are key elements behind gender-based poverty being included in the Concluding Observations.

B. Analysis of Material in the Periodic Reporting Process

(i) Common Core Document

The common core document does not appear to be an influential factor, which is perhaps not unsurprising as it is the only document in the process that is not written in direct response to the state's obligation to report on CEDAW. The Ethiopian common core document contains detailed information on gender-based poverty programmes, whereas the Canadian document contains only broad references to gender-based poverty. Nevertheless, the Committee engages with gender-based poverty to a similar degree in both Canada and Ethiopia.

The Ethiopian common core document explains the two key programmes aimed at reducing poverty among women: the Ethiopian Women's Development Fund (EWDF) and the Plan for Accelerated and Sustainable Development to End Poverty (PASDEP). The EWDF works to 'enable women ... to organise income generating activities with the view to alleviating their economical and social problems'.[46] Women are also central to the goals of the PASDEP. The document explains that: '[T]he Government has moved decisively to advance the agenda on the gender dimensions of poverty ... which forms the core of the gender strategy under PASDEP.'[47] This programme focuses on increasing the participation of girls and women in education, the labour market and political process and improving women's access to land, credit and other productive resources.[48] The common core document also provides statistical information on the real total per capita household consumption expenditure;[49] the national average of calories consumed;[50] the proportion of people below the poverty line;[51] and the food poverty line.[52] However, this information is not disaggregated for gender.[53]

---

[46] 'Core Document Forming Part of the Reports of State Parties: Ethiopia' (2008) HRI/CORE/ETH/2008 [200].
[47] ibid [207].
[48] ibid [205]–[06].
[49] ibid Annex II [2].
[50] ibid Annex II [3].
[51] ibid Annex II [7].
[52] ibid Annex II [11].
[53] ibid Annex II [7]–[13], [22]–[23].

The Canadian common core document does not provide a similar level of detail as the Ethiopian one on gender-based poverty. In three brief paragraphs it discusses women's status and concludes that 'women make up a disproportionate share of the population with low incomes and are much more likely than men to work part time'.[54] The steps Canada is taking to address these issues lack any degree of specification. Canada explains that it is aiming to measure how 'the impact of policies and programmes on women might differ from their impact on men'[55] and that it has identified increasing women's economic security and prosperity as a priority area.[56] No further information is provided. The document does explain how the state calculates the national poverty line, data on housing and food insecurity in Canada in the early 2000s and the anti-poverty programmes the state has developed including income security and family-related benefits.[57] Similar to Ethiopia, none of this information is disaggregated for gender.

The common core documents for Jordan and Turkey provide minimal information on gender-based poverty. The Jordanian document is woefully out of date as it was drafted in 1993 but was still submitted for the periodic review process in 2017. Even this arguably historical assessment of the conditions in Jordan contains no specific information on gender-based poverty.[58] The Turkish document notes, in a few words, that poverty reduction programmes are aimed at improving the conditions of several disadvantaged groups including women.[59]

(ii) The State Report

The state report is an influential element but not determinative. Both Canada and Ethiopia openly engage with gender-based poverty and the manner in which they do so is reflected in the Concluding Observations. A corresponding trend is evident in Jordan and Turkey. The few instances where these reports refer to gender-based poverty are reflected in the Concluding Observations.

The strong impression from reading the Canadian state report is that the state is making extensive efforts to improve the housing, employment and education opportunities, and health of Canadians. A closer reading shows

---

[54] 'Core Document Forming Part of the Reports of State Parties: Canada' (2013) HRI/CORE/CAN/2013 [181].

[55] ibid [182].

[56] ibid [183].

[57] ibid [8], [178].

[58] 'Core Document Form Part of the Reports of State Parties: Jordan' (1994) HRI/CORE/1/Add.18/Rev. 1.

[59] 'Core Document Forming Part of the Report of State Parties: Turkey' (2007) HRI/CORE/TUR/2007 [199]–[200].

that it often fails to appreciate the unique impact of gender. On the positive side, several of the provincial governments have programmes that 'help women in the receipt of income assistance upgrade skills and learn about possibilities in the trade and technology sector'[60] and are developing childcare services for low-income women.[61] To address the link between gender-based poverty and gender-based violence, the state is funding shelters in remote areas of northern Canada and investing C$200 million over five years in, inter alia, economic opportunities for indigenous women.[62] In the Concluding Observations, the Committee does build upon this information and addresses affordable childcare and the high rates of gender-based poverty among indigenous women. However, the majority of the state report does not provide a critical analysis on the measures the state is taking to combat the intersection of poverty and gender. It makes passing reference to maternity and parental leave, but provides no details on these programmes.[63] The state's plans for low-income housing contain no specific steps to address housing insecurity among women. Canada tries to justify this omission with a gendered 'trickle-down' effect. It explains that 'although data on affordable housing are not broken down by gender, government interventions for low income earners and [indigenous] communities benefit women'.[64] Moreover, the report can slip into a self-congratulatory tone. Canada celebrates that there is a small increase in the number of indigenous women obtaining a secondary and post-secondary education but efforts to increase educational attainments are not specifically targeted towards indigenous women.[65] The state is also inattentive to the intersection of race, gender and poverty with respect to indigenous women's employment. Canada does recognise that employment rates of indigenous women are trailing that of indigenous men and non-indigenous women but its efforts to provide skills training, employment opportunities and income assistance are targeted towards indigenous communities as a whole rather than specifically towards indigenous women.[66] The Concluding Observations point out these obvious shortcomings in the state report. The Committee has repeatedly called on Canada to target measures to address the gender-based poverty among women with intersecting identities and include a gender perspective in its national poverty plan and housing strategies. It is also important to note that the state report does not comprehensively engage with gender-based poverty and access to justice, a prominent issue in the Concluding Observations.

---

[60] 'Combined Eighth and Ninth Periodic Report State Parties: Canada' (2015) CEDAW/C/CAN/8-9 [170], [172].
[61] ibid [186], [193]–[194].
[62] ibid [117], [138].
[63] ibid [154].
[64] ibid [200].
[65] ibid [47], [49], [50]–[53], [156], [157].
[66] ibid [54]–[57].

Thus, while the state report guides the Committee, it is not the only factor explaining the inclusion of gender-based poverty in the Concluding Observations.

At the beginning of its report the Ethiopian government explains that: 'The National Poverty Reduction Strategy adopted by the Government was framed in such a way that accords due recognition to women's legitimate share in the country's overall development.'[67] The strategy accounts for women's particular needs and aims to improve girls' education, to provide water and to raise the standard of basic healthcare for women.[68] This initial engagement with gender-based poverty is sustained throughout the report. Unlike Canada, Ethiopia directly acknowledges that gender-based poverty is a serious and continuing obstacle for women and the report is closer to a critical assessment of the de facto situation. Ethiopia directly connects gender-based poverty to women's poor health. The report explains that the long distance from health facilities, the lack of financial resources to pay for transport and healthcare services, and women's heavy workloads limit their ability to access to healthcare.[69] Women's low economic status is also the cause of Ethiopia's high maternal mortality as families do not invest limited resources in obtaining skilled maternity care.[70] Ethiopia explains the measures taken to address these problems: emergency healthcare, family planning services, and prenatal, delivery and postnatal services are provided free of charge.[71] The report also emphasises that women are unable to access financial credit because of their inability to provide sufficient collateral to obtain a loan and institutional stereotypes against lending to women.[72] Ethiopia again explains the programmes it has implemented to remedy these structural barriers and negative attitudes.[73] Lastly, Ethiopia notes how rural women are overworked, that their labour is not recognised or remunerated.[74] The state explains how it is developing technologies to reduce the burden of household work on women. Similar to Canada, the Committee appears to be following the lead of the Ethiopian state report. The Committee, as explained above, makes references to poverty in relation to education, rural women and access to economic resources in the Concluding Observations. Again, however, there is not perfect symmetry between the state report and the Concluding Observations. The Ethiopian state report makes no reference to gender-based poverty and prostitution,

---

[67] 'Sixth and Seventh Periodic Reports State Parties: Ethiopia' (2009) CEDAW/C/ETH/6-7 [3].
[68] ibid.
[69] ibid [131].
[70] ibid [140].
[71] ibid [134].
[72] ibid [157].
[73] ibid [160]–[61].
[74] ibid [167].

but the Concluding Observations do draw this connection. The Concluding Observations do not refer to poverty as a contributing factor to maternal mortality, whereas the Ethiopian state report does.

The Jordan state report appears sceptical on the extent of gender-based poverty. It refers to women as living in geographical 'pockets of poverty', suggesting a perception that gender-based poverty is an isolated problem.[75] The Concluding Observations do not squarely challenge this characterisation as the only time they use the word 'poverty' is in relation to remote rural areas.[76] Implicitly, Jordan also seeks to justify the current gender inequalities by arguing that that the Syrian refugee situation has put unprecedented pressure on the state's resources.[77] Again, the Committee seems to accept this justification. At the beginning of the Concluding Observations it acknowledges that the conflicts in the region and the Syrian refugee crisis have resulted in a sharp increase in poverty in the state.[78] Jordan explains that Syrian girls enter into early forced marriage to improve their standard of living and to reduce their perceived financial burden on their families.[79] The steps detailed in the state report to combat this problem do not include addressing gender-based poverty. The report is also frustrating as it is misleading. All state reports can be criticised for mischaracterising their efforts, presenting half-truths or omitting certain facts. The Jordanian state report is a step beyond as it seems to approbate the efforts of CSOs. At first glance, there is an extensive and impressive assessment of the efforts taken to eliminate gender-based poverty. The report goes into great detail on the amount of interest- and collateral-free loans, the funds provided to support micro, small and medium enterprises, and development programmes to improve the lives of women in poverty.[80] The majority of these programmes and services are not provided by the state but by CSOs. Jordan even relies on the efforts of UN agencies in a report that is meant to be detailing the steps it has taken to implement CEDAW.[81] In reality the efforts Jordan is taking to redress gender-based poverty are largely confined to systemic issues around employment. The state repeatedly affirms its commitment to economically empower women. It explains that it is seeking to: increase women's participation in the labour market, widen the scope of social protection, put legislation in place to eliminate discrimination in pay, and expand the availability of childcare.[82] Jordan is also attentive to the vulnerability of

---

[75] 'Sixth Periodic Report State Party: Jordan' (2015) CEDAW/C/JOR/6 [65], [80], [95(g)], [99], [104].
[76] ibid [49].
[77] 'Concluding Observations: Jordan' (n 7) [6].
[78] ibid [7(b)].
[79] 'State Report: Jordan' (n 75) [12].
[80] ibid [95(a)]–[95(h)], [100]–[104].
[81] ibid [95]–[96].
[82] ibid [65].

domestic migrant workers. It provides details on the efforts of the Ministry of Labour, including regulating recruiting agencies and protecting working conditions.[83] Again, it is easy to detect the role of the state report in shaping the Concluding Observations, as the Committee expresses concerns on migrant domestic workers, employment and the socioeconomic link to early forced marriage among Syrian refugees. The remaining references to gender-based poverty in the state report are brief: assistance to girls for the indirect costs of schools;[84] free contraception but only after counselling;[85] assistance to rural women to improve their family's income and food security;[86] and its commitment to understand how trade agreements impact gender-based poverty.[87] The report concludes by explaining and justifying the different religious laws for inheritance for men and women.[88] This minimal engagement is echoed in the Concluding Observations, which make no mention of trade agreement, affordability of contraception or indirect costs of education, but do broadly refer to the poverty of rural woman and urge the state to apply substantive equality to personal laws.

There are very limited references to gender-based poverty in the Turkish state report. As an outlier, Turkey identifies gender-based poverty as an obstacle to the enjoyment of education,[89] and larger conditional cash transfers are given to families with girls than with boys to ensure girls stay in school.[90] Surprisingly, this issue is not addressed in the Concluding Observations. Other than this example, the report largely ignores gender-based poverty. In the few instances when the Turkish report refers to gender-based poverty it does not always explain what measures are being taken to reduce it. In comparison, when Ethiopia discusses gender-based poverty it consistently reports on remedial measures.[91] An exception to this trend is on women's health. The report notes that Turkish women cannot access health programmes because they do not have sufficient levels of economic independence.[92] However, the state is not working towards economically empowering women; rather it is creating programmes to bring health services into the home.[93] The state report's general silence on gender-based poverty is mirrored in the Concluding Observations, which is further evidence of the critical role of the state report.

---

[83] ibid [67].
[84] ibid [51].
[85] ibid [80].
[86] ibid [100].
[87] ibid [105].
[88] ibid [114].
[89] 'Sixth Periodic Report of State Parties: Turkey' (2008) CEDAW/C/TUR/6[35].
[90] ibid [18].
[91] 'Ethiopia State Report' (n 67) [135], [142]–[49].
[92] ibid[63].
[93] ibid.

(iii) CSO Reports

The CSO reports are a significant source in directing the Committee to consider gender-based poverty. This is most evident in Canada. The Canadian CSO reports overwhelmingly focus on gender-based poverty and are highly critical of the state's efforts. Of the twenty-seven CSO submissions to the Committee, sixteen refer to gender-based poverty. The CSO reports for Ethiopia, Jordan and Turkey do not engage with gender-based poverty to the same extent as Canada. However, even in the more limited instances where these reports do discuss gender-based poverty, the CSO observations tend to be incorporated into the Concluding Observations. This testifies to the importance of CSOs in the periodic reporting process and of the crucial need to prompt CSOs to report on gender-based poverty.

The Canadian CSO reports cluster around certain aspects of gender-based poverty. A large portion of the CSO reports from Canada discuss the high rates of poverty among indigenous and minority women. The CSO community stresses that indigenous women live with food insecurity, lack clean drinking water and are at high risk of violence.[94] Given the dire circumstances of indigenous women, the Native Women's Association of Canada and the Canadian Feminist Alliance for International Action (CFAIA) call the state to task for not developing a national plan to address gender-based poverty among indigenous women.[95] The Canadian state report, apart from indigenous women, makes limited reference to intersectional identities and gender-based poverty. The CSOs provide a richer and more critical analysis of the issue. They repeatedly emphasise that due to racial and gender stereotypes minority women are segregated into low-paid and precarious work which results in inordinately high levels of poverty for African Canadian, racialised immigrant and disabled women.[96] It also highlights that indigenous and minority women shoulder high levels of debt from tertiary education and due to the gender wage gap can have difficulty repaying

---

[94] Aboriginal Legal Services, 'CSO Report Submitted to Committee on the Elimination of Discrimination Against Women' (2016) http://tbinternet.ohchr.org/Treaties/CEDAW/Shared%20Documents/CAN/INT_CEDAW_NGO_CAN_25407_E.pdf; Human Rights Watch, 'Submission on the Combined 8th and 9th Periodic Reports of Canada' (2016) http://tbinternet.ohchr.org/Treaties/CEDAW/Shared%20Documents/CAN/INT_CEDAW_NGO_CAN_22842_E.pdf.
[95] 'Implementation of Recommendation from Article 8 Inquiry on Murdered and Missing Indigenous Women and Girls (2016) http://tbinternet.ohchr.org/Treaties/CEDAW/Shared%20Documents/CAN/INT_CEDAW_NGO_CAN_25418_E.pdf.
[96] African Canadian Legal Clinic, 'Report of African Canadian Legal Clinic' (2016) http://tbinternet.ohchr.org/Treaties/CEDAW/Shared%20Documents/CAN/INT_CEDAW_NGO_CAN_25429_E.pdf; Disabled Women's Network Canada, 'CEDAW Submission' (2016) http://tbinternet.ohchr.org/Treaties/CEDAW/Shared%20Documents/CAN/INT_CEDAW_NGO_CAN_25436_E.pdf; Metro Toronto Chinese & Southeast Asian Legal Clinic, 'The Colour of Poverty' (2016) http://tbinternet.ohchr.org/Treaties/CEDAW/Shared%20Documents/CAN/INT_CEDAW_NGO_CAN_25471_E.pdf.

these loans.[97] The concerns of CSOs are directly incorporated into the Concluding Observations. The Committee has expressed concerns that Afro-Canadian, indigenous, migrant and disabled women have higher rates of poverty, that there is no national poverty plan that incorporates an intersectional gender perspective, and that they are unable to access tertiary education and employment opportunities.

The CSOs report that the amount of social assistance available to women in Canada often results in them living below the national poverty line;[98] that there is a desperate lack of affordable childcare;[99] and that contraception and the new easy-to-use abortion pill are cost prohibitive for low-income women.[100] Amnesty, CFAIA and the Metro Toronto Chinese & Southeast Asian Law Clinic all stress that the closed work permits for migrant domestic workers tie them to their employers, leaving them vulnerable to abusive and exploitative working conditions.[101] There is a sustained discussion by CFAIA on the relationship between gender-based poverty and access to justice. It notes that funding cuts to civil legal aid, especially for family law, disproportionately affect women and that 'income criterion for legal aid is often below the poverty line [which] denies many women access to legal aid, restricting access to only those who live in deep poverty'.[102] The Canadian state report makes no reference to the newly reinstated, federally funded strategic litigation programme but CFAIA asks crucial questions on how it will be used to enhance women's rights. Amnesty and Earthrights International also discuss business, gender equality and poverty. Amnesty observes that the large-scale development of oil, gas and other natural resources has exacerbated gender-based poverty. The 'large number of workers attracted to the region is driving up local prices for essentials such as food and housing'. This pushes women, particularly indigenous women, into economically

[97] The Native Women's Association of Canada, 'Reply to Issue 17' (2016) http://tbinternet.ohchr.org/Treaties/CEDAW/Shared%20Documents/CAN/INT_CEDAW_NGO_CAN_25418_E.pdf; The Canadian Feminist Alliance for International Action (CFAIA), 'Reply to Issues 3, 4, 7, 8, 11, 12 & 13' (2016) http://tbinternet.ohchr.org/Treaties/CEDAW/Shared%20Documents/CAN/INT_CEDAW_NGO_CAN_25417_E.pdf.

[98] Canada Without Poverty, 'Submissions Raising Issues Related to Articles 2, 3, 11 and 14' (2016) http://tbinternet.ohchr.org/Treaties/CEDAW/Shared%20Documents/CAN/INT_CEDAW_NGO_CAN_25381_E.pdf; CFAIA (n 97).

[99] Coalition of Child Care Advocates of BC & West Coast LEAF, 'The Cornerstone of Equality for Canadian Women' (2016) http://tbinternet.ohchr.org/Treaties/CEDAW/Shared%20Documents/CAN/INT_CEDAW_NGO_CAN_25388_E.pdf.

[100] Action on Canada for Sexual Health & Rights, 'Submission to CEDAW' (2016) <http://tbinternet.ohchr.org/Treaties/CEDAW/Shared%20Documents/CAN/INT_CEDAW_NGO_CAN_22744_E.pdf.

[101] CFAIA (n 97); Metro Toronto (n 96); Amnesty International, 'Canada' (2016) http://tbinternet.ohchr.org/Treaties/CEDAW/Shared%20Documents/CAN/INT_CEDAW_NGO_CAN_25352_E.pdf.

[102] CFAIA (n 97).

precarious conditions.[103] Earthrights International is concerned that Canadian mining companies operating in Latin America are undermining the human rights of the poor women.[104] While not all of these issues are discussed in the Concluding Observations, a vast majority are touched upon. It is also interesting to note that the Canadian CSOs demonstrate a sophisticated understanding of gender equality and poverty and appear to be adopting the interpretation of CEDAW proposed in Chapter 4. Several reports point out that poverty creates gender inequality and that women's poverty is a result of gender relations.[105]

A similar trend is evident in Jordan. The CSO reports focus on a small set of gender-based poverty issues that are often included in the Concluding Observations, especially on the situation of Syrian and Palestinian refugees. Numerous CSOs comment on the need to economically empower women refugees.[106] They argue that the state needs to provide employment and education opportunities for women. The lack of such opportunities and the desire to ease a family's poverty is forcing girls into early marriage.[107] There is evidence that women and girls fleeing Syria often do not have formal identity documents and as a result are forced into the informal economy which is precarious and poorly paid.[108] The state report also fails to mention that Syrians must pay a fee before they can access the healthcare system.[109] The exclusion from social services of the children of Jordanian women who married non-Jordanian men is also repeatedly commented on by the CSOs and it is noted that this puts significant financial strain on the home, plunging these women into poverty.[110] The CSOs also report on the appalling conditions of migrant domestic workers who are excluded from labour laws and social protection.[111] With the exception of health fees, all of these issues are discussed in the Concluding Observations.

[103] Amnesty (n 101).
[104] Earthrights International, 'Report to CEDAW' (2016) http://tbinternet.ohchr.org/Treaties/CEDAW/Shared%20Documents/CAN/INT_CEDAW_NGO_CAN_25438_E.pdf.
[105] CFAIA (n 97).
[106] Arab Women Organization and Mosawa Network 'CEDAW Shadow Report' (2017) http://tbinternet.ohchr.org/Treaties/CEDAW/Shared%20Documents/JOR/INT_CEDAW_NGO_JOR_26477_E.pdf; Human Rights Watch, 'Submission to the CEDAW Committee of Jordan's Periodic Report, 66th Session' (2017) http://tbinternet.ohchr.org/Treaties/CEDAW/Shared%20Documents/JOR/INT_CEDAW_NGO_JOR_26376_E.pdf; International Human Rights Clinic at Harvard Law and the Norwegian Refugee Council Jordan, 'List of Issues for Jordan' (2017) http://tbinternet.ohchr.org/Treaties/CEDAW/Shared%20Documents/JOR/INT_CEDAW_NGO_JOR_24312_E.pdf.
[107] ibid.
[108] Harvard (n 106).
[109] Arab Women's Association (n 106).
[110] ibid; Equality NOW, 'Submission' (2017) http://tbinternet.ohchr.org/Treaties/CEDAW/Shared%20Documents/JOR/INT_CEDAW_NGO_JOR_26323_E.pdf.
[111] Arab Women's Association (n 106); Human Rights Watch (n 106).

The CSO reports for Jordan discuss a few additional gender-based poverty issues. Similar to the Jordanian state report, a number of CSO reports assess women's role in the labour market, although unlike the state report, the CSOs are critical of Jordan. Throughout their lives, girls and women face disincentives to participate in the labour market. There is evidence that school textbooks continue to negatively portray women's employment.[112] The Arab Women Association (AWA) and the Mosawa Network explain that the lack of equal-pay laws, women's segregation into low-paid jobs and the high costs of living in Jordan 'discourage women from entering the workforce as [they] end up working hard for little income that barely covers the basic necessities'.[113] In contrast to the state report, which strongly emphasises the availability of microcredit schemes, the AWA argues that the strict lending conditions 'discourage women from pursing their own projects' and that little skills and training support is provided to enable women to use credit effectively.[114] Personal laws in Jordan routinely discriminate against women. A woman still requires her husband's permission to work outside the home, sharia courts only award equal financial support when a woman leaves her husband and there is evidence that women are pressured into giving up inheritance rights.[115] The CSO reports also note that family allowances are automatically granted to married men but only to a woman if her husband is dead or disabled or she is a single mother.[116] There are similar restrictions on women's pension payments.[117] It again appears the Committee draws on the CSO reports as the Concluding Observations highlight the discrimination women face in employment, rural life and personal law, although the Committee does not always provide the same level of detail in the Concluding Observations as the CSOs do in their reports.

To varying degrees the CSO reports for Ethiopia and Turkey are influential. In relation to Ethiopia, the African Rights Monitor points out that only paid workers in Ethiopia are eligible for pensions and that more women than men are unemployed so more women are 'without social security of any kind'.[118] The CSOs note that women's unequal access to land and livestock causes them to be poor;[119] that there is a shortage of clean

---

[112] Arab Women's Association (n 106).
[113] ibid.
[114] ibid.
[115] ibid.
[116] ibid.
[117] ibid.
[118] African Rights Monitor, 'Submission of the African Rights Monitor to the Committee on the Elimination of Discrimination Against Women' (2011) 28, http://tbinternet.ohchr.org/Treaties/CEDAW/Shared%20Documents/ETH/INT_CEDAW_NGO_ETH_49_8757_E.pdf.
[119] Minority Rights Group International, 'Submission to the 49th Session on CEDAW' (2011) 9, http://tbinternet.ohchr.org/Treaties/CEDAW/Shared%20Documents/ETH/INT_CEDAW_NGO_ETH_49_8759_E.pdf.

drinking water and the burden of finding and collecting clean water falls on women;[120] that women's low status in the home means intra-household allocation of resources favours men;[121] and that men abduct girls when the man's family cannot afford to pay the girl's bride price.[122] Some of the CSOs' concerns are incorporated into the Concluding Observations while others are not. For example, the shortage of drinking water, unequal access to land and exclusion from social security protection are all discussed by the Committee. However, the connection between poverty and forced early marriage is not made in the Concluding Observations. The Committee only recommends that Ethiopia 'use innovative measures to strengthen the understanding of [women's] equal rights to freely choose a spouse and enter marriage'.[123] There is also no mention in the Concluding Observations on improving gender stereotypes that affect the intra-household allocation of resources. Similarly, the Turkish CSOs point out that microcredit schemes 'fall short of challenging formal paid wage ... as the male domain'.[124] They call for increasing social security to cover temporary agricultural workers, home and wage worker women.[125] One report notes that the Turkish government used budget constraints and International Monetary Fund targets as justifications to 'narrow the scope of social services'.[126] The Concluding Observations for Turkey do not mention budget cutbacks but do recommend that Turkey ensure women in the informal labour market have access to social services.

(iv) List of Issues

The list of issues is the first chance for the Committee to engage with the state and transcend any gaps in the state or CSO reports by asking questions on gender-based poverty. The briefing template prepared by the country rapporteur and relied upon by the pre-session working group directs the Committee members to ask questions on the state's national gender-based poverty plans and women's entitlement to social protection. Disappointingly, there is no evidence of the Committee asking these cornerstone questions on gender-based poverty. Although it is not taking full advantage of the list of issues, for Canada, Ethiopia and Jordan, the pre-session working group uses this process to gather information on women in poverty.

---

[120] African Rights Monitor (n 118) 35.
[121] Minority Rights Group International (n 119) 7.
[122] ibid 9.
[123] 'Concluding Observations: Ethiopia' (n 6) [19].
[124] 'The Executive Committee for NGO Forum on CEDAW—Turkey: Women's Platform on the Turkish Penal Code, 'Shadow Report' (2010) 14, http://tbinternet.ohchr.org/Treaties/CEDAW/Shared%20Documents/TUR/INT_CEDAW_NGO_TUR_46_10193_E.pdf.
[125] ibid 17.
[126] ibid 15.

With respect to Turkey, in the chapeau to the specific questions the Committee repeatedly identifies gender-based poverty as an obstacle but then frustratingly the pre-session working group does not ask any follow-up questions on how the state is addressing this obstacle. Notably, the aspects of gender-based poverty about which the Committee chooses to ask further questions almost perfectly reflect aspects that have been raised by either the state or the CSOs. This suggests that the Committee is highly responsive to material submitted to it in the periodic reporting process.

The list of issues for Canada raises several questions on gender-based poverty. The pre-session working group requests information on the minimum criteria for gaining access to legal aid services;[127] it asks what steps Canada is taking to provide affordable childcare;[128] on whether it has adopted targeted measures to increase employment opportunities for disadvantaged women;[129] on the impact of the housing shortage on women; and on the plans Canada has to replace the employer-specific work permit for migrant domestic workers.[130] All of these issues were highlighted in the CSO reports and a few are referred to in the state report. Directly echoing the concerns of many CSO reports, the Committee has asked Canada to provide information on indigenous women. It specifically wants to know more about indigenous women and access to healthcare services and safe drinking water, financial support programmes in place to develop income-generating projects for indigenous women; the poor living conditions of indigenous women 'sometimes owing to the expansion of extractive industries'; and the steps Canada is taking to improve their socioeconomic living conditions and the relationship between indigenous women and authorities.[131] All of these aspects of gender-based poverty feature prominently in the state and CSO reports. The reference to extractive industries directly echoes Amnesty's report on mining in Canada. However, it does not ask any questions on the level of social assistance benefits and affordability of contraception, issues touched upon by several CSO reports.

In respect of Ethiopia, the pre-session working group asks for examples of financial incentives for the family to encourage girls to stay in school,[132] information on the level of women's wages,[133] information on any social protection for women's informal and unpaid work,[134] measures taken to protect girls from economic exploitation,[135] efforts taken to ensure affordable

127 The Committee, 'List of Issues: Canada' (2016) CEDAW/C/CAN/Q/8–9 [3].
128 ibid [12].
129 ibid [13].
130 ibid.
131 ibid [16]–[17].
132 The Committee, 'List of Issues: Ethiopia' (2010) CEDAW/C/ETH/Q/6–7 [17(e)].
133 ibid [18].
134 ibid [19].
135 ibid [20].

access to contraceptives,[136] safe drinking water and sanitation,[137] steps taken to reduce risks when women collect water[138] and information on measures to ensure women equally inherit and control productive resources.[139] Education and health are discussed at length in the state report, while informal work and ownership and control of resources are raised by the CSOs. There are no questions on gender-based poverty outside what has been raised in either state or CSO reports.

It possible to detect the influence of the CSOs in the list of issues for Jordan, but there are two instances where the Committee highlights issues that were not prominent in either the state or CSO reports. The pre-session working group asked whether the state is considering establishing a legal aid programme and for information to 'ensure unlimited access for married young women to compulsory and free school education'.[140] The state and CSO community did not significantly engage with access to justice or the costs of education for married women. The Committee's Concluding Observations for Jordan briefly refer to legal aid and only refer to supporting pregnant and young mothers in education without directly referring to costs. These two examples aside, most of the questions do reflect the concerns of the CSO reports and to a certain extent the information in the state report. Similar to both the state and CSO reports, the Committee asks numerous questions on women's employment. It asks questions on equal pay, childcare, women's low participation in the labour force and the steps the state is taking to combat economic and physical exploitation of migrant domestic workers.[141] The list of issues specifically notes that 'it is reported that poverty is higher among females in the countryside' and asks Jordan to provide information on the steps it is taking to ensure capacity-building projects for rural women, and their access to health and education, as well as measures being taken to address discriminatory practices that prevent rural women from inheriting and owning land.[142] These are all issues that CSOs and the state sought to bring to the attention of the Committee.

The list of issues for Turkey does not ask specific questions on gender-based poverty. This is surprising given that in the chapeau to the specific questions the pre-session working group repeatedly identifies gender-based poverty as an obstacle to human rights. The Committee notes that in the state report Turkey explained there was a preference for families to educate boys rather than girls due to economic reasons. The pre-session working

---

[136] ibid [23].
[137] ibid [26].
[138] ibid.
[139] ibid [28].
[140] The Committee, 'List of Issues: Jordan' (2017) CEDAW/C/JOR/Q/6 [5], [15].
[141] ibid [16]–[17].
[142] ibid [19].

group did not follow through and ask what Turkey was doing to address how gender-based poverty negatively impacts girls' education. Interestingly, the Concluding Observations also make no reference to gender-based poverty and education. They only ask what steps are being taken to eliminate stereotypical attitudes in textbooks and the measures taken to promote the importance of girls' education.[143] The list of issues also notes that in the state report Turkey identifies women's economic dependence as a factor limiting women's access to healthcare. However, the Committee does not then ask what Turkey is doing to ensure women are economically independent. Instead, Turkey is only requested to provide information on measures taken to eliminate discrimination in accessing healthcare.[144]

(v) State Reply

The reply to the list of issues only provides a minimal amount of new information. It mostly reiterates information that is in the state report. Perhaps as evidence of the delicate nature of reporting under CEDAW, Ethiopia did not reply to the list of issues. Similar to the state report, the Canadian state reply employs the gendered 'trickle-down' effect. It notes that there are no specific gender provisions regarding access to legal aid but argues that women have benefited from legal aid.[145] It provides information on provincial programmes including training girls for non-traditional careers,[146] and the latest measures to redress the gender wage gap.[147] It only provides limited further information on indigenous women, mostly on the funding of provincial programmes to support employment for indigenous women.[148] It does provide more detailed data on the various monitoring mechanisms to protect the human rights of foreign workers, but this is not gendered.[149] In regards to Turkey, the reply predominantly focuses on gender-based violence and trafficking. However, the reply reiterates that conditional cash-transfer programmes exist to ensure girls go to school[150] and that microcredit schemes are in place for low-income individuals, women in particular.[151] It also explains that rural development programmes which aim at reducing poverty prioritise the needs of women. The Jordanian state reply provides information on the availability of legal aid and similar to the state report it

---

[143] The Committee, 'List of Issues: Turkey' (2009) CEDAW/C/TUR/Q/6 [21].
[144] ibid [25].
[145] 'Response to the List of Issues: Canada' (2016) CEDAW/C/CAN/Q/8–9/Add.1 [14]–[15].
[146] ibid 37.
[147] ibid [97]–[98].
[148] ibid [106].
[149] ibid [107]–[111].
[150] 'Responses to the List of Issues: Turkey' (2010) CEDAW/C/TUR/Q/6/Add.1.
[151] ibid.

explains that CSOs also provide legal aid;[152] it reiterates programmes are in place to support women's employment, reduce poverty and enhance social protection;[153] and that domestic violence shelters supply women with basic needs.[154] With respect to the education of married girls and young mothers, the state reply merely notes that these girls are permitted to return to school without providing any details on how it is addressing any structural barriers or recognition harms.[155]

(vi) UN Agencies

No UN agencies submitted reports to the periodic reporting process for the states in this case study.

(vii) Summary Records

In the Summary Records the state and the Committee discuss in more detail aspects of gender-based poverty that have been emphasised in the state and CSO reports, a list of issues and the state's reply. The Turkish state representative goes into further detail on the steps it is taking to improve the access of poor girls to education.[156] In the session for Canada, Committee members ask questions on the gendered approach to legal aid,[157] on affordable childcare,[158] a gendered approach to the state's anti-poverty plans[159] and the socioeconomic conditions on indigenous women.[160] These are all issues raised in the state report, CSO submissions and list of issues, and ultimately included in the Concluding Observations. When reviewing Jordan, the Committee questioned the conditions of refugees,[161] stereotypes in education,[162] migrant domestic workers,[163] gender job segregation,[164] microcredit schemes[165] and discrimination in personal laws.[166] Again, all of these issues were raised before the oral dialogue session. Similarly, in the Ethiopian session, the Committee asked if the state's income-generating

---

[152] Response to the List of Issues: Jordan' (2017) CEDAW/C/JOR/Q/6/Add. 1 [5.10].
[153] ibid [7.2].
[154] ibid [11.2].
[155] ibid [15.1].
[156] The Committee, 'Summary Record: 937th meeting' (2010) CEDAW/C/SR.937 [6], [23].
[157] The Committee, 'Summary Record: 1433rd meeting' (2016) CEDAW/C/SR.1433 [11].
[158] The Committee, 'Summary Record: 1434th meeting' (2016) CEDAW/C/SR.1434 [6].
[159] ibid [11].
[160] ibid [30].
[161] The Committee, 'Summary Record: 1476th meeting' (2017) C/SR.1476 [10].
[162] ibid [34].
[163] The Committee, 'Summary Record: 1477th meeting' (2017) C/SR.1477 [17].
[164] ibid [16].
[165] ibid [36].
[166] ibid [40]–[42].

activities is yielding any results,[167] the status of social security for informal workers,[168] if there is more current information on poverty among rural women,[169] and actions Ethiopia is taking to increase access to safe drinking water.[170] In one instance Committee members asked questions on gender-based poverty that were not addressed in either the state report or the CSO submissions. In the Ethiopian session, the Committee raised questions on foreign companies leasing lands,[171] and drew a connection between trafficking and economic insecurity.[172]

C. Conclusions

The state and CSO reports are equally vital factors for ensuring that the Committee engages with gender-based poverty in the periodic reporting process. The discussion of socioeconomic conditions of indigenous women in the Canadian Concluding Observations, the focus on how gender-based poverty impacts rural women in the Ethiopian Concluding Observations and the concerns on gender-based poverty among refugees in the Jordanian Concluding Observations can all be traced to both the state and CSO reports. The influence of the state report can also be detected in Turkey where neither the state report nor the Concluding Observations substantively discuss gender-based poverty. The CSO reports provide further information on the aspects of gender-based poverty raised by the state and bring to light new issues that are not included in the state report: access to justice and work permits for migrant domestic workers in Canada; the shortage of drinking water and exclusion of informal workers from social protection in Ethiopia and the inability of Jordanian women to pass nationality to their children when they marry non-Jordanian women. All of these issues were raised by CSOs and included in the Concluding Observations.

There is no evidence that the pre-session working group asks questions on gender-based poverty in the list of issues when it is not first raised by either the state or the CSOs. For example, the Jordanian state and CSO reports do no comment on safe drinking water for women although Jordan has chronic water scarcity issues.[173] So it is surprising that the Committee does not address this issue from a gender-based poverty perspective. However,

---

[167] The Committee, 'Summary Record: 985th meeting' (2011) CEDAW/C/SR.985 [18].
[168] ibid [50].
[169] ibid [19].
[170] ibid [20].
[171] ibid [50].
[172] ibid [31].
[173] USAID, 'Gender Study in Jordan Report No 14' (2010) 6–8, http://haqqi.info/en/haqqi/research/gender-study-jordan-%E2%80%93-desktop-survey.

in the Ethiopian periodic reporting process this is raised by a CSO and the Committee does engage with it. It appears the Committee is reactive and responsive to the material submitted to it. The state reply tends to reiterate information already supplied in the state report and is not an influential factor.

While it is possible to trace the impetus or source for many of the aspects of gender-based poverty included in the Concluding Observations to the state and CSO reports, analysing the publically available material does not explain every reference to gender-based poverty. For instance, in the constructive dialogue process there is one example where the Committee transcends the information provided to it. The Committee asked questions on foreign companies who are expropriating land which is contributing to the feminisation of poverty in Ethiopia. This issue was not raised by the state, the CSOs or the pre-session working group, but by an individual Committee member and it is included in the Concluding Observations. In a similar vein, issues raised by both the state and the CSOs are not automatically included in the Concluding Observations. Turkey discussed the financial incentives it is using to keep girls in school, Ethiopia acknowledged the link between gender-based poverty and maternal mortality, Canadian CSOs emphasized the low levels of social assistance benefits and Jordanian CSOs provided much greater detail on the discriminatory aspects of personal laws and employment benefits than the Concluding Observations. Thus, there are glimmers of other background and behind-the-scenes forces at work in the periodic reporting process.

In conclusion, the essential factor in ensuring that gender-based poverty is discussed by the Committee in the Concluding Observations is the state and CSO reports. The more the state acknowledges gender-based poverty, the more the Committee does. If the state ignores gender-based poverty and the CSO community does not fill this knowledge gap, the Committee does not interrogate the state on the measures it is taking to address how gender-based poverty acts as an obstacle to human rights. The Committee's silence on gender-based poverty in the face of state indifference and CSO inattention only further marginalises women in poverty. The next section in this chapter and Chapters 7 and 8 explore how to engage the state and the CSOs. They also act as a call to action for the Committee to consistently and comprehensively assess the impact of gender-based poverty.

III. REFORMING THE PERIODIC REPORTING PROCESS

The case study in Section II reveals that a key entry point for gender-based poverty in the Concluding Observations is the state and CSO reports. How can these actors be prompted to provide information on gender-based poverty? There are two proposals that can engage these actors and sharpen the use of CEDAW's accountability mechanisms to hold states to account for gender-based poverty. First, through a comparison of the reporting guidelines for the International Covenant on Economic, Social and Cultural Rights (ICESCR),[174] the *reporting guidelines* for CEDAW can be modified so that the state is explicitly requested to include information on gender-based poverty. This hopefully will stimulate the state to take a critical perspective on the steps it is undertaking to address gender-based poverty, and even contribute to a larger conversation on understanding gender-based poverty as a facet of equality and non-discrimination. Although reforming the reporting guidelines is no guarantee that the state will report on gender-based poverty, it is a step towards using CEDAW's accountability mechanisms to shine the international spotlight on the scourge of gender-based poverty. Second, engaging CSOs is challenging as there are no equivalent reporting guidelines for CSOs. A *General Recommendation* on gender-based poverty has strong potential to encourage CSOs to provide the Committee with crucial information. It can also be another tool to engage the state as the reporting guidelines ask states to take into account any General Recommendations adopted by the Committee.[175] According to the Committee, the General Recommendations 'outline matters which the Committee wishes to see addressed in the report of State parties and seek to provide detailed guidance to States parties on their obligations under the Convention and the steps they are required for compliance'.[176] This could potentially have a positive knock-on effect on using CEDAW's other accountability mechanisms—Individual Communications and the Inquiry Procedure—as a General Recommendation, CEDAW's high-profile accountability forum, sends a strong signal on the importance of addressing gender-based poverty in the efforts to eliminate discrimination against women. A General Recommendation on women and poverty is exciting and cutting-edge as it would be the first time a UN treaty body is exclusively examining the relationship between gender equality, poverty and human rights. To ensure this is a persuasive and authoritative statement, the content and structure of a General Recommendation on women and poverty are explored in the next two chapters. This final section of this chapter focuses on reforms to the reporting guidelines.

A. Analysis of the CEDAW Reporting Guidelines

The current reporting guidelines are not optimised to gather information on gender-based poverty. To assist states in the periodic reporting process and

---

[174] International Covenant on Economic, Social and Cultural Rights (adopted 16 December 1966, entered into force 3 January 1976) 993 UNTS 3.
[175] 'Compilation of Guidelines' (n 32) ch 5 [C.2].
[176] 'Overview of the Working Methods' (n 37) [27].

to ensure the Committee has the information necessary to evaluate state compliance with CEDAW, the Committee in conjunction with the other UN human rights treaty bodies and the Office of the High Commissioner of Human Rights have created harmonised guidelines on how to prepare both the common core document and the state report. As a whole, the CEDAW-specific guidelines are vague and do not offer meaningful guidance. The state is only requested to provide information on the implementation of recommendations in the Committee's last Concluding Observations; an analytical and result-oriented examination of the steps taken to implement CEDAW; and information on emerging obstacles to women's human rights.[177] Problematically, there are no requests to include information on gender-based poverty. States are further encouraged to provide information analysing any trends that exist over time in eliminating discrimination against women and to take account of the different experiences of different groups of women.[178] This means that the guidelines rely heavily on the state to identify gender-based poverty as a trend in and obstacle to women's rights.

There are two instances where the CEDAW guidelines require more detailed information. The first example is relatively hidden. A footnote in the guidelines elaborates that the state report should include information on specific issues of gender equality such as the impact of customary and religious law and the existence of gender budgeting. The fact that this important information is requested in a footnote could easily result in it being overlooked by the state. Even more problematic, there is still no direct reference to gender-based poverty.

The second example is that the state should provide information on the implementation of the Beijing Platform and the gender elements of the Millennium Development Goals (MDGs) (now the Sustainable Development Goals (SDGs)). The Beijing Platform is the action plan that came out of the Fourth World Conference on Women held in Beijing, China in 1995. The Platform for Action identifies key areas where state needs to work to promote women's human rights, including 'the persistent and increasing burden of poverty on women' and 'inequality in economic structures and policies, in all forms of productive activities and in access to resources'.[179] Similarly, states are also requested to provide information on the 'integration of a gender perspective … in all efforts aimed at the achievement' of the MDGs/SDGs.[180] The SDGs require states to achieve gender equality and end poverty. It is unfortunate that rather than explicitly asking for this information

---

[177] 'Compilation of Guidelines' (n 32) ch 5, [E.3 (a)], [E.3(c)].
[178] ibid ch 5 [E.4], [E.5].
[179] 'The United Nations Fourth World Conference on Women: Platform for Action', www.un.org/womenwatch/daw/beijing/platform/plat1.htm#concern.
[180] 'Concluding Observations: Ethiopia' (n 8) [47].

the guidelines direct the state representative to secondary sources. Requiring the state to do research to find out what precisely the Beijing Platform and MDGs/SDGs require runs the risk that the state representative drafting the report may overlook these reporting requirements on gender-based poverty. Additionally, having to do research and go to other sources to identify that gender-based poverty is an area of critical concern for women means the CEDAW guidelines miss an opportunity to make an unambiguous statement that the commitment to combat gender inequality entails a commitment to address gender-based poverty. Moreover, the Committee does not appear to be following its own advice. There are only a few limited questions on the Beijing Platform and MDG/SDGs in the list of issues or summary records,[181] and state and CSO reports do not refer to the implementation of the Beijing Platform or the MDGs/SDGs. The reality of the reporting process demonstrates it is insufficient to rely on these sources to gather information on the lives of women in poverty.

In comparison, the reporting guidelines for the common core document are calibrated to gather information on poverty, particularly as most of the data in the document is to be disaggregated for gender.[182] The common core guidelines indicate that: '[S]tates should provide information on specific measures adopted to reduce economic, social and geographical disparities ... to prevent discrimination ... against the persons belonging to the most disadvantaged groups.'[183] In a similar vein, the 'state should provide accurate information on the standard of living of the different segments of the population', including women.[184] Appendix 3 provides a list of indicators to illustrate the standard of living within the state. The common core document appears to be sensitive to gender-based poverty as these indicators should be disaggregated for sex: the proportion of population below the national poverty line, the proportion of population below the minimum level of dietary consumption, in relation to the distribution of income or household consumption to expenditure, enrolment in education, unemployment rates, employment by major sectors of economic activity, including the breakdown between the formal and informal sectors and social expenditures (food, housing, health, education, social protection, etc) as a proportion of total public expenditure and gross domestic product. In practice, however, it appears states are woefully disregarding this advice as none of the common core documents provides this level of detail and data is never disaggregated for gender.

---

[181] 'Summary Record 985th meeting' (n 167) [7].
[182] 'Compilation of Guidelines' (n 32) Appendix 3.
[183] ibid [55].
[184] ibid [35].

B. Reforming the CEDAW Reporting Guidelines

The current situation relies too heavily on states to identify gender-based poverty as an existing and emerging obstacle to women's human rights. States can easily avoid criticisms on gender-based poverty by simply not including this information in the report and still claim that they have respected the spirit of the reporting guidelines. The information in the common core document, even if the data is not disaggregated for gender, is a good starting point and the Committee should be relying on this source more than it currently appears to be doing. The reporting guidelines should also be reformed so as to capture vital information on gender-based poverty. The guidelines for ICESCR serve as a best-practice model. This subsection briefly outlines these guidelines and proposes reforms to the CEDAW guidelines.

The ICESCR guidelines make repeated reference to poverty. When reporting on Article 11 of ICESCR, the right an adequate standard of living, the state should indicate if there is a national poverty line, on what basis this line is calculated or any other tools the state uses for monitoring and measuring poverty.[185] The state is asked to provide information on any national action plans to combat poverty, how these programmes fully integrate economic, social and cultural rights, and how they are targeted to the most disadvantaged groups.[186] For instance, on the right to water, the state must provide information on measures taken to ensure 'adequate and affordable access to water ... for everyone'[187] and 'the percentage of households without access to sufficient and safe water ... disaggregated by region and urban/rural population and the measures taken to improve the situation'.[188] As a further example, under Articles 6 and 7 on the right to work and fair and just working conditions the state is requested to provide information on the employment programmes in place to achieve full and productive employment, the impact of measures to facilitate re-employment of women and long-term unemployed workers, information on the applicability of minimum wages and its ability to provide an adequate standard of living.[189]

The CEDAW guidelines should be reformed so that the state is encouraged to provide information on gender-based poverty. The guidelines should, first, make a very clear and direct request for information on what the state is doing to reduce gender-based poverty. The guidelines should ask that the report include information on gender-based poverty reduction strategies in the state and how they take account of the unique needs of

---

[185] 'Compilation Guidelines' (n 32) ch 2 [42]–[43].
[186] ibid.
[187] ibid [48].
[188] ibid.
[189] ibid [15]–[32].

women in poverty. If the guidelines are reformed using the substantive provisions of CEDAW as a framework, the most logical place to situate the overarching request on gender-based poverty is under Article 13 (equality in economic and social life). Gender-based poverty is a cross-cutting problem and, as argued in Chapter 4, gender-based poverty should not be collapsed into one obligation in CEDAW. Similar to the ICESCR guidelines, the CEDAW guidelines can require that for each provision the state report on disadvantaged and vulnerable women and this should include women in poverty.[190]

For example, under Article 5 on cultural attitudes and stereotypes, the guidelines should ask the state what steps it has taken to address negative stereotypes that contribute to gender-based poverty. The guidelines should request information on the attendance and completion rate of low-income girls at all levels of school and the steps taken to reduce costs associated with attending schools and ensuring girls and women in poverty are able to access education (Article 10). In relation to equal access to healthcare, guidelines should ask the state to provide information on the costs of healthcare services, and especially the accessibility of maternal healthcare with a particular attention to rural women in gender-based poverty (Article 12). Under Article 11 (employment) the state could be asked to provide information on unpaid care work and the informal labour market. These are but a few examples. Chapter 8 and the proposed General Recommendation on women and poverty in the Annex contextualise the obligations in CEDAW to account for gender-based poverty in greater detail. While the level of specificity in the CEDAW reporting guidelines is no promise that states will provide this information, it can be an important prompt to ensure that the Committee has the requisite information on how women in poverty experience human rights violations. It also importantly is a mechanism to ensure consistency on how gender-based poverty is discussed in the Concluding Observations. Finally, reforming the guidelines to refer directly to gender-based poverty sends a message that it is an issue of equality and human rights in CEDAW.

IV. CONCLUSION

A case study analysing how the Committee's working methods in the periodic reporting process influence the discussions on gender-based poverty in the Concluding Observations points the way forward for the Committee to use CEDAW's accountability mechanisms coherently and consistently to tackle gender-based poverty. Reforming the state reporting guidelines so as

[190] ibid.

to require the state to provide the Committee with information on gender-based poverty and releasing a General Recommendation on gender-based poverty can unlock the potential of CEDAW's accountability mechanisms. This still leaves unanswered the underlying question of how to get gender-based poverty on the agenda so that the Committee can send out the necessary signals to the global community. This process is incredibly opaque but the remaining chapters outline how best to produce a definitive General Recommendation on women and poverty that can hopefully act to galvanise the Committee and other relevant stakeholders to be proactive on gender-based poverty.

7

Evolutionary General Recommendations

G ENERAL RECOMMENDATIONS ARE a unique feature in international human rights law. They offer an unparalleled opportunity for the Committee to use its voice to advocate that the commitment to eliminate discrimination and achieve gender equality in CEDAW requires the state to address how gender-based poverty acts as an obstacle to women's human rights. A General Recommendation on gender-based poverty would be ground-breaking. The UN treaty bodies have touched upon gender-based poverty and poverty, as canvassed in Chapters 3, but no treaty body has taken a focused look at gender-based poverty or even more broadly at poverty. This would be a paradigm shift, emphasising that gender-based poverty is a matter of the state's *legal* human rights obligations. Although a General Recommendation itself is not a legally binding statement, it can signify to the state and the larger global community the value of taking a human rights-based approach to gender-based poverty. Experience has shown that General Recommendations can be ascribed great weight by domestic, regional and international courts, lawyers, civil servants and civil society organisations (CSOs).[1] It also has a potential positive spillover effect, prompting the Committee to use CEDAW's other mechanisms to hold states to account for gender-based poverty; and ultimately it could guide the evolution of international and domestic human rights.

To achieve these goals, a General Recommendation needs to provide a rigorous justification as to why CEDAW, a treaty that largely ignores gender-based poverty, now should be used to address it. It needs to be a definitive and persuasive statement not a 'scattered collection' of thoughts on gender-based poverty.[2] Part I of this book provides the arguments for a

---

[1] P Alston and R Goodman, *International Human Rights: The Successor to International Human Rights in Context: Law, Politics and Morals* (Oxford University Press, 2013) 792; see also *Case Concerning Ahmadou Sadio Diallo (Republic of Guinea v Democratic Republic of the Congo)*, [2010] ICJ Rep 693.

[2] P Alston, 'The Historical Origins of the Concept of "General Comments" in Human Rights Law' in L Boisson de Chazournes and V Gowland Debbas (eds), *The International Legal System in Quest of Equity and Universality: Liber Amicorum Georges Abi-Saab* (Martinus Nijhoff, 2001) 764.

compelling evolutionary interpretation of the treaty. Using the established rules for interpreting international treaties, it proposes that gender-based poverty be understood as a matter of non-discrimination and equality in CEDAW. These arguments can be drawn upon when drafting a General Recommendation. To be a convincing statement on gender-based poverty, it is also beneficial to consider the purpose, style and structure of General Recommendations. By examining past General Recommendations from the Committee and General Comments from other UN treaty bodies that have contributed to the evolution of international human rights law, it is possible to derive a structure that can be used to propose a General Recommendation on women and poverty.

Section I assesses how the Committee, other UN treaty bodies and the academic community have articulated the goals of General Recommendations and Comments. This leads to the conclusion that the General Recommendations and Comments are multipurposed and aim: (i) to develop open-textured human rights; (ii) to share best practices; and (iii) to provide directions on how to prepare the state report for the periodic reporting process. Section II analyses evolutionary General Recommendations and Comments that elaborate obligations that are not explicitly articulated in either CEDAW or the International Covenant on Economic, Social and Cultural Rights (ICESCR)[3] to understand how the broad goals of the General Recommendations are channelled into practice and identify key features needed for an authoritative General Recommendation on women and poverty. Drawing these insights together, to be a persuasive statement on gender-based poverty a General Recommendation should include: (i) an *introduction* that justifies the need for a General Recommendation on gender-based poverty and situates itself in the larger evolution of human rights law; (ii) an *explanation* of the legal basis for the interpretation of gender-based poverty into CEDAW; and (iii) a *contextualisation* of the obligations in CEDAW in light of understanding gender-based poverty as a issue of non-discrimination and equality so as to provide guidance to states and the global community on the nature of the obligations in CEDAW. The final chapter then uses this map to propose a General Recommendation on women and poverty.

I. THE PURPOSE OF GENERAL RECOMMENDATIONS

Philip Alston argues that General Comments and Recommendations are 'one of ... the most significant and influential tools available to ... human

---

[3] International Covenant on Economic, Social and Cultural Rights (adopted 16 December 1966, entered into force 3 January 1976) 993 UNTS 3.

rights treaties bodies'.[4] CEDAW only makes passing reference to General Recommendations. Article 21 provides that the Committee 'may make suggestions and *general recommendations* based on the examination of reports and information received from the state'.[5] The Committee has 'drawn on this power to develop a substantial body of interpretive material on specific articles of [CEDAW] as well as cross-cutting themes (such as violence against women …).'[6] On the other hand, the Committee's General Recommendations have been criticised as providing only basic guidance.[7] The Committee has never weighed in on the purpose of General Recommendations. In the late 1980s, General Recommendations 'were relatively short and tended to address technical … aspects of state party reports'.[8] Byrnes argues that due to Cold War politics, canvassed in Chapter 2, 'conservative approaches tended to prevail over attempts to take expansive or innovative approaches'.[9] The General Recommendations are now more substantive. While there has been a shift from the early mechanical recommendations, there is no clear delineation on the current purpose of General Recommendations. Academic study has not yet turned to this issue. Instead it is primarily focusing on the Human Rights Committee (HRC) and General Comments under the International Covenant on Civil and Political Rights (ICCPR).[10] Given the similarity between the HRC and the Committee, it is useful to examine this literature in more detail.

The HRC, similar to the Committee, has a vague mandate to release General Comments. Article 40(4) of the ICCPR holds that the Committee 'shall transmit … such *general comments* as it may consider appropriate to state parties'.[11] Unlike the Committee, the HRC reflects on the aims of General Comments. Early in its history, the HRC explained that General Comments are meant to address 'the obligation to submit reports; the obligation to guarantee the rights in [ICCPR]; questions related to the

---

[4] Alston, 'The Historical Origins' (n 2) 763.

[5] Emphasis added.

[6] A Byrnes, 'The Committee on the Elimination of Discrimination Against Women' in A Hellum and HS Aasen (eds), *Women's Human Rights: CEDAW in International, Regional and National Law* (Cambridge University Press, 2013) 39.

[7] R Cook and V Unduggara, 'Article 12' in M Freeman, C Chinkin and B Rudolf (eds), *CEDAW: A Commentary* (Oxford University Press, 2012) 312.

[8] H Keller and L Grover, 'General Comments of the Human Rights Committee and Their Legitimacy' in H Keller and G Ulfstein (eds), *UN Human Rights Treaty Bodies: Law and Legitimacy* (Cambridge University Press, 2012) 124. See the Committee, 'General Recommendation No 2 (Sixth Session, 1987)' (1987) CEDAW/C/GC/2.

[9] A Byrnes, 'The Convention and the Committee: Reflections on their Role in the Development of International Human Rights Law and as a Catalyst for National Legislative and Policy Reform' (UN Commission on the Status of Women, 2010) 4.

[10] International Covenant on Civil and Political Rights (adopted 16 December 1966, entered into force 23 March 1976) 999 UNTS 171.

[11] Emphasis added.

application and content of individual articles of the [ICCPR]; and suggestions concerning co-operation between state parties'.[12] It further holds that
General Comments are intended to share best practices developed by states
'in order to promote [the] implementation of [ICCPR]; to draw to their
attention insufficiencies disclosed by a large number of reports; to suggest
improvements in the reporting procedure and to stimulate activities of states
and international organisations in the promotion and protection of human
rights'.[13] Although the HRC's assessment indicates that General Comments
are multipurposed, it is not clear if there is de facto uniformity in identifying
these varying purposes. Keller and Grover's recent interviews with past and
present members of the HRC elicited eight different purposes, ranging from
interpretive analysis of the rights in ICCPR to providing support to CSOs in
preparing shadow reports.[14]

The academic assessment echoes how the HRC understands General
Comments. In his historical evaluation, Alston identifies four purposes:
(i) to deepen the understanding of open-textured human rights norms;
(ii) to strengthen the influence of international human rights commitments;
(iii) to consolidate the Committee's learning and insights from reviewing
state reports; and (iv) to provide guidance to state.[15] Keller and Grover,
drawing on extensive interviews with HRC members, conclude that General Comments serve three functions: (i) legal analytical; (ii) policy recommendation; and (iii) practice direction. The legal analytical function directs
the HRC to use General Comments to interpret the content of broadly
articulated rights and to develop legal tests for determining violations of
ICCPR.[16] To achieve this function, General Comments need to be theoretically and analytical rigorous. Keller and Grover argue that General Comments also serve a policy recommendation function. States have discretion
on how to implement their obligations under international human rights
treaties.[17] General Comments are meant to tap into the Committee's expertise by sharing best practices, identifying barriers to the enjoyment of rights
and providing information on how rights violations may be prevented.[18]
The final purpose Keller and Grover identify is practice directions. General
Comments are used to 'indicate the information it would like state parties

[12] (1980) CCPR/C/SR.260 [1].
[13] 'Compilation of General Comments and General Recommendations Adopted by Human
Rights Treaty Bodies' (1989) CCPR/C/21/Rev.1.
[14] ibid 143.
[15] Alston, 'The Historical Origins' (n 2) 763–64.
[16] Keller and Grover (n 8) 124, 126.
[17] See B Schlutter, 'Human Rights Interpretation by the UN Treaty Bodies' in H Keller and
G Ulfstein (eds), *UN Human Rights Treaty Bodies: Law and Legitimacy* (Cambridge University
Press, 2012) 302–08 on the HRC's deference to states on implementing international human
rights standards.
[18] Keller and Grover (n 8) 125.

to include in their periodic report'.[19] While the reporting guidelines also serve this function, the General Comments offer an opportunity to discuss in detail what the Committee desires to see in the state report and, as argued in Chapter 6, they are also a tool to encourage CSOs to submit shadow reports on specific human rights issue. In sum, there is consensus that General Recommendations and Comments are meant to develop the law, share best practices on implementing the rights in the treaty and provide guidance to the state on its obligations. A close examination of General Recommendations and Comments that contribute to the evolution of international human rights law in Section II demonstrates how the treaty bodies flesh out these goals and provide more finely tuned guidance on how to structure a General Recommendation on gender-based poverty.

II. EVOLUTIONARY GENERAL RECOMMENDATIONS

International human rights law is a living tree. It reflects changing social, political, economic and cultural realities. The UN human rights treaty bodies primarily contribute to this evolutionary process through General Recommendations and Comments. Through the work on the UN treaty bodies there is a clear understanding on the right to be free from gender-based violence,[20] the rights of older women[21] and the right to water.[22] CEDAW makes no reference to gender-based violence or intersectionality and ICESCR is silent as to a right to water, yet General Recommendation No 19 on violence against women and General Recommendation No 27 on older women and the protection of their human rights, and CESCR's General Comment No 15 on the right to water examine these issues. These General Recommendations and General Comment are strong examples of UN treaty bodies interpreting international treaties to address newly recognised human rights issues. General Recommendation No 19 is particularly perceived as authoritative and has been ascribed significant weight by domestic and regional apex courts.[23] A General Recommendation on women and poverty would be similarly pioneering new ground.

---

[19] ibid 126.

[20] The Committee, 'General Recommendation No 19: on Violence against Women' (1992) CEDAW/C/GC/19.

[21] The Committee, 'General Recommendation No 27: on Older Women and Protection of their Human Rights' (2010) CEDAW/C/GC/27.

[22] CESCR, 'General Comment No 15: The Right to Water' (2002) E/C.12/2002/11.

[23] *Vishaka v State of Rajasthan* AIR 1997 SC 3011 (India Supreme Court), *Carmichele v Minister of Safety and Security and Another*, 2001 (1) BCLR 995 (South African Constitutional Court) and *R v Ewanchuk* [1999] 1 SCR 330 (Canadian Supreme Court); *Opuz v Turkey* (33401/02) (European Court of Human Rights). See also The Committee, 'General Recommendation No 35: on Gender-Based Violence Against Women' (2017) CEDAW/C/GC/35.

Analysing these three specific General Recommendations and Comments provides a more fine-grained understanding of the broad goals of the General Recommendations and Comments. It pinpoints two insights into structuring a persuasive General Recommendation on women and poverty. First, the treaty bodies do not approach the goals of General Recommendations and Comments as conceptually distinct. General Recommendation and Comments simultaneously seek to provide a legal analysis of the treaty, share best practices by contextualising the obligations in the treaty in light of the proposed interpretation, and provide guidance to the state and the global community. In practice the separate categories proposed by the academic community often bleed into each other. To illustrate legal arguments, CESCR draws on policy recommendations and both the Committee and CESCR are explicitly and implicitly encouraging states to follow their advice and calling on states to provide information on the recommendations it proposes. Second, an evolutionary General Recommendation and Comment begin with an introduction that both justifies and contextualises the subsequent analysis. Following in the footsteps of the past General Recommendations and Comments, a General Recommendation on gender-based poverty needs: (i) to *introduce* the evolution in international human rights law; (ii) to provide a rigorous *legal analysis*; and (iii) to *contextualise* the obligations in CEDAW so as to concurrently provide recommendations on the steps the state should take to combat gender-based poverty and provide guidance on information to submit to the Committee in CEDAW's other accountability forums.

A. Introducing the Evolution in International Human Rights Law

Each evolutionary General Recommendation and Comment begins by justifying the need for a statement on the gender-based violence, the human rights of older women and the right to water. The Committee and CESCR use slightly different methods for explaining the necessity of the General Recommendation and General Comment. The General Recommendation on violence against women begins with a compelling statement: gender-based violence is 'a form of discrimination that seriously inhibits women's ability to enjoy rights and freedoms on a basis of equality with men'.[24] However, the Committee does not set the scene in the opening paragraphs. It does not provide any information on the lived experience of gender-based violence or its prevalence.[25] On the other hand, General Recommendation No 27 on

---

[24] 'General Recommendation No 19: on Violence Against Women' (n 20) [1].

[25] In 'General Recommendation No 35: on Gender-Based Violence Against Women' (n 23) provides detailed information on the many manifestation of gender-based violence.

older women and General Comment No 15 on the right to water, while they do not open with a powerful opening sentence, provide contextual background information. Due to increased living standards and developments in healthcare, people are living longer. General Recommendation No 27 on older women explains that ageing is gendered since women tend to live longer than men. The discrimination older women have endured throughout their lives requires states to pay particular attention to older women's human rights. As a further impetus for the General Recommendation, with shifting demographics there is an increase in older women. The Committee notes that the 'number of older women living in less developed regions will increase by 600 million within the period 2010 to 2050'.[26] The introductory paragraph concludes by addressing the recognition harms associated with older women. It explains that older women are diverse and possess a range of 'experiences, knowledge, abilities and skills' and that they can make unique contributions.[27] In a similar vein, the first paragraph in the General Comment on a right to water notes the crucial role of water. Water is 'indispensable for leading a life of human dignity [and] a prerequisite for the realisation of other human rights'.[28] CESCR then observes that billions of people lack access to basic water supply, a situation that contributes to water-based diseases. As a further justification, all three evolutionary General Recommendations and Comments observe that the state is not attentive enough to the issue in question when preparing the state report.[29]

The opening paragraphs accomplish one further task. They situate the General Recommendation and Comment in broader trends in international law. This not only further illustrates the importance of a General Recommendation and Comment on the subject, it also demonstrates that the treaty bodies' interpretation of CEDAW or ICESCR is not a radical proposal but is contributing to the development and internal coherency of international law.[30] The Committee and CESCR draw on two sources to situate the evolution of international human rights law: (i) the treaty bodies' own work on the subject matter, and (ii) the work of other international bodies. In General Recommendation No 19 on violence against women the Committee refers to the previous General Recommendation on violence[31] and notes that at past sessions it has decided to study 'violence towards women and the sexual harassment and exploitation of women'.[32] General Recommendation

---

[26] 'General Recommendation No 27: on Older Women' (n 21) [6].
[27] ibid [8].
[28] 'General Comment No 15: The Right to Water' (n 22) [1].
[29] ibid; 'General Recommendation No 19: on Violence Against Women' (n 20) [4], 'General Recommendation No 27: on Older Women' (n 21) [1].
[30] Schlutter (n 17) 270.
[31] The Committee, 'General Recommendation No 12: Violence against Women' (1989) CEDAW/C/GC/12.
[32] 'General Recommendation No 19: on Violence Against Women' (n 20) [2]–[3].

No 19 also explains that the Committee is using the periodic reporting process to address gender-based violence.[33] In General Recommendation No 28 on older women the Committee notes that in the previous General Recommendation it recognised age as a 'ground on which women may suffer from multiple forms of discrimination'.[34] The Committee also makes reference to non-binding sources: the Vienna International Plan of Action on Ageing, the Beijing Declaration, UN General Assembly Resolution on Principles for Older Persons, the Madrid International Plan of Action for Ageing, CESCR General Comment No 6 on the rights of older persons, and CESCR General Comment No 19 on the right to social security.[35] CESCR follows the same pattern. It refers to its own consideration of water in the periodic reporting process and notes that states have been asked to include information on water in the reporting guidelines.[36] General Comment No 15 on the right to water also refers to binding legal commitments on water: Article 14(2)(h) of CEDAW (rights to water for rural women), Article 24(2) of the Convention on the Rights of the Child (rights to clean water for children to combat disease and malnutrition) and the Geneva Conventions on the treatment of prisoners of war and civilians. CESCR also references non-binding international commitments: the Mar Del Plata Action Plan from the UN Water Conference, the Dublin Statement on Water and Sustainable Development, and Resolution 2002/6 of the UN Sub-Commission on the Promotion and Protection of Human Rights on the promotion of the realisation of the right to drinking water.[37] Intriguingly, both treaty bodies cite non-binding legal commitments. This indicates that the Committee and CESCR perceive these to be persuasive sources of authority. While the treaty bodies' perception is by no means definitive, it is does reinforce the arguments made throughout this book that in practical terms non-binding international human rights sources, such as General Recommendations, can have substantive weight.

B. The Legal Analysis to Support the Evolutionary Interpretation

After introducing the need for a General Recommendation and Comment and situating it within developments in international human rights law, the Committee and CESCR provide the legal arguments for the new interpretation of the treaty. To be authoritative this section of the General Recommendation and Comment needs to be rigorous and precise. The Vienna Convention on the Law of Treaties (VCLT) interpretative rules,

---

[33] ibid [5].
[34] 'General Recommendation No. 27: on Older Women' (n 21) [2].
[35] 'ibid [3].
[36] 'General Comment No. 15: The Right to Water' (n 22) [1], [5].
[37] ibid [4].

used in Chapter 4 to argue that gender-based poverty is an issue of non-discrimination and equality in CEDAW, provide a legal analytical framework for crafting evolutionary General Recommendations and Comments. Perhaps to remain accessible to non-legal audiences, the Committee and CESCR only appear to be implicitly employing this framework. Even without explicitly using the VCLT rules—the ordinary meaning in light of the context and purpose of the treaty—the General Recommendations and Comments use these rules to present legal arguments for the proposed interpretation. However, the treaty bodies have been criticised for not fully engaging with the legal analysis and as a result the legitimacy of the proposed interpretation has been questioned.[38] Learning from past missteps, it is imperative that a General Recommendation on gender-based poverty provides a thorough legal interpretation of CEDAW.

General Recommendation No 19 is the strongest example of harmoniously using all three elements of the VCLT framework for an evolutionary interpretation of a human rights treaty. It begins with the ordinary meaning. Violence against women is interpreted into the definition of discrimination in Article 1 of CEDAW. The Committee stresses that when an experience is based on gender it falls within Article 1. Violence against women is within the ambit of CEDAW when violence 'is directed against a woman because she is a woman' or 'affect[s] women disproportionately'.[39] General Recommendation No 19 also relies on the contextual element of the VCLT framework. The Committee notes that other provisions in CEDAW—Article 2 (core obligations) and Article 3 (full advancement and development)—establish that CEDAW is an evolutionary treaty. It holds that these two provisions 'establish a comprehensive obligation to eliminate discrimination in all its forms in addition to the specific obligations' in CEDAW.[40] There is also reference to the object and purpose of the treaty. CEDAW is meant to eliminate *all* forms of discrimination, even forms that are not explicitly referred to in the treaty, such as gender-based violence.[41] Importantly, the obligation to address gender-based violence is comprehensively interpreted into CEDAW: '[G]ender-based violence may breach specific provisions of the Convention regardless of whether those provisions expressly mention violence.'[42] This echoes the Office of the High Commissioner's conceptualisation of the relationship between poverty and human rights canvassed in Chapter 1.[43]

---

[38] K Mechlem 'Treaty Bodies and the Interpretation of Human Rights' (2009) 42 *Vanderbilt Journal of Transnational Law* 905.

[39] 'General Recommendation No 19: on Violence Against Women' (n 20) [6].

[40] ibid [10].

[41] ibid [6].

[42] ibid.

[43] Office of the High Commission for Human Rights, 'Human Rights and Poverty Reduction: A Conceptual Framework' (2004) HR/PUB/04/1.

In General Recommendation No 27 on older women, the Committee is implicitly relying on an object and purpose interpretation of CEDAW. The analysis is brief and could benefit from a more sustained assessment of intersectionality in CEDAW. The Committee explains that through the intersection of age and gender, older women experience a unique set of human rights violations.[44] To eliminate discrimination against women it is inherently necessary to protect the human rights of older women, as canvassed in Chapter 4. To achieve CEDAW's aims it is necessary to protect the rights of all women, including older women.[45]

The dangers in not providing a meticulous legal analysis become apparent in respect of General Comment No 15 on the right to water. Similar to General Recommendation No 27, General Comment No 15 only provides a cursory legal explanation of the evolutionary interpretation of ICESCR. CESCR, relying primarily on a mixture of context and object and purpose, argues that a right to water is included in both Article 11(1) of ICESCR (adequate standard of living) and Article 12(1) (health).[46] Water is a necessary for an adequate standard of living and the right to health becomes meaningless without a right to water. CESCR holds that water is required to enjoy many other rights in ICESCR such as food and enjoying cultural practices.[47] That is the extent of the legal analysis. The paucity of legal arguments has resulted in General Comment No 15 attracting criticisms. By interpreting a right to water into ICESCR, CESCR has been accused of interpretative overreach and inappropriate interpretative creativity.[48] It is has been argued that the interpretation in General Comment No 15 is not faithful to the text, state practice or state intention.[49] Although some in the academic community were sceptical, states have not rejected this interpretation. For the October 2016 periodic review process, almost all the states provided information on the right to water.[50] The crucial importance of providing a thorough legal interpretation of CEDAW is a lesson to carry forward when drafting a General Recommendation on women and poverty.

---

[44] 'General Recommendation No 27: on Older Women' (n 21) [14].

[45] Meghan Campbell 'CEDAW and Women's Intersecting Identities: A Pioneering Approach to Intersectionality' (2015) *Revista Diretio GV* 479.

[46] 'General Comment No 15: The Right to Water' (n 22) [3].

[47] ibid [7]–[9].

[48] S Tully, 'A Human Right to Access Water? A Critique of General Comment No 15' (2005) 23 *Netherlands Quarterly of Human Rights* 35, 37.

[49] SC McCaffrey, 'The Human Right to Water' in EB Weiss, L Boisson de Chazournes and N Bernasconi-Osterwalder (eds), *Fresh Water and International Economic Law* (Oxford University Press, 2005) 94.

[50] CESCR, '59th Session (19 Sept 2016–07 Oct 2016)', http://tbinternet.ohchr.org/_layouts/treatybodyexternal/SessionDetails1.aspx?SessionID=1060&Lang=en.

C. Contextualising the Evolutionary Interpretation of the Treaty

As the General Recommendations and Comments used in this analysis are proposing new understandings of the treaty, each places the evolutionary interpretation into context. Specifically, the Committee and CESCR considers how the General Recommendation and Comment affects the state's obligations, provides examples of best practices states should pursue and provides directions on information the state should include in periodic reporting process. These aims are often pursued at the same time. This component of the General Recommendations and Comments is very specific to the human rights issue in question. It is difficult to extrapolate the principles behind contextualising the interpretation that could be used in a General Recommendation on women and poverty. Highlighting a few examples assists in understanding the tone and structure of contextualising the evolutionary interpretation in the General Recommendations and Comments.

Again, the strongest example of this is General Recommendation No 19 on violence against women. Prior to the General Recommendation, gender-based violence in the UN human rights system was still largely perceived as a private matter.[51] As discussed in Chapter 4, up to the early 1990s, there was still confusion as to whether gender-based violence should be dealt with through criminal law or gender equality.[52] The Committee in General Recommendation No 19 addresses this conceptual confusion by holding that gender-based violence is not an abhorrent individual act but part of a larger pattern of systemic abuse based on patriarchal gender norms. It then considers how understanding gender-based violence as a matter of gender discrimination under Article 1 of CEDAW affects the interpretation of the other provisions in CEDAW. General Recommendation No 19 stresses the importance of modifying traditional attitudes which regard women as subordinate to men (Article 5).[53] The Committee interprets Article 2(e) of CEDAW (the duty to eliminate discrimination against women by any person, organisation or enterprise) to hold that the state has a due-diligence obligation to protect women against gender-based violence. It further elaborates that the state 'may also be responsible for private acts if they fail to act with due diligence to prevent violations of rights or to investigate and punish acts of violence'.[54] The Committee is making a bold statement. Gender-based violence cannot be minimised or ignored but is a cornerstone

---

[51] Secretariat of the United Nations, 'Ending Violence Against Women: From Words to Action', www.un.org/womenwatch/daw/public/VAW_Study/VAWstudyE.pdf.

[52] C Chinkin, 'Article 5' in M Freeman, C Chinkin and B Rudolf (eds), *CEDAW: A Commentary* (Oxford University Press, 2012).

[53] 'General Recommendation No 19: on Violence Against Women' (n 20) [11].

[54] ibid [9].

obligation in the fight to eliminate discrimination against women. Under the heading 'Specific Recommendations' the Committee seamlessly integrates recommendations and directions. Unfortunately, it is not always as specific as would be desired.[55] The first recommendation is arguably unhelpfully broad: take 'appropriate and effective measures to overcome all forms of gender-based violence'.[56] The Committee proceeds to provide further examples, with varying degrees of specificity, such as: ensuring that laws against violence protect women and respect their integrity; providing gender-sensitive training to law enforcement officers; and introducing education and public information to eliminate prejudices that hinder women's equality.[57] In this sub-section the Committee repeatedly says 'state parties in their report should ...' and provides a series of directions such as to provide information on and modify the attitudes on violence against women, and information on sexual harassment and the steps taken to eliminate it.[58]

In General Recommendation No 27 on older women, the Committee examines how gender discrimination affects older women: a perception that older women are no longer useful in productive and reproductive roles, a lifetime of gender inequality that becomes exacerbated in old age, unfair resource allocations, maltreatment, neglect and limited access to basic services.[59] As a result older women may suffer from inadequate housing, isolation, income security and lack of access to healthcare. Thus, the state must be attentive to understanding how age and gender discrimination combine to deprive older women of their human rights. The Committee uses the text of CEDAW as a framework to explain how each substantive provision can be interpreted to take account of different aspects of gender equality for older women. The Committee shares a significant number of best practices states should employ: recognising the value of older women; taking account of multidimensional discrimination; preventing forced early retirement; creating non-contributory pension schemes; and social benefits for older women who perform unpaid childcare work.[60] Although the Committee does not explicitly hold this, presumably states should report on these specific rights violations for older women and it would welcome CSO shadow reports on these issues.

CESCR extensively contextualises ICESCR in light of interpreting a right to water into the treaty. It begins by firmly stating that a right to water should not be equated simply to volume but rather 'water should be treated

---

[55] 'General Recommendation No 35: on Gender Based Violence Against Women' (n 23) provides detailed recommendations to states.

[56] 'General Recommendation No 19: on Violence Against Women' [24(a)].

[57] ibid [24(b)]–[24(f)].

[58] ibid [24(e)], [24(j)].

[59] 'General Recommendation No 27: on Older Women' (n 21) [9]–[10].

[60] ibid [30], [31], [41]–[44].

as a social and cultural good'.[61] Each individual must have for personal and domestic use a sufficient and clean supply of water that is both physically and economically accessible.[62] Unlike CEDAW, the rights in ICESCR are to be progressively realised,[63] and the General Comment sets out a minimum core set of obligations that are not subject to progressive realisation.[64] The state is, inter alia, required to ensure a minimal amount of water for personal use; to prevent water-based diseases; and to ensure the right on a non-discriminatory basis. In addition to the core obligations, the state has an immediate, constant and continuing obligation to 'move as expeditiously and effectively as possible towards the full realisation of the right to water'.[65] States are directed to provide information on the steps they have to take to ensure the core obligations and progressively realise the right to water.[66] Unlike the Committee, CESCR also provides guidance on how to set up effective mechanisms to successfully implement the right to water. It recommends that legislation and national water plans should be based on human rights principles, have time-based targets, indicators and benchmarks, be made in a participatory and transparent process, be monitored and periodically reviewed, and have remedies for violations of the right to water.[67] This framework provides more meaningfully guidance for states in translating the right to water into workable laws and policies and for CSOs preparing shadow reports.

III. CONCLUSION

Assessing both the aims of General Recommendations and Comments and how these aims have been operationalised in evolutionary General Recommendations and Comments provides insights into a General Recommendation on women and poverty. To be an authoritative statement that prompts states and CSOs to report on gender-based poverty across CEDAW's accountability mechanisms, that guides the evolution of international and domestic human rights law, a General Recommendation on women and poverty needs: (i) to *introduce* the evolution in international human rights law; (ii) to provide a thorough *legal analysis*; and (iii) to *contextualise* the obligations in CEDAW. It should begin by explaining the need for an in-depth examination into the relationship between gender equality, poverty

---

[61] 'General Comment No 15: The Right to Water' (n 22) [11].
[62] ibid [12].
[63] Art 2(1) ICESCR.
[64] 'General Comment No 15: The Right to Water' (n 22) [37].
[65] ibid [18].
[66] ibid [39]–[44].
[67] ibid [45]–[59].

and human rights, and situate this within the development of an international law. A General Recommendation on gender-based poverty needs to avoid past criticisms. It should draw on the established legal interpretative rules to provide thorough arguments to support the Committee's proposed interpretation. In contextualising the obligations in CEDAW in light of recognising gender-based poverty as an issue of non-discrimination and equality, the General Recommendation should provide specific recommendations and, drawing on CESCR's General Comment No 15 on the right to water, consider broader issues of accountability and implementation at the domestic level. The next chapter follows in the footsteps of these evolutionary General Recommendations and, drawing on the arguments made throughout the book, proposes the content and structure of a General Recommendation on women and poverty.

8

Envisioning Gender-Based Poverty in CEDAW

THIS FINAL CHAPTER brings together arguments made throughout the book to propose a General Recommendation on women and poverty. A General Recommendation is a chance for the Committee to reflect on the intersection between gender equality, poverty and human rights. It is an authoritative tool for the Committee to engage with states, civil society organisations (CSOs), grassroots movements and individuals on the role that CEDAW can play in ameliorating gender-based poverty. A persuasive and compelling General Recommendation on women and poverty has strong potential to be used by legislative bodies, courts, academics and human rights groups in devising and reviewing measures to guarantee the human rights of women in poverty.[1]

Using the insights from Chapter 7 on the structure of evolutionary General Recommendations, this chapter argues that to achieve these aims, a General Recommendation on women and poverty needs to justify approaching gender-based poverty as a human rights issue, provide rigorous arguments using established legal methodologies for interpreting gender-based poverty as a facet of equality and non-discrimination in CEDAW, and contextualise the obligations in CEDAW by sharing best practices and providing recommendations. This chapter acts as an academic commentary or explanatory notes to the proposed text of a General Recommendation in the Annex to this book. An important caveat is that this proposal is a starting point. General Recommendations are the result of a participative and deliberative drafting process. A General Recommendation on women and poverty would be immeasurably enriched with the participation of states, CSOs, academics, UN entities, and specialised agencies and individuals. The proposal here should be understood as a springboard or blueprint for future deliberations.

---

[1] P Alston and R Goodman, *International Human Rights: The Successor to International Human Rights in Context: Law, Politics and Morals* (Oxford University Press, 2013) 728.

I. INTRODUCING GENDER-BASED POVERTY INTO CEDAW

A General Recommendation on women and poverty should begin with a powerful opening statement. It should immediately establish the gender-based nature of poverty and that CEDAW conceptualises gender-based poverty as discrimination against women and a form of gender inequality. Using General Recommendation No 19 on violence against women as a model, the first sentence in a General Recommendation on women and poverty should read: '*Gender-based poverty is a form of discrimination that seriously inhibits women's ability to enjoy their rights and freedoms on the basis of equality.*' In this one sentence the Committee can challenge past assumptions that gender-based poverty is a matter of charity or development and firmly hold that it is a human rights issue. This also implicitly provides a justification for the General Recommendation: since gender-based poverty acts as an obstacle to women's human rights, it is entirely logical that it be addressed by the pre-eminent legal instrument on gender equality, namely CEDAW. After boldly proclaiming its conceptualisation of gender-based poverty, the Committee should explain that the purpose of the General Recommendation is to explore the relationship between gender-based poverty and CEDAW, and to contextualize the obligations in CEDAW by reflecting on the nature of the state's obligations and sharing best practices from the Committee's experience of monitoring the implementation of CEDAW.

To ward off criticisms that this is radical and impermissible interpretation of CEDAW, the introduction to a General Recommendation on women and poverty needs justify itself. There are four compelling reasons: (i) the gendered nature of poverty; (ii) the prevalence and magnitude of gender-based poverty; (iii) the human rights violations that are inherent and contribute to gender-based poverty; and (iv) the evolution in international human rights.

First, similar to General Recommendation No 27 on older women and the protection of their human rights, the General Recommendation on women and poverty should elucidate the gender-based nature of poverty. Poverty is a devastating and pervasive phenomenon that cruelly affects the lives of men and women.[2] Due to the asymmetrical nature of CEDAW, the General Recommendation should clarify it is only examining the gender-based aspects of poverty.[3] It can acknowledge that the causes of poverty are intricate, interlocking and at times hard to pin down with any degree of accuracy. Notwithstanding this difficulty, it is painfully clear that women and girls continue to 'be overrepresented among the world's population

---

[2] UN, 'The Millennium Development Report: 2014' (2014) 8–16, www.un.org/millenniumgoals/2014%20MDG%20report/MDG%202014%20English%20web.pdf.
[3] The Committee, 'General Recommendation No 25: on Temporary Special Measures' (2004) CEDAW/C/GC/25 [5].

living in poverty'.[4] For many women, they are poor because they are women. Gender attitudes and stereotypes condemn millions of women to lives of poverty, indignity, drudgery, hopelessness and despair. These norms are complex, interwoven and deeply embedded in the political, legal, social and cultural fabric, and affect girls and women at every stage of their lives.

The General Recommendation should illustrate the gender-based nature of poverty. Young girls may be denied an education because the family does not want to 'waste' limited household resources on educating a girl.[5] Or parents may be hesitant to enrol girls in school due to the 'belief that is harder for an educated women to get married and concerns that she will remain a financial burden to her family',[6] or there may be significant risks of violence for girls in accessing and attending school.[7] Her time may be seen as being better or more safely spent performing menial chores, care work or subsistence farming.[8] Only 2 out of 130 states have achieved parity in all levels of education.[9] At school, teachers may stress the value of marriage and reproduction over educational opportunities, economic independence and personal empowerment.[10] Pregnancy or early marriage can interrupt a girl's education, condemning her to a lifetime of poor working conditions.[11] Counterintuitively, education for girls does not necessarily translate into decent jobs in the labour market.[12] Women continue to have higher unemployment

---

[4] Working Group on Discrimination Against Women in Law and Practice, 'Discrimination against Women in Health and Safety' (2016) A/HRC/32/44 [44]; Working Group, 'Discrimination against women in Economic and Social Life, with a Focus on Economic Crisis' (2014) A/C/26/39 [8]; UN Department of Economic and Social Affairs, 'The World's Women 2015: Trends and Statistics' (2015) ST/ESA/STAT/SER.K/20 179, ch 8: Poverty.

[5] Right to Education Project, 'Why Aren't Girls in School?', http://r2e.gn.apc.org/node/192.

[6] S Fredman, J Kuosmanen and M Campbell, 'Transformative Equality: Making the Sustainable Development Goals Work for Women' (2016) 30(2) *Ethics and International Affairs* 177, 182.

[7] Office of the High Commissioner of Human Rights (OHCHR), 'Background Paper on Attacks against Girls Seeking to Access Education' (2015) 23, www.ohchr.org/Documents/HRBodies/CEDAW/Report_attacks_on_girls_Feb2015.pdf.

[8] Working Group, 'Economic and Social Life' (n 4) [36].

[9] UN, 'The Millennium Development Report: 2013' (2013) 19 < http://www.un.org/millenniumgoals/pdf/report-2013/mdg-report-2013-english.pdf>.

[10] Naila Kabeer, 'Gender Equality and Women's Empowerment: A Critical Analysis of the Third Millennium Development Goals' (2005) 13(1) *Gender and Development* 13, 17; Shirley J. Miske, 'Exploring the Gendered Dimensions of Teaching and Learning: Background Paper for the Education for All Global Monitoring' (2013) UN Girls' Education Initiative Working Paper No. 6.

[11] Centre for Reproductive Rights, 'Forced Out: Mandatory Pregnancy Testing and the Expulsion of Pregnant Learners in Tanzania' (2013) <https://www.reproductiverights.org/sites/crr.civicactions.net/files/documents/crr_Tanzania_Report_Part1.pdf>; *Head of Department, Department of Education, Free State Province v Welkom High School and Another; Head of Department, Department of Education, Free State Province v Harmony High School and Another* 2014 (2) SA 228 (South African Constitutional Court).

[12] UN, 'The Millennium Development Goals Report 2015' (2015) 25, www.un.org/millenniumgoals/2015_MDG_Report/pdf/MDG%202015%20rev%20(July%201).pdf.

rates than men even when they have comparable levels of education.[13] In the home, women perform a significant and disproportionate amount of unpaid care work, which limits the time and energy they have to invest in employment and cultural activities.[14] Due to the heavy burden of care work, women are segregated into part-time work or into the informal labour market. In northern Africa, and southern and western Asia only 20% of women are in paid formal employment.[15] The majority of women in these regions work in the informal economy and 'usually lack adequate social protection; [and] suffer low incomes and arduous working conditions'.[16] Social attitudes on the role and value of women also contribute to gender-based poverty in the formal labour market as women are continually segregated into traditional 'women's work'.[17] These jobs are perceived as unskilled and less valuable, and as such are not properly remunerated. In both developing and developed countries, women earn less than men,[18] which carries the risk that women will become socially and financially dependent on men.[19] There is evidence that women are less likely to participate in decisions on large household purchases.[20] Where it exists, formal childcare is so unaffordable that it remains illusory for most women.[21] A combination of discriminatory laws and deeply entrenched gender norms results in women being less likely to own and control productive resources or access financial credit.[22] Gender discrimination can become exacerbated in times of economic austerity or financial pressures. Macroeconomic policies 'that aim at "stabilization"—usually through reducing public spending or meeting low inflation targets—tend to reduce employment opportunities'.[23] This can lead to a reassertion of patriarchal norms and practices. For example, 'demands on unpaid care work may intensify during times of economic stress increasing the burden of women'.[24] Elderly women who work part time, in the informal market

---

[13] ibid 8.

[14] UN Women, 'Progress of the World's Women: Transforming Economies, Realizing Rights' (2015) 83–87, http://progress.unwomen.org/en/2015/pdf/UNW_progressreport.pdf.

[15] 'The Millennium Development Report: 2013' (n 9) 20.

[16] 'The Millennium Development Report: 2014' (n 2) 10.

[17] UN Women, 'Transforming Economies' (n 14) 89; International Labour Organization (ILO), 'Women at Work: Trends 2016' (2016) 22–7, www.ilo.org/wcmsp5/groups/public/---dgreports/---dcomm/---publ/documents/publication/wcms_457317.pdf.

[18] Working Group, 'Economic and Social Life' (n 4) [45].

[19] UN Special Rapporteur on extreme poverty and human rights, 'Unpaid Care Work' (2013) A/68/293 [12].

[20] UN Department of Economic and Social Affairs (n 4); 'The Millennium Development Report: 2013' (n 9) 23.

[21] See, for example, Canada Without Poverty, 'Submission to CEDAW Committee 65th Session' (2016) http://tbinternet.ohchr.org/Treaties/CEDAW/Shared%20Documents/CAN/INT_CEDAW_NGO_CAN_25381_E.pdf.

[22] World Bank, 'Voice and Agency: Empowering Women and Girls for Shared Prosperity' (2014) https://openknowledge.worldbank.org/handle/10986/19036.

[23] UN Women, 'Transforming Economies' (n 14) 195.

[24] ibid 194.

or have working patterns interrupted by childcare responsibilities may be excluded from or have reduced pensions. Thus, 'millions of women still find that poverty is their reward for a lifetime spent caring'.[25] Explaining the highly gender-based nature of poverty provides a strong justification for a focused examination on the role that CEDAW can play in combating gender-based poverty.

Second, it is crucial to stress the prevalence and magnitude of gender-based poverty. It is important to push against the perception that can be found in state reports that there are isolated pockets of poverty.[26] This is not a phenomenon isolated to a few unfortunate states but is global and affects an astronomical number of women. In 2016, the World Bank found that in 155 economies there is at least one law impeding women's economic opportunities and across 173 economies there are 943 legal gender differences. In 100 economies, women face gender-based job restrictions.[27] Nearly 200 million older women live without 'regular income from social protection ... compared to 115 million men'.[28] The International Labour Organization (ILO) found that in 142 states women are overrepresented in 'clerical, service and sale workers' and in 'elementary occupations'.[29] The report notes that 'this is particularly the case in developed economies where women constitute 60 percent and nearly 50 percent of total employment in these two lowest paid occupations'.[30] The ILO concludes that the 'gender wage gap is unrelated to a country's level of economic development as some of the countries with high per-capita levels are among those with the highest gender wage gaps'.[31] General Recommendation No 34 on the rights of rural women repeatedly touches upon the links between rural status and gender-based poverty in the developing world.[32] A General Recommendation on women and poverty needs to recognise the global reach of gender-based poverty. It must fill the gap by looking not only at rural gender-based poverty, but also gender-based poverty in urban areas and developed countries, especially as gender-based poverty in developed countries often clusters around other intersecting identities.

Third, after establishing the gender-based nature of poverty and its scope, it is necessary to explain why CEDAW, a legal human rights instrument,

---

[25] UN Special Rapporteur on extreme poverty and human rights, 'Unpaid Care Work' (n 19) [6].

[26] 'Sixth Periodic Report State Party: Jordan' (2015) CEDAW/C/JOR/6 [65], [80], [95(g)], [99], [104].

[27] World Bank, 'Women, Business and the Law: 2016' (2016) http://wbl.worldbank.org/~/media/WBG/WBL/Documents/Reports/2016/Women-Business-and-the-Law-2016.pdf.

[28] ILO, 'Women at Work' (n 17) 33.

[29] ibid xiii.

[30] ibid.

[31] ibid 28.

[32] The Committee, 'General Recommendation No 34: on the Rights of Rural Women' (2016) CEDAW/C/GC/34.

should respond to gender-based poverty. The Committee should acknowledge that besides a concern about women in poverty in the preamble, there is no explicit obligation for states to remedy the gender-based nature of poverty. However, the General Recommendation should state that women in poverty are denied the opportunity for full development and advancement (Article 3) and the enjoyment of their human rights and fundamental freedoms (Article 1) due to the interaction of redistribution wrongs and gender recognition and participation harms. This makes the connection between gender-based poverty and the legal provisions in CEDAW. Drawing on the insights of the UN Special Rapporteur on extreme poverty and human rights, the Committee should clarify that women who live in poverty experience multiple and reinforcing violations of their political, civil, social, economic and cultural rights.[33] Gender-based poverty, akin to gender-based violence, may breach specific provisions of CEDAW, regardless of whether those provisions expressly mention gender-based poverty. This provides a further link to justify a General Recommendation on women and poverty.

The introduction can conclude by situating itself in larger trends in the Committee's own work and in the international sphere on gender-based poverty. The purpose of this is to establish the General Recommendation as part of a larger evolution in international human rights law. The General Recommendation can refer to the work the Committee has done in drawing a connection between gender-based poverty, equality, non-discrimination and human rights in its various accountability mechanisms as examined in Chapter 5. For instance, the Committee can note that it has referred to gender-based poverty in previous General Recommendations on: women's unpaid work;[34] women's unremunerated domestic activities;[35] the economic consequences of divorce and widowhood; and the rights of rural women.[36] All of these substantially, albeit implicitly, assess the impact of gender-based poverty on women's human rights. A General Recommendation on women and poverty synthesises these past Recommendations and insights from the Concluding Observations, Individual Communications and Inquiry Procedures, and takes the next step forward by explicitly and comprehensively discussing the impact of gender-based poverty on the obligations in CEDAW. The General Recommendation can build support for

[33] UN Special Rapporteur on extreme poverty and human rights, 'Final Draft of Guiding Principles on Extreme Poverty and Human Rights' (2012) A/HRC/C/21/39 [2]–[3].
[34] The Committee, 'General Recommendation No 16: Unpaid Women Workers in Rural and Urban Family Enterprises' (1991) CEDAW/C/GC/16.
[35] The Committee, 'General Recommendation No 17: Measurement and Quantification of the Unremunerated Domestic Activities of Women and their Recognition in the Gross National Product' (1991) CEDAW/C/GC/17.
[36] The Committee, 'General Recommendation No 29: on Economic Consequences of Marriage, Family Relations and their Dissolution' (2013) CEDAW/C/GC/29.

itself by citing a variety of international documents, both legally binding and non-binding, that highlight the relationship between gender equality, poverty and human rights. The key binding legal commitments are the right to an adequate standard of living in ICESCR (Article 11), the Convention on the Rights of the Child (Article 27)[37] and the Convention on the Rights of Persons with Disabilities (Article 28).[38] There is also a series of ILO Conventions that it can refer to: Conventions No 100 (equal remuneration), 111 (discrimination in employment and occupation) 156 (workers with family responsibilities), 183 (maternity protection) and 189 (domestic workers). The Committee can also refer to a variety of non-binding commitments: the Sustainable Development Goals (SDG)—to end poverty in all its forms (SDG-1) and to achieve gender equality and empowerment for all women and girls (SDG-5); the Beijing Declaration; the Guiding Principles on extreme poverty and human rights developed by the UN Special Rapporteur on extreme poverty and human rights;[39] and the statement by the Committee on Economic, Social and Cultural Rights, titled 'The Substantive Issues Arising in the Implementation of ICESCR: Poverty and ICESCR'.[40] On a more pragmatic note, a General Recommendation can note that to remain credible and relevant in the eyes of women, CSOs, and domestic and international policy-makers, CEDAW needs to speak to the reality of women's experiences and address one of the 'most abiding and pressing challenges' confronted by women: gender-based poverty.[41] The UN Special Rapporteur on extreme poverty and human rights makes a passionate plea for the human rights system to awake from 'zombie mode' and respond to the reality of poverty and economic insecurity.[42] A General Recommendation on women and poverty is an answer to that call.

II. A NEW INTERPRETATION: THE LEGAL BASIS FOR INTERPRETING GENDER-BASED POVERTY INTO CEDAW

Having established the need for a General Recommendation on women and poverty, the Committee needs to provide rigorous arguments that explain the legal basis for interpreting gender-based poverty into CEDAW. To ensure an authoritative General Recommendation, the Committee needs to candidly

[37] Convention on the Rights of the Child (adopted 20 November 1989, entered into force 2 September 1990) 1577 UNTS 3.
[38] Convention on the Rights of Persons with Disabilities (2007) A/RES/61/106.
[39] UN Special Rapporteur on extreme poverty and human rights, 'Guiding Principles' (n 33).
[40] Committee on Economic, Social and Cultural Rights (CESCR), 'Substantive Issues Arising in the Implementation of ICESCR: Poverty and ICESCR' (2001) E/C.12/2001/10.
[41] The UN Special Rapporteur on extreme poverty and human rights, 'Universal Basic Income' (2017) A/HRC/35/26 [7].
[42] ibid 7.

interpret CEDAW using established legal tools. At the same time, the General Recommendation should avoid alienating its non-legal audience with an overly technical legal analysis. This requires the Committee to strike a delicate balance. Where possible, the General Recommendation should steer clear of overly technical legal jargon. CESCR in its latest General Comments liberally uses footnotes to provide a nuanced legal analysis that still remains accessible.[43] The Committee should also consider the substantial benefits of using footnotes in the General Recommendation. Drawing on the arguments made in Part I, this subsection maps how the Committee can structure its legal analysis in a General Recommendation on women and poverty in a manner that is both legally meticulous and understandable to a wide array of stakeholders.

To frame its legal analysis, the Committee should elucidate its interpretative methodology. The starting point for the Committee's interpretation is its understanding that CEDAW is 'a dynamic instrument that contributes and adapts to developments in international law'.[44] In the past, the Committee has emphasised that CEDAW 'anticipates the emergence of new forms of discrimination that had not been identified at the time of its drafting'.[45] The permissibility of adopting an evolutionary interpretative approach is linked to the drafters' intention.[46] This intention can primarily be found through an application of Article 31 of the Vienna Convention on the Law of Treaties (VCLT);[47] that is, through an examination of the text, context and object and purpose of the treaty.[48] The General Recommendation can cite the VCLT interpretative rules in a footnote and explicitly refer to Articles 1 (the definition of discrimination), 2 (core obligation) and 3 (full advancement and development) of CEDAW. These provisions emphasise that the state has an obligation to eliminate *all* forms of discrimination and advance women's development in *all* fields. The Committee can point out that this means CEDAW is be interpreted in an evolutionary manner. The concept of gender equality and non-discrimination in CEDAW are designed to be responsive to new and newly recognised challenges to women's human rights.

---

[43] CESCR, 'General Comment No 22: The Right to Sexual and Reproductive Health' (2016) E/C.12/GC/22.

[44] The Committee, 'General Recommendation No 32: on Gender-Related Dimensions of Refugee Status, Asylum, Nationality and Statelessness of Women' (2014) CEDAW/C/GC/32 [2].

[45] The Committee, 'General Recommendation No 19: on Violence against Women' (1992) CEDAW/C/GC/19.

[46] See E Bjorge *The Evolutionary Interpretation of Treaties* (Oxford University Press, 2014).

[47] Vienna Convention on the Law of Treaties (adopted 23 May 1969, entered into force 27 January 1980) 1155 UNTS 331.

[48] ibid 92.

The next paragraph can chart the evolution in gender-based poverty. This echoes and amplifies the analysis in the introduction that situates the General Recommendation in the larger evolution in international human rights law. There are two evolutionary streams: one very specific to CEDAW and the other more general to human rights-based approaches to poverty. First, the analysis of the *travaux préparatoires* in Chapter 2 demonstrates that the drafters connected gender-based poverty to rural life in the developing world. The Committee continues to be attentive to this link as evidenced by the discussions on gender equality, poverty and rural status in the developing world in General Recommendation No 34 on the rights of rural women. A General Recommendation on women and poverty should clarify that with the passage of time, it is apparent that gender-based poverty not only affects the human rights of rural women in the developing world but also urban women in both the developed and developing world. Second, human rights violations are inherent to gender-based poverty. Redressing these violations is not only a moral duty but a *legal* obligation in CEDAW. The state cannot ignore the human rights of women who live in poverty. It has to 'has to respect the dignity ... of [women] living in poverty and empower them to meaningfully participate in public life ... and to hold duty bearers accountable'.[49]

The next step in the legal analysis is to define gender-based poverty. The UN system has been alive to the role of gender in perpetuating women's poverty but it has not yet defined this phenomenon. To effectively analyse the legal basis for interpreting gender-based poverty into CEDAW, it is necessary to translate the harms of gender-based poverty into a definition. The Committee can build upon modern definitions of poverty which are moving away from reducing poverty to an issue of insufficient resources. As discussed in Chapter 1, these multidimensional definitions of poverty need to be modified so as to capture the role of gender. The General Recommendation can pioneer a new definition and recognise that gender-based poverty is the redistribution harm of not having access to economic resources coupled with the recognition and participation harms which devalue and exclude women.[50]

The heart of the legal analytical section of the General Recommendation is the Committee's explanation for interpreting gender-based poverty as a facet of equality and non-discrimination in CEDAW. As canvassed in Chapter 4, Article 31 of the VCLT requires CEDAW be interpreted in its ordinary meaning in light of its context and the object and purpose of the treaty. The VCLT is the established and accepted methodology for

---

[49] UN Special Rapporteur on extreme poverty and human rights, 'Guiding Principles' (n 33) [7].
[50] See Chapter 1.

interpreting international treaties. Thus, the Committee needs to use this framework. To remain accessible, the Committee should cite the VCLT framework in a footnote and in the substantive body of the General Recommendation only implicitly apply Article 31. As a starting point, the General Recommendation on women and poverty can analyse the text of CEDAW (the *ordinary* meaning element). Using the definition of gender-based poverty, the Committee can assess how the different models of equality (formal, substantive and transformative) and non-discrimination (direct, indirect and the role of grounds) can redress the harms of gender-based poverty. The General Recommendation can use citations to demonstrate how far these different models of equality and non-discrimination are present in CEDAW (the *context* element). The VCLT directs the interpreter to examine subsequent agreements, subsequent state practice and any other relevant rules of international law. As discussed in Chapter 4, only subsequent state practice is relevant when interpreting gender-based poverty into CEDAW. The Committee can explain that from its experience in reviewing state reports, it is evident that states are working towards a coherent interpretation of equality and non-discrimination that includes gender-based poverty. Finally, the Committee can explain that the goals of CEDAW—eliminating discrimination against women, achieving gender equality and protecting women's human rights—cannot be achieved without addressing how gender-based poverty perpetuates gender discrimination, inequality and human rights violations (the *object and purpose* element). The Committee can conclude that all the elements of the VCLT framework point towards interpreting equality and non-discrimination as evolutionary concepts that include gender-based poverty.

Before contextualising CEDAW in light of this new interpretation, the Committee needs to address how this interpretation impacts the nature of the state's obligations under the treaty. It should clarify that there is no minimum core or progressive realisation in CEDAW. Instead the state is required to demonstrate against an equality and non-discrimination standard or framework that it has taken all appropriate measures to redress gender-based poverty, which can, where appropriate, include international cooperation. Equality and non-discrimination are the analytical rubric against which to assess the state's law, policies and programmes on gender-based poverty. It is tempting to reduce appropriate measures to the allocation of resources. The General Recommendation on women and poverty should stress that the state's obligations also include amending discriminatory laws, taking positive measures to full the rights of women in poverty, improving the management and delivery of public services, meaningful consultation with women who live in poverty, and providing training and awareness-raising campaigns to redress discriminatory norms on gender and poverty. Chapter 4 applies Fredman's four-dimension model of transformative equality to *Texieira*, a decision under the Optional Protocol to CEDAW on maternal health policies, to illustrate these arguments. The Committee can draw on this assessment to enrich its analysis on the impact of the new interpretation of CEDAW.

III. CONTEXTUALISING GENDER-BASED POVERTY IN CEDAW

The General Recommendation should then proceed to contextualise the obligations in CEDAW in light of this new interpretation. The aim of contextualising is to explain in greater detail how each of the provisions in CEDAW should be understood in relation to gender-based poverty, to consider accountability and implementation, to share best practices and provide recommendations to states and to CSOs. While these aims are often pursued simultaneously, for ease of analysis these functions are separated out. This section begins by examining how this new interpretation of CEDAW can be integrated into the substantive obligations in CEDAW and proposes best practices states should pursue; it then considers how the state can be held accountable in the domestic arena for the human rights of women in poverty and concludes by outlining reporting requirements.

A. Gender-Based Poverty and Women's Human Rights

Using the substantive obligations in CEDAW (Articles 4–16) as a framework, this section of the General Recommendation can use equality and non-discrimination as diagnostic tools to illustrate how gender-based poverty negatively impacts women's human rights and to craft remedial measures. The state has discretion to develop laws, policies and programmes to target gender-based poverty. While recognising the space that exists to implement CEDAW in a manner that fits the state's unique political, legal and cultural context, to make a significant contribution the General Recommendation should provide as detailed as possible examples of the human rights violations inherent in gender-based poverty and tailored recommendations. At the same time, a General Recommendation cannot flag every human rights violation that women in poverty experience. The Committee should stress that states need to be attentive to the de facto experience of gender-based poverty and remain attentive to new permutations of discrimination and inequality against women in poverty.

Temporary special measures (Article 4) can be succinctly dealt with in the General Recommendation. Drawing on the work the Committee has previously done, the Committee can stress that the state can be required to take accelerated measures to ensure equality for women in poverty.[51]

---

[51] See 'General Recommendation No 25: on Temporary Special Measures' (n 3).

Article 5 requires the state to modify negative cultural attitudes towards, and stereotypes of, women. The purpose of this is to 'honour the basic choices women make (or would like to make) about their own lives, and enable them to shape their own identities'.[52] The Committee can draw to the state's attention that the interaction between stereotypes on gender and poverty limits the ability of women to shape their lives. Women in poverty are perceived as lazy and promiscuous, and as deviant, unfit mothers who leach off the welfare system.[53] These attitudes manifest in a myriad of ways, including through the law. As one example, in the UK, only women who can prove that their third child is the result of sexual violence can claim benefits for that child.[54] The law operates to classify women in poverty as deserving or undeserving. Only women who have experienced violence are worthy of support for a third child from the state. Furthermore, it requires women to provide private and intimate health information to government bureaucrats, a process that can be humiliating and demonstrates complete disregard for the privacy of women in poverty. Negative gender stereotypes and attitudes can also trap women in poverty. The work women traditionally perform in the labour market is perceived as low skilled and as a result low paid.[55] Deeply entrenched social attitudes dictate that women disproportionately perform unpaid care work.[56] Women may have de jure access to property but may be perceived as selfish or egoistical if they enforce their property or inheritance rights.[57] The President of the World Bank aptly explains this vicious cycle:

> [E]ven when women can legally own property, they may not because those who do become outcasts ... teachers and parents may direct [girls] away from certain studies and jobs for which social norms say boys are better suited. Women then enter jobs ... with lower wages ... overwhelmingly girls and women also perform the unpaid work of care giving, for which they are often penalised with poverty in old age.[58]

A General Recommendation on women and poverty should recommend that states amend any laws that perpetuate negative stereotypes on

---

[52] R Cook and S Cusack, *Gender Stereotyping: Transnational Legal Perspectives* (UPP, 2009) 68.

[53] B Goldblatt, 'Gender, Poverty and the Development of the Right to Social Security' (2014) 10(4) *International Journal of Law in Context* 460, 467.

[54] The Child Tax Credit (Amendment) Regulations 2007, SI 2017/287.

[55] S Fredman, 'Engendering Socio-Economic Rights' in A Hellum and HS Aasen (eds), *Women's Human Rights: CEDAW in International, Regional and National Law* (Cambridge University Press, 2013) 219.

[56] UN Special Rapporteur on extreme poverty and human rights, 'Unpaid Care Work' (n 19).

[57] I Ikdahl, 'Property and Security: Articulating Women's Right to their Homes' in A Hellum and HS Aasen (eds), *Women's Human Rights: CEDAW in International, Regional and National Law* (Cambridge University Press, 2013) 270.

[58] World Bank, 'Voice and Agency (n 22) ix.

gender-based poverty and conduct awareness-raising campaigns that portray the role and value of women positively.

The analysis in Chapter 5 reveals that the Committee is sporadic in identifying the role of gender-based poverty in exploitative prostitution and trafficking (Article 6). This is disconcerting as 'trafficking is a phenomenon *inexorably* linked to the socio-economic impact of globalisation, with wealth disparities feeding increased intra-and transnational labour migration as livelihood options decrease in less wealthy countries'.[59] Poverty can lead women 'to make decisions that increase vulnerability to trafficking'.[60] In states as diverse as the UK and Cambodia, there is evidence that austerity measures have forced women into prostitution.[61] Gender-based poverty explains the 'recruitment of domestic labour from developing countries to work in developed countries'.[62] A General Recommendation on women and poverty must hold that gender-based poverty is an underlying cause of exploitative prostitution and trafficking. The Committee should recommend that the state's measures should be aimed towards redressing women's vulnerability to trafficking and exploitative prostitution, including through adequate social benefits and economic opportunities. Article 6 also raises challenging issues on the state's obligation. It is not only poverty within the state but 'inequality within and between countries ... that further compounds' the risk that women will be trafficked and fall into exploitative prostitution.[63] Almost by its very nature, Article 6 transcends the boundaries of the state. Unlike ICESCR there is no duty of cooperation in CEDAW requiring states to assist each other to eliminate discrimination against women.[64] The Committee seems to be at the early stages of interpreting CEDAW to include such a duty, as discussed in Chapter 4.[65] In the Concluding Observations, it encourages states to enter into bilateral and multilateral agreements to prevent trafficking.[66] Chuang, in her analysis of Article 6, holds that the Committee should encourage states to 'offer assistance to countries of origin to enable them to address inequalities that contribute to trafficking-related vulnerabilities'.[67] The Committee can echo this guidance

---

[59] J Chuang, 'Article 6' in MA Freeman, C Chinkin and B Rudolf (eds), *CEDAW: A Commentary* (Oxford University Press, 2013) 172.

[60] ibid 194.

[61] G Swerling, 'Prostitutes and the Recession: How David Cameron's Cuts Are Affecting British Women', *The Independent*, 30 April 2013; Working Group, 'Economic and Social Life' (n 4) fn 89.

[62] 'General Recommendation No 19: on Violence Against Women' (n 45) [14].

[63] Chuang (n 59) 194.

[64] Art 2(1) International Convention on Economic, Social and Cultural Rights (adopted 16 December 1966, entered into force 3 January 1976) 999 UNTS 3.

[65] The Committee, 'General Recommendation No 26: on Migrant Women Workers' (2009) CEDAW/C/GC/26 [27].

[66] The Committee, 'Concluding Observations: Eritrea' (2015) CEDAW/C/ERI/CO/5 [23(f)].

[67] Chuang (n 59) 195.

in a General Recommendation on women and poverty and encourage states to cooperate to reduce the vulnerability of women in poverty to trafficking and exploitative prostitution.

The Committee has not yet assessed how gender-based poverty acts as an obstacle to women's equal participation in public life (Articles 7 and 8). Gender-based poverty often precludes women from participating in the formation and implementation of government policy and as a result the needs of women in poverty are ignored. The Committee can encourage states to meaningfully consult and ensure the participation of women in poverty in the design, implementation and monitoring of laws, policies and programmes. This can have a positive spillover effect. By listening to the beneficiaries, public policies are less likely to be based on assumptions and instead will reflect women's genuine needs.[68] A General Recommendation on women and poverty can remind the state that women are not homogeneous and may have conflicting perspectives. The state needs to ensure the participation of all women, including women in poverty with intersecting identities. Equal participation in public life also requires the state to empower the voices of women in poverty. It is important to recognise that public participation is increasingly transferring to online spaces. Blogs, Facebook and Twitter are 'opportunities for coalition-building, the transfer of knowledge … and allow for women's movements to more effectively promote gender equality goals'.[69] Digital literacy is essential to effectively participate in these new forums of political activism. Women in poverty may not have the financial resources to gain this knowledge or access new technologies. The Committee can recommend that the state create programmes that address these needs. A General Recommendation on women and poverty should also recommend that states increase the number of women at all levels of decision-making, including at the local and national political level and in international economic, financial and trade institutions.[70] Parity in participation can open up 'sites of economic and social … power traditionally inhabited by men only'.[71] With more women in positions of power and influence, it is hoped that this will result in changes to patriarchal institutions that perpetuate gender-based poverty.[72]

---

[68] UN Special Rapporteur on extreme poverty and human rights, 'Guiding Principles' (n 33) [37].

[69] MA Dersnah 'Global Report for Working Group on the Issue of Discrimination against Women in Law and in Practice' (2014) www.ohchr.org/EN/Issues/Women/WGWomen/Pages/Discriminationinpublicandpoliticallife.aspx.

[70] Working Group, 'Economic and Social Life' (n 4) [127].

[71] R Rubio-Marín, 'A New European Parity–Democracy Sex Equality Model and Why it Won't Fly in the United States' (2012) 60 *American Journal of Comparative Law* 99, 107–12.

[72] R Rubio-Marín, 'Women in Europe and in the World: The State of the Union 2016' (2016) 14(3) *International Journal of Constitutional Law* 545–54.

In the past, the Committee has focused on nationality, marriage and access to state benefits (Article 9).[73] A General Recommendation on women and poverty should reiterate that women should not lose their nationality and access to state benefits and public services upon marrying a non-national. The dramatic influence of migrants, refugees and asylum-seekers means that now 'in practice nationality is frequently a prerequisite for the enjoyment of basic human rights'.[74] Girls and women are 'subject to compound discrimination as women and as non-nationals'[75] and denied access to desperately needed healthcare, education, accommodation, food, clothing, social services and sources of livelihood. Reflecting its recommendations in General Recommendation No 32 on the gender-related dimensions of refugee status, asylum, nationality and statelessness of women, the Committee should recommend that throughout the refugee and asylum process women have access to public services.[76] Naturalisation laws must be sensitive to gender-based poverty. Requiring official identity documents may exclude poor women who never had access to these documents; language requirements may disadvantage women who have limited access to formal education; financial criteria may be impossible for women to meet.[77] Due to these discriminatory laws and requirements, women are forced into statelessness, which increases the likelihood of them being exploited and becoming economically dependent on men.[78] To achieve equality, the structures and institutions on claiming asylum and obtaining citizenship need to be reformed to account for gender-based poverty.

Education is central to measures to combat gender-based poverty (Article 10). Poverty underpins gender inequality in education and the lack of a quality education condemns women to a life of poverty.[79] Schools may have fees or indirect costs (uniforms, food, textbooks) that make education unattainable for girls.[80] Violent attacks on girls attending school are rooted in stereotypes on the role and value of girls.[81] Girls in poverty are less likely to complete primary school,[82] and in times of financial constraint girls are more likely to drop out of school.[83] Girls may be pulled out of school to help with 'domestic responsibilities such as cooking, fetching water and

---

[73] See, for example, the Committee, 'Concluding Observations: Jordan'(2012) CEDAW/C/CO/JOR/5 [33].
[74] 'General Recommendation No 32: on Refugee Status' (n 44)[51].
[75] ibid.
[76] ibid [33], [48].
[77] ibid [55].
[78] ibid.
[79] UN Special Rapporteur on the right to education, 'Girls' Right to Education' (2006) E/CN.4/2006/45 [57].
[80] ibid [66].
[81] OHCHR, 'Attacks against Girls' (n 7) 23.
[82] World Bank, 'Voice and Agency' (n 22) 11.
[83] ibid.

firewood and childcare'.[84] The lack of sanitary facilities can cause girls to drop out of schools when they reach puberty. Schools may expel pregnant learners and even if there is no formal policy, there are 'reports of shaming, punitive measures' that make it impossible for them to return to school.[85] Formal education then 'becomes even more distant [and girls] have virtually no choices other than domestic work and raising their children'.[86] Teachers and textbooks can reinforce regressive gender norms.[87] Girls also experience gender-based violence at school from classmates and teachers.[88] All these forces combine to have a negative ripple effect, 'resulting in poor educational outcomes or the removal of girls from school' and channelling them into low-paid and precarious employment.[89] There are a number of best practices a General Recommendation on women and poverty can highlight. To address the disadvantage dimension, at a minimum primary school should be provided free of charge with no indirect costs.[90] Fulfilling girls' right to education requires the state to provide high-quality affordable public services (water facilities, childcare) so that girls are not burdened with this work. Providing meals at school 'can make a signification contribution to improving access to education for girls'.[91] Cash transfers to families that are conditional on keeping girls in school[92] or 'stipends to girls who agree to delay marriage until they complete secondary education' could also be effective.[93] Conditional cash transfers need to be evaluated to ensure that they do not undermine the girl's agency and reinforce negative stereotypes on gender-based poverty.[94] It is also necessary to address the recognition harms that limit girls receiving an education. Girls should be encouraged to choose non-traditional studies and career paths, textbooks should be revised to depict positive portrayals of women, and discriminatory attitudes on pregnancy and young motherhood needed to be addressed.[95]

---

[84] Working Group, 'Economic and Social Life' (n 4) [36].

[85] R Davis, 'Analysis: When Schoolgirls Fall Pregnant, Why Don't We Talk More About Rape?', *Daily Maverick*, 23 January 2015, www.dailymaverick.co.za/article/2015-01-23-analysis-when-schoolgirls-fall-pregnant-why-dont-we-talk-more-about-rape/#.VcNXpDbbLIU.

[86] UN Special Rapporteur on education (n 79) [78].

[87] Kabeer (n 10) 17; Miske (n 10)19.

[88] Plan International et al, 'A Girl's Right to Learn without Fear: Working to End Gender-Based Violence at School' (2013) 28, www.ungei.org/srgbv/files/Plan_SRGBV_FullReport_EN.pdf.

[89] Fredman, Kuosmanen and Campbell (n 6) 183.

[90] UN Special Rapporteur on extreme poverty and human rights, 'Guiding Principles' (n 33) [88(a)].

[91] UN Special Rapporteur on the right to food, 'Women's Rights and the Right to Food' (2013) A/HRC/22/50 [18].

[92] ibid [15], [17]; World Bank, 'Voice and Agency' (n 22) 28.

[93] Working Group, 'Economic and Social Life' (n 4) [37]. This model was used successfully in Brazil; ibid.

[94] S Fredman, 'Women and Poverty: A Human Rights Approach' (2016) 24(4) *African Journal of International and Comparative Law* 494.

[95] The Committee, 'Concluding Observations: Azerbaijan' (2015) CEDAW/C/AZE/CO/5 [29(c)].

Families may believe it is harder for an educated woman to get married and thus expect her to remain a financial burden to her family.[96] To get at the root of this recognition harm entails deeper structural changes, and decent high-paid employment must be readily available for girls upon graduation. Other structural reforms include the provision of sanitary facilities, space for breast-feeding and childcare facilities at school, and teaching accurate and comprehensive human rights-based sex education. Article 10 of CEDAW also requires the state to regulate non-state actors involved in education.[97] All measures to combat gender-based poverty in education should only be undertaken after the participation and consultation with girls and their families.

The Committee currently tackles core aspects of employment (Article 11) that perpetuate gender-based poverty: the gender pay gap, gender job segregation, and maternal and paternal leave. A General Recommendation on women and poverty needs to confront the latest challenges to decent work. In the developing world, most women work in the informal economy.[98] The Committee should simultaneously advocate for a reduction in informal work through the creation of decent work in the formal economy and for the better working conditions for informal women workers.[99] There is scope here for the Committee to propose innovative legal and policy solutions. For instance, it can encourage the state to extended health and safety inspections to the informal labour market; it can urge states to review urban, planning and zoning laws so that informal women workers who work as street vendors have a safe space to store their wares; and it can recommend that states provide public latrines so that informal women workers have access to sanitary facilities.[100] The so-called 'gig economy' with its flexible working hours is presumed to be attractive to women. There is evidence that traditional patterns of discrimination are replicated in the gig economy and women workers remain vulnerable to exploitation.[101] Labour law is grappling with how to respond to these new employment relationships. The Committee can be a transformative voice and advocate that employee rights should accrue

---

[96] UK Department for International Development, 'Improving the Lives of Girls and Women in the World's Poorest Countries', www.gov.uk/government/policies/improving-the-lives-of-girls-and-women-in-the-worlds-poorest-countries/supporting-pages/helping-to-end-early-and-forced-marriage.

[97] Human Rights Council, 'The Right to Education: Follow-up to Human Rights Council resolution 8/4' (2017) A/HRC/35/L.2.

[98] MA Chen, 'The Informal Economy: Recent Trends, Future Directions' (2016) 26(2) *New Solutions: A Journal of Environmental and Occupational Health Policy* 155, 155.

[99] Working Group, 'Economic and Social Life' (n 4) [90]–[91].

[100] L Alfers et al, 'Extending Occupational Health and Safety to Urban Street Vendors: Reflections from a Project in Durban, South Africa' (2016) 26(2) *New Solutions: A Journal of Environmental and Occupational Health Policy* 271.

[101] AR Barzilay and A Ben-David, 'Platform Inequality: Gender in the Gig Economy' 47 (2017) 47 *Seton Hall Law Review* 393, 420–22.

to the women workers regardless of the precise contractual relationship between the employer and employee. The most pervasive employment and gender-based poverty issue a General Recommendation needs to address is care work. The UN Working Group on Discrimination Against Women in Law and Practice recommends that care work be recognised, redistributed and reduced. *Recognising* care work requires the state to prohibit discrimination on the grounds of care and allow 'care expenses as deductible for income tax purposes'.[102] It needs to be more equally *redistributed* between men and women. The evidence indicates that the uptake of paternity leave is greater when it is well paid.[103] The Committee should encourage states to adopt maternal and parental high-pay leave policies. Unpaid care work needs to be *reduced* through the provision of publically funded care services. These jobs need to be fairly remunerated and have decent working conditions so that care jobs in the formal labour market do not repeat patterns of gender-based poverty. Care services also need to be adapted to women in poverty's working patterns, including informal, shift and rural work.[104] The state also has an obligation to protect care workers in the private sector. Domestic care workers often sit at the intersection of race, gender, class and migration. They are extremely vulnerable to mistreatment and oppression. States need to ensure that their migration policies do not trap women in abusive employment relations[105] and that domestic workers are included in labour law regulations.[106]

A General Recommendation on women and poverty needs to focus on women's health in light of gender-based poverty (Article 12). Women in poverty are at a high risk of maternal mortality.[107] Only 'half of pregnant women in developing regions receive the recommended minimum of four antenatal care visits'.[108] The Committee should recommend that the state ensure women in poverty, particularly poor rural women, are able to access high-quality and affordable maternal healthcare services. This can require the state to guarantee adequate transport systems between rural communities and health centres. Restrictions on abortion negatively impact girls

---

[102] Working Group, 'Economic And Social Life' (n 4) [92]–[96].

[103] ILO, 'Maternity and Paternity at Work: Law and Practice Across the World' (2014) www.ilo.org/wcmsp5/groups/public/@dgreports/@dcomm/documents/publication/wcms_242617.pdf.

[104] N Cassirer and L Addati, 'Expanding Women's Employment Opportunities: Informal Economy Workers and the Need for Childcare' (ILO Working Paper Series, 2007) www.cpahq.org/cpahq/cpadocs/wcms125991.pdf.

[105] J Fudge, 'Global Care Chains, Employment Agencies and the Conundrum of Jurisdiction: Decent Work for Domestic Workers in Canada' (2011) 23(1) *Canadian Journal of Women and the Law* 235.

[106] C 189 Domestic Workers Convention 2011 (No 189).

[107] UN Special Rapporteur on the right to health, 'The Right to the Highest Standard of Health: Reduction of Maternal Mortality' (2006) A/61/338 [10], [28(b)].

[108] 'Millennium Development Report: 2013' (n 9) 28.

and women in poverty. For instance, women in Ireland[109] or the USA[110] simply cannot afford to travel to access safe abortion services. The Committee needs to explicitly recommend that states decriminalise abortion and ensure that women are not denied access to an abortion because of the costs of these services. Sexual and reproductive health services and education are key preventive tools to counter maternal mortality and unsafe abortion. The state needs to ensure these services are accessible, affordable and designed to empower women and girls.[111] The evidence from the Concluding Observations is that poor families do not invest limited resources in maternal health because of women's low socioeconomic status in the home.[112] Therefore, it is also important to recommend that states remedy sociocultural attitudes on the value and importance of protecting women's health and address structural issues that underpin rising health costs.

Equality in economic and social life has not received significant attention from the Committee (Article 13). In the Concluding Observations, the Committee has referred to disadvantaged groups such as women in poverty[113] and to equal access to financial credit[114] under Article 13. There is great potential for the obligation to achieve equality in economic and social life to positively impact gender-based poverty.[115] The most obvious areas are social assistance and welfare schemes. The structure of social benefits can exacerbate gender-based poverty. Women predominate in low-paid temporary, part-time, informal, unpaid care or subsistence work or causal employment and have interrupted work histories.[116] These types of work are regularly excluded from social security schemes.[117] Social assistance schemes can reinforce gender power imbalances by awarding benefits to the head of the household. Programmes that are targeted towards women can 'reinforce existing gender inequalities based on patriarchal assumptions

---

[109] F de Londras, 'Constitutionalizing Fetal Rights: A Cautionary Tale from Ireland' (2015) 22(2) *Michigan Journal of Gender & Law* 243, 277.

[110] Working Group, 'Report on the Working Group on the Issue of Discrimination against Women in Law and Practice, on its Mission to the United States' (2016) A/HRC/32/44/Add.2 [68].

[111] M Campbell, '"The Challenge of Girls' Right to Education: Let's Talk About Human-Rights Based Sex Education' (2016) 20(8) *International Journal of Human Rights* 121.

[112] 'Sixth and Seventh Periodic Reports State Parties: Ethiopia' (2009) CEDAW/C/ETH/6–7 [140].

[113] The Committee, 'Concluding Observations: Canada' (2008) CEDAW/C/CAN/CO/7 [39]; The Committee, 'Concluding Observations: Argentina' (2010) CEDAW/C/ARG/CO/7 [33].

[114] The Committee, Concluding Observations: Kenya'(2011) CEDAW/C/KEN/CO/7 [35].

[115] B Rudolf, 'Article 13' in M Freeman, C Chinkin and B Rudolf (eds), *CEDAW: A Commentary* (Oxford University Press, 2012) 336.

[116] UN Special Rapporteur on extreme poverty and human rights, 'Guiding Principles' (n 33) [85].

[117] UN Special Rapporteur on extreme poverty and human rights, 'Universal Basic Income' (n 41) [38].

about work, family and the economy'.[118] Schemes can be tied to conditions that are stigmatic, implying that women need financial coercion to be good mothers, and burdensome to prove. The monitoring of these conditions can be humiliating and intrusive.[119] Furthermore, under Article 13 the General Recommendation warn of the effects austerity measures have on women. The '"savings" made from cutting back on government funding of public services often increase the demands [on women] on unpaid care and domestic work'.[120] Stimulus measures may target industries and occupations that are primarily male dominated and overlook traditionally female-dominated jobs.[121] To redress these issues a General Recommendation on women and poverty needs to stress the vital importance of non-contributory social welfare schemes that are not connected to regular, formal employment and that recognise the value of care work.[122] Programmes should not be connected to women's relationships 'with male earning members or as part of the family household'.[123] Rates need to reflect the fact that women's resources are often directed towards child and elderly care. Conditional cash transfers should not be used as a tool to punish women or add to their workload. The Committee can urge states to adopt unconditional cash transfers and to invest in public services.[124] The Committee needs to emphasise that in times of economic crisis and austerity it is crucial that recovery measures do not further entrench gender-based poverty. Women should be active participants in the design and implementation of social assistance and welfare schemes.

In General Recommendation No 34 on the rights of rural women, the Committee skilfully uses all four dimensions of transformative equality to address gender-based poverty in rural life (Article 14). It points out that rural women are disproportionately poor and calls on the state to ensure women are able to own, use and benefit from the land by reforming the formal legal system, customary law and sociocultural norms.[125] The Committee also consistently urges the state to ensure rural women are active participants

---

[118] Goldblatt, 'Development and the Right to Social Security' (n 53) 467.

[119] Fredman, 'Women and Poverty' (n 94) 510–11; Goldblatt, 'Development and the Right to Social Security' (n 53) 467.

[120] UN Women, 'Transforming Economies' (n 14) 201.

[121] UN Special Rapporteur on extreme poverty and human rights, 'Human Rights Based Approach to Recovery from Global Economic and Financial Crises, with a Focus on Those Living in Poverty' (2011) A/HRC/17/34 [77].

[122] CESCR, 'General Comment No 19: The Right to Social Security' (2009) E/C.12/GC/19 [4(b)]; Goldblatt, 'Development and the Right to Social Security' (n 53).

[123] B Goldblatt, 'The Right to Social Security—Addressing Women's Poverty and Disadvantage' (2009) 25(3) *South African Journal of Human Rights* 442, 458.

[124] UN Special Rapoprteur on extreme poverty and human rights, 'Basic Income' (n 41) [48]; UN Women, 'Transforming Economies' (n 14) 217; UN Special Rapporteur on extreme poverty and human rights, 'Global Economic and Financial Crises' (n 121) [79].

[125] 'Concluding Observations: Kenya' (n 114) [41].

in the development and implementation of land policies.[126] The Committee should repeat these recommendations in a General Recommendation on women and poverty.

Equality in law requires the state to address how gender-based poverty negatively impacts women's access to justice (Article 15). Women in poverty are unable to afford court filing and legal fees.[127] Income testing for legal aid can ignore women's limited control of household resources.[128] Legal aid schemes may not extend to areas of law of crucial to women in poverty, such as housing or social security entitlements.[129] In General Recommendation No 33 on women's access to justice the Committee is concerned that states are jailing women for petty offences and because of their inability to pay bail.[130] Formal and customary laws can operate to deny women ownership of property. A General Recommendation on women and poverty needs to address these issues. It should encourage the state to extend the coverage of legal aid to cover socioeconomic rights; to reform legal aid criteria to reflect women's de facto income; widen the rules of standing so CSOs can advocate for women in poverty; and consider gender-sensitive alternatives to incarceration. Reforming customary norms to respect women's rights can be challenging.[131] The Committee should encourage states to employ a variety of methods, including empowering women to spark internal reform, bringing customary law under the auspices of the formal legal system and training for traditional leaders.

The Committee has done a significant amount of work to ensure that upon the dissolution of a relationship women do not slip into poverty (Article 16).[132] A General Recommendation on women and poverty can draw on this previous work. It can reiterate that formal and customary law needs to be reformed so that women can equally inherit and own property; that legal aid extends to family law; and that non-financial contributions need to be taken into account when dividing a household's property. Gender-based poverty forces young girls into marriage (Article 16(b) the right to freely enter marriage).[133] Girls who live in poverty are twice as

---

[126] ibid.

[127] UN Women, Progress of the World's Women: In Pursuit of Justice' (2011) 52, www.unwomen.org/-/media/headquarters/attachments/sections/library/publications/2011/progressoftheworldswomen-2011-en.pdf?vs=2835.

[128] ibid 54.

[129] The Committee, 'General Recommendation No 33: on Women's Access to Justice' (2015) CEDAW/C/GC/33 [52].

[130] ibid [17(a)].

[131] M Campbell and G Swenson, 'Legal Pluralism and Women's Rights After Conflict: The Role of CEDAW' (2016) 48(1) *Columbia Human Rights Law Review* 111.

[132] 'General Recommendation No 29: on Economic Consequences' (n 36).

[133] The Committee and Committee on the Convention on the Rights of the Child, 'General Recommendation No 31: on Harmful Practices' (2014) CEDAW/C/GC/31 [21].

likely to be married before they are 18 years old.[134] The Committee should urge states to take a holistic approach and combat child and household poverty. This could be done through conditional cash transfers that require a girl to attend school on a regular basis and through the creation of decent economic opportunities for the family so girls are not viewed as an economic burden.

The General Recommendation needs to highlight the relationship between violence and gender-based poverty. The World Bank notes that 'beyond damage to health, violence reduces women's economic opportunities'.[135] Women who experience domestic violence have 'higher work absenteeism, lower productivity and lower earnings'[136] which can trap women in dependent relationships with abusive partners. Gender-based poverty increases the risk of homelessness for women, which in turn increases their risk of being subject to violence.[137] Women in poverty often cannot afford public transportation, which increases their risk of violence.[138] Domestic workers and women in refugee, asylum and displaced person camps are at an increased risk of violence.[139] If girls face violence at or on the way to school they may be less likely to complete their studies, thereby reducing their ability to compete in the labour market and break cycles of poverty.[140] The Committee should remind states that a commitment to end violence against women necessarily entails reducing gender-based poverty. It can continue to encourage states to provide gender-based violence shelters, ensure affordable public transportation and use a variety of safety techniques (lighting, patrol guards, etc) to ensure girls are not assaulted on the way to school, in the workplace, or in refugee, asylum and displaced persons' camps.[141]

[134] 'Girls Not Brides: What Is the Impact of Child Marriage: Poverty', www.girlsnotbrides.org/themes/poverty/.

[135] World Bank, 'Voice and Agency' (n 22) 65.

[136] ibid.

[137] Working Group, 'United States Mission' (n 110).

[138] The Committee, 'Report of the Inquiry Concerning Canada of the Committee on the Elimination of Discrimination Against Women under Article 8 of OP-CEDAW' (2015) CEDAW/C/OP.8/CAN/1; The Committee, 'Report of the Inquiry Concerning Mexico of the Committee on Elimination of Discrimination Against Women under Article 8 OP-CEDAW' (2005) CEDAW/C/OP.8/MEX/1.

[139] UNIFEM, 'Human Rights Protections Applicable to Women Migrant Workers' (UNIFEM Briefing Paper, 2003) 30; UNHCR and Human Rights Centre University of California, 'Safe Heaven: Sheltering Displaced Persons from Sexual and Gender-Based Violence: Case Study Kenya: May 2013' (2013) 22.

[140] UNIFEM, 'The Facts: Violence Against Women and the Millennium Development Goals', www.unwomen.org/~/media/H$eadquarters/Media/Publications/UNIFEM/EVAWkit_02_VAWandMDGs_en.pdf.

[141] The Committee, 'General Recommendation No 35: on Gender-Based Violence Against Women' (2017) CEDAW/C/GC/35.

B. Accountability for Gender-Based Poverty

The interpretation of CEDAW proposed in this book means that the state is accountable under the treaty's various mechanisms for eliminating discrimination, achieving equality and fulfilling the human rights of women in poverty. Under Article 2 of CEDAW (core obligations), the state also needs to have in place effective *domestic* mechanisms and remedies so that women's rights are protected and upheld.[142] Although the Committee does not have a history of discussing accountability in relation to specific issues of gender equality, the usefulness of a General Recommendation on women and poverty is significantly enhanced if it engages with how the state's domestic accountability mechanisms can tackle gender-based poverty.

The Committee can draw on the Office of the High Commissioner's (OHCHR) guidance to flesh out this accountability obligation in light of gender-based poverty. The OHCHR argues that accountability has three dimensions: responsibility, answerability and enforceability.[143] The responsibility dimension sets out the 'specific obligations which inform [state] conduct'.[144] The Committee can recommend that the state adopt a comprehensive strategy aimed at eliminating gender-based poverty.[145] In developing a strategy, the state can draw on the recommendations and best practices articulated above and consult with women in poverty to develop innovative methods that further implement the state's obligation to tackle gender-based poverty. The Committee can emphasise that the state's responsibility under Article 2 requires it to eliminate discrimination against women in poverty by private parties including individuals, corporations and private providers of traditionally conceived public services. Answerability 'refers to the capacity to demand that those in authority give reasoned justification for their behaviour'.[146] It can come in a variety of forms: courts, administrative hearings, national human rights institutions, consultation, community based, and online interaction and activism. This echoes Article 15 (equality in law). The Committee can reinforce the state's obligation to ensure that the redistribution, recognition and participation harms of gender-based poverty do not act as obstacles to women in poverty, demanding answers for the state's laws, policies and programmes. The third dimension, enforceability,

---

[142] The Committee, 'General Recommendation No 28: on Core Obligations'(2010) CEDAW/C/GC/28 [40]; OHCHR 'Who Will be Accountable? Human Rights and the Post-2015 Development Agenda' (2013) HR/PUB/13/1, 10.

[143] OHCHR, 'Post-2015 Development Agenda' (n 142).

[144] ibid.

[145] UN Special Rapporteur on extreme poverty and human rights, 'Guiding Principles' (n 33) [50].

[146] OHCHR, 'Post-2015 Development Agenda' (n 142) 14.

requires the state to provide effective remedies through compensation for the violations of rights and through the promotion of 'positive structural and institutional change'.[147] This section of a General Recommendation on women and poverty can conclude by reminding the state that accountability applies across the whole lifecycle of the law or policy: planning, budgeting, implementation, monitoring and evaluation.[148]

C. Guidance on Periodic Reporting Process

The last paragraphs of the General Recommendation should provide advice on preparing the state report for the periodic reporting process, CEDAW's central accountability mechanism. Even if the guidelines are reformed as proposed in Chapter 6 to better account for gender-based poverty, it is helpful to reiterate and expand upon this guidance as a General Recommendation is arguably more easily accessible to state representatives preparing the state report. Furthermore, the reporting guidelines direct the state to take account of the Committee's General Recommendations. A General Recommendation on women and poverty can repeat the Committee's call for disaggregated data on women in poverty. In the past states have not responded to calls for disaggregated data on women, but it is still important for the Committee to highlight the importance of understanding the de facto situation of women in poverty. It can also provide guidance on how the state report should be structured. For gender-based violence, the Committee routinely discusses violence under a separate sub-heading and also integrates a discussion on violence into the other substantive provisions in the treaty.[149] The General Recommendation on women and poverty can recommend a similar approach. It should encourage the state report to give specific attention to the issue of gender-based poverty. At the same time, the Committee should emphasise that interpreting equality and non-discrimination to incorporate the harms of gender-based poverty means gender-based poverty is comprehensively interpreted into the CEDAW framework.[150] When preparing the report on each substantive provision, the state should provide information on the de jure and de facto conditions of women in poverty.

---

[147] ibid.
[148] ibid.
[149] 'General Recommendation No 19: on Violence Against Women' (n 45) [29]–[30], [33], [43].
[150] D Budlender and G Hewitt, 'Engendering Budgets: A Practitioners' Guide to Understanding and Implementing Gender-Responsive Budgets' (Commonwealth Secretariat, 2003) 12.

IV. CONCLUSION

A General Recommendation on women and poverty can make a significant contribution to the evolution in the relationship between gender-based poverty and human rights. It ensures that CEDAW remains relevant and speaks to the de facto experience of women all over the world. To achieve this aim, it is essential that the General Recommendation have a firm theoretical basis and that it makes a persuasive argument that gender-based poverty is an obstacle to fulfilling the obligations in CEDAW. This is best accomplished by justifying the need for a General Recommendation, explaining the legal basis for this interpretation of CEDAW, providing meaningful recommendations that are responsive to the complexity of gender-based poverty and providing guidance to the state. It is hoped that an authoritative General Recommendation based on the arguments made throughout this book will prompt states and CSOs to report on gender-based poverty and for the Committee to address gender-based poverty consistently and coherently as a facet of equality and non-discrimination in the treaty's other accountability mechanisms. International human rights law can be a focal point for transformative change and spark discussions on human rights approaches to gender-based poverty by domestic and international policy-makers, CSOs and grassroots movements. It is hoped that all of these actors working together, using the interpretation of CEDAW proposed in this book, can develop best practices on using human rights to ensure that women in poverty can develop, advance, participate and enjoy a meaningfully life.

Annex

Draft General Recommendation on Women and Poverty

I. INTRODUCTION

1.   Gender-based poverty is a form of discrimination that seriously inhibits women's ability to enjoy their rights and freedoms on the basis of equality. Women's poverty is more than insufficient economic resources because poverty is not a gender-neutral experience. Women's poverty is the lack of resources coupled with gendered socio-cultural norms that exclude and devalue women. The Committee on the Elimination of Discrimination Against Women aims to provide authoritative guidance to states parties on legislative, policy and other appropriate measures to ensure the implementation of their obligations under the Convention on the Elimination of All Forms of Discrimination Against Women and the Optional Protocol thereto regarding non-discrimination and gender equality relating to gender-based poverty.

2.   The scope and purpose of this General Recommendation must be determined in the context of the overall scope and purpose of the Convention, which is to eliminate all forms of discrimination against women in the recognition, enjoyment or exercise of all human rights and fundamental freedoms in the political, economic, social, cultural, civil or any other field, irrespective of their marital status. The objective of this present General Recommendation is to explain the relationship between gender-based poverty and the substantive provisions of the Convention and to outline the state's obligations to respect, protect and fulfil the rights under the Convention towards women and girls who live in poverty. The Committee wishes to share best practices it has acquired through reviewing state reports and the Committee's Concluding Observations thereon and Individual Communications and Inquiry Procedures under the Optional Protocol. The General Recommendation aims to guide state parties on how to address all aspects of gender-based poverty in the periodic state report.

3.   Poverty is a serious and pressing problem that affects both men and women. The Convention is a gender-specific human rights instrument that

focuses on women's rights. As such, the Convention provides a gender-sensitive interpretation of human rights law and protects women from sex and gender based-discrimination.[1] In General Recommendation No 19 on violence against women, General Recommendation No 30 on women in conflict prevention, conflict and post-conflict situations, in General Recommendation No 32 on the gender-related dimensions of refugee status, asylum nationality and statelessness of women, and General Recommendation No 34 on the rights of rural women the Committee has recognised that these pervasive and cross-cutting global problems are not gender neutral. The present General Recommendation continues this work and explores the gender-based aspects of poverty.

4.   Gender both causes and contributes to women's poverty. Throughout the developed and developing world women are disproportionately living in poverty. Gendered social norms and cultural attitudes that are based on the idea of the inferiority of women and the superiority of men or on the stereotyped roles of women and men cause and contribute to women's poverty. These gendered norms, attitudes and stereotypes limit women's access to education, healthcare, employment, land, and financial and economic resources. Furthermore, it limits their ability to participate fully in public and private life. This perpetuates a vicious cycle of poverty, powerlessness, social exclusion, inequality and discrimination.

5.   At every stage of their lives girls and women are affected by gender norms that are deeply embedded in the political, legal and social culture. Gender-based poverty is a global phenomenon that impacts a significant number of women in rural and urban areas and in the developed and developing world. Households that live in poverty may be reluctant to invest in girls' education. At school, girls can be pressured into learning traditional occupations and can be expelled if they become pregnant. Women and girls continue to disproportionately perform unpaid care work which restricts the time and energy they have to invest in training, skills, education, leisure and decent employment. The work women perform in the formal and informal labour market is perceived as unskilled and less valuable and is consequentially under-remunerated. There still exist numerous legal restrictions on women's right to work.[2] Due to unpaid care work and discrimination in accessing education and training women are often forced into precarious and exploitative employment.[3] Elderly women who worked

---

[1] 'General Recommendation No 28: The Core Obligations of States Parties under Article 2 of the Convention on the Elimination of All Forms of Discrimination against Women' (2010) CEDAW/C/GC/28 [5].

[2] World Bank, 'Women, Business and the Law: 2016' (World Bank, 2016).

[3] 'Millennium Development Report: 2014' (UN, 2014): 'In developing regions, 60 per cent of women were in vulnerable employment in 2013, compared to 54 per cent of men.'

part time, in the informal market or have interrupted working patterns are often excluded from pension schemes. The undervaluation of women in public life also contributes to women's low socioeconomic status within the private sphere. Women may have limited de facto access to the household's assets and resources. De jure legal barriers and sociocultural norms often combine together to prevent a woman from owning and controlling productive resources, and from making decisions on household purchases and how assets should be used.

6.   There is one reference to women's poverty in the Convention: 'concerned that in situations of poverty women have the least access to food, health, education, training and opportunities for employment and other needs'. Articles 1–3 of the Convention establish a comprehensive obligation to eliminate discrimination in all its forms. Women in poverty are denied the opportunity for full development and advancement and the enjoyment and exercise of their human rights and fundamental freedoms. The Committee firmly holds that women who live in poverty experience multiple and reinforcing violations of their political, civil, social, economic and cultural rights. The Convention, as a gender-specific human rights instrument, covers other rights that are not explicitly mentioned therein, but that have an impact on the achievement of equality of women and men.[4] Gender-based poverty may violate the specific provisions in the Convention, regardless of whether those provisions expressly mention gender-based poverty.

7.   The Convention is a dynamic instrument that contributes and adapts to the development of international law. The present General Recommendation builds upon the work the Committee has done on women and poverty in the Concluding Observations, Individual Communications and Inquiry Procedure. It also builds upon earlier General Recommendations including No 16 on unpaid women workers in rural and urban family enterprises, No 17 on measurement and quantification of the unremunerated domestic activities of women and their recognition in the gross national product, No 29 on economic consequences of marriage, family relations and their dissolution, and No 34 on the rights of rural women.

8.   The Committee affirms previous commitments to women in poverty: the right to an adequate standard of living in Article 11 of the International Covenant on Economic, Social and Cultural Rights,[5] in Article 27 on the Convention on the Rights of the Child[6] and in Article 28 of the Convention

---

[4] 'General Recommendation No 28: on Core Obligations' (n 1) [7]; 'General Recommendation No 19 on Violence Against Women' (1992) CEDAW/C/GC/19.
   [5] International Covenant on Economic, Social and Cultural Rights (adopted, 16 December 1966, entered into force 3 January 1976) 993 UNTS 3.
   [6] Convention on the Rights of the Child (adopted 20 November, 1989, entered into force 2 September 1990) 157 UNTS 3.

on the Rights of Persons with Disabilities;[7] International Labour Organization (ILO) Convention No 100 on equal remuneration; ILO Convention No 111 on discrimination in employment and occupation; ILO Convention No 156 on workers with family responsibilities; ILO Convention No 183 on maternity protection; ILO Convention No 189 on domestic workers; the Beijing Declaration; the Sustainable Development Goals; the Guiding Principles of the Special Rapporteur on extreme poverty and human rights;[8] the Committee on Economic, Social and Cultural Rights statement on the Substantive Issues arising in the Implementation of the International Covenant on Economic, Social and Cultural Rights: Poverty; and the International Covenant on Economic, Social and Cultural Rights.[9]

9.   The Committee observes that not all reports of state parties adequately reflect the close connection between discrimination against women, gender inequality, poverty and human rights. The General Recommendation provides guidance to state parties on the inclusion of women in poverty in their reports on the implementation of the Convention.

10.   The full implementation of the Convention requires states to take measures to eliminate all forms of gender-based poverty. The Committee seeks to ensure that the gender equality and non-discrimination obligations are upheld by state parties to the Convention in respect of women in poverty.

II. LEGAL BACKGROUND

11.   In General Recommendation No 19 on violence against women and General Recommendation No 25 on temporary special measures, the Committee observed that the Convention is an evolutionary instrument that anticipates the emergence of new forms of discrimination that had not been identified at the time of drafting. Article 1 and Article 2 require state parties to eliminate all forms of discrimination, while Article 3 requires state parties to ensure women's development and advancement in all fields of life. The concept of equality and non-discrimination in the Convention are sensitive and responsive to new and newly recognised challenges, such as gender-based poverty, to women's human rights.

---

[7] Convention on the Rights of Persons with Disabilities, A/RES/61/106.

[8] UN Special Rapporteur on extreme poverty and human rights, 'Final Draft of the Guiding Principles on Extreme Poverty and Human rights' (2012) A/HRC/21/39.

[9] Committee on Economic, Social and Cultural Rights, 'Substantive Issues arising in the Implementation of the International Covenant on Economic, Social and Cultural Rights: Poverty; and the International Covenant on Economic, Social and Cultural Rights' (2001) E/C.12/2001/10.

The Definition of Gender-Based Poverty

12. Women's experience of poverty is inherently multifaceted. It cannot be exclusively equated with a lack of income or economic resources. Women's economic deprivation is connected to and reinforced by compromised autonomy, exclusion from social life, political marginalisation, stigma, and bodily and psychological insecurity that are inextricably rooted in their gender. Gender-based poverty is the unique interaction between gendered sociocultural norms and inadequate command over economic resources. The challenges girls face in accessing high-quality education, the gender division of labour, the lack of legal regulation of the informal labour market, the concentration of women in low-paying and often precarious jobs, the low valuation of work traditionally assigned to women, unequal pay for work of equal value, gender power imbalances in the home, the disproportionate amount of unpaid care work they perform, and the limited access to skills training, bank loans and land all combine to create a unique experience for poor women.[10] The definition of gender-based poverty must encompass more than income poverty. For this General Recommendation gender-based poverty is defined as the redistribution wrongs of not having access to economic resources coupled with the gender sociocultural negative stereotypes and attitudes and participation harms that devalue women and girls and exclude them from public and private life. It is the combination of both material disadvantage and gender sociocultural norms that limit the ability of women in poverty to create a meaningful life.

13. Gender-based poverty has historically been seen as an issue of charity or economic development and conceptualised as a gender-neutral phenomenon. It has been perceived as a phenomenon isolated to rural areas in developing countries. With the passage of time, it is now recognised that gender-based poverty is a serious and pressing obstacle to women's enjoyment of their human rights.[11] Gender-based poverty impacts women's rights everywhere in the world. Redressing these violations is not only a matter of charity or a moral duty but a legal obligation under the Convention.[12] State parties need to take appropriate measures to respect the dignity of women in poverty, empower them to create a meaningful life and to participate fully in public and private life. State parties are to be held accountable for respecting, protecting and fulfilling the rights of women in poverty.

---

[10] G Brodsky and S Day, 'Beyond the Social and Economic Rights Debate: Substantive Equality Speaks to Poverty' (2002) 14 *Canadian Journal of Woman and the Law* 184.
[11] UN Special Rapporteur on extreme poverty and human rights, 'Guiding Principles' (n 8) and S Chant, 'Re-thinking the "Feminization of Poverty" in Relation to Aggregate Gender Indices' (2007) 7(2) *Journal of Human Development* 201.
[12] UN Special Rapporteur on extreme poverty and human rights, 'Guiding Principles' (n 8).

Legal Interpretation[13]

14.   The Convention in Article 1 defines discrimination against women. The definition of discrimination prohibits any sex- or gender-based distinctions that impair or nullify women's enjoyment or exercise of their human rights on the basis of equality.[14] The definition of discrimination includes gender-based poverty; that is, poverty which is caused, perpetuated or maintained against a woman because she is a woman.[15] The concept of 'eliminating discriminating against women' and 'equality' permeates all of the Convention. A dynamic interpretation of 'discrimination against women' and 'equality' comprehensively incorporates the harms of gender-based poverty into the Convention.

15.   The goal of the Convention is to eliminate discrimination against women and achieve de jure and de facto gender equality so that women can enjoy and exercise their human rights. The Convention is meant to be responsive to changes in the nature of discrimination against women and gender inequality.[16] Under Article 4(1) of the Convention state parties must be vigilant to women's changing needs.[17] Gender-based poverty is now recognised as an obstacle to achieving women's equality and human rights.[18] Women's unequal share of undervalued care work, their lower levels of education, the inability to seek financial independence, marginalisation in home and society, and negative prejudices and stereotypes create a vicious cycle of social and economic disempowerment and result in women being unable to exercise and enjoy their human rights.[19] For the Convention to achieve its aims, 'discrimination against women' and 'equality' need to be interpreted to include the interaction between poverty and gender to accurately understand how gender-based poverty acts as an obstacle to women's human rights.

16.   The meaning of equality in the Convention is multifaceted. The Convention is based on both formal and substantive equality. Formal equality

---

[13] This General Recommendation uses the interpretative framework of Vienna Convention on the Law of Treaties ((adopted 23 May 1969, entered into force 27 January 1980) 1155 UNTS 331), see Arts 31–33.

[14] 'General Recommendation No 28: on Core Obligations' (n 1).

[15] See 'General Recommendation No 19: on Violence against Women' (n 4) for the basis for an expansive interpretation of Art 1 of the Convention.

[16] 'General Recommendation No 25: on Temporary Special Measures' (2004) CEDAW/C/GC/25 [11].

[17] ibid.

[18] Office of the High Commissioner of Human Rights, 'Human Rights and Poverty Reduction: A Conceptual Framework' (2004) HR/PUB/04/1 [15]. UN Special Rapporteur on extreme poverty and human rights, 'Guiding Principles' (n 8) [23].

[19] S Fredman, 'Anti-discrimination Laws and Work in the Developing World: A Thematic Overview' (Background Paper for World Development Report, 2013).

requires state parties to remove legal barriers that disadvantage women in poverty. State parties are obligated to remove formal legal obstacles that restrict, for example, a woman's choice of occupation, that require a husband or father's permission to travel, work or register a business or that vest control of joint property into the male head of household.

17.   The conception of equality in the Convention goes further than formal equality or equal treatment. The Convention also ensures that women enjoy de facto or substantive equality. In General Recommendation No 28 on the state parties' core obligations, the Committee interpreted substantive equality in a comprehensive manner. Equality in the Convention includes equality of opportunity, equality of results and transformative equality. The Committee uses all three models of equality under its conception of substantive equality. Equality of opportunity requires that state parties take measures to ensure that women be empowered by an enabling environment. This includes taking steps to ensure that girls and women are able to benefit from scholarship opportunities so as to break cycles of gender-based poverty.[20] Equality of results requires state parties to ensure that women enjoy equality in equal numbers with men in socially valuable goods: income levels, decision-making and political influence. This can require the state to set gender quotas in legislative bodies, the judiciary and the board of public companies.[21] Ensuring women's equal participation in public and private institutions can open up sites of power so that laws, policies and programmes do not perpetuate gender-based poverty.

18.   The Convention is also based and committed to achieving transformative equality.[22] Transformative equality seeks four overlapping aims: breaking cycles of disadvantage; addressing stereotyping, stigma, prejudice, negative cultural attitudes and violence; valuing difference by requiring institutional and structural change; and participation.[23] The disadvantage dimension recognises that women have suffered economic, material and social harm for being women. Achieving equality requires specific and positive measures to address this imbalance.[24] The second element requires promoting the dignity and worth of women by addressing stigma, stereotyping, humiliation and violence against women.[25] The structural element seeks to accommodate difference and positively affirm identities by requiring institutions not individuals to change.[26] The final dimension, participation,

---

[20]   Art 10 of the Convention.
[21]   Art 7 of the Convention.
[22]   See Arts 3, 4 and 5(a) of the Convention.
[23]   See S Fredman, *Discrimination Law*, 2nd edn (Clarendon Press, 2011).
[24]   Art 4(1) of the Convention.
[25]   Art 5(a) and 10(c) of the Convention.
[26]   Art 11(1)(d), 11(2)(c) and 14(2)(c) of the Convention.

requires the inclusion of women in all public and private decision-making processes.[27] A transformative equality framework can be used to question whether the design of poverty alleviation programmes truly furthers women's substantive equality. While these programmes target economic disadvantage, transformative equality can highlight how the structure of these programmes can continue to essentialise women as primary care-givers and stereotype them as uncaring mothers.[28] All four dimensions of transformative equality must be used to properly assess whether the law, programme or policy actually improves the lives of women in poverty.

19.   From the Committee's experience reviewing state reports, there is an emerging state practice for understanding the commitment in the Convention to eliminate discrimination against women and achieve gender equality so women can enjoy their human rights to require specific measures to address gender-based poverty. This General Recommendation synthesises state practice and provides a coherent interpretation of the Convention.

20.   States parties are obligated under Articles 1 and 2 to ensure there is no direct or indirect discrimination against women in poverty in their laws, policies and programmes. The Committee in previous General Recommendations has explained that discrimination against women based on sex and/or gender is often inextricably linked with and compounded by other factors that affect women such as race, ethnicity, religion or belief, health, age, class, caste, gender identity and sexual orientation.[29] The Committee has also explained that women experience issues and problems—violence, conflict, statelessness—in different ways than men.[30] Poverty, both as an identity characteristic and as a cross-cutting experience, is similarly linked with gender as a basis for disadvantaged treatment against women.[31] Gender-based poverty is routinely linked to other identity characteristics: age, race, religion, disability, sexual orientation, marital status and nationality. State parties must legally recognise such intersecting forms of discrimination and inequality and their negative impact on the women concerned.

---

[27]   Art 7, 8 and 14(2)(a) of the Convention.

[28]   UN Special Rapporteur on extreme poverty and human rights, 'Conditional Cash Transfer Programmes' (2008) A/HRC/11/9 [58]–[60], [66]–[72].

[29]   'General Recommendation No 28: on Core Obligations' (n 1) [5].

[30]   'General Recommendation No 19: on Violence against Women' (n 4); 'General Recommendation No 30: On Women in Conflict Prevention, Conflict and Post-Conflict Situations' (2013) CEDAW/C/GC/30; 'General Recommendation No 32: On the Gender-related Dimensions of Refugee Status, Asylum, Nationality and Statelessness of Women' (2014) CEDAW/C/GC/32; 'General Recommendation No 35: on Gender-Based Violence Against Women' (2017) CEDAW/C/GC/35.

[31]   *da Silva Pimentel Teixeria v Brazil*, (2011) CEDAW/C/49/D/17/2008.

21.   The Committee holds that a commitment to eliminating discrimination and achieving de jure and de facto equality means state parties are obligated to address the unique human rights violations women in poverty experience.

The State's Obligations

22.   Under Article 2, state parties must address all of their legal obligations under the Convention to respect, protect and fulfil the human rights of women in poverty. The obligation to respect requires that State parties to refrain from making laws policies, regulations, programmes, administrative procedures and institutional structures that cause and perpetuate gender-based poverty. State parties are required to immediately review their laws, policies and programmes to ensure that these respect the rights of women in poverty. This can include removing prohibitions against night work or certain occupations, removing prohibitions on married or pregnant girls and women from attending school, removing the protection for customary or traditional laws that exclude women from owning and inheriting property, and ensuring courts properly account for non-financial contributions in allocating matrimonial property.

23. The obligation to protect requires that state parties protect women in poverty from discrimination and inequality perpetuated by private actors. This can require state parties to enact legislation prohibiting discrimination by private actors; set up organisations that monitor and conduct on-site inspections to ensure equal pay for work of equal value in the private sector; to hold private actors to account when they are involved in the delivery of public services; and to regulate and monitor the informal labour market to ensure women are protected from exploitative working conditions.

24. The obligation to fulfil requires that state parties take various appropriate measures to ensure that women in poverty may enjoy their equal rights. Where appropriate this can include taking temporary special measures in accordance with Article 4(1) and General Recommendation No 25. The state has an obligation to fulfil women in poverty's human rights through public policies, programmes and frameworks that are aimed at meeting the specific needs of women in poverty. This can include social assistance and education grants, and the provision of low-cost healthcare and housing and legal aid.

25.   The state is under an immediate obligation to ensure the measures it takes to respect, protect and fulfil women in poverty's human rights further gender equality and eliminate discrimination against women.

The obligations in the Convention are not subject to progressive realisation.[32] The state is under an immediate obligation to ensure that its laws, policies and programmes are gender sensitive and further women's de jure and de facto equality. In the periodic reporting process and under the Optional Protocol the Committee will evaluate the state party's laws, policies and programmes to ensure that these are consistent with the state's commitment under the Convention to eliminate discrimination and achieve substantive gender equality for women in poverty.

III. SPECIFIC AREAS OF CONCERN

26.　Both men and women who live in poverty experience discrimination because of poverty. Women experience poverty differently. The impact of gender on poverty is often based on deep-rooted cultural and social norms. This negatively impacts resource allocation, contributes to power imbalances between men and women in the home and in the public sphere, and excludes women from fully participating in all fields of life.

27.　The Committee stresses that this General Recommendation only highlights pertinent areas of concern and state parties must be attentive to precisely how women in poverty experience human rights violations.

28.　The discrimination experienced by women in poverty is often multidimensional, with poverty compounding other forms of discrimination based on race, ethnic origin, disability, sexual orientation, gender identity, migrant status, marital and family status, age and literacy.

29.　The full development and advancement of women in poverty can only be achieved by recognising the unique human rights violations they experience. The Committee observes that understanding the way in which women's rights are violated is critical to the identification of those forms of discrimination and inequality and is crucial for creating tailored and transformative remedies. However, in many state parties, gender-based poverty is ignored and tolerated at the individual, institutional and policy level. State parties often disregard how national, regional and global

---

[32] The Working Group on Discrimination Against Women in Law and Practice, 'Discrimination against Women in Economic and Social Life, with a Focus on Economic Crisis' (2014) A/C/26/39 [8] observes that the immediate obligation to achieve gender equality means the state should be concerned about 'the division of existing resources, not the development of resources, and therefore the principle of progressive realisation does not apply'. The findings of the Working Group on Discrimination Against Women in Law and Practice has been adopted by the Human Rights Council. See Human Rights Council, 'Elimination of Discrimination Against Women' (2014) A/HRC/RES/26/5.

macroeconomic policies negatively impact women and increase their vulnerability to economic and social disadvantage.[33] This General Recommendation calls on state parties to approach gender-based poverty as a human rights issue.

Cultural Attitudes (Article 5)

30.   Women who live in poverty are subject to a unique set of pernicious stereotypes. They are often perceived as lazy, promiscuous and unfit mothers who leech off social protection systems. This can make it difficult for women to access social protections that they are legally entitled to. Gender stereotyping, tradition and customary practices can have a harmful impact on women. These can both cause and maintain gender-based poverty. Deeply-rooted social customs often require women to perform the majority of unpaid care work for children and the elderly. In school, women and girls may be discouraged from studying subjects that lead to decent employment which are believed to be better suited to boys and men. If a woman tries to access and enjoy property she legally owns she may be perceived as selfishly acting against the interests of her community. These cultural attitudes trap women in poverty.

Exploitative Prostitution and Trafficking (Article 6)

31.   Gender-based poverty is an underlying cause making women vulnerable to exploitative prostitution and trafficking. States need to appreciate how global inequalities contribute to gender-based poverty. Women in poverty are vulnerable to sex trafficking and sex tourism.[34] The recruitment of domestic labour from developing countries and organised marriages between women from developing countries and foreign nationals can, under certain circumstances, also constitute new forms of trafficking.[35]

Participation in Public Life (Articles 7 and 8)

32.   Women in poverty are routinely denied their ability to participate in public, political and international life. Poverty can be a barrier to voting, particularly if literacy is a requirement to vote and if voting stations are

---

[33] Working Group on Discrimination Against Women in Law and Practice (n 32).
[34] 'General Recommendation No 19: on Violence Against Women' (n 4).
[35] ibid.

situated long distances from where women in poverty live.[36] Poverty is a serious obstacle to participating in the formulation and implementation of government policy. The voices of women in poverty are routinely ignored by state policy-makers. The double burden of unpaid care work and work in the informal or formal labour market mean women often lack the time and energy to participate meaningfully in public life. The lack of digital literacy skills and financial resources means women in poverty are often excluded from online forums of political participation and activism. Women are chronically under-represented in international and national financial and trade institutions. This excludes women from participating in key decisions at both a national and global level, a situation that creates and maintains gender-based poverty.[37]

Nationality (Article 9)

33.   In General Recommendation No 32 the Committee explained the gender dimensions of refugee status, asylum, nationality and statelessness of women. Women and girls are often denied access to food, education, healthcare, accommodation, clothing, social services, and sources of livelihood during the asylum and/or integration process. Due to lack of resources and discriminatory social cultural norms, women and girls may not have identification documents, which further limit their ability to access state-administrated social and economic benefits. States' nationality laws often have literacy and economic sufficiency requirements. Women in poverty may be systematically unable to meet these criteria. Furthermore language and income requirements for nationality may result in women being financially dependent on men and increase their risk to exploitation. Women and their children can be denied access to state benefits upon marrying non-nationals.

Education (Article 10)

34.   Poverty contributes to gender inequality in education. Schools may have fees or indirect costs, such as transportation, uniforms, lunches or textbooks that make education unattainable for girls and women in poverty.[38] While this can affect boys too, families are less likely to invest

---

[36] 'General Recommendation No 23: on Women in Political and Public Life' (1997) CEDAW/C/GC/23.
[37] Working Group on Discrimination Against Women in Law and Practice (n 32).
[38] UN Special Rapporteur on education, 'Girls' Right to Education' (2006) E/CN.4/2006/45.

in a girl's education.[39] In times of household austerity, girls and women are more likely than boys to be taken out of school to help with domestic responsibilities.[40] Families may believe that it is harder for an educated woman to get married and that she will remain a financial burden to their family. Pregnant and married learners can be expelled from school. The risk of attacks girls face when travelling to schools and gender-based violence in the classroom prevent girls from receiving a high-quality education.

Employment (Article 11)

35.   In all states women tend to be paid less than men for the same work or work of equal value. Women's traditional roles in the formal labour market, such as formal care jobs, tend to be poorly paid and have poor working conditions. Women in poverty do not have the skills—literacy, digital literacy, numeracy—to successfully compete in the formal labour market. This can have a devastating impact on the lives of women in poverty. Globally, only 41% of women who had given birth received maternity benefits.[41] Due to childcare responsibilities women are segregated into low-paid, vulnerable and potentially exploitative employment as part-time or causal workers or in the informal labour market. Formal childcare services are simply too costly for many women. New forms of employment and working patterns are repeating cycles of gender disadvantage. All of these types of employment are routinely excluded from legal protection including working time, minimum wage, social security, and workplace health and safety.

Access to Healthcare (Article 12)

36.   Women in poverty are at a significantly higher risk of maternal mortality. They do not receive the necessary prenatal, delivery and antenatal healthcare and services. The disadvantage women in poverty experience are compounded for rural women as they are often long distances from health centres and do not have the resources to access transportation, particularly emergency transportation.[42] Without being able to access affordable contraception and abortion services women and their children can be condemned

---

[39] ibid[66].

[40] Working Group on Discrimination Against Women in Law and Practice (n 32).

[41] UN Economic and Social Council, 'Progress Towards the Sustainable Development Goals' (2017) E/2017/66 [5].

[42] See *Teixeria* (n 31) and UN Special Rapporteur on the right to health, 'The Right to Health and the Reduction of Maternal Mortality' (2006) A/61/338.

to lives of poverty.[43] Women's low position in the home means families will not use their limited resources to address the health needs of women.

Economic and Social Life (Article 13)

37.   The design of social protection schemes can exacerbate gender-based poverty. Attaching onerous and invasive conditions to the receipt of social assistance can stigmatise women in poverty. Programmes that are based on the head of household can result in women not having access to financial resources which re-entrenches gender power imbalances in the home. Social assistance rates do not take account of the financial and time burden on women who have responsibility for caring for children and the elderly. Schemes that have conditions attached have the potential to limit women's time to engage in economic and socially productive activities and to essentialise women as primary care-givers. Women are disproportionately impacted by economic austerity and recovery measures. This is due in part because women are frequently employed in the public sector and rely significantly on public services. In times of financial crisis women's participation in the informal labour market increases and with the reduction in public services women have to perform a greater share of unpaid care work.[44]

Rural Women (Article 14)

38.   In the developing world women are less likely to report owning land or a house.[45] Rural women who live in poverty face legal barriers to inheriting, owning, using and benefiting land. Land certificates may preclude joint ownership. In addition, customary and traditional laws and sociocultural norms also deny rural women access to land.[46] Women are excluded from planning, developing and implementing rural development programmes. Rural women lack easy access to high-quality social services and transportation. Women and girls regularly have to walk long distances to collect clean water. Rural women may not be able to enjoy their right to food, water or housing or participate in community activities.

---

[43] 'Report of the Inquiry Concerning the Philippines of the Committee on the Elimination of Discrimination Against Women under Article 8 of OP-CEDAW' (2015) CEDAW/C/OP.8/PHI/1.

[44] Working Group on Discrimination Against Women in Law and Practice (n 32).

[45] World Bank, 'Voice and Agency: Empowering Women and Girls for Shared Prosperity' (World Bank, 2014) ch 5' Control over Land and Housing'.

[46] *Kell v Canada*, (2012) CEDAW/C/51/D/19/2008.

Equality before the Law (Article 15)

39.   The high cost of obtaining legal advice and of filing court documents can negatively impact a woman's ability to access justice. Legal aid schemes may not extend to areas of law crucial to women in poverty such as housing or social security entitlements. Cuts to legal aid only further remove the ability of women to redress legal wrongs. Income testing for legal aid may not account for women's lack of de facto control of the household assets. Due to illiteracy, court processes and forms may further limit the ability of women to access accountability and enforcement mechanisms. The rules of standing may act in practice to limit the ability of civil society organisations to advocate on behalf of women in poverty. Criminal law may detain women for petty infractions. Customary laws and norms may be exempt from gender-equality guarantees and operate to prevent women from inheriting and owning land.

Family Life (Article 16)

40.   In General Recommendation No 29 on the economic consequences of marriage, family relations and their dissolution, the Committee canvassed how family life can contribute to gender-based poverty. State parties can have multiple legal systems which exempt personal status laws from legal or constitutional guarantees of gender equality. During marriage, laws will designate the man as head of the household, limiting the woman's ability to control and manage the economic assets she has earned during the relationship and more generally the household's assets. Property distribution upon dissolution of the relationship often favours men regardless of whether laws appears neutral, owing to gendered assumptions relating to the classification of marital property subject to division, insufficient recognition of non-financial contributions, women's lack of legal capacity to manage property, and gendered family roles. Women's lack of education and employment skills means they are at further risk of poverty upon dissolution of the relationship. Under statutory and customary laws, women often do not have the right to inherit and administrate marital property on the death of their spouse. Widows can be victims of 'property grabbing'. In General Recommendation No 31 on harmful practices it was noted that girls and women are often forced into marriage. Girls under 18 who live in poverty are more likely to enter into early forced marriage. This also means young girls are more like to become pregnant which limits their ability to gain education, skills and training. Thus, early forced marriage both causes and contributes to gender-based poverty.

Violence Against Women

41.   Violence against women also impacts gender-based poverty. Women who are subjected to domestic violence do not perform as well in the workforce.[47] Women often do not have the economic means to escape from violent partners. The lack of control over economic resources can increase women's risk of violence. For instance, unaffordable transportation can expose women to serious violence. Similarly, violence and harassment at the workplace negatively impacts women's employment opportunities. Women who work as domestic workers may be more vulnerable to violence and sexual harassment.[48] Violence on the way to school or at school from teachers or other students can negatively impact a girl or woman's ability to receive an education. Similarly, women in informal settlements who need to go some distance to perform ablutions or collect water are more vulnerable to violence.[49] Violence against women can trap and encircle women in poverty.

IV. RECOMMENDATIONS

42.   State parties must actively condemn gendered social norms, institutions, patterns and relationships that subject women to poverty. State parties should adopt a comprehensive human rights-based gender-sensitive poverty reduction plan, which includes using temporary special measures in line with Article 4(1) of the Convention and General Recommendation No 25 in order to ensure that women in poverty are able to create and enjoy a meaningful life and to participate fully and effectively in political, social, economic, cultural and civil life and any other field in their societies. State parties have an obligation to ensure the full development and advancement of women in poverty.[50] State parties must be vigilant to the complex and cross-cutting ways that laws and policies, including macroeconomic policies, can contribute to gender-based poverty and limit women's full development and advancement and take all appropriate measures to ensure human rights and fundamental freedoms.[51]

43.   State parties' obligations should take into account the multidimensional nature of discrimination against women in poverty and ensure that the principle of equality and non-discrimination applies to women in poverty.

---

[47] World Bank, 'Voice and Agency' (n 45).
[48] UNIFEM, 'Human Rights Protections Applicable to Women Migrant Workers' (UNIFEM Briefing Paper, 2003) 30.
[49] UNHCR and Human Rights Centre University of California, 'Safe Heaven: Sheltering Displaced Persons from Sexual and Gender-Based Violence: Case Study Kenya: May 2013' (2013) 22.
[50] Art 3 of the Convention.
[51] Working Group on Discrimination Against Women in Law and Practice (n 32).

Gender-based poverty and discrimination of women based on sex and gender is inextricably linked with other facts that affect women, such as race, ethnicity, religion or belief, health, status, age, caste, sexual orientation, and gender identity.[52] As one example, older women experience sex and gender discrimination throughout their life cycle—stereotyping in education, precarious employment and unpaid care work—and as older women this discrimination culminates in gender-based poverty and decreased quality of life, such as limited or reduced pensions. State parties must be attentive to how sex, gender and poverty are inextricably linked to other factors.[53] State parties are urged to repeal or amend existing laws, regulations and customs that discrimination against women in poverty.

44.   In order to support legal reform and policy formulation, state parties are urged to collect, analyse and disseminate data on gender-based poverty disaggregated on the basis of sex and gender, so as to have information on the situation of women in poverty. States are encouraged to collect data on the impact of unpaid work, access to education, healthcare, food, water, social protection schemes, housing, employment, and social and economic benefits.

Cultural Attitudes (Article 5)

45.   State parties have an obligation to eliminate negative stereotypes and modify social and cultural patterns of conduct that are prejudicial and harmful to women in poverty. States are particularly encouraged to address social norms that dictate women perform care-giving. Public awareness, media and online social campaigns should be utilised to explain the value of this work and work that is traditionally assigned to women in the labour force. At the same time men should be encouraged to perform care-giving roles. States are also obligated to address social attitudes that demean and humiliate women who live in poverty, including through repealing and reforming laws based on pernicious gender-based poverty stereotypes.

Exploitative Prostitution and Trafficking (Article 6)

46.   Victims of exploitative prostitution and trafficking need to have access to adequate social benefits and accommodation. State parties should provide training and economic opportunities to break cycles of exploitation and poverty. State parties are under an obligation to be aware of new forms of trafficking such as importing domestic labour from the developing

---

[52] See 'General Recommendation No 28: on Core Obligations' (n 1).
[53] Working Group on Discrimination Against Women in Law and Practice (n 32).

world to the developed world.[54] The Committee recommends that state parties take legal and social measures to regulate domestic work.[55] States are encouraged to cooperate and offer assistance to tackle global conditions that perpetuate gender-based poverty and increase women's risk of exploitative prostitution and trafficking.[56]

Participation in Public Life (Articles 7 and 8)

47.   In protecting and fulfilling the right to vote, state parties need to be aware of the limited time and resources available to women in poverty. State parties have an obligation to meaningfully consult with women in poverty in the design, implementation, funding and monitoring of all poverty reduction programmes and any laws or policies that affect women in poverty. Women in poverty have diverse perspectives on how to tackle gender-based poverty. Meaningful consultation is crucial for ensuring that the state's measures to redress gender-based poverty reflect this diversity and the needs and concerns of women in poverty. State parties are encouraged to empower the voices of women in poverty by providing training and resources so women in poverty can participate in modern forms of political participation and activism. To address global and structural inequalities and ensure macroeconomic policies empower women it is essential to include women at all levels of decision-making in international and national financial and trade institutions.[57]

Nationality (Article 9)

48.   When women marry non-nationals, they and their children should not be denied access to public services. State parties are obligated to ensure that during the asylum and integration process women have access to healthcare, education, accommodation, food, clothing, social services and employment. Registration services for displaced women and girls need to be accessible and recognise that due to the discrimination they experience, women may lack official identity documents and be unable to meet conditions for claiming asylum and citizenship. Nationality requirements must be reviewed to ensure that they do not indirectly discriminate against women.[58]

---

[54] 'General Recommendation No 19: on Violence Against Women (n 4).

[55] International Labour Organization Convention No 189, 'Concerning Decent Work for Domestic Workers' (2011).

[56] 'General Recommendation No 26: on Migrant Women Workers' (2008) CEDAW/C/GC/26.

[57] Working Group on Discrimination Against Women in Law and Practice (n 32).

[58] 'General Recommendation No 32: on the Gender-related Dimensions of Refugee Status' (n 30).

Education (Article 10)

49.   Primary education should be provided free of charge and reviewed to ensure there are no indirect costs limiting the ability of women and girls to access primary education. State parties have an obligation to ensure high-quality and affordable services, such as water facilities and childcare, are readily available so girls are not burdened with the domestic responsibilities that restrict their access to education. State parties are encouraged to adopt school lunches and feeding programmes to ensure girls and women have adequate nutrition so as to perform well in school.[59] Education grants that are conditional on a girl attending school should be considered, but state parties must evaluate these programmes to ensure they do not perpetuate negative stereotypes against families in poverty or further contribute to the time burden of women and girl's or essentialise them as primary care-givers. Scholarships should be targeted towards providing women with training for non-traditional career paths. State parties are obligated to redress socio-cultural norms that devalue educating girls and women by public aware-ness campaigns and ensuring decent employment is available for girls and women upon the completion of education. Furthermore, the state needs to ensure pregnant girls and women are not expelled from school but instead are offered support so as to continue their studies. The rise of private pro-viders in education means the state must ensure that private providers do not perpetuate discrimination against women and girls. The state should consult with girls and their families in the use and design of educational measures to combat gender-based poverty.

Employment (Article 11)

50.   State parties have an obligation to facilitate the participation of women in poverty in paid decent employment in the formal labour mar-ket. State parties should continue to monitor and reduce gender-related pay gaps. State parties are encouraged to require employers to conduct objective gender neutral job evaluation. State parties should adopt a wide variety of methods to combat the gender job segregation of the labour market. At the same time, public awareness campaigns should be targeted towards prop-erly valuing and respecting the work that women have traditionally per-formed. Maternity and paternity leave should be at an adequate level and funded adequately through state or contributory schemes.[60] Paid care leave

---

[59]   UN Special Rapporteur on the right to food, 'Countries Tackling Hunger with a Right to Food Approach' (Briefing Note 01, May 2010) 8.
[60]   International Labour Organization Convention No183, 'Concerning the Revision of Maternity Protection Convention'(2000).

should be equally available to both men and women and the state should use innovative methods to encourage men to use paternity leave.

51.   State parties have an obligation to protect women from exploitation in both the formal and informal labour market. State parties are strongly encouraged to reduce the number of women working in the informal labour market by increasing job opportunities in the formal labour market. To achieve this, the state can take various measures, including targeted skills training and development, to reduce unemployment among women. At the same time, legal regulations should be extended to cover informal employment relationships to ensure that women are not vulnerable to exploitation or work in dangerous conditions. Social protections should be extended to women employees regardless of the type of employment relationship. This includes non-traditional labour arrangements, including part-time work, informal or casual work, new forms of working relationships, and domestic work.

52.   Women's unequal share of care work limits their employment opportunities. Care work should be recognised in the macro-economy. It should be reduced through high-quality, publically funded care services. States need to adapt care services to the working patterns of women in poverty, including informal, shift and rural work. Care jobs in the formal economy need to be fairly remunerated and have fair and just working conditions. Specifically, state parties are encouraged to protect the rights of domestic workers by ensuring that they are not vulnerable to mistreatment by migration policies and included within all labour protections. State parties should adopt policies that both revalue care work and encourage the role of men in caring.

Access to Healthcare Services (Article 12)

53.   States parties are encouraged to review their maternal health policies to ensure they meet the needs of women in poverty. The design, implementation and funding of programmes must pay particular attention to the needs of poor rural women.[61] Reproductive health services, such as contraception, should be physically, socially and financially accessible to all women. State parties are obligated to redress sociocultural norms and power imbalances that give low priority in both public and private life to women's health needs.

---

[61] UN Special Rapporteur on the right to health; see also 'General Recommendation No 24: on Women and Health' (1999) CEDAW/C/GC/24.

Economic and Social Life (Article 13)

54.   Non-contributory social protection schemes that are unconnected to formal employment relationships are crucial to ensure women in poverty are able to enjoy their human rights.[62] This is particularly true for older women who, due to a lifetime of gender-based discrimination, may not qualify for pensions based on continuous employment in the formal labour market. State parties are obligated to ensure their social and economic benefits further substantive gender equality. This can include ensuring women are entitled to receive social benefits in their own names and absent any relationship with men. Social assistance conditions and rates must take into account the time and resources women expend in care work.[63] States parties need to redress sociocultural norms that demonise and penalise women who rely on social benefits. Measures in times of economic austerity should not further women's inequality and poverty. Any austerity measures should be gender sensitive and state parties should ensure that such measures address asymmetries of power and structural gender inequalities. State parties should prioritise investment in education and skill development for women and girls and avoid labour market exclusion, loss of social protection floors and reduction of social services.[64]

Rural Women (Article 14)

55.   Drawing on General Recommendation No 34 on the rights of rural women, state parties are obligated to take all measures to ensure that rural women are able to own, use, enjoy and benefit from land ownership. State parties are encouraged to reform formal legal systems, customary and traditional law, and sociocultural norms through the use of temporary special measures to accelerate women's land ownership. State parties should take measures to ensure that rural women are active participants in the development and implementation of land policies. Furthermore, state parties are obligated to take steps to ensure an adequate standard of living for rural women. This includes the provision of accessible and high-quality transportation, communication systems, water, housing and electricity.[65]

---

[62] See Committee on Economic Social and Cultural Rights, 'General Comment No 19: The Right to Social Security' (2008) E/C.12/GC/19.

[63] UN Special Rapporteur on extreme poverty and human rights, 'Guiding Principles' (n 8).

[64] UN Special Rapporteur on extreme poverty and human rights, 'Human Rights Based Approach to Recovery from Global Economic and Financial Crises, with a Focus on Those Living in Poverty' (2011) A/HRC/17/34; Working Group on Discrimination Against Women (n 32).

[65] Art 14(2)(h) of the Convention.

Equality Before the Law (Article 15)

56.   To ensure women in poverty are equal before the law, the state parties must create and maintain a high-quality legal aid system that meets the needs of women in poverty. The coverage of legal aid must be extended to socioeconomic rights. States should encourage the participation of civil society organisations in ensuring women in poverty are able to access justice. State parties are encouraged to review court procedures to ensure they do not limit the ability of women in poverty to access justice. State parties need to pursue a variety of methods that are sensitive to the local legal, political and cultural context, including empowering women's voice and engaging with traditional leaders to reform discriminatory customary laws and norms.

Family Life (Article 16)

57.   State parties must recognise in their legal systems the equal right of women to own, manage and control assets during the marriage or de facto relationship. Non-financial contributions—household and family care, lost economic opportunities and support of the other spouse's career development—to the relationship must be included in the division of property on the dissolution of the relationship. Post-dissolution spousal payments must take into account women's limited education and employment opportunities.[66] Upon death of a spouse or relative, both men and women should be equally entitled to inherit property. Customary laws that prohibit women from inheriting must be reformed and be subject to gender equality guarantees. 'Property grabbing' must be prohibited. Furthermore, to prevent early forced marriage, the state party must address both the household and girls' poverty. States should consider financial incentives to encourage girls' attendance in schools, and should invest in educational and employment opportunities.

Violence Against Women

58.   State parties are reminded that a commitment to end violence against women necessarily entails reducing gender-based poverty. State parties need to ensure women are protected from domestic violence and have access to domestic violence shelters.[67] State parties are obligated to ensure women

---

[66] See dissent in *BJ v Germany*, (2004) CEDAW/C/36/D/1/2003.
[67] *Yildirim v Austria*, (2007) CEDAW/C/D/39/6/2005.

and girls are able to access education and employment without fear of violence or harassment. State parties need to monitor the employers of domestic workers to ensure their workplace is free of violence. State parties need to take all appropriate measures to ensure women in refugee, asylum and displaced person camps are free from violence. State parties need to invest in public services—such as affordable public transport—to reduce the risk of serious violence for women in poverty.

National Implementation

59.   In General Recommendation No 28, the Committee explained that under Article 2 state parties are required to pursue a policy of eliminating discrimination against women that applies to all fields of life and to public and private actors. This is an essential and critical component of the state's legal obligations under the Convention. State parties must immediately assess the situation of women and take concrete steps to formulate and implement a policy to eliminate discrimination and achieve gender equality so that women can enjoy their human rights. State parties must adopt a comprehensive range of measures and build on those measures in light of their effectiveness and new or emerging issues. These measures include constitutional and legislative guarantees, action plans, monitoring and implementation mechanisms, and a wide range of accountability forums.

60.   The state parties' legal obligation under the Convention means there is a responsibility for the state to have a specific and targeted plan to reduce gender-based poverty. Relying on current economic policies is not sufficient.[68] There must be in place a specific plan to reduce and remedy the gender-based aspects of poverty. The plan should be based on the principles of accountability and transparency. This plan of action must be: (i) based on human rights laws and principles; (ii) cover all aspects of gender-based poverty—economic disadvantage, prejudicial socio-cultural norms, structural and exclusion harms; and (iii) have clearly defined objectives and goals. The plan should also establish institutional responsibility for the process; identify resources available to obtain the objectives; allocate resources appropriately according to need and institutional responsibility; and establish accountability mechanisms to ensure the implementation of the plan. The state should consider drawing on the recommendations provided above, but is also encouraged to use new and innovative methods to reduce gender-based poverty that are consistent with its legal obligation to eliminate discrimination and realise gender equality. The gender-based poverty reduction plan should only be arrived at after the meaningful

---

[68] Working Group on Discrimination Against Women in Law and Practice (n 32).

participation and consultation of women in poverty. This can require state parties to provide transport to consultation meetings, to provide childcare so women have the time to participate and any other necessary capacity-building measures. State parties are encouraged to avail themselves of technical assistance and cooperation of the United Nations' specialised agencies when formulating the gender-based poverty reduction plan.

61.   Women in poverty must be given full and equal access to information concerning the gender-based poverty reduction plan. This is crucial to ensure women are able to hold the state accountable for its obligations under the Convention.

62.   As part of the commitment to end discrimination against women and achieve gender equality, the state is responsible for the delivery of high-quality, affordable and accessible goods and services to women who live in poverty. This means there must be sufficient coordination between different levels and branches of the state. Under Article 2(e) the state remains responsible even if the delivery of goods and services is contracted out to private parties. The state must ensure that private parties do not discriminate against women in poverty.

63.   In the gender-based poverty reduction plan state parties need to identify who is responsible for implementing each element of the plan. The plan should identify the appropriate forum women in poverty can access so the state party can publically account for its law, policies, plans and programmes on gender-based poverty. It is important that forums of accountability are not cost prohibitive for women in poverty. This can require the provision of high-quality legal assistance. State parties are encouraged to respect, protect and support the work of civil society organisations and human rights organisations that assist women in poverty including through adopting broad rules on standing so civil society organisations can assist women in poverty in claiming their rights.

64.   When the state parties are found to have violated the rights of women in poverty under the Convention, the state is obligated under Article 2(e) to ensure that there are effective and meaningful remedies. This can include reparations but remedies should primarily be aimed at promoting positive institutional and structural change.

65.   Gender-based poverty is an interconnected global problem. Article 2 requires states to pursue a policy of eliminating discrimination against women without delay. State parties are encouraged to seek international assistance and cooperation to respect, protect and fulfil the human rights of women in poverty.[69] State parties should avail themselves of the technical

---

[69] 'General Recommendation No 28: on Core Obligations' (n 1) [29]; 'General Recommendation No 26: on Migrant Women Workers' (n 56).

expertise of international agencies. International assistance requires that all relevant domestic and international actors pursue international policies that reduce gender-based poverty. State parties are encouraged to review their international policies, development assistance, loan conditions, trade agreements, taxation, fiscal, investment and environmental policies to ensure that they do not exacerbate gender-based poverty.[70] State parties as actors and participants in international organisations should ensure, as far as possible, that the decisions, policies and actions of these organisations empower women in poverty. State parties are encouraged to regulate transnational corporations to ensure women in poverty enjoy their human rights.

66.   In the state report, state parties are encouraged to follow the guidance provided in this General Recommendation. States should give specific attention to gender-based poverty in the report. Gender-based poverty is comprehensively included in the Convention and states should provide information on gender-based poverty in relation to all of the substantive provisions in the Convention.[71]

---

[70] UN Special Rapporteur on extreme poverty and human rights, 'Guiding Principles' (n 8).
[71] See the Committee's work on violence against women in the Concluding Observations as an example.

Index

Note: Alphabetical arrangement is word-by-word, where a group of letters followed by a space is filed before the same group of letters followed by a letter, eg 'child support' will appear before 'childcare'. In determining alphabetical arrangement, initial articles and prepositions are ignored.

human rights:
  enjoyment denial, 228
  violations reason, 224
income testing for legal aid, 243
indirect discrimination, 232
inheritance, 243
international documents, citing, 228–29
international human rights law,
  establishing as part of larger evolution
  in, 228
interpretative methodology, elucidating,
  230
justice, access to, 243
justification, 224
labour migration, 235
language requirements, 237
law, equality before, 243, 262, 270
legal aid, 243
legal background, 252–58
legal basis for interpreting, 229–33
legal interpretation, 254–57
periodic reporting process, guidance on,
  246
macro-economic policies, 226
magnitude and prevalence of gender-based
  poverty reason, 224, 227
marriage:
  early, 243–44
  to non-nationals, 237
national implementation, 271–73
nationality, 237, 260, 266
naturalisation laws, 237
negative cultural attitudes, 234
negative stereotypes, 234–35
non-binding commitments, citing, 229
opening statement, 224
participation:
  harms, 228
  parity in, 236
  in public life, 236, 259–60, 266
pensions, 227
periodic reporting process guidance, 246
prevalence and magnitude of gender-based
  poverty reason, 224, 227
property, 234
  ownership, 243
prostitution, 235, 259, 265–6
public life, participation in, 236, 259–60,
  266
public services, 237
public transportation, 244
recommendations, 264–73
redistribution wrongs, 228
refugee camps, women in, 244
relationships dissolution, 243
rural women, 231, 240, 243, 262, 269
social assistance, 241–42
social attitudes, 226, 234

social life, 241–42, 262, 269
social welfare schemes, 242
socioeconomic rights, 243
specific areas of concern, 258–64
state benefits, 237
state obligations, 232, 257–58, 265–6
statelessness, 237
stereotypes, 234
substantive equality, 232
temporary special measures, 233
text, draft, 249–73
trafficking, 235
  draft text, 259
transformative equality, 232
transportation, public, 244
unpaid care work, 226, 234, 240
VCLT interpretative rules cited in
  footnote, 230, 231
violence, 244, 264, 270–71
welfare schemes, 241–42
'women's work', 226
General Recommendations:
  CEDAW Committee, *see* CEDAW
    Committee
  UN treaty bodies, 66
generic terms, interpretation of treaties, 61
Geneva Conventions on the treatment of
  prisoners of war and civilians, 216
geographic disparities reduction information,
  205
geographic locations classification, World
  Bank, 108, 109
geographical remoteness, discrimination,
  104
Germany:
  family life, 167
Germany, Federal Republic of:
  CEDAW proposals, 37
Ghodsee, K, 33, 49, 51
gig economy, 239
GII (Gender Inequality Index), 108–10
girls living on streets, discrimination, 105
global concerns, 45
global economic inequalities
  CEDAW *travaux préparatoires*, 37
global governance structures, 11
global issues:
  women's issues separate, 46
global neoliberalism, 131
global reach of gender-based poverty:
  General Recommendation on women and
    poverty, proposal, 227
GNI (gross national income scale), 108–10
goals:
  CEDAW, 115, 117
Goodman, R, 70
governance:
  global structures, 11

Lightning Source UK Ltd.
Milton Keynes UK
UKHW020229301122
413082UK00005B/218